A CITY TRANSFORMED

A CITY

TRANSFORMED

Redevelopment, Race, and Suburbanization in Lancaster, Pennsylvania

1940–1980

David Schuyler

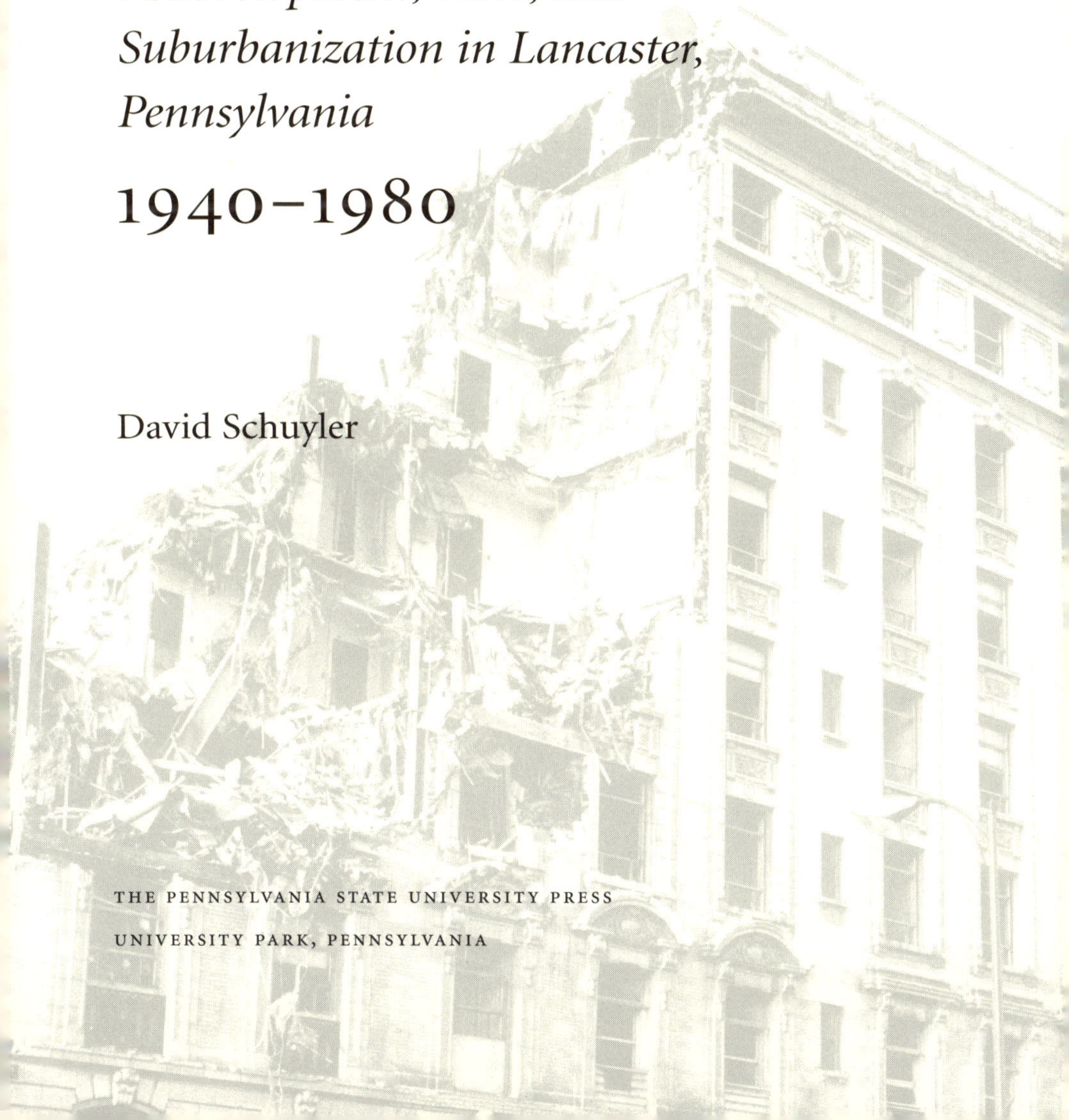

THE PENNSYLVANIA STATE UNIVERSITY PRESS
UNIVERSITY PARK, PENNSYLVANIA

Library of Congress
Cataloguing-in-Publication Data

Schuyler, David.
A city transformed : redevelopment, race, and suburbanization in Lancaster, Pennsylvania, 1940–1980 / David Schuyler.
p. cm.
Includes bibliographical references and index.
ISBN 0-271-02207-8 (cloth : alk. paper)
ISBN 0-271-02208-6 (pbk. :alk. paper)
1. Urban renewal—Pennsylvania—Lancaster. 2. City planning—Pennsylvania—Lancaster. 3. Lancaster (Pa.). I. Title.

HT177.L36 S38 2002
307.3'416'0974815—dc21 2002005320

Printed in the United States of America
Published by
The Pennsylvania State University Press,
University Park, PA 16802-1003

It is the policy of The Pennsylvania State University Press to use acid-free paper for the first printing of all clothbound books. Publications on uncoated stock satisfy the minimum requirements of American National Standard for Information Sciences—Permanence of Paper for Printed Library Materials, ANSI Z39.48–1992.

for Marsha

Contents

Acknowledgments

In important ways this book is the product of almost a decade of studying Lancaster with undergraduates at Franklin & Marshall College. Over the course of that time a number of students have conducted research on important aspects of the redevelopment process and other topics that contributed to my understanding of Lancaster's past. Even before I conceptualized this book the class of 1993 mounted a terrific exhibit on urban renewal and its impact on the city in the college's Rothman Gallery. Two students, James Leach and Sarah Reigner, served as Hackman Scholars and helped immeasurably with research at important stages of the project. In this as in other endeavors, Franklin & Marshall has generously supported my efforts: the college awarded a sabbatical during which I wrote many of the following pages and provided financial support that enabled me to conduct research and assemble the illustrations.

A number of institutions and individuals have been instrumental in making their collections and recollections available. At Franklin & Marshall, Andy Gulati and Tom Karel answered many questions, while Mary Shelly obtained books and articles by means of interlibrary loan with remarkable efficiency. At the Lancaster County Historical Society, Thomas Ryan, Ginger Shelley, Kevin Shue, Marianne Heckles, and Heather Tennies guided me efficiently through their collections, while John W. W. Loose was invariably available to answer questions. City Clerk Janet Spleen helped me find my way through Lancaster's City Council records, while Eric Hinderliter, Paula Jackson, and Stanley Wilk of the Department of Planning and Community Development made information accessible and patiently showed me how planning and redevelopment worked at the local level. Vicki Phillips generously gave me access to the records of the Board of School Directors of the School District of Lancaster, while Robert Schellhamer made the records of the Lancaster Housing Authority accessible. At Lancaster Newspapers, Kathy Cassidy and Sue Sweeney located articles and photographs. I am also grateful to the individuals who have generously shared their time and their recollections of Lancaster with me: Richard H. Barr Jr., Peggy Bender, David

Bucher, the Rev. Louis A. Butcher Jr., Ronald Ford, Gwen Glover, John I. Hartman Jr., Melvin H. Hess, Leroy Hopkins, Tom Hyson, Paula Jackson, Robert Kiernan, Richard Kneedler, Robert Lowing, James McMullen, Charles K. Patterson, Nelson Polite, James Shultz, Scott Standish, John Synodinos, John Vanderzell, and Don Wise.

For permission to publish photographs in their collections I am indebted to Lancaster Newspapers Inc.; the Bureau of Planning, City of Lancaster; Buchart-Horn Inc. / BASCO Associates Ltd., Lancaster and York, Pennsylvania; Fulton Financial Corporation; the Lancaster County Historical Society; and the National Archives and Records Administration, Washington, D.C. Earlier versions of Chapters 2 and 7 were published in *Pennsylvania History* and the *Proceedings of the American Philosophical Society.*

At The Pennsylvania State University Press, I am indebted to Peter J. Potter for his encouragement and ideas, to Peggy Hoover and Patricia Mitchell for bringing the book through its production, and to Lisa Tremaine for its design.

Conversations with a number of historians have shaped my thinking about race, housing, redevelopment, and suburbanization. I am indebted to Henry Binford, Eugenie L. Birch, Lizabeth Cohen, Robert Fishman, Timothy Gilfoyle, Howard Gillette, Tom Hanchett, Clifton Hood, Arleyn Levee, Raymond A. Mohl, Kermit C. Parsons, Gail Radford, John W. Reps, Mary Corbin Sies, Gretchin Sorin, Bruce Stephenson, Tom Sugrue, Alex Von Hoffman, and Tom Winpenny.

A number of friends took time from their own lives to read and comment on earlier versions of this book. Jack Brubaker and Charles K. Patterson gave me the confidence that the Lancaster I portrayed conformed in important ways to their experience and knowledge of the community. John F. Bauman, Whitfield J. Bell Jr., Michael Birkner, Tom Daniels, Sean Flaherty, Scott Henderson, Alison Isenberg, Kenneth T. Jackson, Mark Rose, Nancy Schuyler, and Christopher Silver gave me the inestimable gift of their comments and criticism, for which I am deeply grateful.

I own a special debt to John A. Andrew III, who was a colleague and friend for more than twenty years. John first suggested that I use Lancaster as a classroom, and this book is one tangible result of that encouragement. He was always eager to talk about research under way or sports or politics, and in the midst of his own busy life was invariably the first person to critique what I had written. John had read all of this book in draft before his death in November 2000, some chapters more than once, and I hope that his passion for history, his relentless determination to find meaning in the past, is evident on every page.

In this as in other areas of life, my greatest debt is to Marsha.

INTRODUCTION

In 1980 the Redevelopment Authority of the City of Lancaster, Pennsylvania, emblazoned across the cover of its final report, "This is the story of a city's renewal. . . ." The narrative conceded failure as well as success, though its emphasis was on homes that had been given new life through renovation or restoration rather than buildings that had been demolished. Photographs captured the pride of individuals who were making improvements to their homes, and families that were enjoying renovated domestic spaces, not the anguish of people who had been relocated when their dwellings were condemned and razed. What failures had occurred the report attributed to federal policies that mandated demolition rather than rehabilitation and that limited the range of options Lancaster's leaders might consider. Despite this concession, the title and the photograph of a handsomely restored house on the cover emphasized the Redevelopment Authority's accomplishments, celebrated the city's renewal.[1]

Nowhere was the impress of the Redevelopment Authority more apparent than in the contrast between streetscapes in the 1950s and those of the late 1970s, particularly in the southeast quadrant of the city, which had been home to Lancaster's small minority population at the onset of renewal. In the 1950s, the report reminded readers, "some of our citizens still lived in tar paper shacks at the edge of town"; others endured dwellings without running water and lived along unpaved streets. Twenty years later urban renewal had cleared blocks filled with dilapidated houses and removed junkyards and nuisance industries that once detracted from the quality of life. During the intervening years the city had constructed miles of curbs and sidewalks and a modern infrastructure of sewer, water, and utility lines, while new housing, a modern elementary school, a community center, recreational facilities, and open space replaced decaying old buildings. Two photographs published in the report harkened back to the years before renewal: one depicted a shack literally teetering on the brink of collapse, the other a group of men inspecting conditions along Dauphin Street. "We've come a long way since this tour was conducted," the report noted approvingly, and "eyesores" such as the frame dwelling had been removed.[2]

The Redevelopment Authority's final report also linked urban renewal and suburbanization, acknowledging that the "growth of suburbia spelled hard times for the economy of the downtown business sector." But if competition from a burgeoning suburban retail trade made the need for renewal of the central business district all the more pressing, the report did not mention the city's principal commercial redevelopment project, which involved the demolition of almost the entire second block of North Queen Street. Perhaps because those events were so recent, the report's authors did not feel the need to comment on the years of frustration the city's leaders experienced in attracting a developer interested in erecting a new downtown commercial center, a decade when residents derisively described choice downtown real estate as "our hole in the ground." Perhaps the authority staff did not want to point to the most conspicuous failure of the redevelopment process, Lancaster Square, a retail and recreational space designed by the internationally famous architect and planner Victor Gruen, part of which was demolished only twenty-seven months after its dedication to make way for new office buildings. While the report pointed to the suburbanization of retail as causing the demise of a traditional economic function of downtown, it failed to address the role of various federal and state programs that subsidized growth on the periphery at the expense of the older city. Thus the Redevelopment Authority's final report only hinted at the full dimensions of the urban redevelopment program it had undertaken and left unexamined many of the decisions about downtown revitalization and residential renewal that would have long-term consequences for the city and its people.[3]

Lancaster is a small community with a population of 55,551 in 1990. Located in south-central Pennsylvania, sixty-five miles west of Philadelphia, Lancaster was platted in 1730 and chartered as a borough in 1742. Established as a market town for an exceptionally rich agricultural region, beginning in the 1840s Lancaster evolved into an industrial city. The population grew by 200 percent between 1840 and 1880, and doubled again between 1880 and 1920. These years saw the emergence of a downtown retail district as well as a white-collar economy defined by attorneys who clustered near the County Court House and the banks and insurance offices that located near Penn Square. By the turn of the twentieth century, downtown Lancaster had acquired the attributes of a modern city. Electric and telephone wires looped overhead, horse-drawn wagons and carriages competed with streetcars and automobiles on the newly paved streets, and during the 1920s a skyscraper, the Griest Building, rose fourteen stories above Penn Square and symbolized Lancaster's urbanity even as it affirmed the traditional importance of downtown as the commercial center of the county.[4] But for all the boosterism of the 1920s, beyond the central business district the physical fabric of Lancaster was still predominantly that of a Victorian industrial city in which residents were learning to adapt to changing material conditions. In this Lancaster shared striking similarities with Muncie, Indiana, the representative American city Robert S. Lynd and Helen M. Lynd analyzed in their landmark sociological study, *Middletown* (1929): "It is not uncommon to observe 1890 and 1924 habits jostling along side by side in a family with primitive back-yard water or sewage habits," the Lynds wrote, "yet using an automobile, electric washer, electric iron, and vacuum cleaner."[5]

An important New Deal study documented the degree to which that older Victorian city persisted in Lancaster. A survey of real estate undertaken by the Works Progress Administration in 1936 revealed that, despite decades of prosperity and impressive population growth, only one in four city residences had been erected in the previous twenty years. Almost a third of the city's dwellings were more than fifty years old, while one in three residential structures lacked plumbing, heating, and utilities. As economic conditions worsened in the early 1930s, many owners of city properties deferred maintenance, a pattern that continued through World War II. Thus at the onset of the postwar building boom, many commercial buildings were obsolete, much of the housing stock decaying or worse. In short, Lancaster was an old city whose buildings desperately needed modernization.[6]

As is true of most older cities in the Northeast and the Midwest, Lancaster's population peaked in 1950, when it was home to 63,774 residents, more than 98 percent of whom were white. At that time it retained a thriving industrial economy and a prosperous downtown retail trade. Over the next thirty years, three major changes occurred. The first was demographic. The white population, 62,651 in 1950, declined to 44,373 in 1980, a loss of almost 30 percent. Lancaster's minority population in 1950 was a small African American community of 1,123 with deep roots in the city; in 1980 the black population had increased to 5,052 but was smaller than the Hispanic population of 6,540 residents, virtually all of whom had arrived in Lancaster in the previous twenty years. Together, African Americans and Hispanics (11,592 residents) represented 21 percent of the city's population in 1980.[7] The second major change was the loss of the city's traditional economic base: deindustrialization cost the city 2,200 manufacturing jobs between 1958 and 1977, while the closing of wholesale establishments resulted in the loss of an additional 500 jobs. The third major change was suburbanization, which was a factor both in the dramatic decline of the city's white population and in the loss of jobs and services essential to the economic vitality of Lancaster and its people. Between 1950 and 1980 the white population of six contiguous suburban townships grew exponentially, those municipalities becoming a prosperous ring surrounding a declining core. In each of these developments Lancaster's experience paralleled the trend of other cities, large and small, throughout much of the nation. The decision to undertake a federal- and state-subsidized urban renewal program in the hope of eliminating residential blight and solidifying the downtown retail economy during these years also paralleled choices made in other cities.

How Lancaster's citizens modernized their city would in essential ways shape its future. Whether renewal strategies would strengthen the traditional business district or discourage reinvestment downtown would affect the tax base of the municipality as well as the School District of Lancaster. Whether the Redevelopment Authority could remove substandard houses and eliminate nuisance uses while maintaining neighborhood stability would determine how effectively the residents affected by renewal adapted to change. Early in the twentieth century the Chicago school of sociology adopted biological terms as metaphors for the city, describing buildings or neighborhoods as blighted, transportation routes as arteries, the city as an organism. Writers and urban planners of the postwar generation continued the tradition, often characterizing renewal as surgery undertaken to remove cancerous tissue and restore the health of the urban organism. An important recent study of urban revitalization in the post–World War II era, for example, characterized blight as "this malady destroying the physical tissue of urban America" and as the "archfoe of older central cities." Whether Lancaster would rely on the surgical scalpel or the more blunt instrument of clearance, the bulldozer, whether its actions would be curative or destabilizing, would determine how well the city and its people would thrive at the end of the twentieth century.[8]

Urban renewal was a redevelopment program established under provisions of the U.S. Housing Act of 1949 and state and local enabling legislation. Title I of the act gave municipal authorities power to launch a comprehensive assault on urban blight. Under redevelopment law, blight could refer to individual properties or neighborhoods that were physically deteriorating, or defined by small blocks and alleys, or buildings that were simply too close together. Pennsylvania's 1945 Urban Redevelopment Law, for example, defined blight in terms of patterns of building that did not conform to modern expectations of street width, lot coverage, and open spaces, as well as the "unsafe, unsanitary, inadequate or over-crowded condition of the dwellings" themselves. Blight could also describe buildings or districts where property values or economic uses were declining. In many older cities, such a sweeping definition could be applied to entire neighborhoods and large areas of downtown; in Lancaster it described almost the entire southeast quadrant and much of the rest of the municipality.[9]

After designating an area as blighted, the local authority would then acquire the property, either through purchase or eminent domain, and, after clearance and site preparation, sell the assembled tract to private developers for projects "predominantly residential" in character. The Housing Act of 1949 authorized $1 billion in loans to cities, and an annual appropriation to write down two-thirds of the net cost to the municipal authority—the net cost being the difference between the expense of acquiring and clearing an area and the resale value of the property. Title III established a new public housing program, but like its predecessor, the Wagner Housing Act of 1937, it mandated slum clearance and restricted public housing to the poor. In its containment of the poor from other classes in society, the Housing Act of 1949, along with tax policies and spending programs that subsidized new residential construction in suburbs, was a key component of what historian Gail Radford has termed the nation's two-tiered housing policy.[10]

Although the Housing Act's preamble articulated the goal of "a decent home and a suitable living environment for every American family," subsequent sections of the law contradicted that noble purpose. The result of its tortuous legislative history and battles between housing reformers, planners, and real estate developers, the contradictory impulses and policies embedded in the act ultimately placed too much discretion in the hands of local authorities. Despite the rhetoric of an overbearing federal presence in urban renewal,[11] in Lancaster as in other communities most decisions were made at the local level. In *The Federal Bulldozer* (1964), Martin Anderson conceded that while the federal government provided the bulk of urban redevelopment financing, "the actual execution of the project is left primarily in the hands of local city officials." More recently, a study of redevelopment in Minneapolis and St. Paul, Minnesota, concluded that although urban renewal was perceived as a national program, it was ultimately a local one: "Urban renewal made a vast pool of resources available to cities," Judith Martin and Antony Goddard observed, "but left decisions about where and how to spend the money primarily to local officials' discretion." In Lancaster, the decisions made by local agencies compromised most urban renewal programs, especially residential projects. The combination of a massive infusion of federal and state dollars and generally ineffectual local governments had disastrous consequences. In a study of redevelopment in postwar Detroit, June Manning Thomas has demonstrated that "weak federal and local policy tools and structures stunted redevelopment." The most important federal initiatives—the urban redevelopment and public housing programs of the

Housing Act of 1949 and the Demonstration Cities and Metropolitan Development Act of 1966, which established the Johnson administration's Model Cities program—"suffered because of poorly conceived legislation, antagonistic private interests, congressional and presidential indifference, and erratic funding." These impediments to renewal affected Lancaster just as much as they did larger cities.[12]

Urban redevelopment transformed Lancaster. The comprehensive revitalization program planned and implemented by the Redevelopment Authority of the City of Lancaster changed the physical shape of the southeast quadrant of the city and, through demolition, destabilized the city's African American community. In attempting to solidify the retail functions of the traditional central business district, redevelopment dramatically altered key blocks of the downtown, replacing handsome turn-of-the-century Beaux Arts structures with modernist concrete boxes and a sterile public square. Ultimately, urban renewal affected the quality of life and desirability of distant neighborhoods as well. Perhaps it is a reflection of how desperate planners and elected officials were to stop what they perceived as decline and get Lancaster moving forward again, but during the redevelopment program the city adopted plans, such as Gruen's proposals for Lancaster Square, that were deeply flawed and in retrospect clearly inappropriate for a historic streetscape. The planners and the local political culture failed Lancaster.

Twenty years after the Redevelopment Authority closed its offices, Lancaster is a much different place than it was in 1980. If many of the buildings look the same, residents are poorer, more diverse ethnically and racially, and live surrounded by crime and evidence of societal breakdown. At a time when Lancaster's suburbs are growing rapidly and enjoying a prosperity unmatched in their history, cutbacks in federal and state programs have left the city with few resources to redress physical decline and to promote human welfare. By every standard imaginable, Lancaster is at risk.

The following chapters analyze intersections of local culture and a political framework for redevelopment that was determined elsewhere, in the national and state capitals. Both the local perception and the national context are essential to understanding the impact of redevelopment. Geographer Peirce Lewis has observed that cities and towns are "creatures of very particular cultures and very particular histories."[13] Lancaster's experience with urban renewal was indeed a product of particular circumstances. It was shaped by local actors who determined what areas were designated for redevelopment, who decided what steps would be taken to relocate households and businesses affected by those decisions and what new construction would define the cityscape. These choices were not absolute, of course, for federal and state policies defined the range of options available to public officials and private leaders. Moreover, federal and state bureaucrats evaluated funding applications and attempted to ensure that communities across the nation complied with programmatic goals and policies. But in the interplay of local decisions and federal and state policy, Lancaster's elected and appointed officials largely determined what happened to their city: despite the plague of "institutional modern" buildings that visibly identify redevelopment areas in Lancaster as in other cities, urban renewal was a locally directed program that occurred in a specific place.

If the problems Lancaster confronted were similar to those experienced in urban areas across the nation, the solutions its Redevelopment Authority adopted differed from those of larger cities in terms of scale. How small and medium-sized communities such as Lancaster attempted to halt urban decline and attract downtown the new commercial developments that were spiraling outward from the center is an important though largely unexamined component of our recent history. Indeed, as geographer Wilbur Zelinsky has pointed out, "We know surprisingly little about the form and appearance of the vast majority of the cities and towns of North America," the thousands of small cities and towns that are familiar parts of the American landscape. This study is the idiosyncratic story of a specific community, yet it also presents Lancaster as part of a larger mosaic of policies and trends that have reshaped metropolitan America since World War II.[14]

If this story resonates with the experiences of other places, it is because there is something of more than local importance in Lancaster's urban renewal program. In the preface to *Main Street* (1920), Sinclair Lewis noted that Gopher Prairie's Main Street was "the continuation of Main Streets everywhere." The novelist maintained that his "story would be the same in Ohio or Montana, in Kansas or Kentucky or Illinois, and not very different would it be told Up York State or in the Carolina hills." Lewis's claim is seductive to anyone undertaking a study of a single place, for it asserts a universality to the author's conclusions. Lancaster may not be Main Street transcendent, but in crucial ways its experience was representative of national trends, especially the postwar suburban boom, the persistent pattern of segregation that has afflicted metropolitan America, and, ultimately, the tragic consequences of public policy and private attitudes toward African Americans.[15]

For all the similarity of the problems most older American cities encountered in the post–World War II era, Lancaster commenced its experience with urban renewal long after programs in larger cities were under way. Although this might have been an advantage, Lancaster's elected officials, administrators, and civic leaders appear to have learned little from other places about what makes downtown a successful destination or how to revitalize an old residential area without destroying residents' sense of community. The effort to redevelop downtown Lancaster differed from that of many larger cities because the debate over the future of the central business district in the 1950s did not produce pro-growth coalitions that championed clearance and new construction. As a whole, owners of downtown stores were unprepared for the new competition from suburban retailers. There was not a concentration of large banks, insurance companies, and real estate service corporations downtown—institutions that, in larger cities, had a vested interest in revitalization. Leaders of the city's most important private nonprofit institutions, especially the hospitals and Franklin & Marshall College, did not act as if what happened to the central business district was vitally important to the city as a whole, nor did the owners of Lancaster's largest manufacturing companies, most of which were located along the northern boundary of the city. Lancaster traditionally has been a nonunion community, so what in other cities was a mobilized constituency within the pro-growth coalition was also missing.[16] This may explain the city's inability to build a downtown expressway, a transportation artery advocated in a number of planning studies. Without a powerful pro-growth coalition the political costs of the massive dislocations an arterial highway would have necessitated were simply too high.[17]

In the absence of such powerful groups influencing municipal policy and directing public and private investment toward downtown, Lancaster, and many smaller cities, had to rely on redevelopers from larger cities who sought to profit from redevelopment. It is not surprising that when potential retail tenants decided to locate in suburban malls, the Lancaster Redevelopment Authority, like its counterparts in cities of similar size, proved unable to bring its urban renewal projects to a successful conclusion. The downtown, especially, lost its traditional retail function to suburban malls without capturing a significant percentage of the increase in office and professional employment that the metropolitan area enjoyed. As a result of the failure of commercial renewal, Lancaster has not experienced the prosperity that major downtowns have enjoyed in recent years—the gleaming skyscrapers, hotels, festival marketplaces, gentrified neighborhoods, and other monuments of the construction boom of the 1980s and 1990s, which attract tourists and generate much-needed tax revenues that sustain the municipal government. Visits to other cities, especially in the Northeast, suggest that what happened in Lancaster occurred elsewhere as well. Reading, Pennsylvania; Newburgh, New York (where I grew up) and other mid–Hudson Valley cities that have experienced tragic decline; once-prosperous industrial cities throughout Connecticut; and the rust belt along the Great Lakes—all testify to such national trends as urban population loss since 1950, white flight, deindustrialization, and crime. All bear the scars of a changing metropolitan economy and the failure of redevelopment programs to secure a better future for their respective communities.

In yet another way urban renewal in Lancaster was representative of the experiences of many other communities: it took place in a city with a long history of segregation. The neighborhood in the southeast quadrant of Lancaster occupied by minorities included buildings that were among the oldest in the city, and because segregation severely circumscribed the areas where African American residents could live, the small houses tended to be overcrowded. Many, owned by absentee landlords, were poorly maintained. Segregation framed the boundaries of the neighborhoods designated for residential renewal, which had a devastating impact on the city's African American population. Worse, as a number of dwellings formerly occupied by minorities were demolished, the pressure on nearby blocks increased as African American and a rapidly growing number of Hispanic residents sought decent places to live. As the minority population moved outward from the small area that traditionally had been home to the city's African American residents, the dominant community's long-standing hostility toward citizens of color precluded a rational discussion of scattered-site low-income housing or other measures that might have resulted in an orderly end of segregation and the emergence, over time, of a fully integrated community.

The story of urban renewal in Lancaster, as in other cities, raises unsettling issues of race and discrimination. The experiences common to African Americans only a generation ago seem foreign to many Americans, the majority of whom live in suburbs, and especially to their children. Education and experience have taught the rising generation that segregation was a Southern phenomenon that ended with the Civil Rights movement. Few whites admit the extent to which it existed in northern, midwestern, and western cities and how long it persisted. As a nation we need to recognize that public policies adopted twenty-five and thirty-five years ago continue to affect the lives of minority residents, in Lancaster as in other American cities. Local decisions to undertake residential renewal in specific neighborhoods, and to build public housing projects in the same areas, remain as physical facts that continue to define the places in which individuals live, and continue to circumscribe opportunities for educational, occupational, and social mobility. We need to confront the inequities of the past to understand the shape of our society today. In *A Place to Remember,* historian Robert R. Archibald describes efforts to preserve the Homer G. Phillips Hospital, an institution in St. Louis that trained generations of African American medical professionals. To most white residents of the city the hospital existed outside the realm of everyday experience, and to younger blacks it stands as an abandoned shell, a building without meaning. Archibald believes that the hospital has to be more than a historic building, that it must exemplify decades of African American achievement in the healing arts and stand as a reminder of the community's segregated past: "Our city cannot heal," he asserts, "until this place, its people, and its surroundings become a symbol shared by all St. Louisans."[18]

Lancaster does not have a building that symbolizes the historical experiences of all its citizens, nor does it appear to be seeking one. Instead, the current mayor has spearheaded the acquisition of a historic carousel that once operated as part of Rocky Springs, an amusement park in nearby West Lampeter Township. He hopes to place the restored carousel in Lancaster Square, the centerpiece of Victor Gruen's plan for a revitalized retail district. No one in City Hall seems to think it incongruous that a carousel from an amusement park with a segregated swimming pool—an amusement park that actually closed rather than integrate—should occupy a prominent public space downtown. Memory is elusive. Most of the individuals involved in raising money for the carousel recall happy moments from their childhood but accept those recollections uncritically, disassociate their experiences from those of racial minorities. For many older members of the city's African American community, however, the carousel is a poignant reminder of a time when discrimination was overt, when segregation in housing was nearly absolute. To black Lancastrians the carousel does indeed have a powerful symbolism, though not one shared by most white citizens.

Ironically, for all the pride many citizens take in their community's long history, few discuss recent developments, let alone analyze how the city has changed and why. Most residents think of Lancaster as a unique place even as its pattern of urban decline and suburban prosperity makes it resemble Anyplace. In explaining the limited success of urban renewal in Lancaster, the Redevelopment Authority's final report conceded that its story was not unique. The text emphasized not Lancaster's singularity but the universality of its experience with urban renewal. The "problems encountered were not Lancaster's alone," the report acknowledged, "and the lessons learned in the past 19 years have been the same lessons learned across the country." In compelling ways Lancaster's experience is the nation's drama, played on a local stage.[19]

PART I

The Discovery of Urban Blight

CHAPTER 1

THE POSTWAR HOUSING CRISIS

The photograph is haunting: fifteen houses in a row, six with contiguous walls, then a narrow space, two more houses adjoining, another void, the pattern repeating itself as roof lines, windows, and doors cascade down a hillside (Fig. 1). Two young African American children stare at the lens, perhaps a suggestion that the camera or the skin color of the photographer was an unusual sight. An old man in a rocking chair and another standing nearby exhibit less interest. For them, the presence of the photographer and the reporter was hardly noteworthy; over the years city officials had come to inspect and condemn the houses, then departed. Life continued. Friends had moved away, newcomers had arrived; children had been born, old folks died. This was the 700 block of Southeast Avenue, perhaps the most notorious neighborhood in the city, a place that was known locally as Barney Google Row. City directories indicate a high rate of residential transition in the neighborhood. Of the fifteen structures on the block listed in the 1944 directory, the occupants of six had changed from two years earlier. Only four households remained from as recently as 1939, and one of those had moved from one house to another in the row. Despite the demographic change, the buildings, the squalid conditions, the human misery, remained.[1]

The companion photograph documents another dilapidated frame house, surrounded by discarded furniture and other objects, which was part of a sprawling subcommunity of approximately forty-eight dwellings located on a tract of land owned by the county that formerly had been the city's ash dump. This dwelling, like the vast majority in Shantytown, was constructed by occupants using what one newspaper described as "materials salvaged from the nearby dump, such as old tin, sheet metal, boxes and miscellaneous lumber." Stands of trees cast the buildings in deep shadow, and no humans appear (Fig. 2). This was a wasteland—a forlorn site rendered unsuitable for more traditional urban development by topography and prior use, its buildings little more than shacks rudely fashioned from scraps of discarded material—a desolate landscape, a place devoid of hope.[2]

These photographs, taken in 1944, could have depicted any of hundreds, perhaps thousands of clusters of substandard housing across the United

FIG. 1 *Barney Google Row, photograph published in the* Lancaster New Era, *May 13, 1944 (Lancaster Newspapers Inc.).*

States. But while the poverty they illustrated was widespread, the locale was specific: the photographs accompanied a newspaper article on housing conditions in Lancaster, Pennsylvania. According to the newspaper account, as part of its effort to anticipate community needs in the aftermath of World War II, the Housing Committee of the Post-War Planning Council reported that fully 85 percent of the housing stock occupied by the city's African American population was "unfit to live in." Sixty percent of the houses were without toilets, 40 percent were without electricity, and 30 percent had no running water. Seventy percent of the Lancaster's minority population were renters, another 20 percent were squatters.[3]

As if statistics were not disheartening enough, the Housing Committee's report then described some of the worst dwellings. The fifteen dwellings on the 700 block of Southeast Avenue—Barney Google Row—were simple one-story buildings with flat roofs, approximately sixteen feet square. All the houses were of frame construction, though six had been covered with stucco. Some of the structures were divided into two rooms, others three. A tap of cold running water worked in a few of the houses, but there were "no other

FIG. 2 *Shantytown, photograph published in the* Lancaster New Era, *May 13, 1944 (Lancaster Newspapers Inc.).*

conveniences of any kind." Privies, located about ten feet from the back doors, stood in dusty yards devoid of grass and other ornamental plantings that were no larger than the houses. Shantytown's makeshift dwellings similarly relied on outdoor toilets, and its 144 residents drew water from a single hydrant. Neither the newspaper account nor the photographs depict interiors of the structures, and the report concluded with the telling observation that "vital facts could not be learned because Negroes who have a roof over their heads are afraid to talk."[4]

In 1944 Barney Google Row was an unpaved extension of Southeast Avenue that ran diagonally from Juniata Street to Susquehanna Street in the southeast quadrant of the city. A Sanborn insurance map from the same decade reveals that much of the surrounding area, especially to the south and west, was largely undeveloped. A row of modest brick houses fronted on South Duke Street facing an automobile junkyard. Other nearby structures included gasoline stations, an aluminum and brass foundry, and several concrete block buildings. Several hundred yards to the east was Shantytown, located behind two schools that had been erected in the 1920s: Edward Hand

Junior High and Washington Elementary. This was a neighborhood in transition, with a concentration of frame dwellings that was rare if not unique in a city dominated by red brick. The process of change would continue, indeed accelerate, in the decades following World War II. Shortly after the demolition of Barney Google Row in 1957, the city began proceedings to extend Southeast Avenue across the site, but the street was not built. Barney Google Row has disappeared, seemingly without a trace, as have the houses that once stood along South Duke Street. All that remains is a grass athletic field with several rows of wooden bleachers, surrounded by a locked chain-link fence. Shantytown too has disappeared, the last of its dwellings also razed in 1957, and there is no record of what happened to its inhabitants. Barney Google Row and Shantytown are telling examples of the kinds of neighborhoods and residents that were excluded from the government-sponsored prosperity of the postwar years. Moreover, although they were by no means the only blighted neighborhoods or even necessarily the worst housing in Lancaster, Barney Google Row and Shantytown epitomized the problem of slum housing—dwellings that were a threat to the health and welfare of residents, the inability of the private sector to address a severe housing shortage, especially for lower-income families, and, because of discrimination, the absence of alternative residential locations for minorities. The demolition of Barney Google Row and Shantytown represented the first step in Lancaster's experiment with urban redevelopment. What happened to residents revealed the larger community's attitude toward race and poverty that would shape the housing options made available to the minority population during the process of renewal.[5]

The origins of Barney Google Row and Shantytown are shrouded in uncertainty. The future site of the 700 block of Southeast Avenue was a farm until the early twentieth century, when it was purchased by Anna and Barney Cohn. Fourteen of the structures along Barney Google Row were probably built in the early 1920s as income-producing properties. Manuscript schedules for the 1920 federal census contain no record of the 700 block of Southeast Avenue, and the earliest real estate transaction mentioning the existence of the buildings was recorded in 1934. However, one newspaper account reported that the houses were built in 1922, and a city directory of 1929 lists the occupants of houses along the block. While the precise date of construction has proven elusive, this much is certain: Barney Google Row was substandard housing constructed in response to the acute shortage of dwelling units that existed during and after World War I and to the tremendous demographic increase taking place in the southeast quadrant of the city. This area's population, 9,541 in 1920, had swelled to 11,042 ten years later, a 16 percent increase. According to the city's 1945 comprehensive plan, prepared by Michael Baker and associates of Rochester, Pennsylvania, most of the population growth in the Seventh Ward was the result of new construction on largely undeveloped land south of the older city. Shantytown probably began as a squatter community during World War II, when large numbers of new residents moved to Lancaster seeking industrial work at a time when the housing market was already strained. The findings of an investigation of Shantytown, undertaken as part of the Baker plan, are surely applicable to Barney Google Row as well: "Inquiry reveals that the occupants were forced into these conditions because of the lack of adequate housing accommodations in the city."[6]

The earliest residents of Barney Google Row were probably poor whites. Barney Google was the subject of a Billy DeBeck-King Features comic strip, begun in 1919, and the title of a popular song written by Billy Rose and Con Conrad in 1923. To a later generation of readers he appeared less regularly as the citified cousin of Snuffy Smith, the archetypal hillbilly and engaging ne'er-do-well. The designation "Barney Google Row" may have functioned as a humorous, denigrating, or dismissive characterization of the residents in terms of a comic strip character who came from a poor rural area, spoke a catchy vernacular slang, and was unprepared for the new circumstances of life in a city. Whatever the intent, the association of residents of the row with Barney Google had an important consequence: it enabled public officials, the press, and citizens to depersonalize the issue of substandard housing, to think in terms of stereotypes rather than of human beings.[7]

If the association with Barney Google suggests that early residents were poor whites, by the late 1920s the racial composition of the row had begun to change. In 1929 several African Americans were listed as residents in the city directory, and by the early 1930s, when Leroy Hopkins Sr. lived briefly in a house on Barney Google Row, the transition from poor white to poor black was almost complete: only two or three white families remained. The African American residents of Barney Google Row fit the comic stereotype in one sense. Many, like Hopkins, had migrated to Lancaster city from rural areas of the county. Hopkins had been born in Fulton Township but grew up in Quarryville. At the age of twenty, in 1928 or 1929, he moved to the city of Lancaster. Other early residents of the row migrated there from Conestoga Center, about eight miles south of the city, which had been home to a small African American community at least since the 1880s. The rise of the Ku Klux Klan in rural parts of Lancaster County during the 1920s undoubtedly influenced the decision to migrate. The social "push" impelling black migrants was greater than the economic "pull" of jobs, because most of Lancaster's major industries remained segregated until after World War II. For newcomers, the principal available jobs were as domestics and menial laborers. Shantytown's initial residents may also have been predominantly white; the Baker plan reported that recent migrants to the city were largely whites drawn from rural areas. If that were the case, by mid-century the racial composition of the neighborhood had shifted. Health officer Benjamin F. Charles reported in February 1950 that of the adult residents of Shantytown, twenty-nine were white and forty-four were African American, while there were twenty-two white and twenty-seven African American children.[8]

Throughout much of their history, Barney Google Row and Shantytown were tolerated because of the intense demand for housing. By the mid-1930s federal officials had established minimum standards for housing; in 1936 the Works Progress Administration analysis of real property in Lancaster defined an adequate dwelling as one that provided "at least one bathing unit; an inside flush toilet; a central steam, hot water or warm air heating system; electric lighting; and electricity or gas for cooking purposes." Although both Barney Google Row and Shantytown obviously failed to meet these criteria, the dwellings were a haven for the poor, whites and minorities alike, who had few alternatives in a very constricted housing market.[9]

As federal and local leaders began planning the transition from war to peace in the early 1940s, housing finally became an important component of national policy. Earlier involvement in housing by the federal government had been limited to the emergency housing undertaken as part of the war effort in 1917–18, which was quickly privatized in peacetime, and to the New Deal Greenbelt communities, which were undertaken on such a small scale that the results were negligible. The Housing Division of the Public Works Administration (PWA) built several experimental apartment projects in the 1930s, including the Carl Mackley Houses in Philadelphia, designed by Oskar Stonorov and Alfred Kastner, and the Harlem River Houses, which were erected by the PWA following plans prepared by a team of architects headed by A. M. Brown. But the Federal Housing Administration (FHA), established in 1934 under the first National Housing Act, largely limited its efforts to the restructuring of the mortgage industry, while the Wagner Housing Act of 1937, which authorized a public housing program, was deeply flawed in its imposition of cost limitations per unit on new construction, its linking of slum clearance with public housing, and the income limits it established for tenants. An increasingly powerful conservative opposition in Congress severely limited the number of dwelling units the U.S. Housing Authority could build and effectively ended the public housing program in 1942.[10]

By 1944, however, after fifteen years of depression and war, the shortage of decent housing clearly demonstrated the need for national planning and action. The 1944 Housing Committee study in Lancaster, which highlighted the inadequacies of Barney Google Row and Shantytown, was the product of this postwar planning effort. The following year Michael Baker, who prepared the city's new comprehensive plan, also lamented the persistence of blight in residential areas of Lancaster, particularly in the southeast quadrant, and pointed to federal and state legislation then being considered that would enable the city's leaders to undertake an aggressive program to eliminate blight. Indeed, the Baker plan warned, a continuation of "laissez-faire policy will assure that the new homes will be built in the urban fringe and will leave the over-age, congested, unhealthy, hazardous residential sections of Lancaster for further decay." Urban redevelopment became possible with federal financing upon enactment of the U.S. Housing Act of 1949, which incorporated many of the provisions of the Wagner Act and established the goal of "a decent home and a suitable living environment for every American family." Title I of the act established federal urban redevelopment policies and committed funding to enable municipal authorities to acquire and clear blighted or slum areas as a first step in the revitalization of the nation's cities.[11]

Lancaster launched its war on slums at the beginning of 1950. At the request of City Council, the Board of Health undertook a survey of substandard housing that identified 178 buildings in need of significant repairs. Dr. Horace K. Hogg, executive secretary of the Board of Health, announced that the city was beginning to compile minimum standards of living as the basis for a housing code, and he pointed to Baltimore's widely regarded Waverly project, a code enforcement program, as a model of what Lancaster could accomplish in improving the condition of its housing. In April 1951 health officer B. F. Charles presented a set of criteria to be used as a "yardstick" in the slum eradication program—basic standards such as roof, spouting, exterior walls, porches, and sidewalks in good repair; well-fitted doors and windows; and serviceable sink and toilet. Despite the efforts of health officials, the city did not formally adopt a comprehensive housing code until February 16, 1960, as part of its federally mandated Workable Program for urban renewal. The absence of a housing code during the 1950s was a telling indicator of the lack of a modern administrative structure in the city: Lancaster's leaders had not yet adopted national standards for housing, and the city's planning commission did not have the professional expertise to prepare such a code. In subsequent years critics of renewal would place blame on "experts" from other places who did not understand how Lancaster worked, but in the

1950s it was clear that the lack of professional expertise affected the city's ability to eliminate substandard dwellings.[12]

During the next seven years the city proved unable to act effectively to remove or upgrade housing that failed to meet minimal standards for human occupancy. Barney Google Row continued to stand as rental units, in large part because of the continuing shortage of housing in the city. There was simply no place to move residents permanently displaced by demolition, not even temporary accommodations for residents while owners undertook major repairs to structures that would continue to stand. City officials were reminded of the dire shortage of housing when an owner unwilling to make repairs to condemned properties demolished three dwelling units at the rear of 734 Rockland Street in June 1950: the displaced families moved to Barney Google Row.[13]

To members of the Board of Health, Shantytown's fate was inextricably linked with that of Barney Google Row. Indeed, even as condemnation proceedings against the row were under way, Dr. Hogg insisted that Shantytown "has got to go." Although the Baker plan had identified the neighborhood as blighted in 1945, Shantytown became a political issue four years later, when Democratic mayoral candidate Harry Goodhart cited its continuing existence as one of the Republican administration's "unforgivable blunders." Within a year the Board of Health attempted to eliminate the ramshackle dwellings, declaring the shacks at Shantytown unfit for human habitation and ordering the properties vacated within two months.[14]

Shantytown became a civic embarrassment when Lancaster began construction of its first public housing project, Hickory Tree Heights, in 1950. The new project, a state-financed apartment complex intended principally for veterans and their families, was located uncomfortably close to Shantytown: a "tumble-down shack, fashioned out of odds and ends" and five other structures occupied by squatters stood on property owned by the Lancaster Housing Authority. The authority demolished those six structures beginning on August 1, 1951. According to one newspaper account, residents displaced by the authority "moved, to various parts of the county, taking along most of the wood, packing crates, and tin sheets of which their shacks were built." However, numerous other makeshift dwellings remained standing nearby, on county-owned land. In January 1951 city and county reached an agreement that no new buildings would be permitted, but less than five months later the *Lancaster New Era* reported that new shanties were "springing up."[15]

In ordering these demolitions, members of the housing authority adopted a policy that they hoped would cause Shantytown's population to "melt away." Periodic reports indicate that the strategy of demolishing vacated properties was working, albeit slowly. In October 1951 Shantytown consisted of 49 dwellings with 107 residents. Three months later there were 41 buildings and 90 people living there. Six additional shacks were demolished in April 1952, and on July 1 Mayor Kendig C. Bare claimed that Shantytown had been reduced to 26 structures and 80 residents. Six months later the secretary of the Board of Health reported that fully half of all the buildings in Shantytown had been razed; only 22 structures and 60 people remained. Shantytown was indeed "melting away," without any attempt by city officials to determine where former residents were moving, but progress was slow because residents proved reluctant to vacate dwellings at a time when there was so little affordable housing available in other parts of the city.[16]

At the beginning of 1956 Barney Google Row and roughly half the dwellings of Shantytown were still standing, and the city's annexation of Sunnyside, a peninsula located southeast of the historic boundaries of the city, added still another blighted neighborhood to the city's roster of problems. On other fronts the city claimed great progress in its war on slum housing. Of the 178 dwellings first identified as requiring major improvements or demolition in 1950, action on the part of landlords addressed the problem in half the structures by year's end. At the beginning of 1952 Dr. Hogg of the Board of Health reported that although the city had subsequently identified fifteen other properties as unfit for occupancy, the number of substandard dwellings had been reduced to 68. A year later that number had dropped to 47; by January 1954, despite the addition of seven buildings, the number of substandard houses was 41; and the following year there were but 16 such structures.[17]

Although city officials boasted of continuing success in forcing owners to repair slum properties, the numbers reported annually by the Board of Health did not include Barney Google Row or Shantytown. Thus the row and part of the squatter community remained, testament to the lack of alternative housing and, in the case of Barney Google Row, to the city's impotence in the face of a determined landlord. On August 1, 1956, health officer Charles inspected Barney Google Row once again, and a month later the board determined that the houses "are not fit for human habitation and are a menace to the health of the community." The board described the houses as "a chronic source of complaint" and recommended that the city abate the nuisance because the structures "have been repeatedly brought to the attention of the property owner without adequate corrective action." On September 12, Mayor Kendig C. Bare called for the demolition of Barney Google Row. Bare, who as mayor had targeted the structures for clearance in 1950, asserted that "these houses are symbols of undesirable housing conditions in our community" and pledged that the city would "use all its legal powers" to eliminate blight. A month later Bare ordered the Board of Health to pursue removal of the row aggressively. Given the approach of winter, he cautioned that "not one person will become homeless nor be forced into the cold," a reiteration of long-standing city policy, yet the statement rings hollow: it was precisely the absence of available, affordable, decent housing that had allowed Barney Google Row to stand.[18]

At a special meeting held on November 19, 1956, the Board of Health once again formally investigated the properties along Barney Google Row. Although B. F. Charles testified that the properties were beyond repair, two tenants challenged that assertion. James H. Underwood, a resident of 716 Southeast Avenue, reported that "his house is in good condition and he does some work in some of the other houses such as painting and some work on the roofs." He knew of no tenants of other houses who complained about the condition of their residences, and stated that he had wired his house for electricity the previous January at the request of Mr. Charles. William Shultz, a resident of 714 Southeast Avenue for eleven years, had also installed electricity recently and stated that he was "satisfied to live in the house." An attorney representing the property owner rebutted Charles's characterization of the row as a slum and placed blame for many of its problems squarely on the city: the absence of pavements, streets, and sewer connections should not be held against the owner, he asserted, because it was the city's responsibility to provide those services.[19]

Less than a month later Dr. Hogg of the Board of Health indicated that the city intended to authorize demolition of the row to make way for a new street. The Board of Health nevertheless continued to built its case supporting condemnation as a health hazard. Health officer Charles reinspected the properties on February 16, 1957, and reported that the dwellings were in "a very dilapidated condition." To this report Charles appended the results of a survey he made of the block that listed tenants, period of residence, number of persons living in each dwelling, the physical condition of the structures, and whether the occupant had made arrangements to move from the condemned row. The report is frustratingly imprecise because it contains numerous references to "bad condition," which is never defined. For example, Albert Gray, his wife, and his eighteen-year-old son had lived at 724 Southeast Avenue for fifteen years. Charles described the property in the following words: "Front and back doors bad. Kitchen—ceiling in bad condition, sink in bad condition. paper bad in rear bedroom. Sewer in bad condition—waste from kitchen sink running in yard. Outside toilet working but in littered condition." Similarly, Charles described the house occupied by Violet Milburn at 706 Southeast Avenue: "Living room—Interior bad. Kitchen—paper on walls and ceiling bad. Floor bad. Sink not serviceable. Toilet in backyard overflowing. Yard in very bad condition. Sill under floor rotted out. Back steps in bad condition." Presumably the photographs Charles presented to the Board of Health at the March 13, 1957, meeting captured visually what he described as unacceptable conditions, but the images apparently have not survived.[20]

Although the city ordered the dwellings along Barney Google Row vacated by April 1, 1957, on that date twelve families remained. "The whole problem," city solicitor Bernard M. Zimmerman stated, was "where to put the people." The city threatened legal action to vacate the properties but before initiating that proceeding was sued by Anna Gottleib, owner of fourteen of the houses, and Noah Striver, owner of the fifteenth, who sought a court order restraining the city. When the Court of Common Pleas upheld the municipality, Gottleib threatened to appeal to state courts. The city, anxious to proceed with demolition, instead negotiated the purchase of the properties, acquiring the fourteen owned by Gottleib for $6,000 and the fifteenth from Striver for $1,000. The fourteen properties owned by Gottleib were vacated by July 1, 1957, while Striver negotiated an additional month to find an alternative place of residence. Before demolition, however, two squatter families moved into the vacated dwellings, a reminder of the critical shortage of affordable housing, especially for racial minorities, that continued to affect the city.[21]

On July 10, 1957, a clam-shell scoop crane began demolishing Barney Google Row. B. F. Charles, who had retired from the Health Department, was present with a movie camera to record the scene. "At last the day has arrived," Charles told a reporter. "I worked twenty years to accomplish this. I'm glad I lived long enough to see my fondest dream come true." Equally excited were dozens of young boys who watched the crane level house after house from the top of the row to the bottom. Three days later the site of the first fourteen dwellings had been cleared. The owner of the fifteenth property in the row, Noah Striver, undoubtedly viewed the same scene from a different perspective. Striver, 57, had lived on Barney Google Row for about fifteen years, since he bought a 1,200-square-foot lot and built the house, and every health inspection since 1950 revealed that his was a well-maintained property. Striver, his wife, eight children, and two grandchildren faced the prospect of finding another dwelling. Renting proved impossible, given the size of his family, and so Striver was forced to lease-purchase a property at 449 Atlantic Avenue. The six-room house was similar to the one he had built

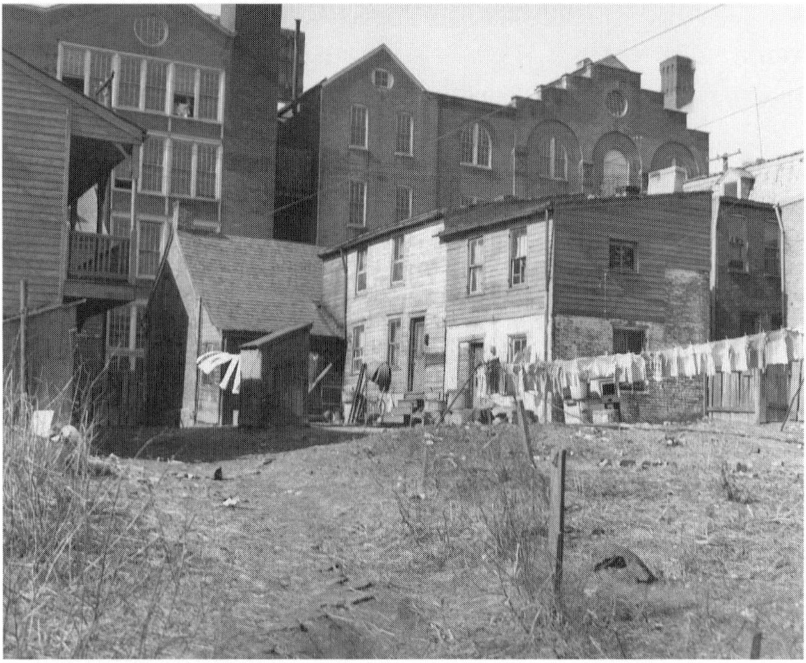

FIG. 3 *Courtyard dwellings behind Howard Avenue. The American Caramel Company building, on the north side of Howard Avenue, looms over the small dwellings (Bureau of Planning, City of Lancaster).*

on Barney Google Row in one respect: it had a cold-water spigot inside and a privy outside.[22]

The demolition of Striver's house on August 26, 1957, marked the end of Barney Google Row. Several dwellings still remained at Shantytown. The city bulldozed three other "shacks" in September, at which time only six dwellings stood. But even as the city neared victory in its struggle to eliminate Barney Google Row and Shantytown, the problem of substandard housing was becoming more acute. Residents vacating Barney Google Row moved into equally deplorable housing in Dunie's Court, a series of dilapidated wooden structures located at the rear of lots facing Howard Avenue (Fig. 3). There, four families shared two outdoor toilets, both of which, while connected to the city's sewer, were in poor condition. Health officer Charles described the deficiencies of these properties as including "doors hanging loosely, windows broken, steps and floors in bad condition." The Board of Health promptly condemned the houses at Dunie's Court and ordered the owner either to make repairs or demolish the structures.[23]

Lancaster's long struggle to eliminate Barney Google Row and Shantytown led eventually to a more comprehensive program of urban renewal that affected every aspect of life in the southeast quadrant of the city. Southeast Lancaster has traditionally been a place apart: it boasts its own name, Musser Town, a legacy of eighteenth-century Germanic origins, as well as a distinctive style of architecture that combines Georgian forms with vernacular building traditions and a grid plan that intersects the city's rectangular street system at an oblique angle. Over the course of more than 200 years the area has been home to the city's poorest residents, its most recent immigrants, and its racial minorities. In the early twentieth century the southeast was a remarkably diverse neighborhood. Degel Israel, the Orthodox congregation of East European Jews, most of whom were recent immigrants, stood on Chester Street, while the Greek Orthodox Church of the Annunciation occupied 219 South Queen Street, on the east side of the block just below German (later Farnum) Street. As if to demonstrate the transitions the neighborhood experienced over time, the Greek congregation occupied a sanctuary that formerly had been a Methodist church. A fixture on East Strawberry Street was Bethel A.M.E. Church, which had been established in 1817 but whose membership had increased in the early twentieth century as the city's African American population grew steadily. A second A.M.E. congregation and Bright Side Baptist Church also served black residents of the southeast. Other churches reflected the continuing presence of mainstream Protestant denominations, though in the years after World War II many of their members had moved to other parts of the city and adjacent suburbs. Throughout the southeast, newcomers from abroad lived on the same streets as American-born children of immigrants from the previous generation and African Americans who could trace their ancestry to the early years of the American republic.

The southeast, an area defined by small lots, narrow streets and alleys, and mixed land use, became the site of the first major residential renewal program in Lancaster. It was in the southeast, where the minority population lived, that the Redevelopment Authority undertook its most extensive slum clearance efforts, where the vast majority of residential displacement occurred and where virtually all of the city's public housing was constructed. The southeast was the crucible in which Lancaster's housing and redevelopment authorities applied the logic of urban renewal. One unspoken but incontrovertible component of the redevelopment process was a policy of containment, the perpetuation of a pattern of segregation in the city by concentrating subsidized housing in the southeast.[24]

Much of the building stock of the southeast quadrant did in fact warrant upgrading. Eighteenth- and nineteenth-century buildings that lined the streets of the southeast were, by the 1950s, aging and in many instances deteriorating. The text accompanying the Residential Security Map of Lancaster, prepared in March 1933, had described the southeast as an industrial and residential area that "holds practically all the aliens and negroes of the city. Houses are row bricks, 50 years and more old. Condition poor." The 1936 Real Property Survey had demonstrated that the southeast was an ethnically and racially diverse area with a concentration of old dwellings, many of which lacked toilets and running water or needed major repairs. An undetermined but significant percentage of the houses were simply unfit to live in. The city's 1945 comprehensive plan had reached the "inescapable conclusion of extremely crowded conditions, with a high portion of aged, obsolete, and crowded homes." The Baker plan described more than a quarter of the city's residential areas as blighted and pointed to slum housing as a cause of social disintegration, juvenile delinquency, poor health, "and a host of other human and municipal ills." While there were substandard houses distributed throughout Lancaster, the worst conditions—in such places as Shantytown, Barney Google Row, and Yanko Court—were in the southeast, as was the greatest concentration of buildings that failed to meet minimal standards for human occupancy.[25]

The campaign against slum housing begun in 1950 had only limited success. Although the Board of Health identified only sixteen substandard structures (other than Barney Google Row) in 1956, a year later Mayor Bare conceded that the problem was much more serious than a handful of dwellings. In his annual report of January 1957, Bare reiterated his longstanding belief that private enterprise should provide adequate housing for all residents, but, keenly aware of the lack of progress in erecting new homes or in renovating existing ones, he added that "it may become obligatory for your city government to take direct action" if the private sector failed to do so. The following March, Bare appointed a Citizen Housing Committee and charged its five members to investigate conditions and submit specific recommendations for improvement. This was an important development, a clear indication that the national interest in housing reform had reached Lancaster. In the course of their first organizational meeting, members of the new Citizen Housing Committee toured the city, beginning in the southeast quadrant.[26]

The four committee members who examined housing conditions recognized the failure of previous efforts to eliminate slums and acknowledged the need for immediate action. Kenneth C. Shelley had reviewed the Baker plan before the tour and was surprised to discover that the blight it described still plagued the city. Donovan K. Smith, chair of the committee and later the longtime chairman of the Lancaster Redevelopment Authority, concurred: "The problem [of slum housing] is serious, and it is complicated and entrenched, through years of ill-fated attempts at solutions." Recognizing that the undersupply of decent rental units was the principal reason for the longevity of substandard housing, Smith and George Zook agreed that the first problem the city faced was finding good, low-cost places for people to live so that slum clearance could begin.[27]

Two factors accounted for the persistence of slums in a booming national economy. One was the lack of construction of affordable housing, which affected Lancaster as well as many other cities. The Residential Security Map had effectively designated most of Lancaster as at risk for federally guaranteed mortgages (Fig. 4). While only three areas were actually redlined—two parcels in the southeast and the small residential community at Sunnyside, which had been annexed to Lancaster in 1955—fully two-thirds of the city was covered with crosshatching, which indicated a pattern of mixed industrial, commercial, and residential use that planners considered inappropriate for homes and that bankers judged detrimental to property values. The Home Owners Loan Corporation (HOLC), established in 1933, adopted a system of evaluation to determine the suitability of residential neighborhoods for federally guaranteed mortgages. Based on reports submitted by bankers, appraisers, and real estate agents, the HOLC prepared Residential Security Maps that colored areas of cities according to the presumed safety of mortgages—from green (the safest, most homogeneous neighborhoods) to blue (stable) to yellow (declining) to red (hazardous). Areas designated red tended to be old, but the housing stock was not necessarily substandard: planners considered neighborhoods characterized by mixed use or racial diversity or large numbers of immigrants at risk for mortgages. Throughout much of Lancaster, potential buyers undoubtedly faced difficulty obtaining the financing that would enable them to acquire and maintain city homes. In what quickly became a self-fulfilling prophecy, the conditions that made an area risky for mortgage-lending also made it unattractive for new residential development, which instead took place in adjacent suburbs.[28]

The other factor was housing discrimination. Lancaster was a segregated community: African Americans, whatever their occupation or income, found it difficult if not impossible to buy or rent housing outside the southeast quadrant of the city. What the Citizen Housing Committee delicately referred to as the "apparent restriction of Negro residents of the community to a specific section of the city" was, to blacks looking for a place to live, a

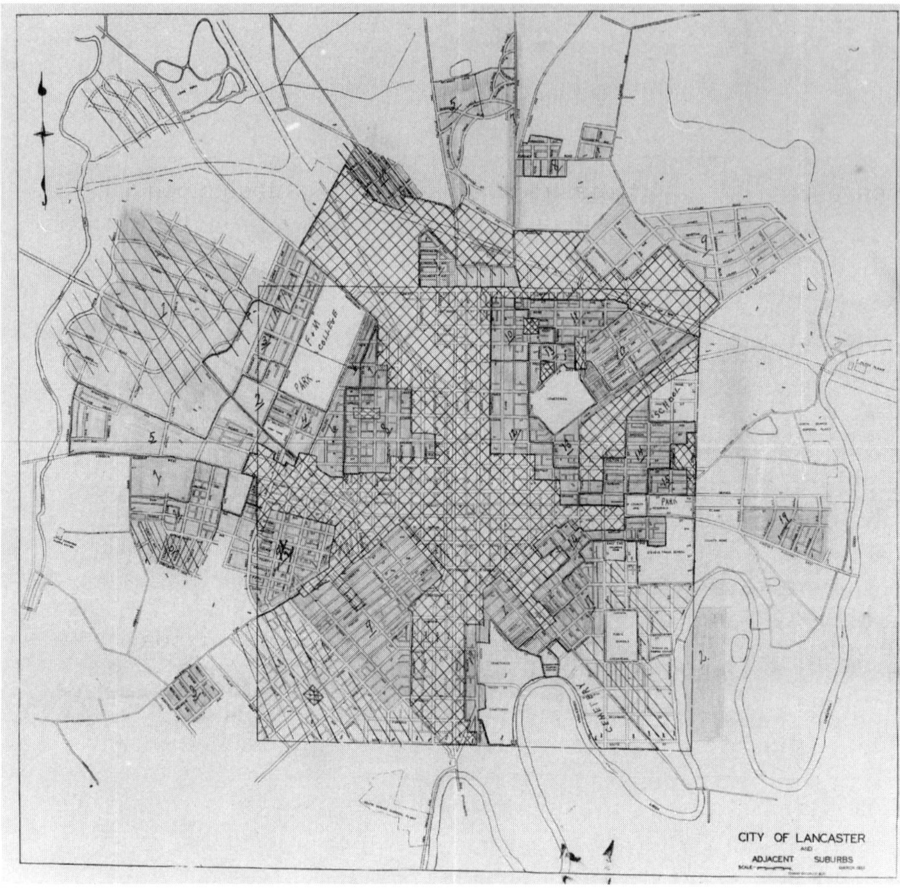

FIG. 4 *Residential Security Map, Lancaster, March 1933, RG 195, Records of the Federal Home Loan Bank Board, HOLC City Survey Files (National Archives and Records Administration, Washington, D.C.).*

harsh reality. Real estate agents routinely steered African Americans away from white neighborhoods and toward "the Ward," as they euphemistically termed the part of the southeast below Howard Avenue, which was the 7th Ward of the city. Consequently, in 1950 the vast majority of the city's African American population lived in the southeast. Only a small number of black households existed in the 1st, 3rd, 4th, and 6th wards, generally on alleys or in small houses close to factories or train tracks. Tom Hyson, formerly executive director of the Crispus Attucks Center and president of the Board of School Directors, vividly recalls his parents' move to a house on the west block of South Duke Street two doors north of Howard Avenue. Although their new home was little more than a block from their former residence on Locust Street, in symbolic terms the move was significant because until that time Howard Avenue had functioned as the boundary separating an exclusively white area from a densely populated, racially mixed neighborhood. The Hysons were not simply moving to a different house but asserting their right to live in a home outside "the Ward." As late as 1960, when the Redevelopment Authority was nearing completion of plans for residential renewal, 96 percent of Lancaster's African American population was living in the southeast quadrant. Any program that attempted to eliminate substandard housing in the southeast would have a disproportionate impact on the city's black residents.[29]

Members of the Citizen Housing Committee did not speak with the Hysons or other African American residents; theirs was a visual tour that focused on buildings and streetscapes, that relied on impressionistic evidence rather than the knowledge and personal experiences of persons who lived in the southeast. The committee's reaction to what they encountered was predictable: shock that human beings were living amid such squalor and a realization that the city had to take steps to eliminate the worst housing. George Zook decried the "alarming conditions of overcrowding, lack of ventilation, and lack of sanitation facilities" he observed in the city. Audrey C. Brodsky's remarks reflected the long-standing reformist belief that a better environment would produce better citizens. The elimination of slums, she asserted, "would be of benefit to the community, from the moral, humanitarian, economic and civic viewpoints." But how to eliminate slums proved vexing. Donovan Smith appeared to speak for his colleagues when he expressed hope that "voluntary individual efforts" would be an important part of any solution to the problem of slum housing, though surely he knew how ineffectual the private sector had been in eliminating substandard housing in the twelve years since the Baker plan had targeted the worst neighborhoods in the city for improvement.[30]

Nine weeks after their tour of residential neighborhoods, members of the Citizen Housing Committee presented their findings and recommendations to City Council. They identified areas where the conditions were obviously substandard, which required immediate attention, as well as neighborhoods that could become blighted. Applying the notion of the city as an organic entity with a natural life-cycle tending toward decay, the committee expressed special concern about areas where the housing was still adequate but that, unless improved, would inevitably become slums and thereby spread the cancerous blight that afflicted the city. The committee's report directly challenged complacency: the efforts of the city and its Board of

Health in attacking the problem of substandard dwellings had "not been able to stem the tide of deterioration and overcrowding—and the social problems that are created by these conditions." The extent of substandard housing was "sufficiently large to call for community-wide efforts and use of the resources of city government and every interested organization and individual." Only a "dynamic, coordinated program" could effectively "preserve property values and prevent physical and social decay."[31]

The committee identified three major problems: a shortage of low-cost housing, which compounded any decision to demolish substandard structures to make way for new construction; the general deterioration of residential neighborhoods throughout the city, which it termed "symptomatic of the cancerous nature of housing blight"; and building, housing, and zoning ordinances that "do not reflect even the minimum standards that should be in force." In addition, the committee identified public sentiment as a major obstacle to urban revitalization, both a widely held skepticism that there were any alternatives to substandard housing and what it termed a "deep-seated opposition in some quarters to the use of certain types of funds, specifically those used to subsidize low-cost housing." The committee then recommended creation of a local Redevelopment Authority with four specific tasks: preparation of a detailed study of housing conditions throughout the city as a preliminary step toward the replacement of substandard dwellings with modern affordable housing; implementation of modern building, housing, zoning, and health codes, with effective enforcement mechanisms; establishment of a neighborhood improvement program to reverse decay in at-risk areas of the city; and a program to educate the public on the need to prevent slum conditions in the city. In presenting the report of the Citizen Housing Committee to City Council, Mayor Bare strongly endorsed the creation of a Redevelopment Authority to tackle the long-standing problem of blight in Lancaster and pledged financial support as the authority organized and began its efforts to revitalize the city. Acknowledging that blighted areas were "harmful to the social and economic well-being," on May 21, 1957, City Council established a Redevelopment Authority, under provisions of federal and state law, with the expectation that its actions would "promote the public health, safety, convenience and welfare of the City of Lancaster."[32]

In the weeks and months following organization of the Redevelopment Authority, the local newspapers promoted a greater awareness of the persistence of substandard housing throughout Lancaster. A five-part series published in the *New Era* in September 1957, for example, presented interviews with residents of blighted buildings, including Noah Striver, owner of the last house standing in Barney Google Row, and tenants throughout the southeast. Although African Americans and Hispanics represented less than 2 percent of the city's population, residents interviewed by the newspapers were almost exclusively minorities, and the photographs published to accompany the articles presented graphic images of deteriorated buildings, squalid interiors, yards filled with discarded tires and other junk, and the seemingly obligatory outhouse. In addition to putting a dark color on poverty, these images have an almost voyeuristic quality, as if the photographer were enabling outsiders to peer into the private lives of minorities who existed apart from the everyday routines of the city's dominant white, middle-class population.[33]

The new Redevelopment Authority began organizing in the summer of 1957. At their first meeting, following yet another walking tour of blighted neighborhoods, members of the authority resolved that the "destruction of Barney Google Row should be our Iwo Jima." They also envisioned new uses for what formerly had been blighted neighborhoods: even before the last of the Shantytown structures fell to the bulldozer, city officials proposed the site as the location for low-income housing for individuals and families displaced as a result of the redevelopment program. Without a hint of concern that Shantytown's reputation might stigmatize residents of the new housing, or that the site's prior use as a dump might present immediate or long-term environmental hazards, local leaders and federal officials alike deemed the former squatter community appropriate for new bricks and mortar. At least in one sense that location was indeed appropriate, because the city's experience with these small areas of substandard housing reflected the community leadership's collective attitude toward the poor, and especially minorities, that would shape urban renewal in the years to come.[34]

Barney Google Row and Shantytown stand as metaphors for the failure of slum clearance, in Lancaster and in other cities. In the years between the first report of housing conditions by the Post-War Planning Council in 1944 and the demolition of Barney Google Row in 1957, Lancaster built no housing for the poor (residents of Hickory Tree Heights would generally be characterized as middle class, at least in terms of income).[35] Nor did the city offer incentives to property owners to improve deteriorated dwellings in the southeast quadrant. Instead, community leaders denounced public housing as a subsidy and a threat to the free enterprise system. When the city finally moved against substandard housing, residents, who were tenants or squatters, were powerless: they did not have the resources to mount a legal challenge to the evictions; they could not defend their homes against the city's bulldozers or demolition cranes. City officials made no attempt to determine what happened to former residents relocated from dwellings along Barney Google Row or in Shantytown, and in neither case did modern housing replace the demolished structures.[36]

Equally important, in subsequent urban renewal programs the city addressed only the physical structures that were symptomatic of a more difficult problem: racial discrimination. Newspaper accounts frequently reported that minority residents were afraid to talk to reporters or public officials, and B. F. Charles informed one landlord that "tenants were very reluctant in furnishing us with any information." To residents such as James Underwood and William Shultz, however bad the conditions on Barney Google Row, a home there was better than none.[37]

Moreover, the so-called shortage of available housing was a narrowly defined deficiency. The city's African American population had increased from approximately 1,800 in 1944 to 2,628 in 1960, but Lancaster's total population had declined from 63,774 in 1950 to 61,055 ten years later. These figures understate the real loss in total population; because of numerous annexations that occurred during the decade, the city's population within the 1950 boundaries declined by 3,893, some 6.1 percent of the 1950 population. The numbers also disguise the startling dimensions of what a 1966 housing study gently termed "white migration out of the southeast area," a suburban exodus aggravated by the city's policy of constructing all subsidized housing in that quadrant. When net natural increase of the population is added to the 1960 figure, it becomes clear that the city was hemorrhaging from white flight. Lancaster experienced the out-migration of 11,400 white persons during the 1950s, roughly one of every six white residents. Most of the natural increase in population resulted from the larger families of the baby-boom generation, which desired more commodious housing accommodations but not necessarily more units. During this time significant new construction, especially in the southwest quadrant, increased the city's supply of housing by 1,140 dwelling units, while annexation accounted for approximately 500 additional units. Thus there should have been ample space to accommodate the people displaced by slum clearance programs.[38]

Ultimately, then, the sheer longevity of the dwellings along Barney Google Row or in Shantytown was testament to the persistence of discrimination, because African Americans in Lancaster and throughout the North were denied opportunities for housing outside carefully circumscribed areas. At a public meeting held in 1956 a realtor expressed consternation over where to find a house for a client he described as being among "the better class of colored fellow," a graduate of Lincoln University, who didn't want to live in "the Ward"—the well-known euphemism for the southeast quadrant of the city—

an implicit acknowledgment of discriminatory practices in Lancaster City and the surrounding suburbs, with the predictable result that 94 percent of the city's African American population lived in "ghetto areas" in 1960, all in the southeast. As late as 1966 a study of housing in Lancaster concluded: "Minority families with the desire and economic capability to move to other area[s] of the city are generally prevented from doing so because of widespread housing discrimination."[39] Together with the failure to modernize existing housing and to construct new dwelling units in older parts of the city, the persistence of discrimination would prove disastrous in the years to come. The same attitudes that tolerated Barney Google Row and Shantytown would continue to characterize Lancaster's collective attitude toward the poor and minorities throughout the city's experience with urban renewal.

CHAPTER 2

THE PROBLEM WITH DOWNTOWN

The discovery of a crisis in housing was the initial step in the development of a comprehensive urban renewal program for Lancaster. Although the years that had transpired between the first identification of residential blight and the demolition of Barney Google Row and Shantytown demonstrate that the condition of the homes of Lancaster's African American population was not a paramount concern to City Hall, the fate of the central business district, traditionally the crossroads of urban life, was more compelling. As was true of many downtowns in the years after World War II, Lancaster's retail core faced a series of problems that included an aging building stock, declining property values, traffic congestion, inadequate parking, and increasing competition from suburban retailers. Confronted with signs of imminent commercial blight, civic leaders made a concerted effort to understand the causes of downtown's troubles. In their quest for solutions, Lancaster's elected officials turned to planners and redevelopment experts who described the city as very much at risk. Lancaster, the planners asserted, needed to take dramatic steps to revitalize its central business district, a conclusion that pointed toward undertaking a comprehensive urban renewal program. Although redevelopment involved risks, and although any project of a scale commensurate with the problems of downtown would have enormous consequences for the physical fabric and social geography of the city in the years to come, proponents of revitalization pointed out that the cost of doing nothing, of allowing the cancerous blight to spread unchecked, was arguably the greater danger.

The location of Lancaster's central business district was the product of geography and economics. The earliest transportation link to eastern markets was the King's Highway, which extended from Philadelphia to the Susquehanna River and which, in Lancaster, became King Street. Later turnpikes also channeled traffic to King Street, which made it the principal commercial thoroughfare of the city. Other roads in Lancaster's grid street system were named for English royalty—Queen, Duke, Prince, and Charlotte, for example—or followed the Philadelphia nomenclature of trees, such as Orange, Chestnut, Walnut, and Lime streets. The major provision for north-south travel was Queen Street. When the Philadelphia & Columbia (later the Pennsylvania) Railroad extended service to Lancaster in 1834, construction of the station on North Queen Street, two blocks north of King, made that street too an advantageous place for business. Penn Square, a recessed square or diamond characteristic of the Pennsylvania culture region, marked the intersection of King and Queen streets and became the commercial and symbolic center of the city.[1] Occupied until 1852 by the County Court House, in 1874 the square became the location for the community's Soldiers and Sailors Monument, erected to honor Civil War veterans (Fig. 5). Handsome church spires punctuated the skyline, but it was the taverns, inns, and commercial establishments that complemented the public functions of the county seat and defined downtown, while most of the city's industries were located adjacent to the railroad.

By the early twentieth century, downtown Lancaster had acquired many of the attributes of a modern commercial center. Within one block of the square were the city's three local department stores and the nation's oldest Woolworth five and dime. F. W. Woolworth had paid homage to the community that supported his first retail success by erecting a large store and office building, topped by a roof garden similar to Stanford White's Madison Square Garden in Manhattan, that stood on the first block of North Queen Street. Other indications of the transformation of the American economy evident near the square were numerous banks, insurance companies, law offices, and other components of a service economy that was becoming increasingly important to cities. Trolley lines that extended to the far reaches of the county converged at Penn Square, bringing downtown the businessmen who worked there and the shoppers from nearby boroughs, villages, and farms who supported the growing cluster of retail establishments. Electric and telephone wires testified to the modernization of American life that had occurred within recent years. As numerous boosters pointed out, by the early twentieth century downtown Lancaster was a modern city. Civic and business leaders were acutely aware of what this meant, as were residents: a local department store advertised itself as the "New York Store" to attract potential customers, and claimed to offer all the goods available in the largest metropolitan area—at reasonable prices, of course. By the 1920s new movie theaters presented the latest releases from Hollywood to an eager public, while the city's first skyscraper, the Griest Building, proclaimed urbanity as it announced downtown's status as the pulsing heart of a growing economic region.

Lancaster's prosperity, however, had brought problems as well as profits to the commercial center. Foremost was congestion, especially as the num-

FIG. 5 *Penn Square, with the Soldiers and Sailors Monument in the foreground. The façade of the Watt & Shand Department Store steps back to conform to the square or diamond that is characteristic of the Pennsylvania culture region. Photograph c. 1958 (author's collection).*

ber of registered automobiles increased dramatically in the early years of the century. If all roads led downtown, many of the city's streets dated from the eighteenth century, and the Germanic tradition of building attached houses close to the sidewalk made the widening of roadways prohibitively expensive. The volume of local traffic was augmented by Route 30, the Lincoln Highway, which became King Street and brought thousands of cars and trucks destined for other places through downtown Lancaster each day. Railroad tracks crossing city streets at grade not only impeded traffic but were an omnipresent danger to vehicles and pedestrians alike, while trolleys also competed with cars and horse-drawn vehicles for space on the narrow streets. Those drivers who successfully negotiated their way downtown faced yet another new problem, parking. Lancaster's first efforts in modern city planning—a 1926 traffic study by Washington, D.C., consultant J. Rowland Bibbins, and a 1929 comprehensive plan prepared by John Nolen of Cambridge, Massachusetts—attempted to relieve congestion and to anticipate the effects of the automobile on city and suburb, but the election of a new mayor and City Council less enthusiastic about the benefits of planning, together with the onset of the Great Depression, prevented the implementation of either the Bibbins or the Nolen recommendations.[2]

One immediate effect of the Great Depression was deferred maintenance, which was especially serious in a city with an aging building stock. A survey of Lancaster real estate undertaken by the Works Progress Administration in 1936 revealed that almost a third of the city's dwellings were more than fifty years old, while 32.4 percent of residential structures were determined to be inadequate because of the lack of plumbing, heating, and utilities. The survey also revealed several ominous trends: that the demand for additional dwelling units had been met by subdividing existing structures into two or more apartments; that most new construction undertaken since the onset of the depression was substandard; and that "the marked rise in population in the adjoining townships indicates a trend toward residential development outside the corporate limits" of Lancaster.[3]

The Great Depression and World War II were years of little investment in downtown Lancaster. Although population increased because of the labor demands of war industries, the additional number of residents crowded within existing structures or found makeshift accommodations. To smooth the transition from war to peace, in 1944 Lancaster's City Council appointed a Post-War Planning Council, headed by businessman A. Z. Moore. Save for the work of the Housing Committee, which investigated the existence of blighted areas such as Barney Google Row and Shantytown, the activities of the council have proven difficult to trace; if it prepared a report, that document apparently has not survived. The council did, however, recommend that the city employ a consultant to update the Nolen Plan, which resulted in the hiring of Baker Engineers, of Rochester, Pennsylvania, to undertake this task. Some of the findings of the Post-War Planning Council were reported in the Baker plan.[4]

Using techniques of demographic, economic, and comparative analysis, growth projections, and other tools that were becoming standard practice in the planning profession, the Baker plan provided a snapshot of Lancaster in 1945. It was an economically diverse city, with a mix of heavy industry, light manufacturing, skilled craftsmen, a full range of wholesale and retail establishments, and a growing service sector, but it was also one of the most densely populated cities in the United States. The product of block after block of brick row houses, this density—almost seventy-eight residents per acre—was more than twice the average the planning profession considered desirable. Although he was confident that Lancaster would continue to be a prosperous community with a skilled work force, Baker urged citizens to recognize that theirs was a "middle age" city and to "face the necessity of planning for a mature community." How the city prepared for that eventuality was essential, because during seventeen years of depression and war the housing stock had continued to age: in 1945 some 56 percent of all dwellings had been constructed in the nineteenth century or earlier, and many had deteriorated in the previous decade because of the lack of money for essential repairs and routine maintenance. "Areas of urban blight will not be absorbed in the future by surging growth and expansion," Baker warned (unaware that the baby boom was already under way), "for population growth in Lancaster, as in the commonwealth and nation, has declined to a relatively insignificant figure."[5]

Given the critical importance of the downtown economy to city planners a decade later, it is perhaps surprising that the Baker plan paid little attention to the central business district. Provisions for suburban development and the construction of new roads to improve traffic flow between urban center and periphery had been important elements of planning since the 1920s, but by the end of World War II better automobile access to downtown became an urgent concern in metropolitan areas across the nation. As John Nolen had done in his 1929 plan, Baker proposed new roads (including an expressway north of the city, a circumferential greenbelt highway, an arterial highway extending to the central business district, and local parkways) as well as alternative traffic patterns in the attempt to eliminate congestion. The absence of close attention to the retail core was undoubtedly also an indication of the lack of real alternatives to, or competition with, downtown stores; there were only a handful of suburban strip malls in the United States constructed before 1945, and the modern, enclosed shopping center was still in its planning stages. Baker's relative neglect of downtown may also have been a reflection of his assessment of the economic vitality of the commercial core and the age of its buildings, the most significant of which dated from the turn of the century. One problem with Lancaster's downtown, Baker conceded, was that too much retail activity took place elsewhere in the city. Largely because of the absence of effective zoning, smaller retail establishments were distributed throughout residential parts of Lancaster, not concentrated in the downtown core. Thus Baker called for the "consolidation of the scattered retail stores into neighborhood shopping centers or into the periphery of the central business district." But for the central business district itself, more attractive window displays, better street lighting, and the introduction of other amenities would be sufficient to maintain downtown's supremacy in retail.[6]

In Lancaster, as in many other older cities, providing adequate parking in the downtown area proved to be a more difficult problem. Baker recognized that "the ability to attract trade depends to a great extent upon the availability of parking space for automobiles," yet also cautioned that curbside parking not only was inadequate for existing demand but also inhibited the free flow of traffic. If traffic and the parking situation worsened, he warned, "the shopper will seek less congested business districts in suburban centers or in neighboring cities." Thus the Baker plan presented a series of "specific and severe recommendations": the reduction in on-street parking and the elimination of surface lots where the entry or exit of cars impeded traffic, the construction of two parking garages (one on the site of Central Market, the other underneath the plaza of a proposed civic center), and the development of new surface lots, most on the interior of blocks but located so that they would not adversely affect traffic flow. These proposals would create an additional 346 downtown spaces, an 11 percent increase over existing facilities.[7]

The Baker plan proved to be a valuable guide in shaping Lancaster's growth in the following decade, especially in the eventual development of a northern bypass and other road improvements. The first stage of the Route 30 bypass was completed in November 1953 and removed a significant though uncounted number of cars from downtown streets, but a comprehensive transportation strategy was never implemented: most notably, the downtown arterial that Baker and other planners advocated, a crucial component of redevelopment in other cities, was never built, nor was an efficient metropolitan public transportation system ever a priority to county planners and elected officials. Nevertheless, as was true of contemporaneous planning efforts in other smaller cities, the plan failed to anticipate the scale and rate of decentralization in the postwar years. Attempting to shore up a declining central business district through better automobile access and underestimating the threat of suburban retail proved to be two of the great miscalculations of urban leaders throughout the United States in the decades after World War II.

Problems of downtown traffic and parking continued to be the focus of planners in Lancaster in decades to come. In 1952, for example, the City Planning Commission proposed once again to relieve congestion in the central business district by diverting some through traffic from downtown. The proposal would have required the extension of several existing streets as well as the widening and repaving of others, but it generated little enthusiasm as a long-term solution. Downtown store owners also feared the potential loss of business as a result of new traffic patterns.[8] More prosaic efforts, such as opening new streets, converting streets to one-way traffic, installing traffic signals, and the like, proved easier to implement, but the Gordian knot of congestion continued to strangle downtown. A 1955 State Highway Department study demonstrated that even after completion of the first stage of the northern bypass, almost six of ten cars entering the central business district were simply passing through Lancaster on their way someplace else.[9] Steps to improve downtown parking were, similarly, half-measures; the lack of progress on a civic center, for example, left the largest component of the Baker plan's proposed solution in abeyance. The city opened its first municipal lot, with seventeen spaces, in 1954, and the following year added a second lot, with fourteen spaces, while moving ahead with plans for a third that would provide twenty-six spaces; it also added parking meters on downtown streets, to increase parking turnover and the availability of curbside space for potential shoppers. But these limited improvements, only a fraction of the additional spaces Baker had insisted were essential, demonstrated that tentative efforts would not solve the parking problem. Given the density of building downtown, demolition of buildings and construction of multilevel garages was the only potentially viable, though obviously highly expensive and disruptive, strategy for additional space. The lack of adequate parking continued to haunt downtown for years to come.[10]

By the end of 1954, Mayor Kendig C. Bare announced that the city should undertake a thorough updating of the Baker plan. As was true of Nolen's 1929 plan, Baker's recommendations had covered an area extending three miles beyond Lancaster's municipal boundaries, all of which was the jurisdiction of the City Planning Commission. Annexation of adjacent land, generally for industrial use, had almost doubled the size of the old four-square-mile city, while the growth of Lancaster's suburbs in the intervening ten years had been dramatic. Thus, in the winter and spring of 1955 Bare recognized that revisions to the earlier plan would not address the real issue facing Lancaster—the fate of downtown in a rapidly suburbanizing society—and called for a document that was more regional in scope.[11] He undoubtedly had in mind the kind of intermunicipal cooperation demonstrated by the Metropolitan Lancaster Commission, a public body consisting of the city and adjacent municipalities that had been established the previous year to develop regional strategies for solid waste disposal. In January 1955 City Council directed the planning commission to discuss the feasibility of a "regional planning unit" with leaders of adjacent municipalities and the Board of County Commissioners. H. M. J. Klein, professor of history at Franklin & Marshall College and longtime chair of the planning commission, enthusiastically supported a broader scope for planning: "The regional plan is the key to effective future planning," he stated, "and then, ultimately, must come the county plan." John M. Groff, another proponent of planning, agreed: although the city had been able to implement many of the recommendations of the Baker plan, the tremendous growth of adjacent suburbs made planning on a metropolitan if not a regional scale imperative.[12]

Adopting one of the suggestions made in the January 1955 discussions, in September the City Planning Commission hired Hugh Pomeroy, director of planning for Westchester County, New York, as consultant. But what appeared to be a bold step forward was actually a temporary retreat from the idea of a regional plan. The commission employed Pomeroy to advise on aspects of the Baker plan that needed to be revised, but not to address broader issues of planning on a county or regional level, Klein reported, because "there still has been no answer to such a proposal from any of the surrounding townships or from the county commissioners." Planning on such a scale was simply not acceptable to Lancaster County voters, who were overwhelmingly Republican and conservative, or to municipalities that jealously guarded home rule.[13]

During the early and mid-1950s, the City Planning Commission, operating without professional staff, approved hundreds of subdivision plans for adjacent suburbs. The Lancaster City Authority extended water and sewer lines to some of these new residential developments and industrial complexes either recently annexed to the city or located nearby, but adjacent municipalities lacked either a planning ordinance or effective zoning. The very problems the Baker plan had attempted to address worsened as unregulated suburban growth sprawled over hundreds of acres surrounding Lancaster City, transforming prime farmland into residential subdivisions. One newspaper described the new pattern of residential growth as the "revolution in our backyards." In the mid-1940s roads leading north from the city through Manheim Township had passed open fields and pastures; a decade later those same roads were lined with housing developments that reflected a startling rate of suburban growth even as the city was losing population. Alarmed by these trends, Mayor Bare initiated a community forum to focus attention on Lancaster's future. The resulting series of public meetings, organized around the topic "Lancaster Looks Ahead," took place on September 18, 19, and 20, 1956.[14]

On the surface Mayor Bare initiated the planning of the Lancaster Looks Ahead forum to obtain the opinions of a diverse group of community leaders on the problems faced by downtown and on potential solutions. The forum consisted of nine sessions, each devoted to a specific subject: Industry; Commerce and Retailing; Positions, Employment and People; Traffic, Parking, Highways, and Transportation; Housing; Public and Social Services; Health; Recreation; and Education. The sessions, chaired by a prominent citizen, consisted of three speakers who presented their considered thoughts on the topics, followed by a question-and-answer session open to all in attendance. The composition of the panels, however, suggests that the forum was less an occasion to debate issues than to generate consensus among community leaders about necessary measures to ensure future prosperity. Only one woman, long active in the local YWCA and Community Chest, served as a member of a panel, to speak about private social services; only one man, an officer of the Central Labor Council, was invited to represent the concerns and perspectives of a highly diverse work force; no one spoke of behalf of the city's minorities. With the exception of a couple of experts from state agencies in Harrisburg who had been invited to provide demographic and other statistical projections, all other speakers were presidents of major corporations, prominent downtown retailers, officers of the local Chamber of Commerce or Manufacturers Association, or members of the boards or executives of social service agencies. At the end of the final session, Mayor Bare praised all participants and noted that he had counted 491 citizens attending the various sessions. But if the people who prepared remarks, asked questions, or otherwise participated in discussions is an indication, the forum represented corporate and official Lancaster, not the working people, not the vast majority of residents, not the poor.[15]

Given the composition of the panels, it is unsurprising that Lancaster Looks Ahead represented a meliorist approach to the city's problems. Yes, downtown traffic was too congested; yes, parking had to be made more available and convenient to shoppers. James Shand, whose family owned the largest downtown department store, testified to the degree to which the automobile had "changed the life and habits" of residents of metropolitan America: "It has made possible the multiplication of suburban housing developments; and conversely, the suburban dweller could not exist without his automobile." The resulting traffic snarls were bad enough, he asserted, but parking had become the "number one problem of the future for retailing, whether downtown or elsewhere." The solutions Shand and other speakers proposed were familiar enough: a northern bypass to route through traffic around downtown, more one-way streets to improve traffic flow, more parking, to be achieved through a variety of strategies, including new surface lots on the interior of blocks, pigeon-hole garages, and park-and-shop initiatives such as that adopted in nearby Allentown. But these were technical problems that could be solved by experts working in collaboration with business leaders.[16]

The panels paid more attention to the need for intermunicipal cooperation and the forging of regional strategies for economic development: how to continue to attract industry to Lancaster, how to develop an educated work force "to the end that an adequate supply of workers may always be available to man our expanding manufacturing plants," how to provide the kinds of cultural and recreational amenities that would make Lancaster more desirable for companies interested in relocating there. Industrial growth would surely continue, one speaker pointed out, because of the "planned de-centralization of manufacturing plants to avoid a crippling atomic blow by the enemy."[17]

And yet, the vast majority of participants in the Lancaster Looks Ahead meetings, even those professing to project twenty years in the future, were unable to perceive a connection between the decentralization of jobs and population on one hand, which they were sure would benefit Lancaster, and the future of downtown retailing on the other. Speaker after speaker implicitly assumed that with the successful implementation of solutions to traffic and parking problems the central business district would remain unchallenged, despite H. M. J. Klein's warning that the planning commission had already received three applications for suburban shopping centers, and a local architect's prediction that "families who leave the cities will do their buying in the suburban areas to which they remove." But whereas Klein insisted that suburban shopping malls were unquestionably the wave of the future, and at least one prominent businessman conceded that the "downtown retailer must meet their competition," other speakers ignored the bad news. Lancaster was simply too small to support department stores both in the central business district and in suburban malls. Retailing in the suburbs, most participants confidently assumed, would never supplant downtown.[18]

Another striking theme of Lancaster Looks Ahead was participants' collective assessment of the proper role of government, at all levels. Whether the topic was federal funding for roads, or state assumption of the cost of building the northern bypass, or the county's responsibility to take the lead in regional planning to promote economic development, or the city's financial assistance in providing the parking that would make downtown more attractive to shoppers (so that retailers, who would most benefit, would not have to bear the burden alone), speakers believed that government must serve the interests of business. They were equally adamant that government must not compete with the private sector, particularly in the area of housing. The chair of the Lancaster Housing Authority, attorney Alfred C. Alspach, echoed Jesse Wolcott, the strident anti–New Deal Congressman from Michigan, and Senator Joseph McCarthy, who had castigated the public housing provisions of the U.S. Housing Act of 1949 as "a key to opening the door to Socialism in America." Any form of subsidized housing, Alspach asserted, was a "socialistic move." Emanuel Murry, a prominent local builder, similarly argued that the solution to the shortage of affordable housing "does not lie in government controls or public housing projects." These "so-called answers," he warned, "would eventually strangle our very precious free enterprise building system."[19]

Neither of these speakers, nor any other participant, noted that the private building industry had done nothing since World War II to alleviate the critical shortage of affordable housing in the city, as Philadelphia mayor Joseph Clark had pointed out the previous year. Nor did anyone mention that the federal government was already subsidizing suburban housing through Veterans Administration and Federal Housing Administration mortgages as well as through the deductibility of home mortgage interest and property taxes. In 1958 William H. Whyte Jr., then editor of *Fortune* and author of the best-selling critique of suburban conformity, *The Organization Man* (1956), described these subsidies, together with the Home Owners Loan Corporation's redlining of cities, as the "discriminatory rules" by which national policy "has been encouraging private investment in suburbia and discouraging it in the city." One speaker suggested that the forum consider establishing a local Redevelopment Authority but wanted to limit that agency's powers: it would use federal urban renewal dollars to acquire and clear a site for a parking garage, which would then be erected by a private developer. Given the conservative political and economic culture of Lancaster, this was the only acceptable area of federal involvement in local affairs, whereas public housing, which at least in theory would compete with the private sector, was simply out of the question. Perhaps more important in the long term, as a result of this conservatism there would be in Lancaster no powerful pro-growth coalition, no effective collaboration of commercial, corporate, and governmental leaders in forging strategies for downtown, as had occurred through the efforts of Pittsburgh's Allegheny Conference on Community Development and Baltimore's Greater Baltimore Committee.[20]

The impact of Lancaster Looks Ahead on the community's attitude toward planning is difficult to assess. To be sure, the local newspapers devoted considerable space to the forum, and particularly to the need for regional approaches to problem-solving (one headline proclaimed, "Municipal Boundaries Viewed as Barriers to Working Together for Area's Progress"), while radio and television similarly provided ample coverage of the proceedings. The discussions may well have succeeded in promoting a united front of commercial interests in support of a regional yet limited approach to planning, but it seems unlikely that the proceedings changed the views of the typical resident.[21]

At the final panel session, forum organizer John M. Groff outlined a plan to pursue the objectives that Lancaster Looks Ahead participants had established. He proposed to classify discussions by topic and to present the findings both to city and county governments and to private agencies. The key to effective planning for Lancaster's future, he added, was "that greater assistance from the county—financial and otherwise—will be required." Mayor Bare similarly expressed hope that Groff's report "will start the county thinking, start the county working, start the county planning."[22] According to *Lancaster New Era* reporter Andrew Torchia, Manheim Township's elected officials also recognized that "suburbia without controls can be a cancer, growing wildly until it kills a community." Despite these calls for county action, and despite the obvious need for planning on a level that could regulate fast-growing suburbs and coordinate the efforts of increasingly interdependent municipalities, the Board of County Commissioners refused to act decisively. The county did not organize a planning commission until 1958, and even then its powers were severely restricted. It was responsible for reviewing all developmental plans but could only advise municipalities about the suitability of applications; local governments retained authority for approval or denial. Moreover, the county planning commission's staff was so limited that it could not provide professional expertise or technical assistance to local governments. Thus by the time the county had developed a vision for the future, in the mid-1960s, the effects of unplanned growth that participants in the Lancaster Looks Ahead forum had warned about had already surpassed the ability of municipalities to control suburban sprawl.[23]

In the absence of any leadership on the county level, efforts to promote regional strategies for managing growth and address problems affecting the city's central business district took two directions. One was the organization of a committee to establish a Regional Planning Commission for Lancaster. This group, apparently a subcommittee of the Metropolitan Lancaster Commission, invited proposals from consultants to prepare a "master plan for the city and ten nearby boroughs and townships." Although the commission did not engage a consultant or employ a professional staff, it continued to emphasize the importance of planning across jurisdictions and tried to influence the policies of the county planning commission.[24]

The other direction focused on the commercial center. The amount of attention devoted to downtown was at least in part a concession that the governmental structure of the surrounding municipalities prevented metropolitan solutions to what had already become metropolitan problems. In late 1956 or early 1957, the City Planning Commission began a series of informal, semi-monthly meetings to discuss strategies for shaping the community's future. Preliminary findings of the group, tentatively entitled "Lancaster—A Vital City, 1965," were published as a fifteen-part series in the *Lancaster Intelligencer Journal* beginning on July 4, 1957. James Todd Baldwin, vice chair of the planning commission and "principal developer of the plans," admitted that the group's proposals were "highly visionary" but nevertheless insisted that the city had to begin tackling long-standing problems if it hoped to maintain the economic vitality of the community.[25]

As had been true of previous discussions about downtown, members of the planning commission began by addressing traffic. Adopting a number of suggestions first presented in the Baker plan, they proposed construction of an outer loop of highways two to three miles from Penn Square as a means of directing through traffic around downtown. They also sketched the lines of an inner traffic loop, roughly corresponding to the city limits, "to permit easy movement between the various segments of the city," as well as a new arrangement of one-way streets to increase the efficiency of travel within the central business district.[26]

The "most radical" suggestion presented by Baldwin's group, an idea that first surfaced a year earlier in meetings of the Citizens Advisory Traffic Committee, was the "elimination of motor vehicle traffic in the downtown area." This was precisely the solution to traffic congestion that architect Victor Gruen recently had proposed for downtown Fort Worth, Texas, which had received considerable attention in the national media. To accomplish the goal of a pedestrian downtown, Lancaster's planners envisioned constructing a network of parking facilities on the periphery of the commercial core and converting the streets in the blocks immediately adjacent to the square into pedestrian malls. If successfully implemented, such an arrangement "would make the downtown area the equivalent of a suburban shopping center" and at the same time, Baldwin asserted, maintain "prime downtown property values and assessments." By emphasizing parking, however, Baldwin's discussion of a downtown pedestrian mall missed a crucial point: the "main purpose" of Gruen's plan, Jane Jacobs observed in 1958, was not to warehouse automobiles but "to enliven the streets with variety and detail."[27]

Paralleling the idea for a pedestrian commercial area was the planning commission's call for construction of a civic center just to the north of downtown. The Baker plan had proposed a new civic center located on a two-block site bounded by North Duke, Chestnut, Walnut, and North Prince streets, and suggested that it include various municipal offices (a new city hall, police and fire headquarters, and a social services building), a public library, county and federal offices, a new public auditorium/sports center, and other functions, including the farmers market. The planning commission's 1957 study envisioned a governmental center on the same site, though without a public library or auditorium/sports complex. Nevertheless, such a civic center would concentrate public services in a single location and remove from the commercial district traditional symbols of downtown, functions that, while essential to a seat of county government, were distinct from retail facilities. "The movement of these offices out of the business district, and out of the shoppers' way," the planners asserted, "would provide additional room for the expansion of retail activity."[28]

The newspaper account of the planning commission's study pointed out that while many of the recommendations were derived from the Baker plan, "in the specifics of these ideas they represent what might be called an up-to-date approach." The proposal to convert downtown into a pedestrian mall, however, was "bold and unprecedented here." The overall tenor of the newspaper accounts, while descriptive, praised the planning commission's efforts. The reaction of the public to the ideas presented, the *Intelligencer Journal* reported, "has been one of recognition of the problems that the ideas attempt to solve." Although even the planners admitted that their suggestions were only a beginning in the struggle to redefine downtown, and that the cost of implementation would be great, "Lancaster—A Vital City, 1965" differed from the Lancaster Looks Ahead forum in its concentration on downtown and its call for specific and energetic efforts to maintain the vitality of the central business district. A number of its suggestions would resurface in the early 1960s as the planning commission and the Lancaster Redevelopment Authority envisioned a new downtown.[29]

The year 1958 marked a break with previous efforts to address the problem of downtown. In the 1957 mayoral campaign, Democrat Thomas J. Monaghan promised to "approach the problems of a greater Lancaster with more imagination" and to "give vigorous wholehearted support to the Lancaster Redevelopment Authority." That November, citizens made Monaghan only the second Democratic mayor elected in the city in the twentieth century. In his inaugural remarks Monaghan emphasized the importance of Lancaster's central business district: "Our cities, most especially Lancaster, have a bright future," he asserted. "The realization of this future, however, will depend on our success in meeting the complex problems of urban life with courage, imagination, and, above all, know-how."[30] To provide a level of expertise commensurate with the challenge, Monaghan made new appointments that resulted in a reorganized City Planning Commission, which, for the first time, could rely on a professional staff headed by Burrell Cohen. Together with the city's newly created Redevelopment Authority, Cohen began a period of intensive study and planning that would result in a concerted program of urban redevelopment. Predictably, the first planning commission document completed by Cohen was *Lancaster's Central Business District: A Study* (1958).[31]

As was true of almost every previous planning document devoted to downtown problems, Cohen first addressed traffic and parking. His purpose was not to identify the dimensions of congestion and parking woes—depressingly familiar topics to anyone concerned with downtown—but to "determine what must be done in order to solve these problems and regain the vigor and vitality of the central business district." The policy recommendations Cohen outlined, however, represented little more than tinkering with the established street system to improve efficiency, and included yet another plea for greater coordination between private parking lot operators, downtown businesses, and the city. More important, he argued for strengthening existing mass transit, which was "responsible for the conveyance of approximately 44 percent of central business district shoppers and an even greater percentage of central business district employees." Increased use of buses was the most effective means of reducing the number of cars entering downtown and alleviating the shortage of available parking spaces. But a focus limited to traffic and parking would be foolhardy, Cohen wrote, because "the answer to the preservation of the central business district does not lie in the solution of a single problem, but rather in the comprehensive planning and revitalization of the entire area." Cohen hoped that the broader strategy presented in this and subsequent reports would "help improve and maintain the central business district and permit it to compete successfully with outlying shopping areas."[32]

Cohen's report provided a compelling economic justification for immediate attention to the central business district. The commercial area adjacent to Penn Square, which occupied approximately 3 percent of the city, accounted for 21 percent of Lancaster's total assessed valuation. "If this district is allowed to deteriorate," Cohen warned, "property value will decrease and the subsequent effects, including tax increases, will be felt throughout the community." The problem, as he perceived it, was not simply traffic or parking but a more general malady he termed "downtownitis," which included "vacant stores, decline in the use of mass transportation into the area and the general deterioration and obsolescence of structures and streets." Lancaster's affliction was not yet at a critical stage, he asserted, but was sufficiently advanced that it required the effective remedy of planning and redevelopment. "The time has come," Cohen wrote, "for the community as a whole and downtown businessmen in particular to organize and plan progressive action to stop its spread which, if not controlled, can spell disaster for the central business district."[33]

In determining that downtown buildings were obsolete and therefore in need of replacement, Cohen introduced a new theme in the discussion of the central business district. Previous studies, which had concentrated on parking and traffic, were predicated on the assumption that if these problems could be remedied, downtown would continue to flourish. But in his preliminary assessment of the central business district, as well as in later documents and addresses, Cohen pointed to the age of buildings as a significant drawback to economic vitality. In *Lancaster Moves Ahead* (1959), for example, he argued that the increasing rate of construction in Lancaster's suburbs, and the lack of modernization to downtown commercial facilities, demonstrated that "the replacement of old and obsolete structures has not progressed with population growth and the increased earnings of business, industry and individual families." To be sure, buildings erected at the turn of the twentieth century lacked off-street loading docks and other features routinely incorporated in more recently constructed retail stores, but many had highly decorated façades that contributed to what Michael Baker termed the "picturesque character" of the city and that were simply irreplaceable given present construction costs (Fig. 6). Although the Urban Land Institute had recently argued for the adaptive reuse of older downtown buildings, Cohen turned the age of structures into a clarion call for demolition. "The future of Lancaster," he claimed, "is entirely dependent upon its ability to remove that which is old and obsolete, that which is undesirable and substandard, whether they be homes, business establishments or industrial facilities and, by so doing, make land available within the city for the construction of new well-built and attractive facilities that will enable the city to effectively compete with its suburban neighbors."[34]

What made immediate action to upgrade the physical condition of downtown essential, Cohen asserted, was the development of suburban retail centers that were "endeavoring to provide the shopper with the same type of shopping convenience once found only within the central business district." Ironically, the planner's assessment of the threat of suburban shopping contrasted with that of most downtown retailers, who interpreted record sales during the late 1950s as an indication of a rosy future for the central business district. Statistics compiled as part of *Lancaster Moves Ahead* confirm that downtown was still a thriving retail area: "Even with the new center in suburban Lancaster, the major merchants in the Central Business District indicate that their total retail sales volume for 1958 surpassed all previous years." But as Cohen and other advocates of redevelopment pointed out, the effect of new competition from the suburban fringe was already evident in an increased vacancy rate in downtown buildings—more than 95,000 square feet of retail space—which, according to Cohen, was "a definite indication that something is wrong within the area itself." Part of the problem was the owners themselves, who were enjoying handsome profits but made little

FIG. 6 *Highly decorated façades along the west side of the 100 block of North Queen Street. Note the storefront for rent, and vacant second and third stories, which planners considered indications of blight. Photograph c. 1962 (author's collection).*

reinvestment to upgrade their stores. Without improved facilities, Cohen argued, downtown would not be able to withstand the challenge posed by new suburban retail centers.[35]

Although downtown merchants followed the position of the Urban Land Institute that suburban retailing did not constitute a threat to the central business district, especially for a small metropolitan area such as Lancaster, the city's commercial core was clearly living on borrowed time, just as H. M. J. Klein and Cohen insisted. Historian Jon C. Teaford has observed that statistics reflecting postwar retail activities in twelve major cities "all pointed to commercial decentralization." What happened in northern New Jersey exemplifies the impact of suburban retail. Bergen County, directly across the Hudson from Manhattan, became, in a remarkably short time, home to the largest suburban retail complex in the world: two malls, Garden State Plaza and Bergen Mall, which in the late 1950s attracted 500,000 shoppers a week.

A survey of shoppers undertaken in 1959 found that more than half the patrons, who formerly had shopped in Manhattan, were spending their retail dollars in Paramus. As historian Lizabeth Cohen has demonstrated, "Nationwide, the trend was the same: retail sales in central business districts declined dramatically between 1958 and 1963, while overall metropolitan sales mushroomed from 10 to 20 percent."[36]

Lancaster was not far behind the national trend. The City Planning Commission reported in 1959 that increased retail sales downtown the previous year were "mainly a result of the greatly increasing population and buying power of the suburban areas" and expressed concern about what it described as "an increasing tendency to develop suburban shopping centers that will absorb much of the retail sales volume now enjoyed by the city's Central Business District." Lancaster's population declined significantly between 1950 and 1960 while that of adjacent suburbs increased dramatically, Lancaster Township's by 46.2 percent, Manheim Township's by 59.9 percent (see Appendix, Tables 1 and 2). Newspaper accounts and subdivision plats filed with the planning commission indicate that suburban Lancaster was experiencing a home-building boom in the 1950s. Indeed, in 1958 one reporter described suburbanization as "the most spectacular happening in this area during the past decade." As the middle class moved to new homes on the periphery of the city, purchasing power, represented by median family income, also migrated from Lancaster to the surrounding suburbs. Although at the beginning of 1958 the increasing concentration of income in the suburbs had not yet translated into new shopping habits in places other than downtown, suburban developers were planning malls that would challenge the continuing vitality of Lancaster's retail core—new stores that were competitive in price and quality of merchandise, and accessible without having to confront the traffic and parking difficulties downtown. In November 1955 local construction executive J. H. Wickersham had proposed a new mall, at the intersection of the Route 30 bypass then under construction and the old Harrisburg Pike (the site of what today is Park City, a regional shopping center), that would include an anchor department store, a supermarket, and numerous other shops. Six months later A. G. Kurtz announced construction of a 52,000-square-foot shopping mall in nearby Ephrata, which would include a W. T. Grant store. Grant's had long been a fixture of downtown, but only months after the decision to build in the suburbs the company announced the closing of its North Queen Store.[37]

The opening of the Lancaster Shopping Center on February 13, 1958, was the first suburban alternative to downtown. Located on a 17-acre site between two major traffic arteries, the Lititz and Oregon pikes, just north of the city, the new shopping center was 766 feet in length and included a parking lot for 1,500 cars. Some 5,000 people braved freezing temperatures to watch a parade, listen to speeches (including one by the city's mayor, Thomas Monaghan), and explore this innovation in retailing. What they confronted was somewhat familiar: among the stores located in the new mall were two large, well-known department stores, W. T. Grant and S. S. Kresge, such national chains as Rea and Derick Drugs, Kinney Shoes, Endicott Johnson Shoes, and Sherwin-Williams Paints, as well as a large supermarket and a smattering of smaller, locally owned stores. But participants in the opening also confronted a new retail environment, one that was vastly different from downtown in terms of accessibility, convenient parking, and such amenities as a covered pedestrian walk. The Lancaster Shopping Center introduced yet another new element in local retailing: absentee ownership. The developers of the shopping center were Food Fair Properties and Max J. Levine, both of Newark, New Jersey. The mall may have represented new investment in suburban Lancaster, but the profits from design, construction, and management, as well as from general operations, would be reaped more than a hundred miles away, while its retail stores would attract shoppers who formerly had patronized downtown.[38]

A year later, developer Max Levine announced plans for Lancaster's second suburban mall, the Wheatland Shopping Center. This 80,000-square-foot retail complex, located on the Columbia Pike just west of the city, would include a W. T. Grant store and an Acme supermarket as anchors, as well as various smaller retail establishments. At the same time, rumors circulated widely about a major addition to the Lancaster Shopping Center. Levine had taken an option on two properties adjacent to the first mall, and newspapers reported that the expansion would include a Sears Roebuck store, long a fixture of East King Street, as well as a Weis supermarket, a nationally known discount store, and a bowling alley. As if competition with downtown retail was not enough, the developers were negotiating with service industries that were also essential to the economic vitality of the city. According to the *Intelligencer Journal,* Levine's rental agent was attempting to persuade the Prudential Insurance Company to move its local offices to the suburban facility and negotiating with the Post Office to establish a substation at the mall.[39]

These suburban malls proved to be attractive investments for developers because of another incentive provided by the federal government. In 1954, in the midst of a slump in the building industry, Congress enacted a law that made possible the accelerated depreciation of newly constructed commercial real estate. Because this provision in the tax code allowed developers to increase net profits, and because it did not apply to the renovation of existing buildings, the effect of accelerated depreciation was to redirect capital investment from downtown to the suburban fringe. According to historian Thomas W. Hanchett, in the years following passage of this provision "shopping plazas sprouted like well-fertilized weeds" across the United States. Although Lancaster's commercial elite, with its traditional ties to downtown, did not turn to developing suburban malls, outside capital took advantage of the opportunity thus provided and constructed new retail facilities in outlying areas to compete with local merchants.[40]

The first suburban strip malls did not, of course, cause an immediate revolution in shopping habits. Downtown retailers retained their supremacy in certain areas—most notably in furniture and the higher end of the department store spectrum, as well as in more specialized retail services that catered to downtown businesses and employees—and at every level of retail activity fought the suburban threat with aggressive advertising. Nevertheless, the development of large retail malls in rapidly suburbanizing areas to the north and west of the city was a serious challenge to Lancaster's central business district. A number of surveys undertaken in major metropolitan areas during the 1950s indicated that women, who did most of a typical family's shopping, still preferred downtown when asked about the range of available merchandise; when questioned about convenience and accessibility, however, they chose suburban malls.[41] Together with the shift in purchasing power to the suburbs, the construction of attractive retail establishments near burgeoning residential subdivisions represented precisely this convenient alternative to downtown. And as shoppers' habits began to change, they spent more time and more dollars in suburban malls than downtown. Between 1958 and 1963 the total volume of retail sales dropped in Lancaster City, while that of the suburbs increased dramatically. Owners of stores in downtown Lancaster, whose businesses recently accounted for more than 44 percent of total county retail sales in 1958, saw their share of the retail trade drop to 28.6 percent over the five-year period. Although downtown retailers enjoyed modest gains between 1963 and 1967, total retail sales in Lancaster in the latter year represented a continuing decline in its proportion of receipts for the metropolitan area (see Appendix, Table 3). The battle for supremacy in the retail arena had been joined, and downtown, only a few years earlier the undisputed commercial center of the county, was by the mid-1960s struggling for its very survival.[42]

The fate of the city of Lancaster was directly tied to the continuing vitality of its downtown. The migration of purchasing power and retail sales to the suburbs adversely affected the assessed value of city properties, especially in the central business district, which as recently as the late 1950s had accounted for 21 percent of total property taxes collected. As sales fell and vacancies increased, the city's income from downtown properties dropped significantly, just as Burrell Cohen had predicted. A countywide reassessment of real estate, completed in 1961, reduced the value of buildings on the 100 block of North Queen Street by $1.86 million, a drop of more than 30 percent. The city and the School District of Lancaster lost approximately $55,000 in annual revenues as a result of reassessment. In August 1962 the planning commission reported that recent real estate transactions demonstrated that downtown properties were selling at prices "considerably less than their market value." As the tax burden shifted to residential properties, the increasing disparity in city-suburban taxes made homes outside the city comparatively more attractive. Equally important, Lancaster did not experience the boom in office construction that occurred in numerous larger cities and that compensated for the loss of some traditional retailing. Although the downtown was "far from being flat on its back," as one consultant observed in late 1959, Lancaster needed to take prompt, aggressive steps to halt the flight of retail activity to the suburbs and to ensure the future of its central business district.[43]

The City Planning Commission and the Lancaster Redevelopment Authority, which had been studying the needs of downtown for some time, were prepared for a counterattack. In October 1959 Clifton E. Rodgers & Associates, consultants to the planning commission, presented an elaborate vision of "Downtown Lancaster 1980," which proposed to modernize and revitalize the central business district through an ambitious program of new construction. Three years later, in October 1962, the Redevelopment Authority completed a survey and planning application for the total redevelopment of the 100 block of North Queen Street. The planners were ready, but the task was formidable. They had to staunch the hemorrhaging of downtown and at the same time break what Lewis Mumford termed the "cycle of environmental impoverishment," especially the "intensified congestion both in the original center and in the suburb, which wipes out the social assets of the city and the rural assets of the country."[44] The stakes in planning a revitalized central business district were enormous: how effective the Redevelopment Authority was in defining a future for downtown, how successful it was in rebuilding the heart of Lancaster, would in many ways determine the future of the entire city.

PART II

Planning a New Downtown

CHAPTER 3

BEST-LAID PLANS

In the late 1950s, the 100 block of North Queen Street was the entertainment crossroads of Lancaster and a critically important component of the central business district. Four movie houses—the Grand, the Hamilton, the Capitol, and Boyd's Colonial Theater—continued to attract patrons to the block, just as they had since the 1920s. Three hotels—the Brunswick, the Wheatland, and the Pennsylvania—still stood, though their function had changed since the passenger train station moved from the northeast corner of Chestnut and North Queen streets to a new location just outside the city limits in 1929. The chaste classical façade of the Lancaster County Farmers National Bank was a familiar landmark to residents, as were the numerous retail establishments along the street—a camera shop, clothiers, two florist shops, two bakeries, a candy store, a drug store, and other small businesses. Several restaurants and bars dotted this stretch of downtown, as did the local telegraph office and the Lancaster YMCA. The streetscape was as exuberant as the diverse functions of the buildings, which ranged in style from high Victorian Romanesque to Beaux Arts classical to 1920s moderne and which varied in height from two to eight stories.

To downtown businessmen and planning commission staff, the most striking characteristic of the 100 block of North Queen Street was not its eclectic architecture or its crowded sidewalks but the evidence of imminent blight (a word borrowed from plant physiology to describe an urban area in which the natural growth had been stunted or that was economically declining). At least one building had already been razed to provide additional parking adjacent to the Brunswick Hotel, a telling indication of the shift from travel by rail to reliance on the automobile. Moreover, the hotels, which once attracted travelers coming downtown to visit, shop, or transact business in the retail core, had a growing population of permanent residents. Equally disturbing to planners was the presence of several vacant storefronts. What a few years earlier had been optimal commercial real estate was experiencing difficulty attracting tenants. To the astute observer, a change in the kind of businesses occupying North Queen Street buildings was also a concern: signs along the street advertised a bowling alley and billiards room, a beauty school, and Figure Tone Studios, uses that were hardly compatible with a prominent commercial area within two blocks of Penn Square (Fig. 7). Still another cause of worry was the lack of reinvestment in buildings, the vast majority of which dated from the turn of the twentieth century or earlier. Peeling paint, years of accumulated dirt encrusted on ornate stonework, and other signs of decline contrasted with the clean new suburban malls just opening outside the city. In short, the 100 block of North Queen Street was becoming functionally obsolete and manifesting the initial symptoms of blight, which Michael Baker Jr., in the 1945 plan of the city, described as "a cancerous tissue." "Like a cancer in a human body," he warned, blighted areas spread outward and cause decay in adjacent neighborhoods. Thus in the summer of 1962 the Redevelopment Authority made the 100 block of North Queen Street the centerpiece of its strategy for downtown renewal, the focal point of efforts to reverse the decline that threatened to overwhelm the entire city.[1]

Before making the decision to undertake an ambitious commercial redevelopment project on the 100 block of North Queen Street, the city planning commission continued to study the larger downtown retail environment. As was true in cities across the nation, most discussions about the problems facing the central business district that occurred during the 1950s focused on traffic congestion and parking. That changed in 1958, however, when the city's new director of planning, Burrell Cohen, echoed developer James Rouse's warning that downtowns were facing a serious challenge which threatened their continuing vitality. Like Rouse, Cohen pointed to the obsolescence of buildings and the threat of suburban retailing as important factors contributing to the decline of the central business district. In late 1959, the consultant employed by the planning commission, Clifton E. Rodgers & Associates, addressed the range of issues facing the retail core. In the report *Downtown Lancaster . . . 1980,* Rodgers observed that between 1954 and 1958 metropolitan Lancaster experienced new construction valued at $78.2 million, but of that total only 12 percent was erected within the city. To dramatize the effects of suburbanization, he demonstrated that whereas per capita expenditure for new construction in the suburbs was $1,283, in the city the amount was only $146. Rodgers did not provide figures on reinvestment in existing buildings, a better indication of how downtown was responding to competition from suburban retailers, but he nevertheless asserted that property owners in the central business district were failing to undertake necessary improvements. Thus he reminded citizens that "a healthy downtown is vital to the economy of the area" and emphasized the "responsibility to replace obsolete facilities in keeping with the needs of the community."[2]

FIG. 7 *Blight visible in declining economic use: the east side of the 100 block of North Queen Street, c. 1962. Note that a building to the left has already been razed to provide parking for the Hotel Brunswick. Photograph published in the* Lancaster Intelligencer Journal, *August 16, 1965 (Lancaster Newspapers Inc.).*

Rodgers's plan envisioned a revitalized downtown that would continue to be the "prosperous hub of the Lancaster Metropolitan Area." The central business district faced difficult challenges, but its condition was far from terminal. Downtown continued to account for 22 percent of all employment in Lancaster County and a significant percentage of retail sales. Land use downtown was changing, however: it was declining in importance as a place of residence, of manufacturing, and of wholesale activity. Rodgers expected that these trends would continue and provide additional space for "expansion of retail trades and services." But, to ensure future prosperity for the central business district, Rodgers argued, two additional steps were necessary: the replacement of "inadequate structures in Downtown" and, together with modern commercial facilities, the construction of high-rise apartments to house the "more sophisticated people" who would work in the expanding service economy and who wanted to live near the center of the city. The latter proposal was similar to strategies adopted in such cities as Boston and Philadelphia as an essential step in downtown revitalization.[3]

As was true of all previous planning efforts, Rodgers devoted considerable energies to the traditional problems facing the central business district: parking and traffic. He pointed to the recently completed northern bypass as a major step in eliminating downtown congestion, but called as well for the prompt development of better north-south traffic patterns through the city and for the completion of the proposed inner loop. Given the plan's focus on the central business district, Rodgers demonstrated that 42,000 vehicles carrying 65,000 persons entered the core of the downtown retail district each day, an increase of 20 percent since 1954. While better traffic patterns would eliminate much of the travel simply passing through downtown, Rodgers insisted that the construction of new roads in the suburbs would not solve downtown's traffic headache. Congestion, though lessened, would remain, and the shortage of parking had long since reached crisis proportions. Although the amount of off-street parking in the city had doubled since 1954 (most of these additional spaces were provided by a single private garage), Rodgers documented an absolute shortage of more than 1,200 parking spaces in the six-block retail core. Moreover, the solution to one long-standing problem—elimination of curb parking to improve traffic flow—would obviously worsen the other.[4]

Rodgers then addressed the physical fabric of the central business district. Downtown buildings enclosed 7.1 million square feet of space, of which 41.6 percent was devoted to retail use or services, 20 percent was residential, 10.8 percent was industrial, and 11.6 percent served public and semi-public purposes. Parking accounted for 10.1 percent of downtown space. Building coverage was highest at Penn Square and decreased with distance from the center, as, in general, did building heights. This area still commanded the highest assessed value of land in Lancaster and contributed 20.8 percent of the city's income from real estate taxes, but the age of buildings, and the increasingly precarious nature of retail trade, had ominous implications for downtown—and for the city as a whole.[5]

Indeed, the signs of blight and obsolescence were unmistakable. Rodgers reported that "inflated property values" had prevented some merchants from undertaking necessary expansion and that obsolete buildings and the high cost of replacing older structures had discouraged the establishment of new commercial uses downtown. The result was an alarming increase in vacancies, even within a block of Penn Square. The overall vacancy rate in the retail core remained seemingly low, 4.6 percent, but the rate for retail was actually 19.3 percent of the total commercial floor space. Director of Planning Burrell Cohen amplified the implications of changing economic uses downtown: although the large department stores were continuing to flourish, other "complementary land-uses," such as specialized stores, theaters, and hotels, were losing their traditional clientele. "These downtown activities," Cohen warned, "are all dependent upon each other for their continued existence and prosperity." The construction of new suburban shopping centers presented a "countervailing force" to the central business district, attracting the kinds of small businesses and shoppers that until recently had contributed to a vibrant retail core. Clearly, if downtown were to retain its traditional role as the commercial center of the greater Lancaster area, the central business district would need prompt, effective attention.[6]

Rodgers's plan, presented, along with a large-scale model of the revitalized downtown twenty years in the future, at a public meeting on October 27, 1959, and published in a glossy brochure shortly thereafter, promised precisely the dramatic action he and most planners nationwide believed was essential to reinvigorate the central business district (Fig. 8). It incorporated several earlier suggestions for addressing the problems of downtown, including a civic center, located at the North Queen Street site designated by Michael Baker in 1945, which, as that earlier plan suggested, would include an underground parking garage. Drawing upon the Victor Gruen's acclaimed plan for Fort Worth and the experiment a number of cities had undertaken in recent years, Rodgers proposed a traffic loop around the six-block heart of the commercial center, which would be redeveloped as a "park-like" pedestrian mall. Parking would be located on the fringes of the central business district, and pedestrians would enjoy a brief, "exciting" walk under arcaded shelters to an attractive retail area (Fig. 9). Buses would deliver employees and shoppers entering downtown within one block of any point in the pedestrian mall. If the proposals for new construction, landscaping, and traffic patterns were adopted, Rodgers asserted, the downtown would be "like a park, but buzzing with excited shoppers."[7]

Rodgers's vision of a revitalized central business district would have transformed the physical fabric of downtown. The plan called for the preservation of several buildings noteworthy for their architectural merit, including the Brunswick Hotel and Watt & Shand Department Store, both handsome turn-of-the-century Beaux Arts structures designed by Lancaster

FIG. 8 Downtown Lancaster . . . 1980, *scale model of the modernist plan prepared by Clifton E. Rodgers (right). Burrell Cohen of the Lancaster City Planning Commission (center) points to a new high-rise building on East King Street (Bureau of Planning, City of Lancaster).*

architect C. Emlen Urban, as well as the Art Deco Fulton Bank, but recommended the demolition of other historically significant buildings, including Samuel Sloan's classical County Court House (1852), the turn-of-the-century City Hall, Urban's ornate Victorian Southern Market (1888), and numerous other structures in the immediate vicinity of Penn Square. In addition, Rodgers called for the removal of all but one structure (the city's recently constructed Public Safety Building) in the two-block area on North Queen Street reserved for the civic center. The plan was predicated upon widespread demolition—literally hundreds of buildings ranging in date from the late eighteenth to the early twentieth centuries—that Rodgers deemed essential to provide space for additional parking, for pedestrian access, for attractively designed open spaces, and for the proper siting of new buildings to be erected according to the plan.[8]

For the new buildings that would be added to the streetscape, Rodgers paid deference to the omnipresent red brick in the city by suggesting the use

FIG. 9 *Detail of cover of the May–June 1960 issue of* Pennsylvania League of Cities, *illustrating Penn Square and its historic buildings: Old City Hall, to the left with the flag, the fourteen-story Griest Building, and the Art Deco Fulton Bank on the northeast corner of Queen Street. Note the pedestrian downtown and the pedestrian shelters. This image also served as the cover of Rodgers's report* Downtown Lancaster . . . 1980 *(Bureau of Planning, City of Lancaster).*

of that material "as a common denominator," enhanced by the addition of "new materials such as glasswalls [*sic*], metal panels, and durable stone." And while he advised that new construction "consciously use shapes, materials, and spaces which take into account the design of the overall area," Rodgers insisted that new structures "should be designed to express their contemporary purpose, and use contemporary technology." To do otherwise, to erect modern buildings that were Georgian in appearance, would "devalue the authentic Colonial structures in Lancaster." Despite this claim of sensitivity to the historical context of downtown, the new construction Rodgers proposed for the civic center (Fig. 10) was hardly sympathetic to the streetscape.

FIG. 10 Downtown Lancaster . . . 1980, *detail of scale model showing modern office building, convention center, and city hall. To the right is the city's Public Safety Building, erected in the 1950s (Bureau of Planning, City of Lancaster).*

The design for a new office building to be located at the corner of West Chestnut and North Prince streets, for example, was an International Style glass box that stood on *piloti* in the midst of parking lots. Adjacent to the east was a convention hall, a structure that clearly expressed its steel and concrete materials in the sweep of its curving roofline. According to one newspaper report, the planners, apparently in all seriousness, explained that the convention center's strikingly modernist shape was "designed to resemble the famed Conestoga wagon at a distance." Farther to the east were the new County Court House, a boxy structure that, like the proposed office building, was elevated on posts, and a nondescript new City Hall. The landscape, in keeping with the architecture, treated the buildings as individualistic expressions of modern art, divorced from each other as well as from the surrounding cityscape. Other proposed downtown buildings—especially two apartment towers located on Vine Street, at the southern end of the central business district, though only suggested in the model and plan—were similarly modernist in expression.[9]

The Rodgers plan would also have transformed the pattern of land use downtown, though not as dramatically as it did the architectural fabric of the city. Space devoted to retail, services, offices, and public uses would have increased slightly, while that allocated to residential, industrial, and wholesale purposes would have declined significantly. The new construction Rodgers proposed would have replaced downtown's mixed commercial, civic, and service economy with a stronger emphasis on retail. The biggest reallocation of space downtown was the acreage devoted to parking, which was projected to increase from 10.5 to 22 percent of the central business district. The buildings demolished, assessed at $8.4 million, would be replaced by new construction erected at an estimated cost of $52 million, which promised to provide a healthy infusion of new tax dollars to the city treasury. Rodgers's figures for new construction, however, included the value of parking garages, which in many cities were operated by a parking authority, and that of the public buildings, all of which would be tax exempt. How much the new private construction would have benefited the city's tax rolls cannot be determined, but the net result surely would have been far less dramatic than Rodgers claimed. Nor did the planner indicate what types of new retail stores would find this revitalized downtown a more attractive location than the suburban malls located closer to the fast-growing residential subdivisions outside the city.[10]

The headline of the October 28, 1959, *Intelligencer Journal* heralded the announcement of Rodgers's plan: "*Downtown Lancaster . . . 1980* Aims for Salvation of Business District." But even if implemented gradually, as the planners projected, the cumulative changes would have resulted in a very different place from the central business district of 1959. Rodgers explained that the proposed new downtown would be a visually exciting, economically attractive area that had successfully deflected the challenge of suburban retailing. Ironically, in determining how to resurrect downtown Rodgers applied the principles of planning that had become standard in the design of suburban malls: everything from peripheral parking, arcaded pedestrian ways, street furniture, signage, and such amenities as cafés, theaters, and plazas. There was apparently no attempt to understand why downtowns had developed as retail centers, what features other than convenience of access had made them dominant commercial areas for generations. For planners of the postwar generation, there was no usable past.[11]

Equally noteworthy, all the improvements projected in *Downtown Lancaster . . . 1980* except the civic center were predicated on private investment. Although Lancaster had organized a Redevelopment Authority in 1957, and although a 1954 amendment to the U.S. Housing Act of 1949 had permitted the use of up to 10 percent of federal urban redevelopment funds for nonresidential projects (which increased to 20 percent as a result of a 1959 amendment to the Housing Act), Rodgers devoted only two sentences in the published plan to the possibility of relying on those tools for land acquisition and clearance. But as the planning commission confronted the daunting task of undertaking a project as ambitious as the Rodgers plan, it conceded that Lancaster might need to take advantage of the extraordinary powers extended to cities in the war against blight. Thus, shortly after the unveiling of the Rodgers plan a newspaper reported that the Redevelopment Authority "may be asked in the future to play a major role in the large-scale renovation of the central business district." Still, the city's reluctance to use eminent domain and federal dollars was underscored a week later, when a group of businessmen announced the formation of a private nonprofit corporation to carry out plans for downtown revitalization. This group, the Central Lancaster Development Corporation, had the enthusiastic support of planning director Cohen, who believed that a "private development corporation is the only way that a downtown plan can be implemented." Its organizers expected that the new association would have the power to "acquire land, accept gifts and promote downtown projects."[12]

Despite the uncertainty about how to carry out the downtown revitalization, other members of the business community generally endorsed the plan as well. In October, Rodgers had urged downtown businessmen to "think in bold terms, in terms of market demand and competition and what other cities are doing." Within two weeks he received precisely the response he wanted: Richard H. Barr Jr., chair of the Chamber of Commerce's committee on planning and zoning, informed the press that his group had studied the Rodgers proposal and concluded that it "was a step forward, merited attention and should be implemented." In the initial stages of renewal planning, at least, a consensus emerged that something had to be done to save the central business district.[13]

At the presentation of the Rodgers report and model, planning commission chair John Vanderzell described it as possessing "much merit," while his predecessor, H. M. J. Klein, termed it "very fine." Although the *Intelligencer Journal* praised the "city-that-could-be" as "a wonderfully attractive, airy, delightful place with malls and fountains and trees," it nevertheless described public reaction as mixed. Even if the plan ultimately proved beneficial to downtown, one person at the presentation remarked, "They'll never be able to get that kind of money." Given the magnitude of projected changes to the city, what was mixed about the response to the Rodgers plan reflected doubts about feasibility, not concern over whether it was the best, or even an appropriate, strategy for revitalizing downtown. The $52 million cost of the project was indeed formidable: less than a year later, Boston, a city more than ten times the size of Lancaster, announced the beginning of a $90 million redevelopment program. As was true of Lancaster's plan, Boston's renewal was predicated on solutions to parking and traffic problems as well as on construction of a complex of governmental buildings adjacent to the commercial center. But in addition to the revitalization of downtown, the anticipated expenditures for Boston's renewal included improvements to housing in outlying neighborhoods, costs not reflected in Rodgers's estimate for Lancaster.[14]

Downtown Lancaster . . . 1980 presented a series of recommendations that attempted to ensure the economic vitality of the central business district. According to Burrell Cohen, the plan represented "our professional thinking on what is best for the Downtown." Cohen clearly hoped that the Rodgers model and plan would spark discussion and debate, that its projections for the future would "develop thinking on the part of other people interested in the preservation of Downtown." Much of the conversation took place in private meetings of the Central Lancaster Development Corporation, but planning commission staff also made a series of presentations to small groups of businessmen and service clubs to explain the plan, answer questions, and generate support for renewal. To determine the feasibility of commercial revitalization of the 100 block of North Queen Street, the city, using funds contributed by local businesses, also employed marketing consultants to survey shopping habits, public opinion, and expected response to a new retail complex downtown.[15]

In the months following the release of the Rodgers plan there was little overt opposition to its conceptualization of a new downtown. This may have been the result of the sheer scale of the project and the length of time over which the plan would be implemented, a period of twenty years or more. Without a scheduled commencement of demolition and new construction, even owners of buildings slated for the wrecker's ball undoubtedly would not have felt an immediate threat. Moreover, given the preliminary nature of Rodgers's presentation, owners of affected property may well have anticipated that the plan would change, and perhaps spare their buildings, as it came closer to consummation. But ultimately the greatest doubt was whether Lancaster's elected officials and its businesses had the resources and will to carry out so ambitious a plan, especially given the conservatism of the city's leadership. What best characterized the response to the Rodgers plan was a wait-and-see attitude.[16]

Nevertheless, the fate of the central business district was an important consideration to many Lancastrians. In the mayoral campaign of 1961, Republican George B. Coe, owner of a small downtown camera store, criticized Monaghan's administration for its lack of progress in revitalizing

North Queen Street, for its reliance on "high priced experts from out of town," for poor management and financial stewardship, and for numerous other alleged transgressions. A political novice, Coe campaigned on the theme of "A Better Lancaster," and insisted that the city "must move ahead" aggressively with urban renewal programs. Without revealing anything specific about goals or strategies, he promised to lead the city in a somewhat different direction from that which Monaghan had followed. Whether Coe swept the election because he appealed to nascent citizen dissatisfaction with urban renewal, or because he capitalized on the public's resentment of recent tax increases and coalesced the Republican majority behind his candidacy, he took office in January 1962, while additional studies for a revitalized downtown were moving forward. To be successful as mayor he would have to demonstrate progress in solving long-standing problems with the central business district, beginning with the North Queen Street block where his camera shop stood.[17]

The announcement of specific plans for the redevelopment of North Queen Street in the summer of 1962 sparked a renewed debate about strategies for revitalizing the city's retail core. On August 2 Coe announced the next stage in the process of downtown revitalization begun by his predecessor, a "most dramatic and significant" $10 million clearance and construction program for the 100 block of North Queen. Coe described existing buildings as "old, tired and worn out" and promised that the renewal project, "more than any undertaking in the City's history, will have a dramatic and important effect on the future of the City." The details of the plan were indeed stunning, especially when announced by a mayor who as a candidate had pledged a less grandiose renewal program that was in keeping with the city's traditions. Although *Downtown Lancaster . . . 1980* had proposed the retention of approximately half the structures on the block, including the YMCA and the Hotel Brunswick, and the construction of a hotel-motel, a retail center, and a parking garage, the new plan, prepared by the New York architectural firm Abbott, Merkt & Company, called for the total clearance of buildings facing North Queen Street as well as the construction of a massive parking garage adjacent to the site, at the corner of North Prince and West Orange streets. "While some of Lancaster's history, some of its nostalgia," would be destroyed, Coe admitted, "what is planned to replace them will, hopefully, give Lancaster a bright and prosperous future." Whereas the Rodgers plan called for the preservation of a number of buildings on the block, the Abbott, Merkt proposal followed both federal urban renewal policy, which allowed total clearance so that extant structures would not interfere with large-scale redevelopment projects, and Le Corbusier's famous dictum—a rallying cry of modern architecture—to tear down the old and reject any local traditions in new construction.[18]

Based on First Research Corporation's assessment of downtown retailing, Abbott, Merkt proposed the construction of a fourth department store at the northwest corner of North Queen Street, at Chestnut, as well as an enclosed mall for smaller retail shops, a new thirteen-story motor hotel, an office building, a movie theater, and a public theater. The key, Thomas Dieterele of First Research insisted, was a 100,000–150,000-square-foot department store—a commercial magnet that, he predicted, "would be a tremendous benefit to the downtown area; not only to existing department stores but also to variety stores in bringing more people downtown." Shoppers had already begun taking their consuming habits to suburban malls, Dieterele reported, which had resulted in a 15.6 percent decline in downtown retail sales between 1957 and 1960, a period when the rest of the metropolitan Lancaster saw such receipts increase by 32.5 percent. The addition of a large new department store would prevent the location of a competing full-service store in the suburbs and solidify downtown's retail base by attracting more suburban customers to the central business district (Fig. 11). Several weeks after presenting the preliminary plan for North Queen Street, the city announced an expansion of the property to be included in the project to make space for a second parking garage.[19]

The city's planning director described the proposed department store as the "true test" of downtown revitalization. Both Cohen and Dieterele, however, pointed out that commercial revitalization was part of a package, that it was predicated on solutions to traffic and parking concerns. Thus, on the same day that Abbott, Merkt presented preliminary plans for North Queen Street, Cohen released a study that called for a limited-access roadway to carry north-south traffic through the city. A high-speed arterial to the central business district had been a component of Victor Gruen's plans for Fort Worth, Texas, and Midtown Plaza in Rochester, New York, and was becoming a predictable part of the planning profession's downtown redevelopment repertoire. The road Abbott, Merkt proposed in Lancaster would eliminate most of the through traffic that had clogged downtown streets and also improve access from suburban subdivisions. In conjunction with the northern bypass and the parking garages proposed in *Downtown Lancaster . . . 1980* that were included in the Abbott, Merkt sketches, the north-south route was the final piece in improving automobile access to center city.[20]

In proposing to locate the new department store at the northwest corner of North Queen Street, the Redevelopment Authority anticipated that it

FIG. 11 *The suburbanization of downtown: sketch depicting the new commercial center envisioned by Buchart Associates Ltd. for Second North Queen Inc. Photograph published in the* Lancaster New Era, *May 28, 1965 (Lancaster Newspapers Inc.).*

would be the centerpiece of new construction that would eliminate blight. At the same time, the plans suggest that Abbott, Merkt envisioned a different kind of downtown from the historic retail core that had taken shape at the intersection of streetcar lines. Gone was the pedestrian mall that figured so prominently in discussions held during the late 1950s and in the Rodgers plan. But this was not necessarily a retreat from a suburban downtown: the location of the fourth department store would anchor the new retail complex on North Queen Street, much as mall developers followed Victor Gruen's influential dumbbell plan and placed the largest department stores at opposite ends of new suburban shopping centers. Shoppers would then traverse the two-block area of smaller storefronts to Penn Square, where the three older department stores clustered. Moreover, the new store would effectively mark the northern terminus of the central business district: the next block to the north was the proposed site of the civic center, a group of government buildings.[21]

On August 15 the city planning commission completed a survey and planning application that certified the entire area as blighted, and the Redevelopment Authority adopted those findings the next day. In conformity with federal and state requirements, the planning commission reported that

46 of the 55 structures in the project area were substandard or obsolete. As Planning Director Cohen explained, "the buildings have enough physical and functional deficiencies to justify their clearance." Although some physical decline was evident even to the untrained eye, the most compelling evidence of blight was economic, a decline in property values on the 100 block of North Queen Street. Recent real estate transactions demonstrated that property values had fallen dramatically, a development confirmed by the recent countywide reassessment, which reduced the appraised value of the block by $1.86 million. "If physical and economic conditions in this area continue to deteriorate," the planning commission warned ominously, "it is safe to assume that subsequent reassessments will result in more severe tax losses." Thus, funding on a level adequate to ensure completion of the project was "overwhelmingly important to the future of the City," the planning commission insisted in requesting $2.85 million as the federal share of the net cost for land acquisition and clearance. The state and the city would each assume half the remaining cost of $1.4 million, with private-sector investment of $8.2 million bringing the cost of the project to $12.45 million.[22]

The publication of the Abbott, Merkt plan for the second block of North Queen Street generated the first widespread reaction to urban redevelopment and the first wave of dissent against the proposals the city was considering. On August 9 the *Intelligencer Journal* published a lengthy editorial commenting on the Abbott, Merkt plan. The sheer scale of the concept was "a bit breathtaking," the newspaper conceded, "especially to an essentially conservative community such as this one." But the evidence of blight on the block made dramatic action necessary, both to reestablish the downtown retail district and to shore up the city's declining tax base. Lancaster's business leadership needed to shake off the effects of "long years of relative contentment and prosperity" and aggressively support downtown redevelopment. Given the "intelligent understanding and cooperation of our community leaders," the *Intelligencer Journal* concluded, "there is no reason why the vision cannot be translated into a reality."[23]

The *Intelligencer Journal* editorial had warned that there might be a "hornet's nest" in the North Queen Street proposals, and the publication of specific plans for the block made downtown redevelopment a hotly contested issue. Letters to the editor, particularly in the *New Era*, the more conservative afternoon newspaper, denounced the plan, while a survey of merchants and property owners raised significant questions about the overall merit of the Abbott, Merkt proposal. The majority of downtown businessmen continued to favor renewal, though several expressed reservations about the specific plan or rejected it entirely. The objections fell into one or more categories: that the plan was simply too expensive to be feasible; that the city should first solve traffic and parking problems, and only then turn to redevelopment; that the downtown could not support a new department store competing with the three existing ones; and that the plan would result in the destruction of historically significant buildings. Although there was general consensus that something needed to be done about downtown, these objections pointed toward stasis. On the one hand, demolition of historic buildings was necessary to provide space for a parking garage, something the central business district desperately needed; on the other hand, a number of critics insisted that no buildings be razed until the parking and traffic problems had been solved. Dissenting voices included a member of the Redevelopment Authority who questioned the appropriateness of building a motel in the midst of a retail district, as well as several citizens who urged the inclusion of a medical and dental center instead of other elements of the plan. Thus a challenge to the overall consensus about downtown revitalization was emerging: a recognition that whatever was wrong with the central business district, the present plan—and, apparently, any remedy dramatic enough to cure blight—would necessarily destroy the familiar cityscape and disrupt long-standing patterns of social or economic interaction.[24]

Planning director Cohen dismissed this first significant opposition to the North Queen Street project as "diversionary tactics." Visibly irritated, he castigated the citizens who expressed concern about the pace of redevelopment planning as chronic complainers. The city needed the "full hearted cooperation of all segments of Lancaster" in its revitalization efforts, he stated, not the resistance of "a few retail merchants" whose self-interested concerns would delay implementation of a vital program. The Redevelopment Authority moved quickly to incorporate the Abbott, Merkt proposals for the block in an information packet for prospective developers and set a timetable for land acquisition, clearance, and commencement of construction. The schedule established a deadline of December 31, 1962, for receipt of proposals for the redevelopment of North Queen Street, announcement of the selection of the developer a month later, and, after review of the Redevelopment Authority's application for funding by federal and state officials, the beginning of construction in June 1964.[25]

This was an ambitious schedule—in bureaucratic time a headlong race toward project implementation. And yet as a candidate who criticized the glacial progress of renewal under Monaghan, Coe was in some respects captive of the planning then under way. He could not scrap what had already been accomplished and start anew if he had hope of seeing any substantial progress in construction, let alone completion of the project, within his four-year term. Thus as Mayor Coe confronted the same criticism of North Queen Street redevelopment that his predecessor had endured, especially concerns about the timing and the component parts of the plan. Prominent businessmen continued to insist that the city needed to address parking and traffic concerns before commencing demolition and reconstruction, and once again challenged the economics of a fourth department store as the centerpiece of the proposed new North Queen Street.

In January 1963 James Shand, president of Watt & Shand, raised a series of issues challenging the city's redevelopment plans. He conceded that "there is a potential for additional retailing in the City of Lancaster and the downtown area" but questioned the need for a fourth department store in the 100 block of North Queen Street. Such a major store, he predicted, would "create a situation where the present retailers in the other blocks are hurt and driven out of business." Shand then asserted that awarding a redevelopment contract to an outside firm without clear assurance that a department store had agreed to locate on North Queen Street would leave the city hostage. Lancaster "may be required to accept anything in order not to have vacant land," he argued, "or have absolutely no development." Instead of wholesale clearance, which would be a financial burden on the city, Shand called for the more limited renewal of the west side of the street. Better to resolve traffic congestion first, and pursue a less ambitious plan "in an orderly fashion," than to strain the city's financial resources and destroy existing businesses while pursuing "'pie in the sky' promises of redevelopment."[26]

Shand's testimony notwithstanding, on February 6, 1963, the city and the Redevelopment Authority announced the selection of National Land and Investment Company, a Philadelphia firm, as developer of the North Queen Street site. The Redevelopment Authority had received six proposals, only one from a local developer, and chose National Land based on its sixteen years of "proven experience, design ability and imagination, reputation, and financial capabilities." National Land's previous involvement in urban renewal included Park Towne Place, North Triangle, and Eastwick in Philadelphia, as well as projects in San Francisco, Santa Monica, and Washington, D.C. According to Redevelopment Authority chair Donovan Smith, National Land had the financing to proceed with redevelopment and "a design winning urban renewal architect heading its design team," Milton Schwartz & Associates.[27]

National Land's proposal, which placed a 100,000–150,000 square foot prestige department store at the northwest corner of Chestnut and Queen streets, was the only submission that adhered to Abbott, Merkt's plan for a major retail facility on this site. Other elements of the plan included a new, six-story motor hotel at the northeast corner of Chestnut and Queen streets, a movie theater complex, a 250-seat restaurant, a swimming pool–ice skating facility, and another large building for retail stores on the east block. The west side of the street would include a 1,200-car, six-story parking garage, an exhibition hall, and dozens of specialty shops. Two pedestrian malls were the centerpiece of the plan, one located at ground level, the other a full story above the street. National Land President Bernard Weinberg predicted that his firm's $18 million project would "reinforce the basic economic soundness of the entire downtown Lancaster area." Although he presented only preliminary site plans at the February 6 press conference, Weinberg promised that the design of the complex would be "fresh yet complementary to the flavor of local tradition with the tasteful use of materials and through the design of signs and symbols."[28]

Mayor George B. Coe pledged the city's "enthusiastic endorsement and wholehearted support" of National Land, but local reaction proved to be far less favorable than he anticipated. In a rare front-page editorial, the *New Era* called the proposal "bold and imaginative" but suggested a more cautious approach. While it acknowledged that public opinion supported some redevelopment of North Queen Street, the newspaper was reluctant to gamble with the city's future. To ensure that National Land's proposal was the best solution to Lancaster's needs, the *New Era* suggested that an independent group—"the best business, industrial, banking, legal and tax men of our community"—analyze and evaluate the plan. As the *New Era* printed dozens of letters hostile to National Land's proposal, members of City Council publicly stated that they had not yet approved the plan and presented a series of questions ranging from the city's financial liability to the need for a fourth department store to the treatment of existing businesses during the period of clearance and construction. Until they received satisfactory answers, City Council would not authorize any action on the plan.[29]

Planning director Cohen was "rather amazed" at Council's position and accused its president, attorney W. Hensel Brown Jr., of "innuendoes and verbal charges." Council had been apprised of the Redevelopment Authority's deliberations all along, Cohen insisted, and had informally approved of the selection of National Land. But the public outcry over the plan demonstrated that the proposed redevelopment did not resolve the major differences some business leaders had with the North Queen Street plan. Thus Coe, following the suggestion of the *New Era,* appointed a Special Review Committee to assess the city's actions and ensure that contracts with the developer protected the city's interests. He undoubtedly also hoped that the committee would find common ground between redeveloper and downtown leaders. When the review committee met, Shand reiterated his argument against a new department store and insisted once again that solutions to traffic congestion be undertaken before urban redevelopment began. Citing the success of Midtown Plaza in Rochester, New York, as well as Jacksonville's redevelopment program, which was accomplished without federal dollars, Shand expressed doubt that Lancaster's urban renewal program was well suited to the needs of the community. Two prominent commercial organizations representing downtown interests similarly expressed reservations over the National Land plan. The Central Lancaster Development Corporation retreated from its earlier enthusiasm for redevelopment. While it pledged continued support for renewal, it questioned the need for a department store, which would "cause economic dislocation to existing facilities in the remainder of the downtown area," and urged that remedies for traffic congestion precede the commencement of any redevelopment program. The Chamber of Commerce similarly reiterated its support for the renewal of North Queen Street but distanced itself from National Land's proposal.[30]

Coe anticipated that the Special Review Committee would limit its role to the "legal aspects" of redevelopment, but several members insisted that "they should delve into the merits of the entire project." Although several citizens expressed the fear that this would be a "white-wash committee" that would rubber-stamp the Redevelopment Authority's decision, resistance to National Land's plan was increasing. Upon hearing testimony from businessmen about the impact of the proposed renewal on downtown, on March 25, 1963,the review committee asked the Pennsylvania Economy League to analyze the redevelopment plan and especially its "impact on city taxpayers." The Central Lancaster Development Corporation firmly rejected the need for a large department store in the North Queen Street project, which, it predicted, would have a "bad economic effect on the remainder of the downtown area." The group also challenged the need for a 1,200 car-parking garage, reasserted the importance of traffic improvements in the downtown area, and insisted that when redevelopment began it not cause "economic dislocation to existing facilities." Still another form of resistance surfaced when approximately twenty people met to form an organization to oppose the North Queen Street project. Headed by Earl Rebman, a local businessman and outspoken foe of urban renewal, which he called a "planned effort to bankrupt America," the group included Hyman Mishkin, a former member of the Redevelopment Authority, and attorney Owen P. Bricker.[31]

Despite significant questions about the appropriateness of the downtown renewal plan, the Redevelopment Authority prepared a preliminary agreement with National Land. The agreement called for National Land to make a good-faith payment of $100,000 to the city, which reserved the right to approve all major tenants in the new facility. Following review by Coe's committee of business advisers and city approval of the contract, the Redevelopment Authority and its consultant, Abbott, Merkt, would begin preparation of a final plan for North Queen Street that was in conformity with the proposal submitted by National Land. The agreement further specified that the city would not acquire buildings until after completion of the plan and a public hearing to provide comment on its contents, which would cause a delay of at least six months to a year. In addition to these provisions, the contract was subject to three conditions: federal approval of financing, City Council approval of the overall plan, and economic feasibility.[32]

Progress on North Queen Street redevelopment finally seemed assured on June 14, 1963, when the Special Review Committee released its report and that of the Pennsylvania Economy League. The Economy League generally praised the Queen Street renewal plan for its conceptual and fiscal soundness, though it admonished the Redevelopment Authority for the absence of what it termed a "total city renewal program" and for its emphasis on residential clearance rather than the rehabilitation of existing structures. The review committee's report similarly contained several important reservations: it called for revisions to the preliminary contract between the Redevelopment Authority and National Land, which, it insisted, "does not adequately protect the city's interests"; it expressed strong aversion to the project's reliance on federal funds and recommended that, if possible, future projects be undertaken using only local financing; and it advocated appointment of a Design Review Committee to advise the Redevelopment Authority during preparation of the final plan. Despite these criticisms, the committee acknowledged that the announcement of redevelopment had "accelerated the deterioration" of North Queen Street and recommended that the project move forward "with all reasonable speed to lighten as much as possible the impact on property owners and tenants in the area." The ultimate success of renewal, it warned, would depend on broad support from the business community and from the public at large.[33]

Ironically, the Special Review Committee called for united support of renewal at a time when consensus had evaporated. The Redevelopment Authority nevertheless went ahead with planning as if it had received complete endorsement of its actions. Coe and Paul F. Miller, who had replaced the outspoken Cohen as the city's redevelopment coordinator, predicted that the project would now move into "high gear" and announced the hiring of three additional persons to conduct appraisals of properties to be acquired and to assist businesses and families forced to relocate. Coe reiterated his belief in the importance of the project to the city's tax base and asserted that its completion would "strengthen and revitalize both the downtown area of Lancaster and the entire community."[34]

The city and the Redevelopment Authority signed a revised contract with National Land on July 17, 1963. What followed was a period of eighteen months when the Redevelopment Authority applied for federal and state funding for the project and completed plans for redevelopment, while National Land sought, in vain, a department store tenant to anchor the new construction. In May 1964 Paul Miller had confidentially informed members of the board, "we must realistically face the possibility that there may be no department store, at least in the first stage of the Renewal Project." The Redevelopment Authority maintained a public stance that plans for North Queen were proceeding without problems, and the following month submitted its application for federal funding. That document enumerated a department store among potential uses within the overall project, but the illustrative site plan for the redevelopment area identified the location previously reserved for a fourth department store only as "Commercial (Retail)"—the same designation applied to all other new construction in the blocks facing North Queen Street.[35]

Since the presentation of Rodgers's *Downtown Lancaster . . . 1980* plan in 1959, the foundation of all downtown redevelopment planning had been retail. In 1962 the Redevelopment Authority announced that a new department store was essential to the future of downtown as a commercial center. But potential department store tenants, who studied the same marketing trends the planners had, did not see a bright future for retailing in downtown Lancaster, and by 1964 the authority confronted the possibility of redevelopment without such a commercial anchor. During the intervening period many businessmen who supported revitalization in principle began to fear that the specific plan, with a large department store, would have an adverse impact on other commercial endeavors and result in the decline of sales elsewhere in the central business district, spreading the very blight urban renewal was supposed to cure. The inability of National Land to secure a tenant for the department store also confirmed what many businessmen must have been thinking all along, that the outside experts hired by the Redevelopment Authority simply did not know enough about Lancaster to be trusted to make decisions about its future.[36]

Doubts about the feasibility of the National Land plan and the ability of the Redevelopment Authority to advance the best interests of the city were central themes expressed by citizens at a September 30, 1964, public hearing about the North Queen Street plan. A *New Era* story announcing the ground rules for the public hearing explained that the Queen Street project was "keyed to a department store, if one is found," while the *Intelligencer Journal* reported that the application for federal funds "permits development of the area with or without a proposed department store"—the first public acknowledgment of a retreat from the long-standing position that a major retail facility was an essential part of the renewal plan. Details about the ultimate disposition of space and potential tenants were so sketchy that they aroused even greater suspicion that the Redevelopment Authority was holding the city's future hostage to speculative plans for revitalization. Articles published in the two local newspapers predicted that the hearing would be "extremely well attended and controversial," which proved to be an understatement given the overflow crowd of some 200 citizens and the loud applause that followed statements by opponents of the plan.[37]

At the public hearing several speakers supported revitalization in principal, but the overwhelming majority expressed hostility to the National Land plan. Downtown businessman Douglas Darmstaetter, for example, argued against the acquisition of property until the redeveloper had assembled a complete list of tenants for the project. To do otherwise, to begin condemnation without a comprehensive understanding of how a new North Queen Street would take shape, would be tantamount to issuing a "blank check for National Land to do what they wish regardless of the effect on the community." Nathaniel Hager, a well-respected retailer whose family owned the oldest local department store, similarly argued against acquisition of land until the redeveloper had commitments from all major tenants. Frank H. Simpson, a public affairs officer for Armstrong Cork Company, opposed any steps that would irrevocably commit the city to "an indefinite building project," while attorney John I. Hartman Jr. denounced the authority's intent to begin acquisition of land without specific plans for redevelopment. As was true of several other speakers, Hartman doubted that National Land would be able to secure the tenants to make wholesale revitalization feasible and urged the Redevelopment Authority to "develop the area on its own in piece-meal fashion," which, he suggested, would probably result in renewal that was more in keeping with Lancaster's needs. Still other citizens protested awarding the North Queen Street project to a developer from out of town, investors who were motivated by profit and not necessarily what was best for the community.[38]

At the beginning of the public hearing, Redevelopment Authority director Paul Miller announced that the city would hold a second hearing after National Land had secured all major tenants and finalized financial and architectural plans for North Queen Street, probably in December or January. In the meantime, Miller, who was listening closely to public sentiment, established a deadline of January 13, 1965, for National Land to present a plan that included all major tenants. Were it unable to comply with the deadline, the Redevelopment Authority would be "prepared to submit alternate plans for the expeditious development of the Queen Street project." Given the public resistance to its plans, the increasingly strained relations with the city and the Redevelopment Authority, and its inability to find a major department store willing to locate in the project, National Land & Investment Company withdrew from the North Queen Street agreement on January 6, 1965.[39]

More than five years had passed since Clifton Rodgers presented his vision of a revitalized downtown. During that time the City Planning Commission and the Lancaster Redevelopment Authority had spent thousands of dollars in planning a massive commercial redevelopment project for North Queen Street. One crucial outcome of the planning process was a vigorous debate over the best strategy for redevelopment, which sounded the death knell of the initial consensus that something had to be done to restore the economic vitality of the commercial center. The fragmentation of support, together with the withdrawal of National Land, left the city and its mayor with a profound dilemma. Four years earlier Coe had castigated Democratic Mayor Thomas Monaghan for the city's lack of progress in revitalizing North Queen Street. In January 1965, at the beginning of an election year, Coe faced the prospect of having to go before the city's voters once again, but this time he would have to defend his record. The buildings along the 100 block of North Queen Street were still intact, but on numerous occasions Paul Miller, whom he had appointed to head the Redevelopment Authority, pointed out that the area was continuing to decline as long-standing businesses moved to more hospitable locations. Given the prominence of the North Queen Street project to the downtown economy and to his administration's urban renewal program, Coe was in serious political trouble. Thus, on the same day that Redevelopment Authority officials described the withdrawal of National Land as only a temporary setback to Queen Street plans, Coe announced that he would not be a candidate for reelection.[40]

In the aftermath of National Land's withdrawal from the Queen Street project, the Lancaster Redevelopment Authority had two alternatives. The first was to seek another developer willing to undertake the entire project, a problematic choice given Lancaster's experience with National Land. The second, suggested by several speakers at the September 1964 public hearing, was to divide the North Queen project into smaller components and contract with local developers for individual parts of the overall plan. Although National Land warned that a "piece-meal" approach to development "will not successfully accomplish the objective of revitalization of the North Queen

Street area," on January 6, 1965, Redevelopment Authority director Paul Miller announced an "alternative land use plan [that] divides the project into a number of segments," including the motor hotel, theaters, restaurants, retail shops, and perhaps an office or apartment building. The withdrawal of National Land, he stated, had resulted in several expressions of interest by local investors eager to undertake redevelopment of North Queen Street.[41] But whether the Redevelopment Authority was prepared to rethink its assumptions of the role of downtown as a retail center in a suburban age, and whether local developers had the experience to assemble plans and the resources to move the project forward quickly, remained highly problematic. The fate of the central business district hung in the balance.

CHAPTER 4

A NEW HEART FOR LANCASTER

The withdrawal of National Land & Investment Corporation on January 6, 1965, proved to be an acute embarrassment to the mayor and members of the Redevelopment Authority. The announcement forced local officials to reconsider their downtown revitalization strategy and redouble their efforts to attract a suitable developer or developers for the North Queen Street project. Nine days later, the Redevelopment Authority reluctantly decided to subdivide the site into seven parcels, a concession that its previous determination to rely on a single developer was no longer feasible, and published a new schematic that illustrated the subdivision of the property as part of a newspaper advertisement. "LANCASTER WANTS ACTION!" read the boldface heading of an ad that trumpeted the North Queen Street project as "a great Opportunity for Developers." In a significant change in policy, Lancaster's City Council also eliminated a previous requirement that prevented the Redevelopment Authority from acquiring property until Council had approved the land-disposition contract and citizens had expressed their opinion in a public hearing. The same day, January 15, the U.S. Housing and Home Finance Agency awarded the Lancaster Redevelopment Authority $3.9 million to begin acquisition of North Queen Street properties, the first step in the redevelopment process. Despite National Land's inability to secure tenants for its project, there was "heavy interest" in the site, City Development Coordinator Paul F. Miller optimistically assured local newspapers: he reported that ten developers had contacted the authority about the North Queen project. During the next five months, while the authority undertook appraisals and commenced the taking of property, the city searched for a new developer or team of builders who would undertake specific parts of the larger downtown project.[1]

On February 19, 1965, the Redevelopment Authority invited proposals for new plans for the North Queen Street site. The revised site plan accompanying the call for proposals differed from the 1962 North Queen Street Renewal Study in two principal ways: it moved the location designated for a department store from the north end of the west block to the south, and it enlarged the pedestrian plaza at the center of the two facing blocks. By the

May 10 deadline the Redevelopment Authority had received nine proposals, three of which included plans to develop the entire site, the others limited to specific buildings in the renewal area. One proposal was local, Second North Queen Inc., which consisted of J. H. Wickersham Engineering & Construction and Hyman Mishkin, a major investor in Lancaster real estate and a former member of the Redevelopment Authority who had opposed the earlier National Land plans for the commercial site. That Mishkin emerged as a major underwriter of the project exemplifies the blurring of traditional boundaries between the public and private spheres in the redevelopment process. A key component of the Second North Queen proposal was a locally owned department store, Hager & Company, which would move from its West King Street location to a new 120,000 to 150,000 square foot building within the renewal project. A second proposal came from Mrs. Goldie Hoffman, in partnership with Albert M. Greenfield & Company, Philadelphia, with a site plan prepared by Victor Gruen Associates, while the third was submitted by the Rosemont Construction Company of Rosemont, Pennsylvania. Proposals for individual parcels within the project area included a hotel, a movie theater, and an office building.[2]

The Redevelopment Authority and other stakeholders in downtown revitalization, especially the business community and the city, quickly narrowed the choice to two developers: Second North Queen and Hoffman. Rosemont received scant consideration because it failed to provide information on site plan, building design, and prospective tenants that the Redevelopment Authority considered essential; proposals for the development of single parcels received even less attention. Of the two developers who emerged as finalists, Second North Queen followed the February 1965 site plan and placed a department store at the southern end of the renewal area and a motor hotel at the north (Fig. 12). Its proposal also called for a multilevel shopping mall on the east side of North Queen Street, which one spokesman for the developer described as a "festive market place reminiscent of the famous Lancaster farmers' markets," and a public plaza in the middle of the block. Two multistory office buildings and a theater flanked the retail complex on the east block. The key to the success of the redevelopment proposal was its Lancaster genealogy. Clinton Clubb, president of Wickersham Engineering & Construction, emphasized the commitment of local investors to the future of the city: "It is our belief that local people, residents of Lancaster and adjacent counties, are most sincerely interested in and will do what is best for Lancaster City." He drew a sharp contrast between out-of-town investors and the principals of Second North Queen, who were "local people who have been and are here to stay" and who "will not take our profits from the project and then sell out and be gone."[3]

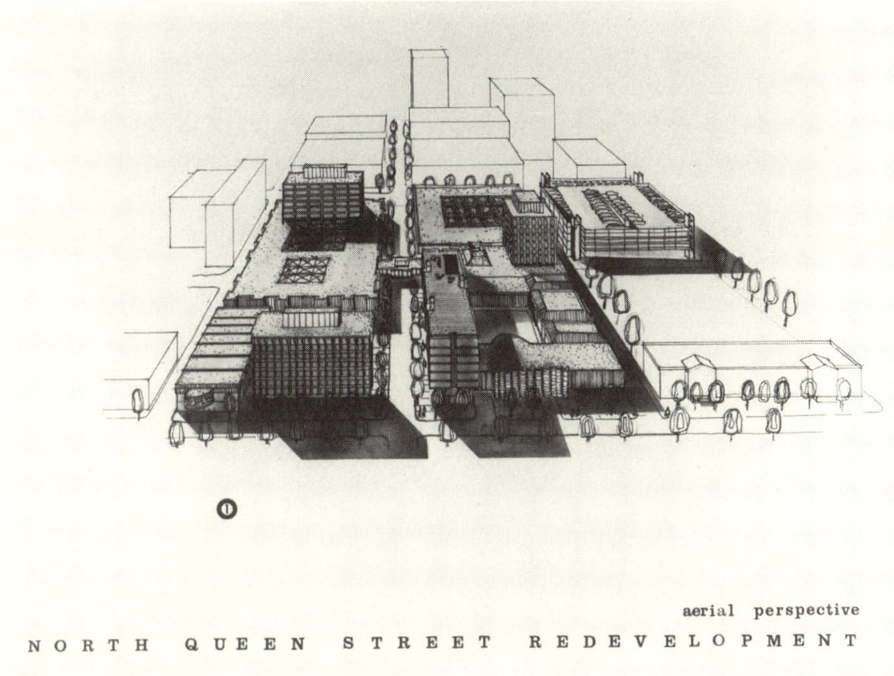

FIG. 12 *North Queen Street from above, sketch looking south with Chestnut Street in the foreground, the taller buildings around Penn Square in the distance. The drawing, by Buchart Associates Ltd., May 1965, captures the vision of downtown as suburban mall proposed by Second North Queen Inc. (Buchart-Horn Inc./BASCO Associates Ltd., Lancaster and York, Pennsylvania).*

Hoffman's proposal adhered to the original 1962 site plan and located the department store at the north end of the block, opposite a new hotel to be erected on the site of the old Brunswick. It incorporated a shopping mall for smaller retail stores on the west side of Queen Street, framed by a public square, as well as the office buildings, theater, and other facilities specified in the plan. The Hoffman plan also called for construction of a publicly financed parking garage. Implicit in the composition of Hoffman's team was the importance of expertise. Where Second North Queen emphasized its local ties, Hoffman highlighted her twenty-five years of development work in Philadelphia and her experience as treasurer of the Philadelphia Redevelopment Authority, and she included in her team the architect and planner Victor Gruen, who was nationally known for urban renewal projects he had designed in other cities.[4]

Downtown business leaders were divided over the choice. The Urban Renewal Committee of the Chamber of Commerce favored a local developer and endorsed Second North Queen's proposal, while the Architectural Design Review Committee, a citizen group appointed by the Redevelopment Authority, judged the Hoffman plan "substantially superior." Donald Reidenbaugh, the authority's consulting architect, strongly favored the Hoffman plan because he believed that the northern location of the department store would establish a "northern nucleus of commercial activity" downtown and because of the "experience and talent" of Gruen and his associates. Some downtown merchants, such as A. C. Darmstaetter, were more willing to trust Lancaster's future to local developers and advocated adoption of the Wickersham proposal, while others undoubtedly believed that Hoffman's team was best able to revitalize the city. At its meeting of June 15 the Redevelopment Authority chose Second North Queen as developer, largely, the *Intelligencer Journal* reported, because it was a local company, because it did not require municipal expenditures to construct the parking garage, and because it had a tenant for the department store. The following day City Council endorsed the choice of Second North Queen and designated the southwest corner of the intersection of West Chestnut and Queen streets as the site of the motor hotel.[5]

Even as the Redevelopment Authority was reviewing proposals for the Second North Queen project area, it was beginning the process of acquiring properties on the west block as the site for the motor hotel. On April 9, 1965, the Redevelopment Authority filed a declaration of taking, the first step in exercising the power of eminent domain, and in late June it initiated condemnation proceedings on the Brunswick Hotel, the northernmost property on the east block. Although the Redevelopment Authority had pledged that no buildings would be demolished until a developer had commitments from tenants for the site, it stepped up the pace of acquisition despite the fact that the developer had not yet been incorporated and had not revealed details of its finances. And although the *Intelligencer Journal* emphasized the need for safeguards to protect the city's interests in redevelopment, on August 2, 1965—three years to the day since the announcement of the North Queen Renewal plan—a demolition crane began razing buildings on the west block. Three days later, on August 5, the Redevelopment Authority adopted a resolution of condemnation for properties on the northern half of the east block. At the same meeting the Redevelopment Authority gave preliminary approval to a contract with Second North Queen and sent it to the federal Urban Renewal Administration for review and approval.[6]

These were momentous decisions: the city began demolition without any guarantee that development would follow. There were 92 businesses, 20 families, and perhaps 100 individual residents of the project area who had already been affected by designation of the North Queen Street blocks as blighted, and when the implementation phase—destruction—began, their lives and livelihoods would be irrevocably changed. Also at stake was the city's financial well-being, which relied on a thriving downtown to generate essential tax revenues. The city's future as the retail center and point of destination of the county hung in precarious balance. The decision to proceed involved great risk, but the Redevelopment Authority and the city government emphasized what they anticipated would be positive outcomes rather than the negatives and committed the city's future to a developer's intent. What seems in retrospect to have been an inexplicable decision, an unacceptable risk, may have been the result of a desire to move forward quickly after years of frustrating delay; perhaps it reflected the certitude that a well-connected local developer would act in the best interest of the city. Nevertheless, the city did not have a developer under a legally binding contract, and the developer with whom it was working did not have the commitments from prospective tenants that would enable it to secure financing for new construction. According to Richard H. Barr Jr., then chair of the Architectural Design Review Committee, the decision to demolish was made at the behest of Mayor George Coe, who believed that a blank slate would demonstrate that Lancaster meant business in redeveloping downtown. Certainly Paul F. Miller, executive director of the Lancaster Redevelopment Authority, lent credence to that position: in May 1964 he told a newspaper reporter, "I'm quite sure we could get a department store"—the lynchpin of the North Queen project—"if we had a site cleared" and a parking garage under construction. Despite the concerns citizens voiced at the September 1964 public hearing, and despite editorials that warned against turning downtown into a rubble-strewn wasteland, Coe, members of City Council, and the Redevelopment Authority abandoned a policy that had prevented premature demolition and adopted a new one that ensured it. Among the many mistakes Lancaster's civic leaders made in the urban renewal process, the decision to commence demolition in the summer of 1965 was undoubtedly the greatest. The west block, the first demolished, remained vacant for most of a decade and became known as "our hole in the ground."[7]

Since the 1950s the bulldozer and the scalpel have stood as metaphors for urban redevelopment. The choice of words to represent the process is telling. One is noisy, dirty, powerful, and destructive; the other is silent, antiseptic, and, in the hands of a skilled surgeon, curative. The bulldozer disrupts urban life even as it clears large blocks of land to enable new construction to follow; the scalpel carefully removes blighted buildings, the diseased tissue of the organic city, in the hope of allowing adjacent structures and blocks to prosper. A machine reduces a complex human endeavor to rubble; a simple instrument restores life, vitality, to the fabric of the city. Edmund Bacon, the legendary architect of Philadelphia's post–World War II renewal, often described the scalpel as his instrument of choice; other cities, such as Boston and New York, where Edward Logue and Robert Moses adopted different renewal strategies, relied on the bulldozer to a much greater extent than Philadelphia did.[8]

The process of urban redevelopment in Lancaster involved both the bulldozer and the scalpel, though wholesale clearance was the strategy of choice for North Queen Street. Elected officials saw the demolition crane that began dissembling 148 North Queen the morning of August 2, 1965, not as a demonic machine but as a symbol of hope. Certainly Mayor Coe climbed into the operator's cab and commenced the razing of the building that had housed his own camera shop with the expectation that the new structures to be erected in its place would improve Lancaster. In pursuing a strategy of clearance and redevelopment Lancaster's elected officials and planners were ignoring the devastating if polemical critique of urban renewal, *The Federal Bulldozer,* that Martin Anderson had published the previous year. Just to the south of Coe Camera stood the Lancaster County Farmers National Bank (Fig. 13), a majestic Roman Revival building erected around 1920. On September 6, 1965, a wrecking ball ripped through its monumental entrance, framed by two columns, and left its handsome vaulted ceiling in rubble (Fig. 14). As the crane moved northward along the street, it encountered the Capitol Theater, the Romanesque Revival Wheatland Hotel and to its rear the Hamilton Theater, then Boyd's Colonial Theater. At the corner stood Tony Faranda's Imperial Bar. Faranda, who opposed the designation of his property as blighted, sued to reverse the Redevelopment Authority's condemnation. Although the authority prevailed in the local Court of Common Pleas, Faranda's appeal to the State Supreme Court effectively halted demolition. An aerial photograph taken on November 6, 1965, shows the site of the motor hotel cleared save for the tiers of seating of the Colonial Theater and the roof of Faranda's bar. Because of litigation, the small structure would continue to stand for more than a year after demolition had begun on the west block.[9]

The Redevelopment Authority anticipated that construction of a motor hotel would commence shortly after completion of demolition. Moreover, it expected that the process of site-clearing would shift to the east block once the razing of the north half of the west block was completed. As the legal proceedings that delayed the demolition of the Imperial Bar and the lack of a leasee for the motor hotel made clear, the Redevelopment Authority's timetable proved hopelessly optimistic. It began condemnation of the east block in August 1965, and the following November initiated eminent domain proceedings against the five properties at the south end of the west block, which it designated as the site of a new Hager's Department Store. Included in this parcel was the Lancaster YMCA, a handsome Beaux Arts structure at the corner of North Queen and West Orange streets. But while maintaining that the list of prospective tenants for each of the sites was "extremely good," the Redevelopment Authority had difficulty translating interest into legal and financial commitment.[10]

On September 1 the *Intelligencer Journal* once again expressed the fear that urban renewal was turning downtown into a wasteland: "The only part of the renewal project that appears to be proceeding according to schedule," the newspaper editorialized, "is the demolition of the buildings on the west side of North Queen Street." As delays and missed deadlines continued, the optimism that accompanied commencement of demolition began to fall with the autumn leaves. Then former mayor and Democratic candidate Thomas J. Monaghan made the lack of progress on urban renewal a campaign issue, decrying the "mess" the Coe administration had created and the "vacant lots" and "broken promises" that were its major accomplishment.[11]

Monaghan handily won the mayoral contest in November 1965 but proved unable to bring the North Queen Street project to a speedy and successful completion. Between the November election and his assumption of official duties in January, the redevelopment picture worsened as Hyman Mishkin, one of the principals in Second North Queen Inc., withdrew from the partnership, leaving the developer in need of another investor to help meet the $15 million cost of the project. Until financing was secured, federal law prohibited the Redevelopment Authority from transferring land to the developer.[12]

The new partners who came to the rescue of Second North Queen had a familiar look; the principal investor was Goldie Hoffman, joined by her associates at the Greenfield company, Maurice Lichtenstein and Robert K. Greenfield, who together controlled 50 percent of the newly reconstituted development corporation. Although these were the very individuals who had competed with Second North Queen in the summer of 1965, and although Clinton Clubb had then emphasized the importance of local money and local leadership in the development process, he nevertheless professed great optimism about the project and praised the dynamic background and experience of his new partners. The infusion of new capital came with strings, however: Second North Queen now insisted, as Hoffman had in her 1965

FIG. 13 *Erected in the early twentieth century, the chaste classical façade of the Northern Savings & Trust Company (later the Lancaster County Farmers National Bank) was one of the most beautiful buildings in the city. Photograph by Ed Sachs, July 1965 (Lancaster Newspapers Inc.).*

proposal, that the city parking authority bear the cost of constructing a parking garage. Because litigation involving the Imperial Bar continued, the new partnership also requested a different building program, one that would begin with the construction of a new Hager's Department Store at the northwest corner of Queen and Orange streets.[13]

Hoffman's group insisted on one other concession: the determination of the architect and planner. Although Second North Queen already had Buchart Associates, a local architectural and engineering firm, preparing schematic plans for the new department store and motor hotel, in April 1966 Clubb announced that Victor Gruen Associates, which had been a member of Hoffman's original team, would be the designers who would determine the overall shape of the project.[14]

FIG. 14 *Partially demolished Lancaster County Farmers National Bank, with the two Corinthian columns standing majestically over the rubble. Photograph by Ed Sachs, September 6, 1965 (Lancaster Newspapers Inc.).*

Gruen, a Viennese-born architect and planner deeply influenced by the European modernists Camillo Sitte and Le Corbusier, is perhaps best known as the principal architect and philosopher of the regional shopping center. His first shopping center, constructed in Los Angeles in 1947 for Milliron's Department Store, and the more famous Northland Center outside Detroit and Southdale Complex near Minneapolis, constructed in the early and mid-1950s, codified the design and function of the new retail environment. In its fully matured form the shopping center was a large though architecturally nondescript structure that sprawled over the landscape. Surrounded by a system of access roads and acres of asphalt for parking, it was a building that turned inward on interior courts or pedestrian malls. The crowds that visited Northland, even on Sunday when the stores were closed, convinced Gruen that these new malls were not simply palaces of consumption but were also places of social activity, town centers for the automobile age. The shopping mall became, in his estimation, the symbolic as well as economic focal point for the seemingly scattered subdivisions of post–World War II suburbia.[15]

By the end of the 1950s Gruen had become equally prominent as a critic of suburban sprawl and a champion of revitalized downtowns. "The flight to the countryside has effectively destroyed the landscape," he asserted, "and many feel now that suburbia is a place which offers neither the advantages of the city nor those of the country." With evangelical enthusiasm he delivered speeches to chambers of commerce and professional groups and wrote numerous articles promoting the role of planning in creating exciting new commercial centers for the nation's cities. The future of downtown retailing was bright, he insisted, for the center of the city "will again become the best location for retailing wherever decisive action is taken." That action, he believed, must make downtown areas, which too often were "outmoded and outdated and outflanked," into truly modern and efficient environments adapted to the myriad demands of the second half of the twentieth century.[16]

Gruen explained his views on revitalized downtowns most systematically in his 1964 book, *The Heart of Our Cities.* The problem, as he perceived it, was that central business districts were old, congested, and decaying as the "scatterization" of once-urban functions on the periphery of cities accelerated. Employing the human body as a metaphor for the metropolitan region, Gruen portrayed downtown as the "tired heart" of the "urban organism." The remedies he prescribed were dramatic: concentric rings of concrete around downtowns, along with expressways that penetrated the heart of the city like those depicted in Norman Bel Geddes's Futurama exhibit at the 1939 New York World's Fair; construction of massive parking garages just outside the traditional core (the provisions for highway construction and parking were part of a strategy he termed "taming" the automobile); new circulation patterns that emphasized public transit; and higher-density building and attractive pedestrian malls in what traditionally had been the central business district.[17]

The remedy for what ailed downtown, for recentralization, Gruen explained with more than a touch of irony, could be found in the very regional shopping malls that had contributed to the flight of traditional retail activities from cities. The separation of utilitarian from human functions so successfully incorporated in suburban malls was equally applicable to the central business district. The peripheral highways and parking, separation of service access, and pedestrian amenities that had proven so attractive to shoppers and so remunerative to merchants contributed to a better understanding of how a reconfigured downtown could work. "What is novel and revolutionary" about the new suburban malls, Gruen explained, "is the manner in which the store buildings are placed. Instead of being arranged conventionally, directly bordering the surrounding highways, they are located in the space theoretically least visible from the public roads and least directly accessible to automobiles: in the center of the site." As the stores turned inward on pedestrian areas rather than outward toward the surrounding parking lots, merchants quickly learned the obvious: it was not the volume of passing automobiles that determined the desirability of retail space but the number of pedestrians who entered stores. And, as the public areas within such malls quickly became centers for human interaction, Gruen explained, they performed the unexpected function of recentering suburban life.[18]

The same principles, Gruen asserted, could be applied to tired downtowns. In his famous though unexecuted plan for Fort Worth, Texas, as well as in designs that were successfully implemented in Rochester, New York, and Fresno, California, Gruen proposed precisely the new highway systems, parking facilities, transit services, and pedestrian amenities that worked in the design of suburban malls. The Fresno downtown mall, for example, designed in collaboration with landscape architect Garrett Eckbo, was not simply a street from which the automobile had been banished, a tendency Gruen characterized as planning by subtraction. Instead, it was a carefully designed pedestrian space, full of amenities, intended to serve as "a focus of community interest and events, a promenade and rendezvous for friends, a play area for children and meeting place for teenagers." For Gruen, much as the retail mall served as a community center for suburbanites, so could a revitalized downtown recentralize metropolitan life.[19]

Second North Queen presented Gruen's plan for Lancaster (Fig. 15) at a special meeting of the Redevelopment Authority on July 28, 1966. A large gathering of public officials, business and civic leaders, and anxious citizens listened to a slide presentation by Abbott Harle, director of Gruen's New York office, and John Beyer, head of the firm's design department, and had the opportunity to ask questions of developers Maurice Lichtenstein and Clinton Clubb. The Gruen plan differed from earlier proposals for North Queen Street in several significant ways. One was its larger scope, particularly the inclusion of a second department store and a second parking garage, which increased construction costs to an estimated $20 million; another was a major

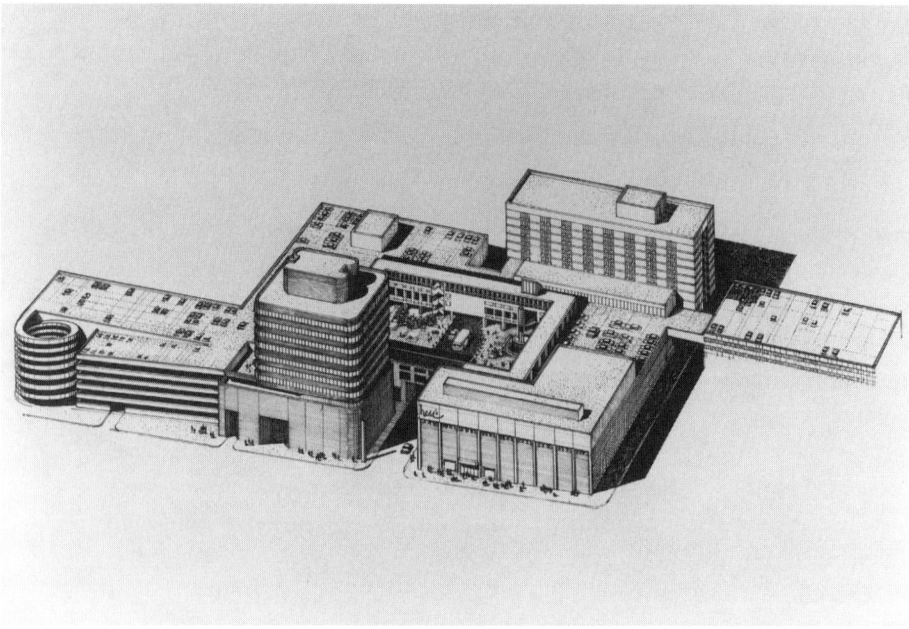

FIG. 15 *Schematic of Victor Gruen's plan for the 100 block of North Queen Street. The near buildings—the parking garage to the left, the office building and Hess's Department Store, face Orange Street; North Queen extends northward between the office building and the department store, while the new hotel is in the upper right and the second parking garage is to the far right. Note the outlines of Lancaster Square, defined by a three-story concrete walkway, in the center of the block (Buchart-Horn Inc./BASCO Associates Ltd., Lancaster and York, Pennsylvania).*

design feature, the organization of the building program around a large new public square that physically as well as symbolically united the east and west blocks of North Queen Street into the new retail heart for Lancaster. Gruen designated the corner of Chestnut and Queen, opposite a new motor hotel on the site of the Brunswick Hotel, as the location of the northernmost department store and placed the second department store on the east side of Queen Street, at the corner of Orange, opposite an office building. One garage occupied the corner of Orange and Prince streets, while the second, which necessitated the condemnation of additional land, stood at the corner of Duke and Chestnut streets. Smaller retail stores and a movie theater flanked the new public space, which the developers named Lancaster Square. Beyer described the square as "a new center for public activities" such as art shows, dances, and political rallies, and suggested that it be designed and planted "in keeping with the character and atmosphere of Lancaster." In much the way that the pedestrian amenities and quasi-public spaces of the mall proved attractive to suburbanites, Gruen anticipated that the public square in the middle of North Queen Street would quickly become a new center for social activity in the city. A third, equally critical element of the Gruen plan was the oft-proposed (but never constructed) downtown expressway, which, proponents argued, would make the central business district accessible to increasingly suburbanized consumers.[20]

The key to the Gruen plan was a thriving retail economy. The inclusion of two department stores, and the decrease in available office space, was an attempt to solidify downtown as the retail center of Lancaster County. Indeed, Gruen adapted his well-known "dumbbell plan" for shopping centers to the larger scale of an older city center. If the optimal arrangement of a suburban mall was a pedestrian concourse extending between two large department stores, with rows of smaller retail establishments on either side of the pedestrian way, so would the second block of North Queen Street anchor the northern end of a downtown commercial center. Older department stores clustered around Penn Square—Watt & Shand, Garvin's, and Hager's—would anchor the southern end, and smaller retail establishments would line North Queen Street, which would function as a suburban mall. Pedestrian activity was the key to the success of the plan and explains why Gruen shifted the department store from the west to the east block along Orange Street, away from the parking garage—to ensure that shoppers entered a larger downtown retail environment, not simply an adjacent department store.[21]

The presentation of Gruen's plan, and the extensive publicity it received, captured the imagination of many Lancastrians. After months and years of anxious waiting, here was a vision of a revitalized downtown, in a three-dimensional model, that projected an economically healthy, socially vibrant city. Clinton Clubb enthusiastically described the Gruen plan as "the best possible solution to the development of North Queen Street," and most local officials agreed. Yet amid what one reporter described as the "unanimously favorable" reactions to the design, there lurked other worries. At the presentation of the plan Maurice Lichtenstein indicated a lengthy timetable for project implementation—perhaps fourteen months of preparation, marketing, and design before construction could begin. Under the most optimistic scenario it would be late 1968 before any part of the project might be ready for occupancy, under less favorable conditions perhaps 1970 until completion of the work. Moreover, when questioned about finding tenants for the project, particularly department store anchors, Lichtenstein flatly refused to give guarantees of success: "You just have to assure yourself that you're in strong, competent hands and then tell us to go ahead," he explained. To a community that had been discussing downtown renewal for seven years and that was being asked to defer dreams for another three or four, strong hands, however competent, provided little comfort.[22]

Moreover, the Gruen plan shifted a number of financial obligations from the developer to the municipality or its constituent authorities. The Redevelopment Authority would have to act quickly to acquire additional property for the Duke Street garage, while the parking authority would have to borrow money to erect the structure and hire additional staff to operate it. A privately owned garage would generate revenues for the city and the school district, whereas property owned by the parking authority would be tax exempt. And the city would have to bear at least some of the cost of acquiring land, building, and maintaining a downtown expressway. Urban renewal was supposed to strengthen the tax base of the downtown area, yet the cost of implementing the Gruen plan would strain the city's resources, and its patience.

The long years of waiting for redevelopment to commence were a troubling time for downtown Lancaster and for cities across the nation. The growth of suburban retail threatened to render the traditional downtown department store a relic of an earlier time. Historian Lizabeth Cohen has demonstrated the impact of recently constructed shopping malls in suburban Paramus, New Jersey, on older downtowns such as Paterson and Hackensack. Whereas in 1950 Paterson was a vibrant shopping district, the malls constructed in 1957 siphoned customers away from downtown and the city began a tragic decline; Hackensack too saw a significant decrease in the number of merchants who had businesses on Main Streets, as did other traditional retail centers throughout Bergen County, and despite energetic efforts storeowners could not stop or even slow the flight of shoppers to the new malls. In Lancaster the earliest type of suburban retail was the strip mall, the first of which opened in 1958, yet even these rudimentary facilities caused a substantial drop in downtown's percentage of total county retail sales over the next five years. Since the announcement of the North Queen urban renewal project in 1962, the dislocation of so many businesses surely contributed to the shift in shoppers' loyalties to suburban stores. At the very time that Greenfield was trying to market retail space in the North Queen Street renewal project, two new shopping centers were being developed on the periphery of the city, one of which, Park City, was a vast regional center located on a 127-acre site at the intersection of Route 30 and the Old Harrisburg Pike. The suburban malls, the *New Era* reported, "are matched with downtown Lancaster in a race to secure department store tenants, small stores and, ultimately, shoppers."[23]

In the race for retail ascendancy Lancaster was quickly falling behind its suburban neighbors. Hager's, a West King Street establishment since 1821, had been a key supporter of downtown revitalization; indeed, its verbal commitment to relocate to the Queen Street site had been one of the strong factors in the selection of Second North Queen over the Hoffman group. But following the reorganization of the development corporation and the presentation of Gruen's plan, Hager's abruptly lost interest. John C. Hager doubted that downtown could support a fourth department store, let alone the fifth the Gruen plan included, and was furious that planners had designated the site long promised to his firm for use as an office building and relocated the department store across North Queen Street, which he considered too distant from a parking garage. Hager sounded an emphatic no to the Queen Street plan, and before the year was out signed a twenty-five-year lease for a 149,888-square-foot store in Park City, the new regional shopping mall being constructed northwest of downtown. In joining the nationwide exodus of downtown retailers who were moving to malls, Hager explained that the suburban location would enable the store "to better serve the shopping public, and protect its share of the local retail market." Hager's became the second department store to lease space at Park City, joining J. C. Penney, another refugee from King Street seeking a more advantageous location for its Lancaster business.[24]

The long period between presentation of site plan and commencement of construction, the uses proposed for the project, and the shifting of costs from the developer to the municipality, were real concerns, yet Lancaster's leadership had tied the city's commercial future to Second North Queen. The developers presented the Gruen plan on July 28, and four days later the Redevelopment Authority met to decide whether to approve the plan. Over the weekend, authority staff pored over the model, the schematics, and the descriptions, as did members of other interested groups. The urban renewal committee of the Lancaster Chamber recommended approval of the site plan, though it suggested a specific timetable for completion of leasing, design, and construction; the Redevelopment Authority's Architectural Design Review Committee judged the plan excellent and particularly praised the "keen understanding of both the pedestrian and vehicle traffic problems posed by the project location and the solutions projected." Donald Reidenbaugh, consulting architect for the Redevelopment Authority, commented, "With few exceptions, the design concept approaches excellence with its potential for becoming a successful urban shopping center for the city of Lancaster, the individual shopper and the retailer." Even the most cursory scrutiny revealed important unresolved issues—the necessity for and cost of a second parking garage, the feasibility of two department stores in the renewal area, whether retail was the key to downtown's future, the cultural and social significance of historic buildings that stood in the project area—but there was no time for careful study. On August 1 the Redevelopment Authority approved the Gruen site plan for Second North Queen, though it imposed ten conditions on the developer, the most important of which was a six-month deadline for securing commitments from major tenants.[25]

Discussion of the Gruen plan swiftly shifted to whether Greenfield would be able to secure the commitments from such major tenants as a department store, a motor hotel, and a movie theater. As the deadline neared, the developer submitted a list of seventeen companies that had indicated "serious interest" in the project, but publication of that list sparked controversy: several of the firms claimed they had never been contacted by the developer, while others had already signed leases at Park City. Redevelopment Authority Executive Director Paul F. Miller and Mayor Monaghan made frequent public statements about the city's ability to take over North Queen if the developer failed to present leases by the February 1 deadline, and the mayor even promised to set aside some of his official duties and make downtown renewal a personal crusade, but such posturing was hardly convincing. On January 31, 1967, the authority gave the developer authorization to proceed even though it had no legally binding commitments from major tenants and apparently not even an expression of "strong interest" from a department store. Lancaster officials expressed satisfaction with Second North Queen's pledge to begin construction of the motor hotel by September 1, 1967, and assurances that the entire project would be completed within four years, a schedule that added six months to the timetable the developer had promised the previous July.[26]

Less than a week after retaining Second North Queen as developer, the Redevelopment Authority turned to site preparation. Only the northern two-thirds of the west block had been cleared of buildings, and in addition to extensive demolition the authority needed to acquire the site at the corner of Duke and Chestnut streets for the second parking garage included in the Gruen plan. During the night of May 1, 1967, a wrecker's ball slammed into the Hotel Brunswick, the handsome Beaux Arts structure designed by C. Emlen Urban that was a popular downtown destination for generations. A sign on the wall separating the building from the sidewalk bore the legend, "TEARING DOWN—TO MAKE WAY FOR PROGRESS" (Fig. 16). Six weeks later, bulldozers cleared the last of the rubble from what had been a landmark structure and several adjacent buildings and moved west across Queen Street to continue their work. The largest building still standing there was the YMCA (Fig. 17), another downtown landmark. On Monday, July 11, a steel wrecking

FIG. 16 *"Tearing Down—To Make Way for Progress" was the optimistic message that heralded the demolition of C. Emlen Urban's Beaux Arts Hotel Brunswick, for sixty years a downtown landmark and destination (Lancaster Newspapers Inc.).*

ball smashed into that Beaux Arts structure and sent bricks and other debris flying into the night air (Fig. 18). A month later, all that remained of a once vibrant block was the rumbling of bulldozers leveling the ground.[27]

The signboard at the Brunswick site promised progress but did not define what progress would be, what shape a new downtown center might take. Nor could it account for the sense of loss so many Lancastrians experienced—the death of a familiar streetscape, the destruction of buildings associated with important events that defined their lives. More than thirty years after the demolition of the second block of North Queen Street, many Lancastrians fondly recall learning to swim or participating in other athletic events at the Y, or family dinners at the Brunswick as special occasions. Others cherish memories of wedding receptions, graduation parties, formal dinners and dances, or retirement celebrations. To them what was demolished was not

FIG. 17 *The YMCA, located at the northwest corner of Orange and Queen streets, was another signature Emlen Urban building and, like the Brunswick, a repository of the community's memory. Photograph c. 1925 (Lancaster County Historical Society).*

simply a block of buildings but a special place. The Y and the Brunswick were repositories of the community's collective memory, to paraphrase historian Robert R. Archibald's description of a hotel in his home town on Michigan's Upper Peninsula. Their meaning went deeper than the skin of brick and handsomely cut stone: for generations of residents these buildings defined place and time.[28]

What would be erected in place of these familiar landmarks would be the true test of progress. The questions were significant: whether the new buildings and spaces would contribute to a thriving downtown economy, solidify the city's tax base, and create momentum that would lead to revitalization throughout Lancaster; whether the new structures on the second block of North Queen Street would contribute to a humane landscape, one that dignified the city and its people, or whether the project would be designed and constructed in a way that diminished the human presence; whether the new public square would become a tranquil oasis in the midst of a bustling downtown or an inhospitable, empty space. The answers would, to a large

FIG. 18 *Demolition of the YMCA, one of Lancaster's landmark buildings, began on July 11, 1965 (Bureau of Planning, City of Lancaster).*

extent, determine the success of urban renewal in revitalizing Lancaster's central business district (Fig. 19).

During the summer of 1967, as architects worked on plans, the Redevelopment Authority, Second North Queen, and the city's parking authority negotiated an agreement for the construction and operation of a parking garage adjacent to the motor hotel, while the city and the developer submitted amended applications for federal funding and agreed to a phased schedule of construction. Phase I, or parcel A, was the site of the motor hotel and theater at North Queen and East Chestnut streets; construction was to begin on November 1, 1967, and be completed within two years. Phase II, or parcel B, was located at the corner of Queen and West Chestnut streets, opposite the site of the motor hotel. Designated for a department store, the tentative schedule of construction on this parcel called for groundbreaking in August 1969 with completion approximately eighteen months later. Phase III included parcels C and D, with a second department store to be located on the southern half of the east block and an office building designated for the

FIG. 19 *A symbol of redevelopment: the Prince Street Parking garage, erected adjacent to Lancaster Square, one of four garages that ring the central business district (Buchart-Horn Inc./BASCO Associates Ltd., Lancaster and York, Pennsylvania).*

southern half of the west block. The timetable established June 1970 as the tentative commencement of construction, with project completion in December 1971, a schedule predicated on federal approval of applications for increased funding and the developer's ability to secure tenants, especially for the two department store sites and the office building.[29]

Groundbreaking for the Statler-Hilton motor hotel and the theater complex took place on November 1, 1967. Redevelopment Authority Chairman G. Theodore Storb began the ceremonies by recognizing the long years of uncertainty that surrounded the project and asserted that with the onset of construction the patience of citizens "at long last will be rewarded." He was followed by state and federal officials and local business leaders who congratulated the city on its excellent project and the mayor for his leadership. Clinton Clubb, president of Second North Queen, thanked all who supported the redevelopment effort and pledged his corporation to the revitalization of the downtown. "We want to show that shoppers do prefer center city," he told the audience, "and not the widely scattered stores within acres of asphalt." Finally, Mayor Thomas Monaghan spoke. He graciously acknowledged the many individuals whose efforts made this day possible, and particularly former mayor Kendig C. Bare, whose administration first declared war on urban blight in the 1950s and who launched urban renewal in 1957. The mayor must have felt great relief that the redevelopment of North Queen Street was finally moving forward. While he admitted that there were still obstacles to the successful completion of the project, he expressed confidence that the city and the Redevelopment Authority would be able to bring North Queen Street to successful completion.[30]

Given the series of difficulties that had beset the North Queen project, it is perhaps fitting that the groundbreaking too became an occasion for controversy. The day before the long-anticipated event, Republican City Chairman Robert J. Broucht derided the ceremony as political grandstanding, designed to impress citizens with the progress of redevelopment and the administration's accomplishments, only days before a municipal election. "Is the North Queen Street groundbreaking a Halloween trick, or will real construction follow?" he asked. Whether or not the event was scheduled to impress voters, it was a symbolic beginning rather than the start of building: the developer still had not taken possession of the ground because HUD officials had not approved the documents signed by the redevelopment and parking authorities and the developer. Not until January did HUD officials assent to the contract between Lancaster and Second North Queen Inc. and authorize a grant to meet the additional cost to the project of the second parking garage and Lancaster Square. Not even these favorable actions bore immediate results, however; because of the delays, the developer acknowledged that construction would not begin until the spring.[31]

Before that happened the local partners in the development corporation—Clubb, his firm, Wickersham Construction, and Elmer Hansell, chairman of Wickersham's board—sold their interest to Hoffman and the other Philadelphia investors. Clubb attributed the sale to record-high interest rates, which, together with the local investors' share of the $3 million construction cost for the hotel and theater were straining his company's ability to pursue its construction business. Although Clubb expressed great confidence in Hoffman, and Milan and Monaghan insisted that the ownership change would not affect the project, this was a stunning event. The city and the Redevelopment Authority had chosen Second North Queen over Hoffman's group and other potential redevelopers because they were local, because they would not burden the city with the cost of erecting a parking garage, and because they had a tenant for the department store. Yet in late March 1968, before the foundations had been poured and a single brick laid, Second North Queen was in the hands of absentee owners, the city's parking authority had agreed to build and maintain two garages for the project, and the developer still lacked commitment from a single department store, let alone the two called for in the plan. Moreover, the developer had shifted two additional costs to the city: financial responsibility for the construction of Lancaster Square, which had a pricetag of $2.8 million, and architects' fees of $125,000 for Gruen's firm for planning the square. Perhaps because the fate of North Queen Street was essential to that of Lancaster's downtown, perhaps because a tenet of political culture in Lancaster held that government must serve the interests of business, few voices questioned whether public-sector investment of this scale should be used to generate private-sector profit.[32]

Construction of the motor hotel began in mid-1968 and revived a debate over the architectural style and materials to be used on new buildings in the urban renewal area. In 1965, Redevelopment Director Paul Miller predicted a "conservative approach" to design: "We would want to see something appropriate that would not become obsolete and ugly in ten years," he assured citizens attending a meeting of the authority. In succeeding months, as planning of the North Queen project shifted from concept to design, architectural style became a lightning rod for controversy. Donald W. Reidenbaugh, the Redevelopment Authority's consulting architect, advocated "an architectural image which is consistent with our times" and denounced the use of a contemporary Georgian style as "1966 colonial." While declining to take sides in the debate, the *New Era* conceded that there was "considerable sentiment in the community in favor of colonial" and argued for an architectural style that would stand the test of time. There was also public debate over the appropriate materials for new construction downtown. A rumor that the proposed parking garage on Duke Street would be built of concrete drew derisive comments from speakers, eliciting a defense of the material from Abbott Harle, of Gruen Associates, who pointed to Boston's new city hall, an inverted Mayan pyramid designed by the architectural firm of Kallman, McKinnell & Knowles, as "an example as one of the finest structures built in the Northern Hemisphere [that] is totally concrete." Despite Harle's aesthetic claims for concrete, local sentiment clearly favored a material that was more in keeping with the historic cityscape.[33]

The design of the Statler-Hilton Inn (Fig. 20) might best be described as conservative modernism: a rectangular box built of red brick with concrete trim. The choice of building material may have been a concession to the dominant red-brick architecture throughout the city, or perhaps it was a reflection of local enthusiasm for the colonial style, but the design was bland, especially in comparison with the hotel that had stood on the site for more than six decades. Where rusticated stone and generously detailed entrances distinguished the street level of the old Brunswick, flat walls of concrete and plate glass defined the new; where the façade of the Beaux Arts building was enlivened by handsomely carved keystones, cartouches, and other details worthy of a Renaissance palazzo, the modern hotel was accented by horizontal banding and vertical window frames—what one reporter described as "strips of natural colored structural cement." The adjacent movie house, which was the first new theater built in downtown in twenty years, was to be constructed by the developer and leased to Sameric Corporation as the Lancaster Eric Theater. At the ceremonial signing of the lease, Sameric president Samuel Shapiro promised that "no expense will be spared in making the Eric a downtown showplace," yet the building as erected was a nondescript box standing behind the concrete frame of Lancaster Square.[34]

As construction moved forward, Monaghan and Philip I. Berman, president of Allentown-based Hess's Department Store, announced that Hess's would erect an 180,000-square-foot facility directly south of the hotel and theater. Attracting a department store to North Queen Street had eluded developers since the early 1960s, so the March 1969 announcement of Hess's commitment to Lancaster was a major event. It marked the culmination of efforts, led by Monaghan and Fulton Bank Chairman Harold J. Frey, who solicited the support of eighteen local investors and raised $5 million toward the cost of erecting the new store. One newspaper reported that Hess's Lancaster store was "the first major full line department store designed for a downtown business district in a Pennsylvania city in more than 30 years," and local officials and merchants alike saw it as the key to the survival of retail trade in the city.[35]

With the beginning of Hess's construction, downtown took on a "new spirit . . . a sense of revitalization," according to Lancaster Newspapers reporter David J. Hladick. Interviewing merchants in May 1969, he discovered a pervasive optimism. Particularly enthusiastic were merchants on the first block of North Queen Street, which, Hladick noted, "will be sandwiched between two major traffic generators," the Watt & Shand department store at Penn Square and the new Hess's store at Lancaster Square. With the completion of the renewal project, the manager of a local shoe store predicted, "N. Queen Street will become the main street again," the center of the downtown retail district. A number of storeowners described major improvements they were undertaking to give their storefronts or interior spaces a facelift in anticipation of returning shoppers, including Bill Bash, owner of a jewelry store, who described the renewal project as "a bonanza for downtown." Local merchants realized the logic of Gruen's urban dumbbell: the shoppers who

FIG. 20 *The Lancaster Hilton Inn and Victor Gruen's concrete superstructure defining Lancaster Square, 1971. Compare with the Hotel Brunswick, which formerly stood on the same site, Figure 16 (Buchart-Horn Inc./BASCO Associates, Ltd., Lancaster and York, Pennsylvania).*

parked in garages adjacent to Watt & Shand or on either side of the North Queen Street project would stroll past their doors, just as the volume of pedestrian traffic would benefit smaller stores located between the anchors of a shopping mall. Hess's executive vice president Roy J. Hertz predicted that the area extending from Penn Square to the new hotel two blocks north would become the "dominant shopping center" in Lancaster.[36]

Unfortunately, the building Hess's erected on North Queen Street (Fig. 21) did everything possible to discourage shoppers from returning downtown. Its architects, Copeland, Novak & Israel, a New York City firm, had designed a number of suburban retail facilities, and they clearly thought of Hess's Lancaster store as if it were in a suburban mall. They produced a building

FIG. 21 *Hess's Department Store, designed by the New York architectural firm Copeland, Novak & Israel. Compare the blank façade with the elaborate detail of the Watt & Shand store, Figure 5 (Lancaster Newspapers Inc.).*

with a four-story red-brick exterior accented by vertical strips of concrete and a broad horizontal band of concrete at the top. Other than street-level display windows on either side of the small entrances on Queen and Orange streets, the new department store had no exterior windows, and the façade gave no indication of its retail function or even the number of floors within. Indeed, one newspaper described the building's "blank effect" and termed its lack of windows a "radical break from local department store design." Ironically, a building that was supposed to be a major piece in the revitalization of center city turned its back on the downtown as completely as the stores in a contemporary shopping mall turned inward, away from the parking lots that surrounded them. As designed and constructed the new department store did nothing to dignify the public realm of the street or provide visual delight to a passing pedestrian.[37]

For all the shortcomings of its design, construction of the new Hess's lent momentum to the North Queen Street project. At the unveiling of the department store plans, Monaghan indicated that an agreement to erect an office building on the site opposite Hess's would be finalized within three months, and in August the Redevelopment Authority advertised for bids to

FIG. 22 *Aerial view of Lancaster Square under construction. The Hilton Inn is to the upper left of the square, Hess's Department Store to the upper right, and the Prince Street Parking Garage under construction is at the lower right. Photograph by Ed Sachs c. November 1970 (Lancaster Newspapers Inc.).*

construct Lancaster Square. Edward Schwar, the Redevelopment Authority engineer, described the square as "a two-level covered pedestrian walkway encircling an attractively landscaped city park." Defining the square was a three-story concrete superstructure that carried the pedestrian walkways around the new public space and across North Queen Street, which bisected the square (Fig. 22). The smaller retail spaces were somewhat unconventionally located—away from the street, just as Gruen had explained in his 1964 book, *The Heart of Our Cities,* and behind a concrete screen—but the architect explained that pedestrians walking in or around the square would provide the clientele merchants needed. The interior of the square included a fountain and a playground on the east side and a skating rink and stage complex on the west (Fig. 23). Beda Zwicker, the Gruen partner responsible for the design of Lancaster Square, described it as a "neighborhood activity center," a place that provided "all the human amenities for the revitalization of the heart of the city." Here was Gruen's answer to suburban malls, a large downtown retail space that had the same features as malls—covered walkways, fountains, seats, and other attractions—as well as convenient parking. The plan was ambitious and attempted to emulate, on a smaller scale, a

FIG. 23 *Gruen's vision for Lancaster Square included an attractively landscaped commercial center as well as a space suited for recreation and entertainment. A photographer documented the square in September 1971, on the eve of its dedication (Buchart-Horn Inc./BASCO Associates, Ltd., Lancaster and York, Pennsylvania).*

world-famous mixed office, retail and public recreational space: when two sketches of Lancaster Square were published in April 1970, the *Sunday News* reported that "Architects and developers are predicting it will resemble a miniature Rockefeller Center."[38]

As the superstructure of Lancaster Square rose, the second block of North Queen Street began to fulfill some of its promoters' aspirations. The new Eric Theater began screening films over the Christmas holiday, the Hilton Hotel opened on April 3, 1970, the Duke Street Garage began operations in August, and Hess's greeted its first shoppers in April 1971. The culmination of the dramatic strides Lancaster had made came on September 25, 1971, when public officials from all levels of government joined civic leaders and

FIG. 24 *U.S. Senator Hugh Scott speaks at the dedication of Lancaster Square, September 25, 1971 (Buchart-Horn Inc./BASCO Associates, Ltd., Lancaster and York, Pennsylvania).*

citizens in the dedication of Lancaster Square (Fig. 24). The event took place three days after the dedication of Park City, the new regional shopping center that contained four department stores and more than 100 smaller shops (Fig. 25). Perhaps as a result, despite the brilliant sunshine, only a sparse crowd attended the ceremonies, which included the obligatory remarks by local politicians, the unveiling of a plaque, and the burying of a time capsule. In the keynote address, a speech largely devoted to promoting President Nixon's urban agenda and attacking Congressional Democrats, U.S. Senator Hugh Scott praised the new downtown square as "the beginning of a plan

FIG. 25 *Aerial view of Park City, the regional shopping center northwest of Lancaster's downtown that opened the same week as Lancaster Square's dedication (Lancaster Newspapers Inc.).*

that will make Lancaster second to none in its urban renewal." In words that could have been written by the builder or the architect, he described the "dramatic redevelopment of a onetime area of obsolescence" into a "showplace of design with dramatic firsts."[39]

For all the words celebrating Lancaster's progress, the absence of an enthusiastic crowd was perhaps more noteworthy than Scott's address; certainly the years of frustration at the glacial progress of the North Queen Street project, and the empty space on the west block (the area Lancastrians still described as "our hole in the ground"), should have tempered any overly optimistic thoughts. The office building designated for the corner of Queen and West Orange streets, announced in the summer of 1969 with a projected completion date of February 1971, remained in limbo, as did the thirteen-story apartment tower to be located at the northwest corner of the project, which developer Goldie Hoffman unveiled in July 1970 and scheduled for summer 1972 occupancy. Hoffman had changed the site plan from a department store to a luxury apartment building, with retail on the street level and the second floor, as a way of qualifying for Federal Housing Authority funding, but before plans could be completed and federal approvals obtained, Hoffman died at her Philadelphia home. The largest investor in Second North Queen Inc., and the partner most deeply involved in Lancaster affairs, her death at the age of fifty-two was a major setback to the development of the west block. Mayor Monaghan paid homage to Mrs. Hoffman, with whom had had often clashed over schedules and projects, praising her efforts and her faith in Lancaster's future. "She believed in Lancaster," he said, "and felt that she had passed the peak of the difficulties she had faced in the project."[40]

Hoffman's death added to the obstacles the developer encountered in bringing the North Queen Street project to a successful conclusion. Philadelphia attorney Abraham Gafni assumed responsibility for the developer and within several weeks announced that Bresler & Reiner Inc., a Washington, D.C., development corporation well known for its Waterside Mall project in the southwest quadrant of the capital, had contracted to erect buildings on the west block. Bresler promptly submitted an application for an $11 million construction loan to the Department of Housing and Urban Development (HUD), but the Philadelphia regional office rejected the request. Bresler, a close associate of Vice President Spiro T. Agnew, apparently convinced the Washington office to override the decision made in Philadelphia and grant preliminary approval of the loan for the Lancaster project. Expecting a funding commitment from FHA imminently, Bresler promised an early beginning to construction, as did Monaghan, who predicted that groundbreaking for the office tower would take place before the end of the year.[41]

No activity had occurred when, on January 4, 1972, Second North Queen announced the formation of a new limited partnership to complete the project, which would delay commencement of construction until mid-April. As he had done on previous occasions, Monaghan once again expressed displeasure with the developer—he was "fed up," according to one newspaper—and set a deadline of April 14. If the developer did not consummate the transfer of land by that date, Monaghan threatened to turn the project over to a new developer. While the city as a whole was disappointed at yet another delay, Philip I. Berman, the president of Hess's, was particularly concerned about the lack of progress in finishing the square, which left his new building in a retail netherworld: the adjacent smaller retail spaces were largely vacant, and without highly populated buildings on the west block, the square lacked the level of downtown activity that would make the new department store viable. Berman nevertheless professed optimism that a completed Lancaster Square would be an enormous benefit to downtown: "The square is unique and impressive," he told a *New Era* reporter. "It will become an attraction when it is finished that everyone will want to see." But, he added, "half a square isn't going to serve the purpose"—especially, he didn't need to add, when competing against completed, fully occupied suburban malls.[42]

The spring of 1972 saw the end of Second North Queen's role as developer. Despite Bresler's Washington connections, the FHA canceled the loan application for lack of essential information, and the developer allowed the April 14 deadline to pass without any activity. Less than a month later, Transamerica Investment Group, an Omaha, Nebraska, development company, and National Central Bank, a new institution formed by the merger of several smaller banks from Lancaster and nearby counties, announced plans to build a skyscraper of twelve to eighteen stories on the west block site designated for an office building. The bank would sell its East King Street headquarters to the city for use as a new city hall and lease at least three stories of the new building from Transamerica. As designed, the proposed building was a thirteen-story structure of brick and dark-tinted glass, with brick piers giving the building a strong vertical emphasis. A Transamerica spokesman explained that the use of brick, rather than marble, as originally suggested, was an attempt "to dovetail with the city's colonial architecture." With a projected commencement of construction in late 1972 (later pushed back to January 1973) and completion in September 1974, the new office tower promised just the infusion of white-collar workers downtown retailers needed. In an editorial entitled "The Future Brightens," the *Intelligencer Journal* praised not only the economic impact of the proposed National Central Bank Building but also its aesthetic contribution to the cityscape. The newspaper particularly noted the use of brick "to keep the building in harmony with the Colonial appearance of Lancaster" and the office tower's "contemporary design," which it judged "compatible with what has already been completed in Lancaster Square."[43]

Prospects for the west block seemed even brighter two weeks later, when Lancaster builder E. E. Murry, in partnership with Crossgates, a western Pennsylvania development company, announced that he had taken an option on the remaining parcel of the North Queen Street project area and would erect a twelve-story apartment tower with retail at the base. Together, the office building and the apartment/retail complex seemed a real solution to the problem of downtown Lancaster: the office tower would significantly increase the number of workers in the retail core, while the presence of 136 apartment units would give downtown a residential population it sorely lacked. The construction of these two buildings, the *New Era* editorialized, will make possible "a full demonstration of Lancaster Square's capabilities."[44]

Once again, best-laid plans came to naught. Although merchants and civic leaders were optimistic in the spring of 1973, the mood soon soured. By

June the Redevelopment Authority had grown frustrated with Transamerica's delays and threatened to terminate its contract, and, in July, Murry and partners, unable to provide evidence of adequate financing, sought a fourth extension of their project. Transamerica subsequently announced that it had cut the size of the building to ten floors—apparently an attempt to increase the likelihood of obtaining funding, which surely was predicated on commitments from tenants—and the following month Murry, unable to obtain tenants for the commercial space in his building, allowed the option on the North Queen site to expire. Before the end of August, Transamerica's plans for the office tower collapsed because the firm was unable to secure tenants. By the summer of 1973 Lancaster's redevelopment plans were being affected by rising oil and gas prices, the combination of slow economic growth and high inflation that pundits called stagflation, and a sense of economic uncertainty that touched all areas of the United States. Moreover, the North Queen Street project, conceived a decade earlier, was by 1973 a relic of an earlier approach to solving the urban crisis. As the economic boom of the 1960s faded into memory and budget deficits increased, a new political economy devalued downtown redevelopment projects. Indeed, throughout 1973 the Nixon administration was working to dismantle urban renewal and replace it with community development block grants.[45]

Discouraging as these developments must have been, Philip I. Berman's surprise announcement of the closing of Hess's North Queen Street store on August 27, 1973, twenty-eight months after its opening, was devastating. Berman attributed the unprofitability of the store since its opening to the city's failure to complete Lancaster Square. Raymond G. Herr, chair of the Board of County Commissioners, told a newspaper reporter that Berman was disappointed in the city and quoted Hess's president as feeling betrayed: "We had been promised that the other portions of Lancaster Square would be completed at the same time our store was." The lack of progress on the west block, together with the success of Park City, Berman conceded, was simply too much for the new downtown store to overcome. Local officials interpreted the announcement as a blow to urban revitalization and sprang energetically to work in the hopes of attracting another tenant for the building. But the final sentence of the Hess's announcement was perhaps the most telling assessment of retail's future, not only for Lancaster but for downtowns across the nation. Termination of the Lancaster operation, Berman stated in a press release, would enable the company "to review plans for additional Hess's suburban convenience stores, which have proved so successful."[46]

Downtown Lancaster was at a crossroads even as a mayoral election heated up. Republican candidate Richard M. Scott, a retired Air Force general, termed Hess's "one of the few bright spots in the downtown picture" and deplored the announcement of its closing, while the Republican *New Era* blamed Monaghan for the failure to complete the development of Lancaster Square. As the leaves turned to autumnal hues, Monaghan desperately attempted to get the North Queen project back on track. When National Central Bank (NCB) and Armstrong Cork Company expressed interest in undertaking a feasibility study for building on the west block, at the mayor's insistence the city acquired options on the site from Second North Queen to ensure the availability of the land. Announcing the study, NCB president Wilson D. McElhinny stated: "If at all practicable, it is our desire to play a major role in the revitalization of center city Lancaster." Conveniently ignoring the failure of a local development company in the revitalization of North Queen Street, the *New Era* sought to make political capital of the announcement by contrasting Armstrong and NCB with outside investors recruited by Monaghan, who, it charged, had "turned the block into a concrete and brick desert." This was a familiar refrain: in 1961 Republican mayoral candidate George B. Coe had criticized Monaghan for his administration's reliance on "high priced experts" from elsewhere rather than listening to local voices. Twelve years later, using the same tactics, Scott and the *New Era* successfully identified Monaghan with the failure of urban renewal, especially the North Queen Street project, and the Republicans won a convincing victory at the polls on November 6, 1973.[47]

On April 9, 1974, Armstrong and National Central Bank announced their decision to build on the west block. The bank determined to erect a five- or six-story structure at the corner of Queen and Orange streets, while Armstrong would build an interior-design center on the west side of Lancaster Square and an office building at the corner of Queen and Chestnut streets. According to McElhinny, the feasibility study demonstrated that "downtown Lancaster has the potential for making an exciting recovery" and predicted that it "will become a vibrant center for cultural events, commercial business, retailing and tourism." James H. Binns, Armstrong's president, expressed hope that individuals and businesses alike would become supporters of the downtown. Preliminary plans called for construction contracts to be finalized before the end of the year with completion some time in 1976. An overwhelmed Mayor Scott called the decision "the big spark" that would result in a "turnaround for our city." Other downtown leaders were similarly delighted. Among the numerous commentators the newspapers quoted, R. Wesley Shope, president of the Lancaster Chamber of Commerce, explained the Armstrong-NCB decision as part of a national trend, the transformation of downtowns from retail to financial and business centers.

The result, he predicted, would be "a giant step toward reversing the decline in center city."[48]

On August 30, 1974, Armstrong and NCB unveiled their plans for the North Queen Street site. The principal speaker was architect Alexander Ewing, a senior partner in the Philadelphia firm Ewing, Cole, Erdman, Rizzio, Cherry & Parsky, who presented the concept of the west block and the design of the three structures proposed for the site, each of which enclosed approximately 80,000 square feet of space. The NCB building, Ewing explained, was a five-story brick structure defined by strong horizontal windows, with public banking areas on the first floor and offices for some 200 employees above. Armstrong's three-story interior-design facility stood on the west side of the square, while its seven-story office building occupied the site at the corner of Queen and West Chestnut streets (Fig. 26). Together the two buildings would provide space for approximately 350 Armstrong employees, so the total impact of the project on the downtown work force, and at least potentially on the downtown retail and entertainment economy, was considerable. Ewing described the buildings as "contemporary" and compatible with structures on the east side of Lancaster Square. While he rejected a Colonial style as inappropriate for the scale and site of the buildings, he nevertheless expressed hope that the red brick chosen as the material and the contemporary design would have the "proper restraint to blend with the other surroundings, to achieve the quiet dignity for which we are working."[49]

Reaction to the Armstrong-NCB plans was overwhelmingly enthusiastic. Chamber President Wesley Shope praised the plan both for the substantial new presence it would make in the downtown and for the positive psychological effects he expected the filling of the west block streetscape would have. James Shand, president of Watt & Shand, described the plan as a "great incentive" to downtown and a step that would "help get things back on a positive track." To Theodore A. Distler, former president of Franklin & Marshall College and vice chair of the Redevelopment Authority, the prospect of these buildings on North Queen Street "portends a great future for the city." Donald B. Hostetter, executive director of the Redevelopment Authority, praised the Armstrong-NCB decision to build on Lancaster Square as "tangible evidence of the rebirth of downtown development." Mayor Scott was particularly upbeat: the proposed buildings would complete Lancaster Square, make downtown a vibrant place, and attract a new tenant for the vacant Hess's store. Construction of the bank and office complex, Scott exclaimed, would "make Lancaster even more beautiful and prosperous" and mark the beginning of a new era downtown.[50]

FIG. 26 *Armstrong House, designed by Alexander Ewing, with design studio to the left. Armstrong has abandoned its downtown presence for the suburbs, and its former building now houses corporate offices, including Smith Barney (author photo).*

That new beginning required the demolition of an earlier new beginning—the concrete superstructure defining the west half of Lancaster Square—and removal of the skating rink, stage area, and furnishings of the public plaza. Gruen's plan for the square was "a good idea for the development of a retail complex," Ewing explained, but was inappropriate for office buildings because the covered walkways that provided shelter for pedestrians would block the view from windows in the new structures proposed for the site. In addition to the demolition of Gruen's concrete superstructure, which the Queen Street Design Review Committee termed a "concrete cage," Ewing's plan called for replacing the plaza with a grove of trees and the skating rink with benches for passive recreation. Scott particularly praised the park planned for the site and compared it with Mellon Square in Pittsburgh, a park the size of a city block created in 1949 on top of an underground parking garage that stood between two skyscraper office towers—the Alcoa Building and the Mellon Bank–U.S. Steel Building. Scott and the architects clearly expected that what had been an urban wasteland would become "a place for people to gather."[51]

FIG. 27 *Demolition of the west side of Lancaster Square, December 17, 1974. Photograph by Ed Sachs (Lancaster Newspapers Inc.).*

On December 17, 1974, twenty-seven months after the dedication of Lancaster Square, a wrecking ball smashed into Gruen's concrete superstructure (Fig. 27). Over succeeding weeks the west side of Lancaster Square, as well as one of the two Queen Street overpasses, tumbled to the ground. Ironically, Clinton Clubb's Wickersham Construction Company, which proved unable to get the North Queen urban redevelopment site built, won the contract for demolition. As bulldozers removed the vestiges of Gruen's square on the west block, they shattered a widely held but misguided faith in the future of downtown retail. Local tradition, however, holds a different, more symbolic interpretation of its demise: Lancaster Square, and urban renewal in general, became key actors in a conservative morality play. Lancaster Square failed because it was the product of a government program, whereas the new buildings that would revitalize downtown—the city's "second chance" at renewal, in Scott's words—would be paid for by private capital. Lancaster Square failed because its fate was dependent on the work of outside experts and developers, whereas the new construction reflected the commitment of two prominent local firms. Ultimately, Lancaster Square failed because it just wasn't Lancaster.[52]

Thus the symbolic interpretation of Lancaster Square's demise celebrates a local perspective over a national program, hometown ability over cosmopolitan expertise, private-sector initiatives over public investment. But this is folklore rather than reality, a reinterpretation of events to make them consonant with political and cultural ideology. Lancaster Square did not fail for these reasons. Lancaster Square failed because, massive though the project seemed to contemporaries, it was dwarfed by the amount of new retail construction on the periphery of the city. Upon its opening, Park City enclosed perhaps as much space devoted to retail as did the traditional downtown shopping district, and there were at least four other strip malls in suburban Lancaster that also competed against downtown, and each other, for the shopper's dollar. Given the explosive growth of Lancaster's suburbs in the 1950s and 1960s, and with it the relocation of a substantial percentage of the metropolitan area's purchasing power away from the city, the North Queen Street project simply could not halt the rapid decline of downtown as a retail center. Moreover, easy though it has been to dismiss Lancaster Square as a caricature for wasted federal tax dollars, the simple truth is that far more generous federal tax subsidies underwrote the cost of suburban development across the United States, not just homes and retail space but corporate offices as well. By 1975 it was clear that the pattern of suburban development in the thirty years since World War II had resulted in the "environmental impoverishment" Lewis Mumford feared at the very onset of the economic boom of the 1950s, a sprawling, formless growth on the urban periphery that consumed vast amounts of farmland and undermined the economic and social viability of older central cities. Thus while official Lancaster celebrated the steel and brick that rose on the west side of Lancaster Square, the revitalized downtown Scott promised did not ensue. The calculus of the new suburban economy had no sympathy for the tired heart of an old retail district.[53]

PART III

Race, Housing, and Renewal

CHAPTER 5

RACE & RESIDENTIAL RENEWAL

The Adams-Musser Towns Projects

Paralleling the process of downtown revitalization was neighborhood renewal, which throughout most of the urban redevelopment era in Lancaster was concentrated in the southeast quadrant of the city. In 1957 the Citizen Housing Committee had recommended the creation of a local Redevelopment Authority as the key to eliminating substandard housing in Lancaster and preventing the spread of blight into other neighborhoods. At that time Mayor K. C. Bare strongly endorsed the creation of a Redevelopment Authority and pledged financial support as it began its efforts to revitalize the city. Acknowledging that blighted areas were "harmful to the social and economic well-being" of Lancaster, City Council established a Redevelopment Authority, under provisions of federal and state law, with the expectation that its actions would "promote the public health, safety, convenience and welfare of the City of Lancaster."[1]

The newly created Redevelopment Authority began organizing in 1957, but its role intensified when Thomas Monaghan became mayor the following January. In his inaugural address Monaghan promised to confront the city's problems with courage and expertise, and no problem demanded greater energy and ability than the physical condition of the city. By the end of January the Redevelopment Authority's consultant, William Harkins, presented a preliminary plan for redevelopment of an area bounded by South Queen, Vine, East King, South Ann, South Duke, Chesapeake, and Strawberry streets. His plan called for the total clearance of sixteen blocks, which would have necessitated the demolition of 622 buildings, 516 of which were residential, and projected limited clearance on twenty-two additional blocks. On April 1, 1958, City Council authorized the application for federal funds to prepare surveys and redevelopment plans for the Adams-Musser Towns Urban Renewal Area, which reduced the clearance area to twelve blocks but retained the overall project boundaries Harkins had sketched. Two months later the planning commission designated the project area as blighted and recommended that the Redevelopment Authority plan for its total renewal. Before the end of October the city had completed and submitted a General Neighborhood Renewal Plan Application for the Adams-Musser Towns project area.[2]

This preliminary Adams-Musser Towns plan (Fig. 28) sketched the future of a predominantly residential area of eighty-four blocks on approximately 245 acres. Bounded roughly by Strawberry and South Queen streets to the west, East King Street to the north, South Ann Street to the east, and the intersection of South Ann and South Duke streets to the south, the Adams-Musser Towns area contained 2,371 residential structures with 3,042 dwelling units, some of which were 200 years old. In addition to homes and apartments, 195 commercial, 26 industrial, and 31 community buildings stood in the project area. The data assembled by Redevelopment Authority staff determined that 32 percent of the residential structures (780 buildings) were dilapidated and substandard, while 10 percent (278) lacked running water. Compounding age and neglect was density: the Redevelopment Authority found that the area was overbuilt, with an average of 50 to 60 percent of the blocks covered by buildings, while on some blocks buildings occupied as much as 80 percent of the land. Moreover, because of the "irregular, unbalanced and antiquated building lots," what open space remained was inaccessible or occupied by such nuisance uses as junkyards or automobile graveyards. Together, the age of structures, density of building, and existing nuisance uses made the southeast area particularly prone to fire. One terrible conflagration in June 1956 left the American Caramel Company building on Church Street a brick shell that loomed ominously over adjacent residential structures (see Fig. 3). Still other deficiencies of the area included narrow, irregular streets and the lack of adequate recreational facilities. Here was an area, the Redevelopment Authority asserted, that fully met federal criteria for urban renewal.[3]

In its first formulation the General Neighborhood Renewal Plan Application anticipated the use of four strategies for residential renewal. The first was total clearance of all buildings, which was the treatment projected for twelve blocks containing 397 structures (342 residential, 44 commercial, 5 industrial, 6 community facilities). The clearance area extended from Church Street south along the east side of Duke Street to Juniata and included most of the blocks on the west side between North and Juniata streets. This area was the site of most of the alleys and courts that advocates of housing reform had identified as blighted for a generation. Based on findings of the 1950 Census of Housing, the renewal plan classified 300 of 465 dwelling units in the twelve-block area as "unsanitary or in substandard condition," and subsequent field surveys confirmed that assessment. On three of these blocks more than 70 percent of the structures were occupied by nonwhite residents; five other blocks had a nonwhite population of 30 percent or more.[4]

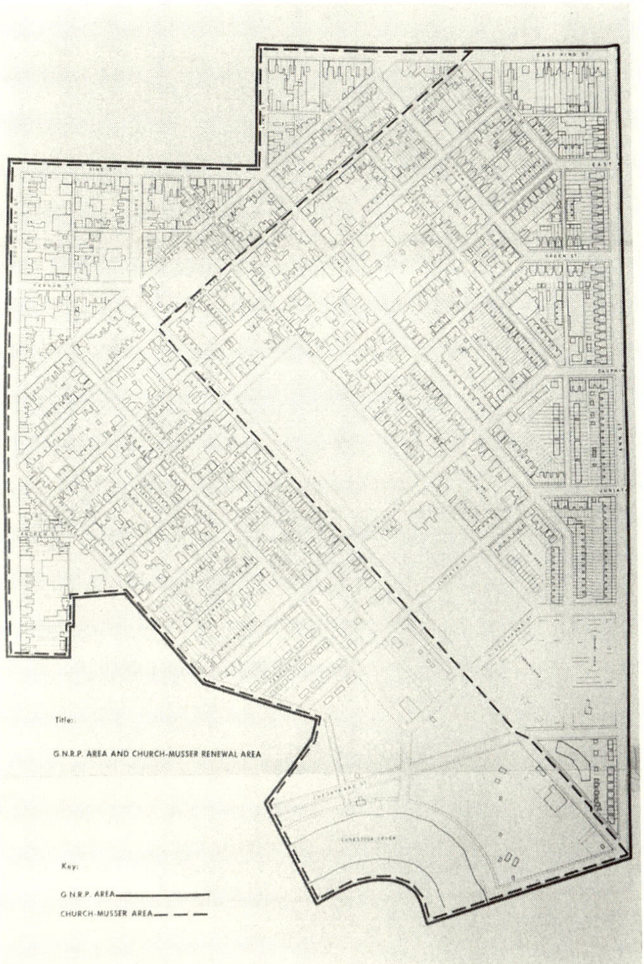

FIG. 28 *General Neighborhood Renewal plan for the Adams-Musser Towns Urban Renewal Area. From Drayton S. Bryant Associates,* Ongoing Neighborhood Self-Renewal: Recommendations for Housing Programs and Related Services, Church-Musser Renewal Area, Lancaster, Pa., *May 1967 (Bureau of Planning, City of Lancaster).*

The second treatment strategy outlined by the plan was limited clearance and rehabilitation, which involved twenty-two blocks, all but one adjacent to the Duke Street spine or contiguous to other blocks designated for total or limited clearance. What the planners termed "spot," or limited, clearance meant the removal of "the many very old substandard, wood-frame structures that are interspersed among standard brick residential 'row house' structures." The plan called for the demolition of 230 structures, 176 of them residential. Together the first two treatment strategies affected an area roughly four blocks wide by seven blocks long—a small part of the city, to be sure, but an area that because of segregation contained most of Lancaster's African American population.[5]

The third strategy advocated the rehabilitation and conservation of virtually all existing structures. Most of these blocks were at the northern and eastern edges of the Adams-Musser Towns renewal area, where the population was overwhelmingly white. The plan acknowledged that some structures were "showing the first signs of blight and deterioration," but it anticipated that with proper repair and conservation only a few demolitions would be necessary. The fourth strategy called for clearance of the blighted and sparsely populated southern part of the renewal area, which the plan designated as the site of new public and privately financed housing. These new dwellings would meet the housing needs of families to be displaced from other parts of the renewal area.[6]

Lancaster's first comprehensive residential renewal document called for dramatic alterations in one of its oldest neighborhoods, a program that would affect the lives of thousands of citizens. As planning for the southeast as well as the downtown commercial district advanced, the city launched a six-part public education forum entitled "Community Improvement Through Urban Renewal." The first speaker, John P. Robin, who had played prominent roles in the revitalization of Pittsburgh and Philadelphia, reminded listeners that cities have traditionally fulfilled important functions in human history—the marketplace, the capital, the focal points for social and cultural institutions—and asserted that despite growth on the suburban fringe the historic role of cities as centers of civilization remained. In remarks punctuated by practical advice, such as keeping urban renewal nonpartisan, and the need for vision ("Don't clear two blocks for a parking lot and call it urban renewal"), Robin explained the process of redevelopment and patiently answered audience questions. Other speakers included Edmund Bacon, executive director of the Philadelphia City Planning Commission, whose illustrated presentation emphasized the need for long-term, comprehensive planning and strong linkages between the public and private sectors; Francis J. Lammer, executive director of the Philadelphia Redevelopment Authority, and Drayton S. Bryant of the Housing Authority, who spoke on the difficult yet essential task of relocating individuals and families displaced by urban renewal; William Wilcox of the Greater Philadelphia Movement, who addressed the role of citizens in urban renewal; and Harold Grabino, counsel for the New Haven, Connecticut, Redevelopment Authority (substituting for executive director Edward Logue), who described how his city's ambitious redevelopment program had created a vital, thriving commercial center that, he claimed, vanquished the challenge to the traditional downtown economy presented by suburban sprawl. As a whole the forum attempted to educate Lancastrians, but it seems unlikely that the speakers influenced public opinion in any meaningful way. According to newspaper accounts, sixty-five "governmental and civic leaders" attended the first forum, fifty individuals were at the second, forty the third and fourth. The newspaper did not bother to publish attendance figures for the final presentations—perhaps an indication that, despite the magnitude of the problems the city faced and the size and cost of the projects planners envisioned, the forum generated little citizen interest.[7]

Another way of informing public opinion was through an extensive survey. The Adams-Musser Towns Committee interviewed more than 70 percent of the 2,500 households in the project area, both as a way of explaining how renewal worked and as a means of assembling data for the planners. The information generated by the survey revealed family size, housing needs, and family finances, which would enable planners to determine what new housing would have to be constructed to replace the units they hoped to demolish. The survey revealed the existence of a significant number of families with incomes too low to qualify for federally subsidized mortgages, which led consultant William Harkins to conclude that some public housing would be essential in the southeast.[8]

Throughout much of 1959, Redevelopment Authority staff and consultants studied the housing needs of residents of the southeast and refined the preliminary plan for the neighborhood. The product of almost two years of study was the General Neighborhood Renewal Plan (GNRP), prepared by Harkins and completed in November 1959. This blueprint for the renewal of the southeast sketched an eight-year program of improvement that would cost an estimated $8.1 million. The plan addressed general concerns such as the density of building, the absence of recreational spaces, and the need for modernized streets and adequate parking as well as significant improvements in the available housing stock. Components of the plan (Fig. 29) included a widened South Duke Street flanked by a greenway, the Duke Street Mall, which the planners envisioned as a space for passive recreation, other improvements to roads and the area's utility infrastructure, a municipal parking garage, a renovated or newly built elementary school with capacity for 900 students, a public housing project containing at least 240 units, and privately developed row houses and apartments. Smaller pocket parks distributed throughout the southeast would provide recreational opportuni-

FIG. 29 *Scale model showing intended redevelopment of the Adams-Musser Towns area. Note the new building corridor adjacent to the Duke Street pedestrian mall, as well as the amount of open space elsewhere in the renewal area that would result from selective demolition (Bureau of Planning, City of Lancaster).*

ties for children, and several sites were designated for neighborhood commercial development.[9]

As the preliminary application for funding had done, the GNRP divided the 244-acre renewal area into four projects. In succeeding months, as the planning moved from general to specific, the first of the residential renewal projects to move toward implementation was the site at the southern end of the Adams-Musser Towns area. Project I, a slightly smaller version of the area initially designated for clearance in August, encompassed an eight-block area with approximately 200 residences, more than three-fourths of them substandard, as well as several commercial facilities. The site was an irregularly shaped parcel of 33 acres bounded by South Lime, Susquehanna, South Ann,

Duke, and Dauphin streets. This was chosen as the location of the first project because of the low density of buildings and population. By undertaking Project I in the thinly populated neighborhood with a significant amount of vacant land, the Redevelopment Authority hoped to clear large tracts that could become the site of new single-family homes and apartments. Project I plans called for the acquisition of 90 structures for clearance and site improvement, the elimination of alleys and narrow streets, and modernization of infrastructure as the first step in what planners anticipated would be a major new residential development. The elements of the plan included spacious, well-designed row houses, a 111-unit public housing development intended "for those families within the Adams-Musser Towns area that lack enough income to rent or purchase on the private market," a wide pedestrian promenade or mall along Duke Street, and a one-acre neighborhood commercial center. The project "will serve as a bold and inspiring example of what can and must be done throughout the Adams-Musser Towns Area," Donovan Smith predicted. "It will re-establish the desirability and nourish the desire of future generations of live and raise a family in this area."[10]

One component of Project I sparked intense debate even as the plans were evolving: the Redevelopment Authority's recognition of the need for public housing. This became a major issue in the spring of 1960, when the Redevelopment Authority requested that the city, county, and school district accept payment of 10 percent of rents collected in lieu of property taxes on the public housing complex. Although Redevelopment Authority executive director Robert Going assured school directors that the payment would generate more revenue for education than taxes on generally dilapidated properties, the school board balked. John C. Truxal, vice president of the Lancaster County National Bank and a school director who was also chair of the Lancaster Housing Authority board, strenuously opposed federally subsidized public housing, which, he asserted, would become the slums of the future. Truxal conceded that Lancaster needed low-income rental housing, but he insisted that it be privately constructed and called upon local banks and corporations to help underwrite the cost. He drew a sharp distinction between a local subsidy for construction, which he supported, and a federal subsidy for rent, which he rejected outright. Pointing to Hickory Tree Heights, Lancaster's only public housing project, which had been erected with state funds to provide housing for veterans after World War II, Truxal noted that tenants who failed to pay their rent were evicted. The same, he argued, should be true of any public housing. As the debate over public housing filled the columns of local newspapers, Truxal called for appointment of a committee to study alternatives to the Redevelopment Authority's proposal, and without any apparent sense of impropriety or conflict of interest he promptly agreed to serve as chair of the committee and selected its members. At the same time, the Housing Committee of the Lancaster Chamber of Commerce advocated private rather than publicly financed low-income housing.[11]

The idea of privately financed low-income housing appealed to the conservative political philosophy of Lancaster, particularly because the cost of public housing would be significantly higher than comparable dwelling units constructed as a private development. This was not necessarily a matter of governmental inefficiency or layers of bureaucracy; the cost of public housing included site and infrastructure improvements as well as the construction of community facilities that private developers rarely if ever included in low-rent projects. Still, comparative costs weighed heavily on many residents, including Mary Fischer, vice president of the school board, who suggested that it would be "much more economical for all of us citizens of Lancaster to finance this [low-income housing] ourselves." In effect, Truxal and other opponents of public housing held up the image of a self-reliant community that could use local resources to solve its own problems, that didn't want or need an intrusive federal government wasting tax dollars in its midst. Attractive though this self-image was for many Lancastrians, no one in the city had built a substantial number of low-income housing units in the southeast in a generation, and no bank or corporation announced its willingness to play a leadership role in financing such private construction. This preference for privately financed low-income housing over public was not unique to Lancaster—similar arguments appeared in communities across the Northeast and Midwest—but as consultant Harkins pointed out, "no one in the United States has been able to do it," at least on the scale anticipated. The rhetoric of opponents of public housing in Lancaster conformed to what historian Michael Katz has described as "unrealistic expectations for the capacity of private action to ameliorate public problems."[12]

The Redevelopment Authority found itself in a difficult situation: if the school board or the county withheld the tax waiver, the city could not provide adequate housing for families relocated from other parts of the renewal area, which was required by the federal Urban Renewal Administration. Based on redevelopment programs in other Pennsylvania cities, the state Bureau of Community Development similarly considered public housing "essential to the success of any renewal program." Thus at their meeting of June 13, 1960, members of the Redevelopment Authority board defended public housing as the only way of ensuring the relocation of residents displaced by renewal. Moreover, they suggested that the school board's failure to grant tax relief to the public housing project imperiled all other redevelopment efforts in the city. Monaghan concurred, calling public housing absolutely essential to any total renewal of blighted areas. Concerned that "minority and lower income groups have safe and sanitary housing," the Interracial Council of the Lancaster County Council of Churches denounced the school board's position as "extremely short-sighted." Compounding the issue of public housing was the fate of the Higbee School, a turn-of-the-century structure that stood at the corner of Dauphin and Rockland streets in the Project I area. Construction of a new school as part of neighborhood renewal would count as a local contribution toward the project's total cost, which would benefit the city and the Redevelopment Authority. But the school board temporized while Truxal's special committee deliberated, using the decision on the location of the new school as a means of delaying any resolution to the question of a tax waiver.[13]

On June 24 the school board committee discussed alternatives to the Redevelopment Authority plans. Realtor John B. Kendig Jr. suggested the creation of a local fund to assist families displaced by renewal. He also described how a private agency might use contributions or interest-free loans to purchase and improve houses that it would rent to individuals and families who could not find suitable accommodations on their own. Following Kendig's presentation, Philip Schmehl, executive director of the Reading Housing Authority, provided the committee with an assessment of how public housing had worked in his community, but his assertion that public housing could be "good, sound, and workable" drew the ire of attorney Owen P. Bricker. Bricker, who apparently saw no conflict between his self-described role as attorney for "some of the biggest renters in Lancaster," his personal belief that public housing was antithetical to the American way, and his membership on a committee seeking solutions to the city's low-income housing needs, denounced the entire redevelopment program as injurious to property values. Following Bricker's outburst, Truxal, who had traveled to York to examine a recently constructed federally subsidized housing project, decried public housing for fostering "immorality and illegitimacy."[14]

Monaghan seethed as opponents of public housing placed the city's renewal program at risk. At the next City Council meeting he denounced Truxal and his committee as "self-styled statesmen" who had overstepped their authority even as they ignored the fate of "several hundred destitute families and children" who desperately needed public housing. Monaghan patiently explained the efforts of City Council, the planning commission, and the Redevelopment Authority in determining a strategy for renewal and the importance of public housing to the overall success of that effort. But all this might come to naught because of the efforts of a small handful of ideologues who refused to realize that public housing was an essential tool in urban revitalization. Members of the Truxal committee were engaged in fanciful dreaming at a time when the city needed decisions: "Let them give their green light while there is time to save our slum clearance program," Monaghan thundered, "and then let them retreat to their search for the angels." Later that day he warned that the city was in danger of losing state aid for residential slum clearance because of the school board's delay and expressed exasperation that any public official would act as if low-income residents had no right to expect decent housing.[15]

The Truxal committee report, presented to the school board on July 14, 1960, reluctantly recommended the waiving of property taxes on public housing, but in explaining its contents the chairman's tone was patently oppositional. Truxal informed the board that in the committee's "considered opinion," public housing was "not the only method to provide for the displaced persons, in the proposed redevelopment area" and urged a private-sector alternative strategy for low-income housing. Three contractors were ready to build on cheap land in the renewal area, he reported, which together with the renovation of some properties and rigorous code enforcement would ensure an adequate supply of dwelling units for families that would be relocated. In a lengthy minority report Owen P. Bricker reiterated his opposition to public housing and urged the full board to deny the tax waiver. During the ensuing discussion, Mary Fischer denounced Redevelopment Authority publications as propaganda and public housing as an unfair imposition on tax-paying citizens who would have to subsidize it. As was true of several of her colleagues on the school board, Mrs. Fischer advocated a Lancaster solution to Lancaster's housing needs rather than one imposed by bureaucrats in Washington and Harrisburg: "Let us lend our support to our own citizens who will find a way to house our citizens." Planning Director Cohen and Redevelopment Authority Director Going strongly supported the tax waiver, as did Tell B. Nussbaum, chairman of the Interracial Council, who urged the board to support public housing "in the name of human needs," but their voices went largely unheeded.[16]

Truxal persuaded the school directors to vote 6–2 against the recommendation of his own committee and deny the tax waiver. One school director vigorously dissented. William Schaeffer described how Truxal, unwilling to accept the committee's recommendation, "obtained 'new facts' [which] purported to show that the majority's decision was in error. With the new evidence, he has succeeded in convincing the Board to reject the committee's recommendation." Schaeffer pointed to Bricker and other opponents of public housing as working "to scuttle the entire Redevelopment Program," which they considered a "radical New Deal scheme." Donovan Smith, chair of the Redevelopment Authority, took the school board's vote as effectively blocking federally mandated relocation of displaced residents, which he considered the death knell of residential renewal in Lancaster. The following morning all five members of the Redevelopment Authority board resigned in protest against the school board's action. Smith portrayed the school board's vote as yet another manifestation of the "'old saw' of Lancaster doing much talking but very little real action on our blighted areas" and charged those opposed to public housing with the moral obligation of improving housing conditions throughout the southeast quadrant of the city. The president of the school board, A. Hugh Forster, praised his colleagues for their "sincerity and conviction" and derided the Redevelopment Authority board's action as "very dirty politics" and a blatant attempt to pressure the school directors.[17]

As Monaghan struggled to forge a compromise acceptable to all parties, the focus of attention shifted to the Chamber of Commerce's Action Committee on Necessary Housing, which had been hastily organized after the school board committee initially voted to recommend support of the tax waiver. The appointment of Truxal, the highly vocal opponent of public housing, as vice chair, was a telling indication that the committee's purpose was anything but action. Faced with the loss of $112,498 in state Bureau of Community Development funds should the city fail to meet a September 1 deadline for submission of a program for relocating residents displaced by renewal, Monaghan persuaded the Redevelopment Authority board to continue. He also brought representatives of state and federal urban renewal agencies to Lancaster to explain the federally mandated "firm guarantee" of available housing for citizens relocated by urban renewal and to describe what private developers of low-income housing would have to do to meet federal guidelines.[18]

All these efforts appeared to be wasted when the Action Committee presented its report on July 26. The most interesting recommendation was that the Hickory Tree Heights housing complex "be made available for the housing of qualified, carefully screened welfare family units displaced by the housing portion of the Urban Renewal program." The Redevelopment Authority had determined that a minimum of 240 low-income housing units would be necessary to relocate families displaced by renewal, so the 100 units in Hickory Tree Heights were only a partial solution to any relocation program. This discrepancy notwithstanding, the Action Committee claimed that its strategy might completely eliminate the need for additional public housing in the city. Further, the committee expected that the redevelopment and housing authorities could assist current residents of Hickory Tree Heights in purchasing homes of their own. Other recommendations included the reuse of all sound residential structures, reliance on local builders to erect housing on vacant land in the renewal area, and a rigorous program of code enforcement. The Action Committee described its report as a "good faith" attempt to "meet the needs of our own community and accomplish our purposes in our own way—with a minimum of hardship and a maximum of results," but what the report did not state was as revealing as what it did. Unmentioned was the fact that Hickory Tree Heights was a segregated, white-only housing development, while most of the families who would be displaced by renewal were African American. The report was effectively asking for public subsidies that would enable white families with an average income of $5,294—only $351 less than the median family income in the city—to purchase their own homes, and then devoting the public housing units they vacated for Lancaster's most needy minorities. Few of Lancaster's African American residents would have considered this a "good faith" proposal.[19]

The Action Committee report neither endorsed federally subsidized public housing nor presented a viable strategy for private-sector solutions to the shortage of affordable housing. Monaghan might have castigated the Action Committee report as long on rhetoric but short on action; instead, he simply noted that it failed to mention any potential source for the private-sector money that opponents of public housing argued was available and that, they suggested, "could be used to subsidize the low-income families of our community." The next day the mayor attacked the Achilles' heel of those who championed a nongovernmental solution to the city's housing needs: he released the results of a meeting with three local banks, which Truxal had suggested might provide subsidized financing for private low-rent housing. The bankers rejected that proposal out of hand, going so far as to dismiss the idea as "impractical and contrary to sound banking practices." Monaghan was carefully educating citizens about the realities of low-income housing, which proved to be very different from the claims made by opponents.[20]

Monaghan's strategy of deflating expectations for a private-sector solution produced results. At an August 1 forum on urban renewal sponsored by the Lancaster Interracial Committee, School Board President Hugh Forster assured the large audience that the principal unresolved issue was how much urban renewal would cost the school district. The question was not simply or even mainly public housing, he conceded, but the fiscal impact of a larger student body on school district expenses and on taxpayers. Monaghan and Redevelopment Authority officials responded by explaining that the residential renewal projects would disperse a highly concentrated population throughout a much larger area of the southeast. The number of housing units would increase only slightly, they assured the public, and the additional costs would be more than offset by tax revenues that reflected increased property values. Losing the battle for public opinion on the public housing question, and endangering a renewal program that many if not most citizens and civic leaders supported, Forster was ready to compromise. So was Monaghan, who feared that the city would lose state and federal renewal dollars if the controversy continued.[21]

After several meetings, Forster and Monaghan reached an agreement acceptable to the city, the school board, and other interested parties—the Board of County Commissioners, the Lancaster Housing Authority, and the Redevelopment Authority. In the cooperation agreement the school board agreed to waive property taxes on all public housing units constructed in the renewal area but received several concessions in return. First was establishment of an absolute limit of 300 units of public housing in the city. Second was a restriction that limited public housing to tenants "who have been bona fide residents of the City of Lancaster for a period of two years" and who lived in the Adams-Musser Towns renewal area. The city reiterated its commitment to a rigorous program of code enforcement, and all parties agreed that upon retirement of the construction bonds, they would pursue steps that would enable the Lancaster Housing Authority to sell the units to tenants. The terms of the agreement were designed to safeguard the interests of the school district, Forster declared. The school board's actions had not been obstructionist, he insisted, but were sincere efforts to protect the city's taxpayers. Although he anticipated that public housing would increase its expenses by a million dollars over a ten-year period, Forster conceded that "public demand for the renewal program to go forward" had persuaded the school board to sign the tax waiver. A crucial omission from the agreement was a provision, long supported by Truxal, that the city seek private local financing for the low-income housing project. The school board had surrendered. On the afternoon of August 11, 1960, Lancaster's City Council and Redevelopment Authority met separately to approve the cooperation agreement, and the school board voted its assent that evening. Monaghan, and the vision of a revitalized residential neighborhood, had triumphed over a small but outspoken group of opponents of public housing.[22]

Hard-fought as it was, the cooperation agreement was a victory only in the sense that it allowed the urban renewal process to go forward. Within hours the Redevelopment Authority staff was working to finalize applications for state and federal funding, which were due within weeks, but almost a year passed before plans were finalized. A critical step along the way was a public hearing to ascertain citizen reaction to Project I. The city scheduled two hearings: the official hearing on the morning of May 19, 1961, and an informal hearing held the previous evening for individuals who could not attend a meeting during the workday. At the beginning of each session Burrell Cohen made a trenchant presentation detailing the need for renewal. His hour-long remarks were illustrated by slides that depicted some of the worst conditions in the southeast. The tenor of his commentary was negative: "Here's a typical alley shot showing you the accumulated junk and the deplorable housing conditions," Cohen stated as the audience peered at one slide, and as another appeared on the screen he added, "Here's some more trash, cluttered alleys, very, very poorly maintained fences which I think gives you some indication as to what the homes must be like." Cohen then attempted to explain how Project I would work. During the clearance phase, blocks containing 90 structures would be razed and the nuisance uses such as junkyards would be removed; then new housing and a small commercial center would be built in the project area, as would such amenities as the landscaped pedestrian mall along South Duke Street.[23]

Although most of the statements made at the hearing were by representatives of twelve civic organizations such as the YMCA, the YWCA, the Chamber of Commerce, the Lancaster Recreation Commission, and the Council of Churches, all of which supported urban renewal, there were dissenting voices. Foremost among these were black Lancastrians, who would be most directly affected by renewal. Several individuals asked questions that probed how redevelopment would take place within a segregated community. Herbert Cooper, a longtime resident of the southeast, described how housing discrimination worked in Lancaster. When a young African American couple sought his help in finding a place to live, they "went to every real estate man in the city and checked every ad in the newspaper. Some offered housing, he said, but when we got there their minds were changed," with the result that the young couple was frustrated in their quest to find the home they desired. Cooper then asked whether the Redevelopment Authority would help residents of the southeast, regardless of color, secure housing in other parts of the city. He also predicted that the combination of demolition and discrimination was "going to cause a racial problem" and urged the city to use the recently adopted state Fair Housing Act as a tool in the relocation process. James Underwood, a former resident of Barney Google Row who was then lease-purchasing a home several blocks away, at 721 Rockland Street, questioned how the Redevelopment Authority had the "power to take our house away from us" yet did not have the power to help his family live in whatever neighborhood they chose. Cohen conceded that the concentration of African Americans in the southeast was a long-standing problem, and added that while he personally deplored discrimination he did not believe the Redevelopment Authority was responsible for it. The authority's role, Cohen insisted, was "to remove substandard and undesirable houses, improve the environment and the living conditions of everyone in Lancaster in this area whether they be Negro, White or any other race or religion." He steadfastly maintained that the Redevelopment Authority could not coerce owners of properties to rent to minorities, which many black Lancastrians took to mean that housing discrimination would persist. The minority population, which would bear the greatest burden from demolition and dislocation, would find in urban renewal no relief from discrimination.[24]

Immediately following the public hearing, City Council held a special meeting and voted unanimously to adopt Project I, which shifted from the planning to the execution phase. Selection of a developer for the first new residential construction occurred in May 1962, and demolition began in the summer. The first step in the project was the construction of 119 dwellings over a two-and-a-half-block area bounded by Dauphin, Rockland, Susquehanna, South Lime, and South Duke streets. The western end of the plot, along South Duke Street, would be devoted to a pedestrian mall or linear park (Fig. 30). The Bogar Lumber Company, a local building-supply firm, was the developer. Bogar, the only prospective developer to submit a proposal acceptable to the Redevelopment Authority, had been in the building-supply business for more than forty years, but Project I was its first venture into construction. Nevertheless, Donovan Smith praised the Bogar company for its "willingness to cooperate and produce a proposal of the highest quality" and its "desire to do the best possible job in redeveloping this land in keeping with the Authority's original objectives." Following extensive review, the Redevelopment Authority approved the sale of land to Bogar on November 28, 1962, and four weeks later the Urban Renewal Administration gave final authorization to the project.[25]

The Bogar houses (Fig. 31) were "a mixture of contemporary and semi-colonial design," one newspaper reported. They were a lighter brick than the traditional deep red used on so many Lancaster buildings and were set back from the street in staggered rows. Each dwelling was twenty feet wide (four feet wider than the typical Lancaster row home) and twenty-eight feet in depth, and would enclose ample space for a kitchen, living, and dining room on the first floor and three bedrooms on the second. In addition, the site plan provided a parking space for each residence. Because the Redevelopment Authority assembled the property and sold it to the developer at

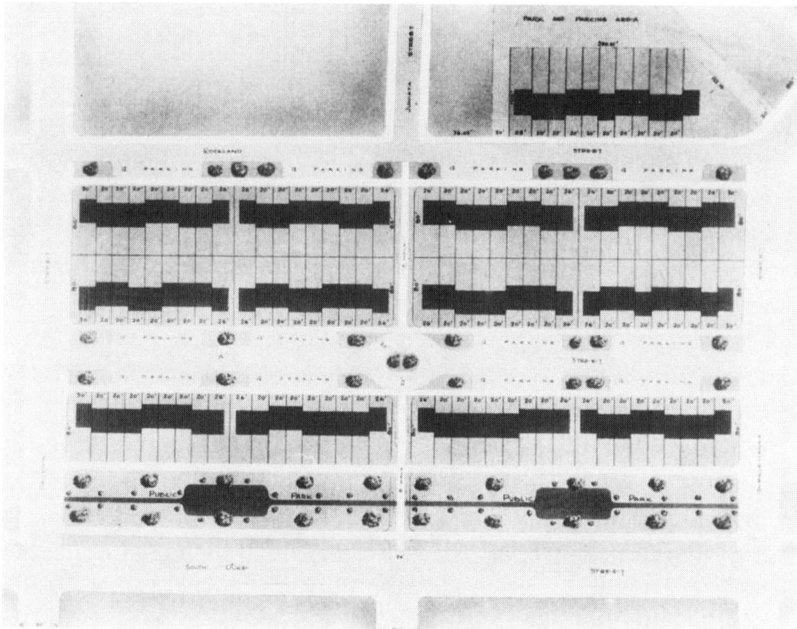

FIG. 30 *Schematic showing site plan for Bogar houses and the Duke Street Mall. The eleven Bogar homes that were constructed are at the top; the Duke Street Mall, identified as Public Park, is at the bottom. The drawing shows the intended location of 108 additional Bogar homes, but these were never built (Bureau of Planning, City of Lancaster).*

reduced cost, and the city assumed responsibility for construction of some of the infrastructure, Burrell Cohen expected the houses to sell for $10,300 to $10,600. With a $350 down payment and $150 in closing costs, the monthly payment for mortgage and real estate taxes would be $80 to $85, a cost that would exclude low-income residents. The Bogar homes, Cohen noted, would achieve one of the "most important objectives of the planning program—the creation of quiet pleasant residential streets, attractively landscaped so as to provide moderate income families with the privacy and atmosphere they seek for residential purposes."[26]

Construction of the first eleven Bogar houses marked an optimistic beginning for residential renewal. Despite Bogar's success in constructing the first eleven homes,[27] the remaining 108 units would not be built as planned. The city and the Redevelopment Authority executed a contract with Bogar for the next phase of construction and approved the site plan for the area bounded by Dauphin, Rockland, and Susquehanna streets and the Duke Street Mall to the west, but the discovery of an ash dump on the prop-

FIG. 31 *The first eleven Bogar houses, with part of the site containing the ash dump in the foreground (Bureau of Planning, City of Lancaster).*

erty during groundbreaking, together with what the *New Era* described as "red tape and other factors," led to a different redevelopment strategy. The presence of ashes necessitated caissons and special foundations, which increased construction costs beyond the amount the local housing market would bear. The other factors the newspaper mentioned included a federal program, FHA Section 221(d)(3), that promoted partnerships between developers and nonprofit organizations to build low- and moderate-income rental housing. Taking advantage of the opportunity this program presented, the Redevelopment Authority decided that garden apartments would better meet the housing needs of low- and moderate-income families displaced by renewal than attached single-family dwellings. Then the Redevelopment Authority accepted a proposal from the Bell Development Corporation and the Penn Central Conference of the United Church of Christ (UCC) to erect a garden apartment complex on the site and sought federal funding to enable a nonprofit developer to undertake the construction. After lengthy delays, groundbreaking for the first 80 units of a 160-apartment complex took place on July 12, 1968; thirteen months later the UCC dedicated the five three-story brick buildings (Fig. 32). In his dedication address, the Rev. Dr. Ben M. Herbster, president of the denomination, praised the residential development as an expression of Christianity's social responsibilities. Despite altruistic intentions, the UCC Apartments had a troubled start; operating costs exceeded income from rent and shoddy construction caused

FIG. 32 *Duke Manor Apartments, an FHA-subsidized complex erected by the Bell Development Corporation and the United Church of Christ (author photo).*

problems for tenants and owner alike. Facing bankruptcy, the apartments were eventually taken over by HUD, managed by a nonprofit housing provider, and renamed Duke Manor Apartments.[28]

The other major component of Project I was the much-debated public housing complex. The Lancaster Housing Authority initially planned to erect a 111-unit high-rise complex on a 5.5-acre tract bounded by Susquehanna, South Duke, Chesapeake, and South Ann streets, just to the south of the Bogar homes site, but the federal Public Housing Administration rejected tall buildings as incompatible with the surrounding cityscape. The Lancaster Housing Authority then reduced the proposal to ninety-six and eventually to 75 units in a series of two-story buildings. The site was the largest tract of vacant land in the southeast and was critical to the overall renewal plan because the buildings constructed would serve as relocation housing for families displaced as demolition occurred in the more densely populated blocks of Project II. Once again, however, a former use of the site affected development plans: the land had been a sand quarry for close to a century, and over the last thirty years the extensive pit had been filled with ashes and cinders. Test borings revealed depths of 40 and 50 feet, and one former owner estimated the size of the dump as 80 by 200 feet with a maximum depth of 90 feet. The presence of ashes over so large a part of the site, and the depth of the ash, would make construction much more difficult and more expensive.[29]

The ash dump was a grave threat to the Adams-Musser Towns urban renewal project. If the Public Housing Administration rejected the site, either because of prior use or the additional cost entailed by the presence of the ash, it would cause "utter confusion," in Burrell Cohen's words: because there was no readily available alternative site for low-income housing elsewhere in the Project I area, such a decision would necessitate the preparation of an entirely different residential renewal plan and set the Adams-Musser Towns redevelopment program back several years. In March 1963, engineers estimated that construction on the ash dump increased the project cost by $110,000, which led the Lancaster Housing Authority to consider an alternative site. Fearing the consequences of delay, the Redevelopment Authority persuaded the Housing Authority to purchase the land at a substantially reduced price, with the savings in land acquisition offsetting the increased cost of construction resulting from the condition of the site. When construction began, recreational facilities and parking lots stood on the part of the site that had been an ash dump, while the new two-story brick-and-frame apartment buildings faced the surrounding streets. Construction was delayed at least once when contractors had to sink concrete columns and pour a concrete platform to stabilize three units that had collapsed because of the ash pit. But after years of public debate and the long process of condemnation, clearance, site preparation, and construction, tenants moved into the first 25 units on December 1, 1965. The fifteen-building garden apartment complex, Susquehanna Court, was completed on April 29, 1966.[30]

The second stage of the Adams-Musser Towns renewal program, Project II, consisted of two components, the first of which was to acquire and clear a site for the new Higbee School, an elementary school to be located between North, Rockland, and Dauphin streets and the Duke Street Mall. The area contained 149 residential structures, mostly row houses, and 17 commercial buildings; it was subdivided by narrow interior streets and alleys that provided access to dilapidated housing. The Redevelopment Authority's proposal for the Higbee project reported that 98 percent of the buildings were "structurally deficient." Of the 114 families that lived on the Higbee site at the end of 1963, the Redevelopment Authority estimated that 73 were eligible for public housing.[31] While there were some handsome, well-maintained buildings in the project area, total clearance was essential, a Redevelopment Authority executive told citizens and civic leaders. The new Higbee school

FIG. 33 *The new Higbee School, now the Martin Luther King Jr. School (Lancaster Newspapers Inc.).*

and playground were "vital facilities for the total program of uplift and regeneration" and would serve residents who lived in newly constructed homes as well as rehabilitated dwellings throughout the Adams and Duke Street project areas. Following demolition and site preparation by the Redevelopment Authority, the School District of Lancaster took possession of the land on September 9, 1965. The new Higbee School (the present Martin Luther King Jr. Elementary School), a state-of-the-art facility with twenty-eight classrooms for more than 900 students, was completed on May 8, 1967, and dedicated on January 7, 1968 (Fig. 33).[32]

The second component of Project II was the Adams Project, an area of approximately 85 acres bounded by Duke Street to the west, Howard Avenue and East King Street to the north, Ann Street to the east, and Project I properties to the south and west. Adams marked a new direction for the Lancaster Redevelopment Authority. Instead of the wholesale clearance that had been the renewal strategy in previous projects, rehabilitation was the goal of Adams: 78 of the 85 acres in the project area were slated for some kind of conservation or restoration treatment. Philadelphia architectural historian Charles E. Peterson, a consultant to the Redevelopment Authority, praised the Adams neighborhood as being "loaded with homes of the Civil War period or older, the majority of which are worthy of preservation." Based on his enthusiasm and a careful inspection of every structure in the project area, the Redevelopment Authority determined that roughly 900 of the 1,200 buildings were suitable for renovation, with the remaining blighted sites to be cleared for redevelopment, parking, or open space uses. Paul Miller, who had succeeded Cohen as head of the Redevelopment Authority, was especially enthusiastic about the Adams Project. Pointing to eighteenth- and nineteenth-century buildings along Howard Avenue as examples of how renewal could be accomplished, he described the area as "one of the great resources of Lancaster." The renovated buildings would not be "museum pieces" but would be "lived in and used."[33]

The Adams Project promised to substitute the artisan—the carpenter and bricklayer, the plumber and the electrician—for the bulldozer that had leveled so much of the area along South Duke Street. Here was an urban renewal strategy that required capital, expertise, and imagination. The Redevelopment Authority would provide the expertise, and did so through a series of information meetings that sought to reach every resident of the rehabilitation area. Each meeting included remarks by redevelopment officials, the mayor, and rehabilitation-conservation coordinator Carl H. Simmons. Collectively, the speakers attempted to explain how rehabilitation would work and what role the city and the Redevelopment Authority would play in the project. The city assumed responsibility for widening and improving streets and in creating parking lots, open space areas, and playgrounds in the eight areas where substandard buildings would be demolished. In addition to removing substandard buildings, the Redevelopment Authority would provide technical assistance to residents, such as architectural and engineering services, and would review contracts between owners and building contractors. Grants and low-interest loans would help homeowners who otherwise could not afford the cost to upgrade their properties.[34]

Following an extensive series of public meetings with residents as well as the preparation of applications and supporting documents for federal and state review, the Redevelopment Authority released a plan for the Adams Project in November 1964. The Adams plan called for the demolition of approximately 300 structures, the relocation of 245 families and 30 businesses, and the renovation of 900 buildings, most of which were single-family homes. New construction included a sanctuary for the Faith United Church, at the corner of South Duke and North streets, to replace the congregation's church that stood in the Higbee project area, as well as a new facility for the Lancaster Boys Club, a small neighborhood commercial center, and a scattering of apartments and houses on cleared sites. Most buildings in the project area would be renovated, and to assist homeowners the

FIG. 34 *Historic houses along Howard Avenue restored as part of the Adams Project (author photo).*

Redevelopment Authority prepared a booklet explaining the city's housing codes and establishing standards for rehabilitation. A year later, Redevelopment Authority head Paul Miller described Adams as "urban renewal in its best sense, saving those parts which can be saved, replacing those which are uneconomical to save, and at the same time providing public housing, off-street parking, an industrial park and historical restoration." A major component of the Adams Project was the creation of Lancaster's first local historic district, a two-block area bounded by Howard Avenue and Shippen, Locust, and Lime streets (Fig. 34).[35]

The Redevelopment Authority also renovated two houses on Locust Street as an example of how the rehabilitation process could work. In an similar effort, Armstrong Cork Company, the largest industry in Lancaster, acquired seven single-family homes on the 500 block of Rockland Street. Armstrong hoped that the work undertaken on the seven homes would "determine which of our present products can serve this part of the housing market best, and what new products we may need to develop," according to

F. S. Donnelly, who coordinated the effort. What the project demonstrated most clearly was that the cost of renovations exceeded the market value of the homes. Nevertheless, with more than $4.5 million in public spending as well as money from individual homeowners and investors pouring into the area, the Adams Project achieved a number of its objectives: it demolished 283 of the worst buildings in the neighborhood, as well as a series of alleys or interior streets that were lined with dilapidated structures; and it constructed new streets and other infrastructure, paved parking lots, and established small parks for children. This rehabilitation program extended the life of 710 houses and several churches that were more than a century old.[36]

Promising though the rehabilitation of historic homes was, a continuing inability to secure sites for low- and moderate-income housing bedeviled the several Adams-Musser Towns projects. Approval of the Susquehanna Court complex left a shortfall of 225 dwelling units needed as relocation housing for residents displaced as the renewal program moved to the more densely populated blocks to the north. In September 1963 the Lancaster Housing Authority sought the aid of the Redevelopment Authority in identifying sites for additional low-income housing. A month later the Redevelopment Authority recommended two locations. The first was a 10-acre tract west of South Duke Street overlooking the Conestoga River, which Paul Miller believed was appropriate for a 125-unit low-income housing complex. Miller was particularly enthusiastic about the site because it would require very little demolition and relocation, so that new housing could be constructed quickly. The second site was a tract on Church Street, where the American Caramel Company's factory (see Fig. 3) had stood and where, following Miller's recommendation, the Housing Authority erected a high-rise residential tower for the elderly. The Public Housing Administration rejected the first location because the excessive fill found on the property would increase construction costs. The Housing Authority then secured an option on a 15-acre site between Franklin Street and the Conestoga River, which the Redevelopment Authority had previously rejected because it was outside the boundaries of the General Neighborhood Renewal Plan. Redevelopment Authority and Planning Commission staff were caught off guard by the announcement of the Housing Authority's action. Miller was particularly concerned because the site was not within an approved redevelopment area and the cost of infrastructure would not count as part of the city's match for federal urban renewal grants. The Housing Authority nevertheless erected a 124-unit apartment complex, Franklin Terrace, on the site, much of which was a floodplain.[37]

On September 13, 1963, the day the housing and redevelopment authorities announced their collaboration in seeking sites for low-income housing, Paul Miller proposed scattered-site housing as a solution to Lancaster's housing needs. He was enthusiastic about using renovated homes in the Adams renewal area instead of large-scale projects, which, he suggested, could ensure that "at least some public housing could be scattered throughout the renewal area." Miller cited two advantages of scattered-site housing. First, and most important, scattered-site units would not stigmatize residents as "public housing families"; second, experience in Philadelphia and other communities that experimented with rehabilitation demonstrated considerable cost savings—as much as $5,000 per unit—over new construction for larger projects. While conceding that administrative costs for individual units tended to be higher than projects, Miller believed that the savings in construction and the social benefits of scattered-site housing made it a viable and exciting alternative.[38]

Scattered-site low-income housing would become a persistent and divisive issue in Lancaster. Miller's initial remarks had suggested that scattered-site housing would be confined to the renewal area itself, which would continue a long-standing pattern of discrimination. At an April 28, 1965, public hearing devoted to the Adams Project, Betty Tompkins, a member of the executive board of the Lancaster NAACP, demanded that the Redevelopment Authority pay particular attention to the human dimension of renewal. She urged the board to "become more sensitized to the families that are being up-rooted" by redevelopment, and fellow citizens to become more accepting of "those persons wishing to move out of the renewal area." Tompkins was a persistent voice urging the desegregation of Lancaster's housing market. She and other proponents realized that scattered-site housing was at least potentially a powerful tool in accomplishing that goal, but in succeeding years the Lancaster Housing Authority and many white residents would adamantly attempt to restrict low-income housing to the southeast quadrant of the city.[39]

The impetus to create scattered-site housing outside the renewal area persisted. A year after Tompkins's statement, the Lancaster Human Relations Committee advocated an ambitious program of "scattered-site public housing, throughout the community, in new and existing structures, in owned and leased structures and in single family and multi-family structures." In August 1966 the Redevelopment Authority recognized the need for 600 additional units of public housing to meet relocation needs as the renewal program progressed. In a memorandum urging the Housing Authority to commence planning for those needs, Paul Miller advised against erecting large projects like Susquehanna Court or Franklin Terrace and also rejected the idea that any additional public housing be constructed in the southeast quadrant of the city. Instead, he proposed to the Housing Authority that a minimum of 100 scattered-site units be occupied in 1967, another 200 in the following two years.[40]

On November 10, 1966, the Redevelopment Authority formally requested the Housing Authority to provide 375 additional units of public housing. Miller also "asked that the Housing Authority consider dispersing them throughout the city." The Housing Authority tabled a resolution authorizing application for federal funding to provide the additional units, and a newly elected, Republican-dominated City Council sought to slow the implementation of what its president, Richard Filling, termed "spot housing." As the implications of a community-wide scattered-site program became clear and as public housing became increasingly politicized, opposition erupted. Leading the opposition was David B. Bucher, a member of the Housing Authority. Bucher rejected scattered-site units on two grounds: because of the higher cost both to build and administer, and because of what he termed a "social problem"—the "peculiar nature of the people who don't have basic training in health and community living." He also expressed concern that scattered-site housing would undermine the stability of neighborhoods. When Thomas Monaghan, who had succeeded Coe as mayor in 1966, wrote Bucher and urged him to be broad-minded rather than obstructionist, Bucher vigorously defended his point of view and called for a thorough public discussion of housing issues. Claiming the high ground, he argued that "no declaration of urgency, no plea for expedient action, should take precedence over the right of the people to know"—and then promptly released the text of both letters to the *New Era*.[41]

Scattered-site housing divided the Lancaster community. The League of Women Voters came to its support. "Project-type housing tends to make a ghetto for the poor," wrote League president Mrs. Leonard Sloane, and ultimately failed to "change the psychological and social outlook of the poor." Scattered-site housing, in the League's estimation, offered the poor "the opportunity to break out of this pattern." Rejecting critics who asserted that residents of scattered-site units would bring the problems of the ghetto to different locations, Mrs. Sloane instead pointed out that the "opportunity to live where neighbors are more responsible may . . . engender a new feeling of self-respect and a new desire to participate positively in the community." The Lancaster City–County Human Relations Commission similarly insisted that "ghettos are bad for our community and bad for our nation" and called for a Housing Authority with county-wide jurisdiction as the most efficacious way of achieving scattered-site housing, which it considered a just solution to housing discrimination.[42]

But a host of voices denounced scattered-site housing. A resident of Prospect Street who lived in the southwest quadrant near a site proposed for such units conceded that applicants for public housing needed help but strenuously objected to his neighborhood as the caregiver. "If you or anyone else think these people will be accepted by the surrounding neighborhoods," Robert Esbenshade wrote Mayor Monaghan, "I think you are badly mistaken. These sites will become like islands even in the best Christian-like neighborhoods." Other opponents expressed fear that scattered-site tenants would lack "basic training in health and community living" and thus have a negative impact on the area and on property values. Still other critics believed that scattered-site housing was simply bad public policy because its costs outweighed the benefits it would provide.[43]

The debate over scattered-site public housing took place ten years after the Citizen Housing Committee first examined substandard dwellings in the city and called for the creation of a redevelopment authority to eliminate blight. By January 1967 the Redevelopment Authority had brought the eleven Bogar houses to completion and the Housing Authority had opened the 75-unit Susquehanna Court complex, which it operated along with Hickory Tree Heights. Other housing projects then being built were the 124-unit Franklin Terrace apartments, the 101-unit Church Street high-rise project for the elderly, and the first half of the 160-unit middle-income apartments being developed by the United Church of Christ along South Duke Street. Urban renewal had already eliminated more than 400 dwelling units by the summer of 1966 and projects then under way called for demolition of 500 more—twice the number of housing units then planned to provide shelter for low-income residents. In a study of the Lancaster housing market released on January 30, 1967, in the midst of the debate over scattered-site housing, John O. Shirk calculated that the completion of demolitions already planned by the Redevelopment Authority would reduce the housing supply in the General Neighborhood Renewal Area by more than 25 percent from what had been available only three years earlier.[44]

Shirk's study graphically demonstrated that the progress of the Adams-Musser Towns urban renewal projects had a disproportionate impact on the city's minority population, particularly those most in need. The Bogar homes and the United Church of Christ apartments were intended for middle-income families, while the Church Street project for the elderly would serve more whites than blacks for the simple reason that the white population was significantly older (Housing Authority data released in October 1970 revealed that 95 percent of the residents of Church Street Towers were white and 5 percent were black.) Even the projects clearly intended for lower-income residents did not meet the housing needs of the minority community. Indeed, relatively few of the households forced to move from homes in the southeast turned to public housing: according to figures incorporated in the *Lancaster Housing Study,* by the end of 1966 public housing had "provided standard housing for about 54 Negro and Puerto Rican families from the G.N.R.P. area," a number far below demonstrated need. In part this was the result of strict screening of applicants. The Housing Authority routinely rejected potential tenants who were unmarried, had credit problems, or had experienced brushes with the law—even if those applicants were sponsored by local social service agencies—arguing that without such policies the "city faces the danger of exchanging old slums for new slums." For reasons unexplained in surviving records, only sixteen of forty-one families displaced by the Higbee project who applied for apartments in the Susquehanna Courts complex were accepted by the Housing Authority. A majority of the other "problem families," as they were called, apparently sought inexpensive housing elsewhere in the southeast but were paying higher rents for lesser accommodations. In desperation the Redevelopment Authority moved some relocated families into other condemned homes and then, as those buildings were about to be demolished, moved them again into still other condemned dwellings, a practice that reduced human beings to pieces on a game board.[45]

Taken together, the Housing Authority's screening policy and the Redevelopment Authority's demolition program resulted in the persistence, perhaps even an increase, in the percentage of minority population living in the southeast. In April 1966 Paul Miller, executive director of the Redevelopment Authority, expressed concern over a new "Negro ghetto—a donut-shaped ghetto that is growing on the fringe of the old ghetto that we are demolishing." The housing study data released the following January confirmed Miller's sense of how discrimination was resulting in the formation of a second ghetto: in a city with 3,200 African American and 750 Puerto Rican residents, only 39 black families and 55 Puerto Rican families lived outside the southeast. With demolitions clearly outpacing the construction of new units that would be affordable by and accessible to the minority population, the study noted that "Renewal has broken down the concentration of the minority population in a few blocks and dispersed it throughout the southeast area." Blacks and Puerto Ricans displaced by renewal were migrating toward the eastern and western edges of the renewal areas. The housing study concluded, "Residential segregation has been the consistent pattern for the Lancaster Negro," and that the "discriminatory pattern in housing has intensified in the past 25 years."[46]

The rehabilitation of historic houses in the Adams Project preserved an important part of the city's architectural fabric, but at the expense of eliminating low-income housing. Rehabilitated buildings were either purchased as homes or rented at a much higher cost than low-income families could afford. With the exception of several blocks of the Adams Project that became the city's first historic district, the white population declined dramatically throughout the southeast. Demolitions also had a significant impact on the neighborhood's demographics. The Redevelopment Authority had purchased the property of homeowners, the majority of whom were white. Many whites took the equity they had accumulated in their houses and purchased new dwellings elsewhere in the city or in adjacent suburbs; others moved to apartments in other parts of the city. Neither of these options was readily available to blacks, who continued to face discrimination in the local housing market. Analysis of the 112 white families relocated as a result of the Duke, Higbee, and Adams projects reveals that 75 percent moved outside the General Neighborhood Renewal Area whereas more than 85 percent of nonwhite families relocated within the GNRP boundaries. Urban renewal, the Shirk study concluded, had "intensified residential segregation" in Lancaster.[47]

As a potential remedy for a pattern of residential segregation that had evolved over decades, scattered-site housing in essence became a debate over the future of Lancaster. Argued in letters to the editors of local newspapers, in forums sponsored by local business and service clubs, in City Council and public agency meetings, on street corners and in neighborhood bars, even in the pulpits of Lancaster's churches, the issue of scattered-site housing crystallized residents' attitudes toward race, civil rights, and segregation. As Lancastrians debated how best to meet the housing needs of all citizens, they were wrestling with those broader issues as well as the role of public housing and public policy in reshaping the built environment of the city. Unresolved was how citizens would confront a legacy of their collective history: whether Lancaster would maintain the invisible barriers that had created a segregated city or overcome the fear of racial differences and embrace fair housing.[48]

CHAPTER 6

CHURCH-MUSSER

Race and the Limits of Housing Renewal

Throughout the winter and spring of 1967, while citizens debated the necessity for and location of public housing, Redevelopment Authority planners were moving ahead with the city's largest renewal project, Church-Musser. The Adams-Musser Towns projects encompassed only part of the southeast quadrant of Lancaster, the 78-acre area east of South Duke Street and south of Howard Avenue. Much of the rest of the southeast, which had been included in the original General Neighborhood Renewal Plan (1958), resembled the Adams-Musser Towns area in its narrow streets, building density, deteriorating housing stock, and diverse population. In 1965 Redevelopment Authority staff had prepared applications for federal funding to undertake the survey and planning stages for the renewal of Church-Musser, an irregularly shaped area of 120 acres that framed the Adams-Musser Towns projects to the north and west. This ambitious project extended urban renewal two blocks north of Howard Avenue and from the west side of South Duke to South Queen Street, an area that encompassed approximately 1,266 buildings and 5,000 residents. Preliminary plans called for clearing 36 acres in the project area and conservation-rehabilitation treatment for the remaining 84 acres. Upon approval Church-Musser became Lancaster's second predominantly residential project.[1]

As was true of most neighborhoods in Lancaster, Church-Musser was characterized by structures that were more than a century old and by a pattern of mixed uses—residential, commercial, and industrial—that the postwar generation of planners found inappropriate in a modern city. Many of the same challenges that were present in the Adams-Musser Towns projects extended into Church-Musser. Especially vexing was the requirement to provide adequate housing for residents displaced by the renewal process. But Church-Musser would be different from earlier redevelopment projects in Lancaster: as renewal moved through the planning stages to implementation, residents proved far less receptive to planners and became more assertive in protecting their neighborhood.

Race relations in Lancaster in the mid-1960s were different from what they had been at the commencement of urban renewal. Lancaster's small

African American community followed the national Civil Rights movement closely, and beginning in 1963 an energized local NAACP chapter became an active voice in the city. In that year it staged protests against the hiring practices of two locally owned department stores and demonstrated at Rocky Springs, a popular amusement park that operated a segregated swimming pool. As redevelopment progressed in the southeast the NAACP protested Housing Authority policies that were excluding the majority of relocated families, decried the persistence of junkyards and other nuisances in areas where a preponderance of minorities lived, insisted that the Redevelopment Authority adequately maintain its properties, and called for fair-housing and scattered-site housing policies.[2]

The combination of discrimination, frustration born of a housing shortage caused by a redevelopment program that was more adept at demolition than at getting new dwelling units constructed, and a plan to erect a high-rise apartment tower for the elderly on a site that necessitated the displacement of a number of African American households and businesses heightened racial tensions in Lancaster in the summer and fall of 1967. So did riots in Detroit, Washington, D.C., and numerous other cities, including New Haven, Connecticut, generally regarded as the most successful urban redevelopment program in the nation. Lancaster was not immune to civil disorder: the Rev. Ernest E. Christian, minister at Bright Side Baptist Church and president of the local chapter of the NAACP, was exasperated at the slow pace of renewal, the promises of better housing to come that never seemed to materialize. "I hate to resort to this type of thing," he told a chapter meeting on housing and redevelopment in October 1967, "that we have to get violent and radical to get things moving. . . . This is what you might get." At the same meeting, Kenneth Bost, a former chapter president, attributed the housing problem to racism; it was the product of bigots who refused to rent or sell to minorities "simply because we are black men."[3]

The anger so evident at the October NAACP meeting was a product of years of frustration, to be sure, but it was also an assertion by the African American community that it would be heard, that it would not tolerate urban redevelopment policies that destroyed homes and communities in the southeast but did nothing to ensure better housing opportunities for all citizens. Yet even as the Redevelopment Authority proposed strategies that would place public and low-income housing outside the southeast, angry white residents who lived close to the designated sites organized to defend their homes and neighborhoods. When the Redevelopment Authority announced the Church-Musser project, planners were confident that a combination of demolition, new construction, and housing rehabilitation would improve the quality of life in the southeast; instead, the federally mandated relocation program polarized the city along racial lines. A decade later the southeast was still home to the vast majority of the city's African American population and virtually all its public housing. A project that began with the hope of creating a racially diverse and economically mixed neighborhood failed to overcome the legacy of segregation.

Church-Musser, a neighborhood defined by red-brick row houses, was home to more than half of Lancaster's minority population. Philadelphia housing consultant Drayton S. Bryant, who had visited Lancaster in 1959 as one of the speakers in the six-part "Community Improvement Through Urban Renewal" forum, returned eight years later to prepare a preliminary plan for the redevelopment of Church-Musser. In his report Bryant described the area's "particular historical functions" as "housing non-white families and low-income families in lower cost housing." The 1960 census demonstrated that 53 percent of Lancaster's African American residents lived in Church-Musser, as did 183 people of Puerto Rican birth or heritage. Half of all dwelling units occupied by nonwhites were in Church-Musser, and the dislocations caused by demolition in the Adams-Musser Towns projects since 1960 undoubtedly swelled the minority population significantly—and increased population density—in intervening years. The vacancy rate in the project area, 1.4 percent in 1960, was surely lower seven years later, as an exceedingly tight housing market strained under the influx of households migrating across South Duke Street into Church-Musser. Given the lower rate of home ownership in Church-Musser compared with the city as a whole, and the significantly lower income level for nonwhite residents, it is not surprising that in 1966 more than one in five of the residences in the neighborhood was substandard.[4]

The Lancaster Redevelopment Authority probably selected Bryant for the Church-Musser plan because of his efforts, while public relations director of the Philadelphia Housing Authority, to desegregate that city's public housing. The preliminary plan, released in May 1967, attempted to transform the southeast quadrant of the city into a thriving community. Conceding that the neighborhood suffered from years of decline and disinvestment, and acknowledging the difficulties any ambitious redevelopment program encountered, Bryant nevertheless described Church-Musser as "a prime location and desirable residential section with much character and strength." Church-Musser presented an "outstanding opportunity" for urban revitalization that would "change the character and direction of the Southeast quadrant."[5]

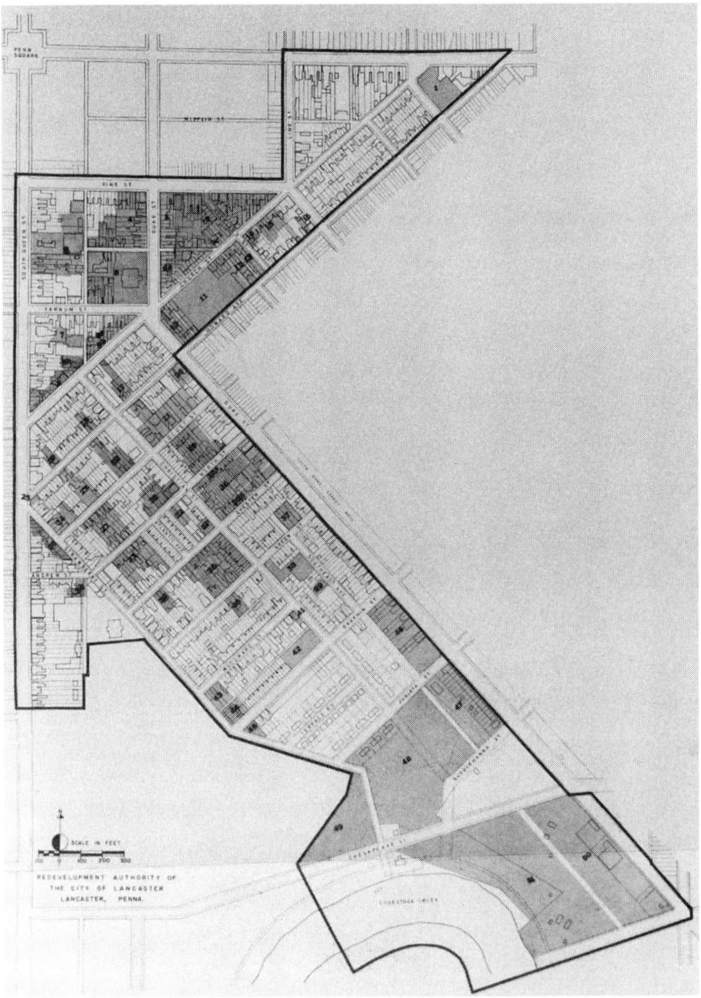

FIG. 35 *Church Musser boundary map. From Drayton S. Bryant Associates,* Ongoing Neighborhood Self-Renewal: Recommendations for Housing Programs and Related Services, Church-Musser Renewal Area, Lancaster, Pa., *May 1967 (Bureau of Planning, City of Lancaster).*

Bryant's vision for Church-Musser (Fig. 35) revolved around the concept of the "self-regenerating neighborhood." A healthy neighborhood, he argued, had to be economically and demographically diverse; it had to possess the "capacity to replace itself," to maintain a strong sense of community in the face of constant change. If all blocks and areas in a city confronted evolving physical and social conditions, healthy ones found in these transformations the opportunity for a continual process of regeneration. Thus the proposals Bryant outlined for Church-Musser attempted to avoid the twin dangers of ghettoization and segregation that had contributed to neighborhood decline, in Lancaster as in other cities. Renewal, he warned, "should not create a new and heavier 'lock-in' of low-income families in the same area," which would perpetuate the "many negative aspects" of an impoverished community. Instead, it should result in a neighborhood that would be attractive to a wide range of people, with housing appropriate to different economic levels and for individuals and families at different stages of life.[6]

The key to achieving this vision was to make Church-Musser a neighborhood of homes for upscale and middle-income families as well as its traditional population. This would require a number of initiatives. Crucial to the success of renewal was the population that would have to be relocated: the planned demolition of 36 acres and spot razings of dilapidated dwellings throughout the area would necessitate finding new homes for perhaps as many as 450 families, two-thirds requiring "special means" to obtain decent, adequate housing at an affordable price. Bryant realized that many relocatees would be unable to obtain suitable dwellings in the conventional housing market, but he adamantly rejected construction of traditional public housing projects, which were already too heavily concentrated in the southeast. Relocation of all displaced residents simply could not be accomplished within the renewal area at the same time neighborhood revitalization was taking place. Thus Bryant advocated a comprehensive housing strategy that included scattered-site units and federal rent subsidies to enable relocatees to live in neighborhoods throughout the metropolitan area.[7]

Within Church-Musser, Bryant advocated a range of housing choices. Half the dwellings in the project area were owner-occupied, and Bryant proposed using rehabilitation grants and low-interest loans to enable 300 owners to renovate their homes. This program would stabilize the existing housing stock, however, not add to it. Other strategies, such as cooperative housing developments, rent supplements for the elderly and families, and the rehabilitation of old houses and construction of new dwellings for sale, would increase the available housing stock by roughly 500 units. A key component of this strategy was the creation of a nonprofit housing corporation, which could take advantage of federal funding opportunities to erect or rehabilitate buildings within the project area and help renters make the transition to homeownership.[8]

A program of demolition and the renovation of buildings, however well conceived, did not inevitably result in a self-renewing community. To become a healthy, sustainable neighborhood, Bryant explained that Church-Musser needed to attract new residents, especially families from the business and professional classes who otherwise might live in a suburb. Given his

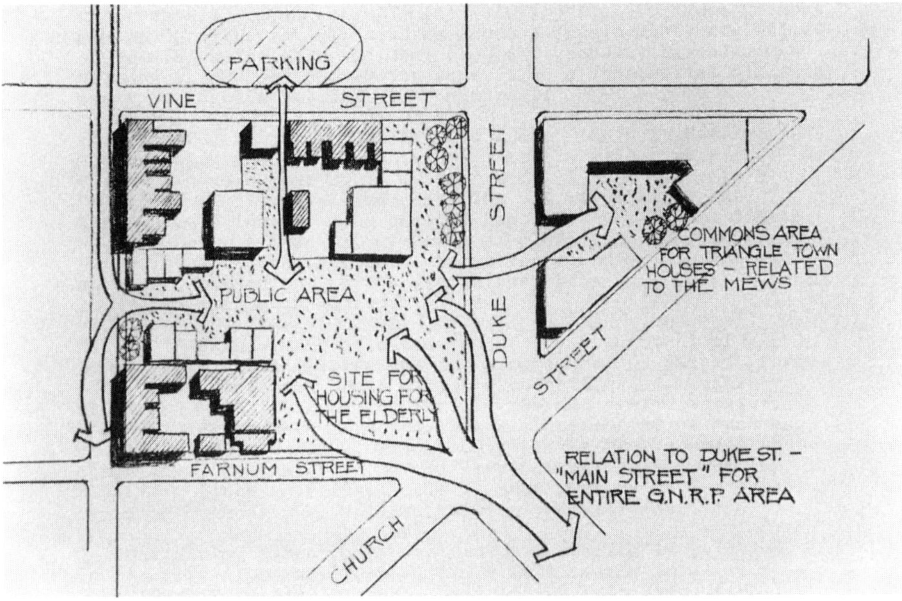

FIG. 36 *Church-Musser, plan for townhouses and mews. From Drayton S. Bryant Associates,* Ongoing Neighborhood Self-Renewal: Recommendations for Housing Programs and Related Services, Church-Musser Renewal Area, Lancaster, Pa., *May 1967 (Bureau of Planning, City of Lancaster).*

familiarity with the importance of historic preservation to the transformation of Society Hill in Philadelphia, it is perhaps surprising that Bryant considered the principal attraction of Church-Musser its proximity to downtown, not its historic streetscapes of vernacular structures almost two centuries old and a range of nineteenth-century architectural styles and building types. As a result, the most striking aspect of his plan was a proposal to demolish a two-block area bounded by South Duke, Vine, Church, and Farnum streets and transform it into an expensive residential and commercial enclave (Fig. 36). The square bounded by Duke, Vine, Farnum and Queen streets—only a block from Penn Square, the center of downtown—presented "an outstanding opportunity for small shops of quality, a small-sized theatre for films of quality, the most attractive pedestrian walk-ways in the city and interesting architectural design." The streetscape would resemble that of a traditional downtown, with narrow roadways and two- and three-story dwellings above the street-level shops, rather than the more typical renewal project that transformed both the scale and the ambience of neighborhoods. Adjacent to the east was a triangle bounded by Duke, Vine, and Church streets, which Bryant proposed as the location for eighty modern two- and three-story townhouses that would appeal to "professional, white collar and managerial persons connected with the core of the city and its institutions."[9]

Although the term "gentrification" had not yet been adopted to describe the transformation of poor, largely minority residential areas to affluent white neighborhoods, this is precisely what Bryant was suggesting. The demolition of old buildings and construction of a carefully designed commercial block and mews, together with the new townhouse development, he argued, would change the popular perception of the southeast from the "bottoms" of the city to a more positive impression. The commercial square would bring a new vitality to Church-Musser—economic activity, to be sure, but also the socializing and incidental gatherings that might contribute to the development of a sense of community among residents—and would bring workers from downtown and residents from other parts of the city to its specialty shops and restaurants. Implicit in his report was Bryant's belief that individuals and families living in the townhouses and mews, who would be better educated and possess higher incomes than the traditional residents of Church-Musser, would provide the leadership that was so essential to a self-regenerating neighborhood.[10]

Bryant proposed a second neighborhood shopping center (Fig. 37) for a 1.6-acre site along South Duke Street, between Chester and North streets opposite the new Higbee School. This 30,000– 35,000-square-foot commercial development would have a supermarket as anchor and from five to nine other tenants, principally to serve residents who lived within walking distance, but also for drivers who traveled South Duke Street, a major traffic artery entering the city from the southeast. Small parking lots faced South Duke and Christian streets, and the stores faced inward, along pedestrian walkways and landscaped spaces. With stores and essential service businesses as well as a shaded lawn with benches, the shopping center would "serve as a neighborhood gathering place," a combination of the commercial and the public that had long characterized cities but that was being lost in private suburban shopping malls.[11]

The other residential component of Bryant's plan for Church-Musser was South Park Towers, a complex of three or four apartment buildings on a large tract of land between Chesapeake and South Duke streets (part of which was the former site of Barney Google Row). Much of this area had been an ash dump, which made the cost of foundations for row houses unacceptably high, so the complex of tall buildings was designed to minimize site-preparation costs, and the intended high-rent units would amortize

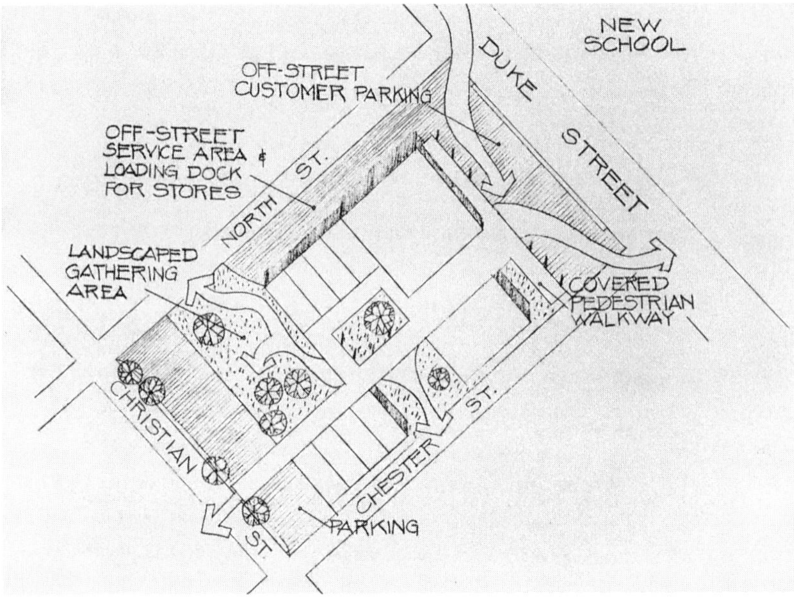

FIG. 37 *Church-Musser, plan for neighborhood shopping center along South Duke Street. From Drayton S. Bryant Associates,* Ongoing Neighborhood Self-Renewal: Recommendations for Housing Programs and Related Services, Church-Musser Renewal Area, Lancaster, Pa., *May 1967 (Bureau of Planning, City of Lancaster).*

development costs. Because the site was at the southern end of the GNRP, a considerable distance from downtown, Bryant anticipated that the 200 apartments in the complex would attract an "automobile-based population" of singles, couples, and couples with one young child. Like the triangle townhouses, these apartments would appeal to tenants who came from the higher end of the "broad range of income groups" that Bryant considered essential to a successful redevelopment program.[12]

The final piece of Bryant's proposals for Church-Musser was a new multipurpose community center that, he anticipated, could be erected using a special federal grant. A number of social service agencies and nonprofit institutions were scattered throughout the southeast, many of which served the needs of children and the elderly. Bryant suggested that city and Redevelopment Authority planners survey those service providers to determine whether a new community center would be attractive. Such a building, he believed, could "serve a basic and important need for community organization," strengthen the morale of residents, and contribute to the greater success of the service organizations grouped under its roof. A neighborhood center, located along Duke Street in the heart of the redevelopment area, he predicted, would be especially valuable as a bridge between traditional residents of the southeast and the higher-income newcomers moving into the houses and apartments Bryant projected for the area.[13]

Bryant's proposal for Church-Musser would have decreased the population density of the area even as it introduced a new group of upper-income residents to the southeast. It attempted to meet federal requirements for relocation housing by moving most displaced families to other areas of the city, which in subsequent years would prove to be its political undoing. Redevelopment officials and consultant Bryant explained the highlights of the plan in two public meetings held in the afternoon and evening of July 13, 1967. Despite the effort to schedule meetings at times when most people could attend, only twenty-five residents were present at the first session, and thirty-five at the second. Redevelopment Authority Executive Director Louis G. Milan announced several modifications of the Bryant plan, including construction of a high-rise apartment building for the elderly on the triangular site Bryant proposed for townhouses and subsidized low-income housing in place of the market-rent apartments. With little fanfare, and apparently without any sense of how essential the mixed-income housing was to its overall success, Milan changed the very nature of the redevelopment plan he was presenting to the public: those modifications eliminated the higher-income residents and the range of housing options Bryant considered essential to a self-regenerating community.[14]

Redevelopment Authority staff then began the lengthy process of preparing surveys, interviewing all residents of the project area, and completing the formal application for federal and state funding of a multiyear, multimillion-dollar project. The city hoped to have the Church-Musser project under way in early 1969, but Redevelopment Authority staff members were already overseeing the Duke, Higbee, Adams, and North Queen Street projects as well as a code-enforcement program in the King-Manor neighborhood. As the application process dragged on, the planners also encountered changes in federal urban renewal policy, especially with the beginning of the Nixon administration in January 1969. But the most difficult impediment to completion of the plan was the need to provide relocation housing for the more than 500 families and individuals the Church-Musser project would displace. One provision of the Civil Rights Act of 1964 mandated nondiscrimination in all federally assisted programs, which Public Housing Administration officials interpreted to apply to location as well as to admission: Lancaster Housing Authority Chair Edward C. Goodhart explained federal policy as requiring that new housing projects be located "in areas of other than minority or ethnic concentration." Redevelopment Authority executive Louis Milan conceded that Church-Musser presented "the most serious problem for relocation" because of the families and individuals from other urban renewal projects who had moved into an already densely populated neighborhood. Unable to relocate displaced persons within Church-Musser, planners had no choice but to propose moving minority residents to other parts of the city. In so doing they angered a large number of whites who organized to resist scattered-site housing and to maintain the invisible barriers that had restricted housing opportunities for blacks.[15]

On March 9, 1967, the Lancaster Housing Authority took the first step toward meeting the relocation needs of the Church-Musser project by authorizing the application for federal funding to erect or acquire 360 units of low-cost housing and to lease an additional 40 units. The following September the Redevelopment Authority submitted to the Housing Authority a list of ten potentially viable sites for public housing. Because of the federal mandate prohibiting discrimination in the location of public housing, all ten of the potential sites were outside the southeast. In an attempt to overcome resistance to scattered-site housing, Mayor Thomas Monaghan called for a public forum that was held on November 29, 1967. The thirteen speakers presented a range of opinions on what a local realtor described as Lancaster's "very severe housing problem." The Rev. Ernest Christian of the NAACP described discrimination from the perspective of his personal experiences; James S. Sheaffer, supervisor of operations for the Redevelopment Authority, pointed to the paradox that the "largest supplier of housing for the low-income family in Lancaster is the slum lord" and called for public policies that would provide better housing at affordable prices; Theodore Schwalm, chairman of the Lancaster Housing Authority, reiterated a main thrust of Bryant's recommendations for the Church-Musser area, advocating strategies that would "move middle income and upper income people into the southeast area and move some of the lower income people out of the area." Building contractors, a member of the Lancaster Human Relations committee, and a field representative from HUD also gave presentations on how best to address the shortage of low-income housing.[16]

Two speakers emphasized that Lancaster's housing problem had causes and consequences that extended beyond municipal boundaries. Thomas R. Wenger, assistant director of the city's planning and development department, attributed the concentration of low-cost housing in the city to "restrictive zoning and building standards in suburban townships, which are feasible only because of the large amounts of governmental subsidies, [and which] have zoomed construction costs and priced low-income families completely out of the suburban housing market." The shortage of low-income housing was a metropolitan problem, not exclusively a local one, he asserted, and would only be solved on a metropolitan scale. Consultant Drayton S. Bryant summarized what he considered the obstacles and opportunities for revitalization in Lancaster and pointed to a consequence of the lack of a national urban policy: "In our actual planning there is no real relationship between suburban sprawl, the location of total new development, or the demolition or conservation of older areas." Only truly regional strategies that embraced city, suburbs, and countryside would make possible the organic, self-regenerating communities he considered essential to the life of cities. The forum was Monaghan's effort to educate the community on the need for a comprehensive city housing policy, and the *New Era* distilled the deliberations of the evening into four recommendations: establishment of a county Housing Authority; an end to ghetto conditions in the southeast quadrant of the city; scattered-site public housing "outside the southeast section, in the city and county"; and assistance from the real estate profession in helping lower-income families find homes outside the southeast. But apparently few outside the auditorium supported the idea of public housing throughout Lancaster County or endorsed Wenger and Bryant's portrayal of the interdependence of city and suburb.[17]

In still another attempt to end the gridlock over scattered-site housing, on June 19, 1968, Jim Moore, a representative from HUD's regional office in Philadelphia, visited Lancaster to tour potential locations for public housing. HUD had completed a preliminary review of the application for the units submitted in March 1967 but wanted to assess the sites. Robert T. Schaffner, a planner with the Redevelopment Authority, accompanied Moore and Housing Authority Executive Director Howard Riegert on a tour of the ten sites the Authority had recommended. Riegert proposed three additional sites, two in the southeast and a third at Sunnyside. Schaffner wrote in his account of the tour, "Mr. Moore said his interest in the tour was to determine that the 360 units for which Howard had reservations will not be built in areas where minority groups are concentrated. . . . Mr. Moore made a point of instructing Howard that public housing is not to be considered minority housing." Based on the tour and the discussions that transpired, Schaffner concluded that Riegert "desires to keep all public housing in the general Southeast Area."[18]

Moore must have left Lancaster with the same impression. Four weeks later HUD halted the Church-Musser planning process because of the lack of progress in solving the housing issue. What Alexander Short of HUD's

Philadelphia office termed a "get tough" approach was not a new policy, as the *New Era* indicated, but an attempt to enforce a long-standing federal requirement that local public agencies provide adequate replacement housing for people relocated during urban renewal. HUD had begun to insist that families be relocated before commencement of demolition because in Lancaster, as in other cities, the construction of new housing lagged far behind the destruction of homes. Church-Musser was the fifth urban renewal project undertaken in Lancaster since the organization of the Redevelopment Authority in 1957, yet at the time of Moore's visit the local Housing Authority had completed only the Susquehanna Court apartments, which could not accommodate more than a fraction of the displaced families who qualified for public housing. HUD had reason to require that relocation precede the razing of Church-Musser properties.[19]

When HUD did commit the funds for the construction of 360 units of public housing in Lancaster, on July 12, 1968, it made explicit the requirement that all had to be outside the southeast. In explaining the need to comply with the federal mandate, Edward Goodhart announced the authority's endorsement of the "scattered-site concept that large concentrations of low-income families should be avoided." The Housing Authority board then adopted a resolution bringing its policies in line with federal ones. The board determined that "insofar as possible, distribution of projects shall be made to balance the total program, geographically, in the City." It further recognized that a housing project proposed for a neighborhood with a preponderance of minority residents was "'prima facie' unacceptable" and ranked accommodations for families as a more pressing need than public housing for the elderly. In forcing local officials to comply with the nondiscrimination provisions of the Civil Rights Act, federal officials were attempting to redraw the social geography of the city.[20]

The Housing Authority board narrowed the potential sites to eight and released the list to the public on October 28, 1968. One site, adjacent to a new high-rise apartment for the elderly, Church Street Towers, was in the southeast and was reserved for as many as 100 apartments for senior citizens. The other sites were in the southwest (four) and northeast (three) quadrants of the city. In publishing the locations the Housing Authority noted that the sites had been reviewed by all appropriate local agencies and officials, including the mayor, City Council, planning and redevelopment boards, and the school board. The construction of 260 units for low-income families at these locations, a spokesman for the Housing Authority stated, "could go a long way in assuring Lancaster of a multi-ethnic population in years to come, rather than reducing our community to the problems of other large urban areas which in reality have become minority communities."[21]

There were only a few objections to the October list, probably because no specific projects were linked to each location. But a sharp public outcry greeted the announcement of federal approval for four sites, two in the southwest and two in the northeast, on March 12, 1969. The Housing Authority had picked the sites carefully: each was vacant, to avoid the cost of demolition and to speed the process of construction; each was small enough that the project would not introduce a heavy concentration of low-income residents into the neighborhood or overwhelm the local elementary schools. In the first phase of an ambitious construction program, the Housing Authority proposed the development of 212 housing units. One site was a 1.2-acre tract in the 800 block of Fremont Street in the southwest, which was designed to accommodate 16 units; another, larger site in the southwest, on South Pearl Street, could accommodate 92 units and a community building on 7.1 acres; forty units would be constructed on the third site, a 2.6-acre tract on the south side of East Walnut, between Broad and Reservoir streets in the northeast; the remaining 62 units would be built on a 6-acre tract along Pitney Road at the eastern edge of the city. During the second phase of construction the Housing Authority would erect the high-rise for the elderly and 48 garden apartments in the northeast quadrant of the city. In announcing the sites, Edward Goodhart explained the evolution of the scattered-site program and once again stated that it had been reviewed by the mayor, the Redevelopment Authority, planning commission staff, and the school board, as well as by officials at HUD.[22]

If the Housing Authority's site-selection process represented careful planning, its public relations efforts proved disastrous. No one consulted with residents of the four areas to explain how the scattered-site units, and residents, would be woven into the fabric of the neighborhoods. As a result, reaction to the proposed sites was swift and pervasive. As was true in other cities where federal mandates for nondiscrimination clashed with long-standing patterns of neighborhood segregation, residents of the southwest were "boiling mad" because public housing was "being shoved down their throats without even the opportunity of a public hearing." City Council President Richard Filling, who rose to the defense of white property owners, urged the Housing Authority to hold such a hearing, both to explain the plan to residents and to listen to their concerns. Mayor Thomas Monaghan, a resident of the southwest, denied that he had approved the locations for scattered-site housing and denounced Howard Riegert for "insensitivity and reckless disregard" in not consulting with citizens of each of the proposed neighborhoods before releasing the list. He rejected Filling's call for a city-wide public hearing and instead urged a series of smaller meetings in each of the affected neighborhoods. "We're dealing with people and emotions," the mayor insisted. "And I think the authority should do a better public relations job with its plans." Monaghan then conceded that Lancaster City alone could not accommodate the low-cost housing needs of the metropolitan area and called for the establishment of a county Housing Authority to address the problem on a broader scale.[23]

The political leadership engaged in partisan charges and finger-pointing, Monaghan denouncing Riegert as incompetent and Republican County Chair K. L. Shirk Jr., blasting the mayor for blaming the county for the city's problems. What would have been predictable behavior in an election year was aggravated by a peculiar facet of Pennsylvania's municipal code: members of the Housing Authority were appointed by the governor, Raymond P. Shafer, a Republican, while the Redevelopment Authority board was appointed by Democratic mayor Monaghan, with the result that the two agencies often seemed to work at cross-purposes. In this already heated political atmosphere, citizens in the southwest and northeast quadrants organized to defend their neighborhoods. Although the plan for the 16-unit complex on Fremont Street consisted of three groups of attached buildings roughly the scale of typical Lancaster row houses, nearby residents who met at a neighborhood elementary school rejected the idea of public housing in the 8th Ward. In part they were concerned about the perceived impact of public housing on property values: "I worked hard to earn my place and I don't want to see it lose value," stated one resident to loud applause. Letters to the editor published in the *New Era* were filled with outrage that a public housing project was being imposed on the neighborhood, predicted that it would have a devastating effect on the value of homes, expressed fear that classrooms in nearby schools would be severely overcrowded, and accused the Housing Authority of "creating slums throughout the city." Clearly, residents of Lancaster had adopted what historian Scott Henderson has termed the "almost entirely negative image of public housing that had emerged in the mid-1960s." And although opponents of public housing tried to keep race out of the public discussions, someone burned a five-foot cross—the hallmark of the Ku Klux Klan—on the 800 block of Fremont Street, the site in the southwest quadrant that sparked the most heated opposition.[24]

Residents of the northeast quadrant similarly protested the Pitney Road tract, which, they asserted, was remote and inaccessible, was located in an area zoned industrial, and would have an adverse impact on the value of houses in Eden Manor, a recently developed subdivision of expensive homes.

Still another group organized to oppose other sites in the northeast. Pervading each of the citizens meetings was an "unspoken but apparently deep resistance to integration by some residents." Opponents circulated petitions, which they presented to City Council and which Filling took to Washington, where, together with Congressman Edwin D. Eshelman, he attempted to persuade HUD Assistant Secretary Lawrence Cox to overrule the local authority because of widespread opposition to scattered-site housing.[25]

Some individuals wrote in defense of public housing or objected to stereotypical characterizations of the city's poor and minorities. A number of civic groups and social service agencies also came to the support of scattered-site housing. The League of Women Voters reiterated its belief that scattered-site homes would help break the cycle of poverty and give residents "a new opportunity to move into the mainstream of society rather than being separated and restricted." Other voices of support included Neighborhood Services of Lancaster, the Urban League, the NAACP, the Community Action Program, and the Lancaster City-County Human Relations Committee, which believed it expressed the "view of all fair-minded citizens that racial ghettos are bad for our community and bad for our nation."[26]

Race was at the heart of the scattered-site housing dispute, and these expressions of support could not span the chasm separating their views from those of white residents who opposed public housing in their neighborhoods. Republicans on City Council attended the meetings of opposition groups and openly sympathized with residents who feared the introduction of low-income housing in their neighborhoods. Indeed, in telling one group that he opposed "putting public housing outside the southeast area while all the redevelopment land there remained idle," Council President Filling lent legitimacy to the efforts to block scattered-site housing. Council even approved a resolution to extend Poplar Street through the Fremont Street site, which, together with building setback requirements, would have forced the Housing Authority to reduce the number of units in the complex and perhaps abandon the site altogether. Monaghan reiterated his support of public housing but added, "I am in favor of making the Housing Authority responsible to the needs and wishes of the community it serves." However, what he meant by community—the city as a whole, or residents of areas designated for public housing, or the low and moderate income families who were most immediately served by the Housing Authority—was so imprecise (and politically astute) that the statement could have been interpreted favorably by both supporters and opponents of the scattered-site locations. Amid all the posturing, one thing was certain: "We're right back where we were two years ago," Howard Riegert of the Housing Authority told a reporter.

"We thrashed out the scattered-site idea then, and now we're going through it again."[27]

At this point Monaghan asked HUD for a six-month extension to resubmit the city's public housing development plans and urged City Council to formally endorse that request. Council instead resolved that "No public body wants to accept the responsibility for the initiation of scattered-site housing," and insisted that the Housing Authority withdraw its request for a change in the zoning of the sites selected. At the same time, the mayor appointed a Fact-Finding Committee on Public Housing, chaired by educator John A. Jarvis, to study the subject. The committee's report, presented in July 1969, called for public housing as the only effective means of meeting the critical need for low-income housing in Lancaster. It identified a shortage of 260 units of public housing that, it asserted, should be met immediately—100 in a high-rise apartment building for the elderly, 160 in family units. Hoping to avoid the impact of a large project in any neighborhood, the committee recommended that the family housing be located on a least ten sites throughout the city. It further admonished the city to employ a variety of means to increase the supply of low- and moderate-income housing, including private nonprofit corporations subsidized by HUD, rent-supplement programs, and turnkey programs in which private contractors erect housing that is then sold to the Housing Authority, presumably at a lower cost than if the Housing Authority itself were to do the construction. The ultimate goal of all public housing, the committee insisted, was "to help break the cycle of poverty by giving those in need a base to start a new life."[28]

While the Jarvis committee studied the issue, public attention shifted to the Zoning Board of Appeals. Although each of the proposed sites was vacant, none was zoned for multifamily dwellings. Thus the Housing Authority had to seek approval of a nonconforming use. In the case of the Pitney Road site, the city planning commission as well as the mayor and council favored industrial development and opposed the zoning change. Opponents of public housing on the Fremont and East Walnut street sites argued strenuously against the zoning change as a way of derailing the project, and in June 1969 the Zoning Board of Appeals agreed. Because so many residents of the affected areas protested the introduction of public housing into their midst, by a 2-to-1 vote the zoning board denied the special exception as contrary to the general welfare of the community The board used the same rationale in denying the rezoning request for the South Pearl Street site, even though no one spoke against it or presented any evidence that it was unsuitable for public housing.[29]

Over the course of the next several years, variations on the scattered-site theme recurred. In January 1970 the Court of Common Pleas reversed the zoning board's ruling against scattered-site housing. The board had erred in placing more weight on the number of protesters than on the "nature and quality of their objection"; it had also erred in placing the burden of proof on the Housing Authority rather than on the opponents of public housing, who should have been required to demonstrate how public housing would "damage the health, safety and morals of the community." The court then granted the special exception for the three sites the Housing Authority had selected, a ruling that infuriated opponents, who had organized as the Southwest Lancaster Citizens Council. Three months later the Regional Office of HUD informed the Lancaster Housing Authority that "unless plans are presented in the very near future, funds reserved for providing additional public housing units in Lancaster may be withdrawn."[30]

On October 7, 1970, the Housing Authority unveiled yet another plan, an ambitious $6 million housing program. The three components of the program included a 100-unit high-rise apartment building for the elderly, at the South Duke and East Farnum Street site adjacent to Church Street Towers; the purchase of 110 existing homes throughout the city for scattered-site public housing; and the construction of 101 new low-income housing units on three sites in the southwest quadrant of the city. The three sites included the 800 block of Fremont Street that residents found so odious, on which the Housing Authority proposed to erect 26 two-story brick dwellings; the block bounded by Hershey Avenue, Hager and Wabank streets, and Hilton Drive, which would become the site of 41 units; and a plot of land near the intersection of Fairview and Hershey avenues at the southern end of the city, which would contain 34 units. Housing authority executive director Peter Lucia, who had replaced Riegert, hoped that private contractors would commence construction on the three sites in January and that the buildings would be ready for occupancy within a year and a half.[31]

Once again, residents of the southwest were outraged. Citing public housing as the cause of declining property values and rising crime rates as well as overcrowding in neighborhood schools, John W. Rutherford, president of the Southwest Lancaster Citizens Council (SWLCC), called for a massive demonstration of opposition to the program at the next meeting of City Council, which would take place on October 27. Approximately 500 residents of the southwest marched from the Fremont Street site to the Public Safety Building, where they crowded into City Council chambers to express their objections to the Housing Authority's program. SWLCC Vice President John Pecuch likened the introduction of public housing to the "assassination of a neighborhood" and predicted that scattered-site housing would effectively destroy Lancaster City. SWLCC board member John Koogler contended that the placement of the three housing sites in the southwest was not scattered-site housing, "where family assimilation into a neighborhood is more readily and easily accomplished," but rather was punishment inflicted on residents of the southwest for having resisted previous proposals to locate public housing in their neighborhood.[32]

The following morning, members of the all-Republican City Council voiced their opposition to the Housing Authority proposals. Although the three complexes of 26, 41, and 34 units respectively would have had a lower density than typical blocks in much of the city, Councilwoman Julia F. Brazill characterized the proposed developments as large-scale projects that would harm the fabric of urban neighborhoods and expressed support for a different strategy, which she termed "scattered-site, owner-occupied housing." So did Jack B. Metzger, president of City Council: "I'm not in favor of any kind of large concentrations of housing in any area of the city," he stated. "I favor scattered-site, owner occupied public housing." Neither Brazill nor Metzger or other members of City Council offered to explain how low-income families who desperately needed public housing could afford to acquire those dwellings.[33]

Ultimately, the battle over scattered-site housing was fought not over density or building type or impact on school enrollments but over race. The Southwest Lancaster Citizens Council demonstrated this when it proposed a compromise: residents would accept a high-rise apartment complex for the elderly in their neighborhood if the Housing Authority built the scattered-site units in another quadrant of the city. Residents of the southwest as well as the southeast knew what this meant: Church Street Towers, the elderly project already completed, was 95 percent white, while the Franklin Terrace garden apartments for low-income families were 75 percent minority. So did federal officials: when City Council met with members of the Housing Authority board on November 3 to discuss the housing situation, Wagner Jackson, assistant director of HUD's Office of Equal Opportunity in Philadelphia, rejected the SWLCC proposal because it would necessitate the location of more family housing in the southeast. The premise of scattered-site housing, he asserted, was to diffuse low-income and minority residents, not concentrate them in ghetto conditions.[34]

A month later HUD informed the Housing Authority and City Council that they had ninety days to develop a revised housing plan that "balanced" public housing throughout the city. Almost immediately the Housing Authority sketched the outlines of a different allocation of the units. The new plan called for construction of a 90-unit low-rise apartment complex for the elderly, 60 new family units, at least forty of which were slated for the southwest, and 110 scattered-site houses throughout the city, as well as the 100-unit apartment tower at the Farnum and South Duke street location. When the Housing Authority sought developers and sites for the projects, five different companies proposed eight sites, five in the southwest, including the Fremont Street site and another along Hershey Avenue between Wabank and Hager streets.[35]

When the Housing Authority finalized plans for the 150 units of low-income housing, in March 1971, it proposed that 90 units be constructed in the northwest, as a five-story apartment complex for the elderly at the corner of West Lemon and North Mulberry streets, and that 59 units be located on three sites in the southwest. Fifteen would be built on the 600 block of Union Street, 10 on the 500 block of Beaver Street, and 34 units, in semi-detached houses, would be erected on the Hershey Avenue site between Hager and Wabank streets. The "low income" turnkey houses would cost between $22,000 and $26,000 to build—in a city where the median value of an owner-occupied home was $11,700. Despite that price, Edward Sager, the new chairman of the Housing Authority, announced that all the new houses would be sold to tenants. The 800 block of Fremont Street, which had sparked the most heated opposition, had been dropped as a potential site.[36]

Before these plans could be evaluated carefully, HUD rejected the Housing Authority's proposal to acquire 110 existing homes for scattered-site dwellings as too vague. When the Housing Authority then rescinded a contract with the Redevelopment Authority to find and rehabilitate the buildings, a senior official at the Philadelphia regional office of HUD characterized the city's quest for public housing as a charade. Apparently unfazed by HUD's public criticism of its program, the Housing Authority announced that it would be able to commence construction of 224 units by July, all but 34 of them units for the elderly. These remaining 34 would be constructed on the Hershey Avenue tract in the southwest.[37]

By this time it must have been clear to all parties that Lancaster officials had no interest in constructing new public housing units in the southwest, or anywhere other than the southeast. A year later Robert Kochel, then the executive director of the Housing Authority, announced that the Murry project on Hershey Avenue and a second project at the southern end of the city were dead because HUD objected to the acquisition price of the land. HUD "wants housing in prime locations," Kochel told *New Era* writer Jack Pollard, "but isn't willing to pay the freight." In November 1972 Kochel again publicly criticized HUD for failing to release money to start construction of projects for the elderly. At a time when 400 families were on a waiting list for public housing, most of them for three years, the Housing Authority head accused HUD of stalling. There were only a couple of suitable sites left in the city, Kochel warned, ominously noting that public housing was "sick, if not dead" in Lancaster.[38]

Public housing had in fact been reduced to a death watch. When the Lancaster County Development Corporation, a subsidiary of the Urban League, received a HUD-guaranteed loan to construct a 133-unit low- and middle-income housing project in the southwest in 1974, the Southwest Lancaster Citizens Council organized resistance to the development. Once again the zoning board of appeals killed a subsidized housing project in the southwest by refusing to grant a special exception. Zoning Board Chair Lawrence Stengel told a reporter, "We feel the applicant's proposed use isn't compatible with adjacent properties and other properties in the area." Stengel conceded that the concerns of area residents were a significant factor in the decision. Local opposition to scattered-site housing had triumphed over federal officials intent on integrating the city.[39]

There would be a few other attempts to create public housing in the southwest quadrant of Lancaster, but none would succeed. Indeed, no other family units of public housing were erected in the city, and in 1974 the Nixon administration imposed a moratorium on all public housing subsidies. Together, the extensive demolitions undertaken by the Redevelopment Authority and the failure of the Housing Authority to provide affordable replacement housing had a devastating effect on the African American population of Lancaster. What contemporaries remember as a close-knit community characterized by face-to-face relationships was rent by bulldozers, and in the absence of vigorous enforcement of state and federal fair housing laws that would have effected the integration of Lancaster and its suburbs, the city's minority population moved to adjacent blocks, spreading outward from the urban renewal area, just as John O. Shirk surmised in his 1966 study of housing conditions. A new ghetto replaced an older one, but without the fabric of community, the network of institutions and patterns of human interaction that had characterized the southeast in the decades preceding urban renewal. The failure to establish an effective scattered-site public housing program would haunt Lancaster in the decades to come.[40]

The battle over relocation housing for people displaced by the Church-Musser project delayed implementation of redevelopment. An update of the Shirk housing study completed in December 1969, two and a half years after Bryant's plan, characterized the extent of blight in the project area as extreme: 60 percent of all structures were in "deteriorating condition or worse," while almost a third fit the worse category, "deteriorated and dilapidated" buildings that were too far gone for repair and reuse. The Redevelopment Authority initially expected that the project would commence in early 1969, but funding authorization was complicated by changing federal procedures. The Johnson administration's Neighborhood Development Program, which attempted to improve the performance of local renewal agencies by allocating funding on an annual basis, was an attractive option to the Redevelopment Authority because it would allow commencement of work on the initial stages of the project and defer most of the anticipated relocations to the final two years (at which time, presumably, newly constructed public housing units could accommodate a significant number of relocatees). When the Nixon administration returned to the conventional five-year application procedure in 1969, the Redevelopment Authority had to resubmit a different proposal that factored inflation into the five-year budgetary projections and that produced a viable relocation plan for more than 500 families affected by the project. Not completed until late 1969—more than four years after the beginning of the planning process and months after the anticipated commencement of improvements—the final piece of the Church-Musser application proposed the relocation of 523 families and individuals, 372 of whom would require public housing (120 units in elderly housing, 252 in family units). As project implementation neared, Mayor Monaghan expressed appreciation for the patience of residents of the Church-Musser area. "Now we'll make it one of the most beautiful sections of the city," he predicted.[41]

The strategy for renewal in Church-Musser involved demolition of substandard buildings, commercial and industrial as well as residential. Some structures, such as the burned shells of the American Caramel Company on Church Street and the old Sanitary Food Market on South Duke, were obvious candidates for the wrecking ball. Demolition was also a strategy for assembling sites and clearing the way for new construction. In addition to the Sanitary Food Market, the Sturgis Hotel, a laundry, and a vacant building were demolished on the 400 block of South Duke Street so that the site could be redeveloped as a neighborhood shopping center, first proposed in the Bryant report, that was never constructed. The Salvation Army building—the former Muhlenberg School on South Duke Street, which the *Sunday News* described as one of the city's "foremost landmarks"—was demolished, and the Farnum Street East apartments for the elderly were erected in its place. To continue its work in the neighborhood, the Salvation Army constructed a utilitarian building of brick and concrete on South

Queen Street, a couple of blocks away. The new building was set back a considerable distance from the sidewalk, which created a void in the streetscape, and was derided by a member of the Redevelopment Authority's architectural review committee as having a "cheap, industrial flavor."[42]

Church-Musser also included an extensive program of rehabilitation for the remaining houses. Based on careful inspection of all structures in the project area, and surveys of families and individuals to determine housing needs and financial ability, the Redevelopment Authority prepared a comprehensive strategy for financing renovations that included a combination of grants and low-interest loans. HUD Section 115 grants were available to families with annual incomes of less than $3,000, while 3 percent loans with repayment plans of up to twenty years were available to families whose income exceeded the $3,000 limit. The Redevelopment Authority also promoted the rehabilitation of homes by nonprofit housing corporations and institutions through a variety of federal programs.[43]

Unfortunately, as the lengthy delays, the problems that resulted from shoddy construction, and the ultimate insolvency of the United Church of Christ Homes in the Duke Street project demonstrated, the private nonprofit sector in Lancaster did not have the expertise to become a major force in the low-income housing market. As a result, the Redevelopment Authority turned to for-profit developers both to undertake new construction and to rehabilitate substandard dwellings. Alas, the for-profit sector was no more successful than the nonprofits had been in meeting the housing needs of the southeast. The most ambitious proposal for new residential construction from a private builder was submitted by Neal Mitchell Associates of Cambridge, Massachusetts. Mitchell, who taught at the Graduate School of Design at Harvard, had developed a house-framing system that used lightweight structural components. Columns, beams, and slabs were reinforced cellular concrete, factory produced for on-site assembly by workers who needed little if any construction experience. Given the simplicity of the structural system, houses could be built rapidly, inexpensively, and as boxlike modules that could be expanded to three stories, which allowed for maximum flexibility in meeting the needs of families and individuals. In May 1968 the Mitchell firm outlined plans to erect 150 to 180 low-cost housing units on 6.5 acres on five tracts along Rockland Street, in the Adams Project area but immediately adjacent to Church-Musser. Because of the cost-savings associated with precast concrete and other types of prefabrication, the developer and city officials expected that the houses could be built for approximately $10,000. The Redevelopment Authority sold the land to a Washington, D.C., company, Mid-City Developers, which contracted to build 156 units according to the Mitchell system. Mid-City then erected three all-electric demonstration units on Locust Street, financed by Pennsylvania Power & Light (PP&L), but needed to pre-sell 150 additional homes—to take advantage of economies of scale and to guarantee a return on investment—before it could commence construction of the remaining units. Whether because of location, their strikingly modernist appearance, or their price, which exceeded the resources of most minority residents of the southeast, those buyers failed to materialize. The project collapsed, although the three pilot units still stand on Locust Street, the concrete façades covered by siding as if to repudiate a vision of affordable housing through technological innovation.[44]

Mid-City then proposed to erect a complex of 152 units on the site set aside for the Mitchell houses. Mid-City executives initially expected that the houses would be sold through a cooperative ownership program, but when too few potential buyers made a commitment to purchase unbuilt homes, the developer shifted to rental units. FHA approved the financing of the complex in June 1971, and construction began in October. Completed two years later, the Hillrise Apartments (Fig. 38) proved to be an unmitigated disaster. Despite warnings from PP&L, the developer built the structures without adequate insulation, which made heating costs prohibitively high. As operating and maintenance costs increased, Mid-City defaulted on its mortgage obligation, and the project had to be taken over by HUD. In February 1978 one-third of the Hillrise units were vacant and so badly vandalized that they could not be rented, which Mayor Richard M. Scott called "a terrible thing." Redevelopment Authority Executive Director Charles K. Patterson agreed: "One thing we don't need here, is 153 housing units boarded up in a five-year-old housing project." But that is what Mid-City wrought.[45]

For-profit rehabilitation was the principal housing strategy the Redevelopment Authority adopted in the Church-Musser project. Another venture was the rehabilitation of 18 dwellings on the 500 block of Dauphin Street by the Rock-Towne Development Corporation. Rock-Towne stripped the roofed wood porches from the buildings and replaced them with a concrete pad, added aluminum siding to the rear of the houses, and replaced the dilapidated interiors with new walls, floors, and windows as well as new plumbing, wiring, and heating systems. The firm, which had purchased 16 of the dwellings from the Redevelopment Authority for $850, hoped to sell each house for $14,950. Prospective purchasers were eligible for FHA mortgages as low as 1 percent. Redevelopment Authority official Patterson praised the renovated homes as examples for others to emulate: "If we had more of this kind of work and interest by private developers," he stated, "many of our nation's problems would be solved." Unfortunately, this kind of project—18 attached

FIG. 38 *The minimalism of subsidized housing for the poor: Hillrise Apartments (author photo).*

houses on a single block, with a small company renovating one house a month at what it anticipated would be a modest profit—was not easily replicable on a larger scale.[46]

The difficulty of undertaking rehabilitation on a scale commensurate with the number of houses needing work became evident in the mid-1970s. In the spring of 1973 the Redevelopment Authority contracted with BHAR Builders Inc., a Philadelphia developer, to rehabilitate a large number of deteriorating houses in the southeast. BHAR, headed by Eugene M. Howard, was then rehabilitating more than 60 structures in the Mount Airy section of northwest Philadelphia. Howard proposed to demonstrate the efficacy of mass production methods in rehabilitation, first through a 10-house pilot project, and then a much larger 90-house effort. Donald B. Hostetter, who had succeeded Milan as executive director of the Redevelopment Authority, emphasized that the ten demonstration houses would have to meet city housing codes and be approved by the authority before BHAR would receive title to the additional properties and begin work. Upon completion of the rehabilitation BHAR would sell the houses at market rates, with purchasers using conventional financing. Ambitious though the BHAR proposal was, the rehabilitated houses would not be affordable for low-income families.[47]

BHAR commenced renovations to more than 50 houses in the next two years. In May 1975, however, owners and tenants of 24 houses recently completed by BHAR, all in the Church-Musser project area, complained to the Redevelopment Authority about the poor quality of the work. One member of the authority board, Thomas Armstrong, inspected several of the homes and concluded that the work was indeed deficient. At a meeting with Redevelopment Authority staff and Howard, Armstrong explained: "I found serious defects. And I found them not being corrected in a reasonable length of time." In one house on South Duke Street, the living room ceiling was damp and stained from leaks, the kitchen walls were stained with mildew, and the plastic baseboards were peeling from the walls. A hole in the floor was covered with carpet. In another house on South Duke Street, water from a leaky roof discolored the ceiling and walls of the master bedroom, and improperly installed plumbing caused sewage to back up into the house. Casual inspection revealed signs of water penetration, tile walls and floors that were cracking, and similar examples of inferior workmanship in recently rehabilitated dwellings. Some of the homes had been acquired by the Housing Authority as turnkey projects; all should have been inspected by the Redevelopment Authority before they were occupied.[48]

In succeeding weeks, investigations of the BHAR homes became a staple of local newspaper coverage. When the Redevelopment Authority released a statement that its investigation of the houses revealed only a few major problems, two former BHAR employees told a *New Era* reporter that many of the houses suffered from "shoddy workmanship" or "defective materials." One of the employees gave the reporter, Jack Pollard, a list of 24 rehabilitated houses along with specific owner or tenant complaints. Pollard then visited 30 houses in the Southeast and asked about problems. Twenty-six owners or tenants complained about defective workmanship in their houses, including leaking roofs and the lack of adequate heat, three others were unavailable or refused to comment; only one expressed satisfaction with the condition of her home. Disaffected residents marched to City Hall to register their complaints with the mayor, who demanded that the Redevelopment Authority investigate and remedy the defects it identified. Meanwhile, the NAACP rushed to the defense of BHAR, a black-owned firm, as did Patrick Kenney, director of the Human Relations Committee, who praised the BHAR project as essential to Lancaster in making homeownership possible for individuals and families of modest means. Then city housing inspectors reported major as well as minor deficiencies in the BHAR homes: poorly repaired or newly constructed roofs; improperly installed heating systems, ductwork, and radiators; sinks that didn't function properly; as well as a lengthy list of minor problems, all resulting from poor workmanship. City inspectors found what they considered ample justification for residents' complaints.[49]

The dispute over the BHAR homes simmered throughout the summer and fall of 1975. A thorough inspection of BHAR work completed in June revealed that 43 of the 45 houses rehabilitated by BHAR needed repairs. By October the Redevelopment Authority reported that the contractor had completed almost half of the repairs and was making good progress on the remaining work. The following month, Eugene Howard asked the Redevelopment Authority for a guarantee of 50 houses a year to continue the rehabilitation work in Lancaster. The Redevelopment Authority replied that it could not turn over additional properties until BHAR satisfactorily completed the repairs to the first homes it had rehabilitated. By mid-December, when repairs to almost half of the 45 houses sold by BHAR were still not complete, the Redevelopment Authority board voted to hold up the sale of any additional buildings to Howard unless those houses were brought up to code by the end of January 1976. The board also conceded that it could not guarantee a steady supply of 50 houses, which Howard insisted was essential to the success of his business. Six months later Fulton Bank foreclosed on the mortgages of 14 properties owned by BHAR, which effectively ended Howard's efforts in Lancaster.[50]

The failure of BHAR Builders to rehabilitate houses in southeast Lancaster successfully had several causes—an undercapitalized company that apparently needed to turn over completed projects rapidly to finance ongoing work; the lack of adequate oversight on the part of the Redevelopment Authority and city housing inspectors; and inadequate counseling of new homeowners—but the largest cause was the inability of the private, for-profit sector to rehabilitate housing affordable by low- and moderate-income families. The legacy of the BHAR homes persisted; several years later a number of buildings once owned by BHAR had not yet been renovated, others were boarded up and vacant following mortgage foreclosure, still others bore the scars of poor workmanship. At a time when direct and indirect federal subsidies were helping to finance the construction of new housing in the suburbs, the Redevelopment Authority was frustrated in its program of rehabilitating homes for resale in the southeast—as were residents who endured the demolition and the wrenching dislocations caused by urban renewal without an increase in the supply of good and affordable housing.[51]

The Church-Musser project resulted in the demolition of 304 buildings, the vast majority of them houses. Long-term residents of the southeast were also displaced from approximately 70 dwellings in the two-block area roughly bounded by South Duke, East Vine, and Church streets that were later renovated as expensive townhouses. The Church-Musser project accomplished the complete rehabilitation of 649 housing units, though that number translates into significantly fewer than 649 buildings. Church Street Towers and Farnum Street East provided apartments for the elderly, though residents came from all parts of Lancaster City and were predominantly white, so the new units did not replace a significant percentage of houses lost through demolition. Drayton S. Bryant's 1967 plan for Church-Musser had called for an increase of 500 units to compensate for demolitions and to provide better housing for residents. The final Church-Musser funding application, which outlined a comprehensive strategy for relocating displaced residents, called for construction or acquisition of 252 family units of public housing. Not a single unit of family housing was built in the project area during the decade of Church-Musser. Given the wide disparity between housing needs, demolition, and new housing construction, Church-Musser worsened the severe shortage of affordable housing in the city.[52]

The Church-Musser project lasted almost ten years, twice the time planners projected as necessary to complete the renewal of the area. The final pieces were two small tracts north of Church Street. In September 1976 the Redevelopment Authority announced it would seek bids for the sale of a 2.5-acre tract bounded by South Duke, East Vine, and Church streets. The triangular site contained 42 structures, virtually all residences. Redevelopment Authority head Charles K. Patterson described the surviving buildings on the site as "representative of old Lancaster" and expressed hope that developers would undertake a "faithful restoration" of the area. Three months later the Redevelopment Authority announced that it would also be selling the 1.1-acre tract directly across South Duke Street, a half-block between East Vine and Washington streets, which contained 24 buildings, all but one of them residences. Patterson described this as the "last major parcel of undeveloped property in a redevelopment area program begun 17 years ago" and explained that the successful redeveloper would remove formstone siding from many of the buildings while preserving their "unique and antique appurtenances, such as the handcarved lintels over the windows."[53]

The two blocks Patterson described were a small but important part of the Church-Musser project. Almost a decade earlier, Bryant had recommended that the triangular block be redeveloped with 80 expensive two- and three-story townhouses, while the proposed treatment for the tract across South Duke Street was for upscale shops and restaurants in a kind of commercial mews only a block from Penn Square (see Fig. 36). Redevelopment Authority planners favored a different use of the space. Their December 1969 amendment to the Church-Musser funding application called for the total clearance of the two blocks and the construction of high-rise apartments for the elderly. The Redevelopment Authority had acquired all but two properties and relocated a number of residents, but by the mid-1970s had not demolished the buildings or constructed the new ones outlined in the 1969 plan. Many of the dwellings were boarded up, several had been vandalized, others had burned under circumstances the fire department termed suspicious.[54]

By late 1976, political and administrative elites in Lancaster recognized that clearance and project-type redevelopment had not improved housing opportunities and the quality of life in the southeast. One part of the problem, Patterson told a reporter, was that "inner-city land is not so attractive to a developer as it was originally thought to be." But in many cities the rehabilitation of substantial, well-built dwellings had proved to be economically feasible and had resulted in the physical improvement of whole neighborhoods. Patterson hoped that two contiguous tracts near the heart of downtown would be attractive to developers and to prospective residents. They were given the names "The Triangle" and "Washington Square."[55]

When the deadline for bids for the Triangle passed, however, not a single developer was willing to pay the $242,000 minimum the Redevelopment Authority had placed on the parcel. Patterson, clearly disappointed, pledged that the authority would negotiate with HUD to reduce the sale price of the land and strive to generate interest in the project. A second round of bidding took place in March 1977, when both the Triangle and Washington Square were available to developers. The prospectus prepared by the Redevelopment Authority cautioned that price was only one criterion in the selection process; when opened, the bids for the Triangle ranged from $247,000 to $69,828 while the bids for Washington Square were $43,200 to $37,040. Perhaps surprisingly, in each case the Redevelopment Authority awarded the contract to the low bidder, Old Town Lancaster, a corporation headed by local architect John deVitry and interior designer Tom DePaul, whose backers included Calvin and Dale High, scion of a major steel fabricating company that had branched into real estate development; Phares Martin, a local builder; and Sidney Kevich, a real estate investor.[56]

What made the deVitry-DePaul proposal so attractive to the Redevelopment Authority was its pledge of accurate historical restoration, which included incorporating the two blocks in the city's local historic district, and the sound financing behind the package. Old Town Lancaster, as the restoration was called, was decidedly upscale: the smallest homes would be priced at $31,500, the cost of the largest dwellings would escalate to more than $69,000. Patterson described the proposal as "a very costly, dramatic upgrad-

FIG. 39 *Nineteenth-century houses along South Duke Street, part of the Old Town restoration (author photo).*

ing on these properties," which, he believed, would "reverse the character of a neighborhood." The developers likened Old Town Lancaster to Society Hill in Philadelphia, and upon gaining favorable review from federal and city agencies began the process of transforming long-neglected buildings into gentrified homes (Fig. 39). Local newspapers celebrated the rebirth of Old Town. The *New Era* predicted that the entire community would benefit from "a project which restores an early part of the city to new usefulness and new high visual quality." As groundbreaking neared, the *Intelligencer Journal* praised the "courage as well as vision and creativity" of those who would revitalize an entire block of boarded up homes.[57]

Old Town was hardly affordable housing, though, and the people who had the resources to purchase the renovated homes represented a totally different economic group from those displaced by the Redevelopment Authority several years earlier. In words similar to those Drayton Bryant had used to describe a "self-regenerating neighborhood," which was predicated on attracting middle- and upper-class residents to Church-Musser, Redevelopment Authority Chairman David L. Gockley praised the expensive houses at

Old Town as a counterweight to the public housing erected elsewhere in the southeast. "The idea of a full spectrum is rather important," he stated. Mayor Richard M. Scott, a resident of downtown, wholeheartedly endorsed the project: "This is the way to go." A rehabilitated Old Town, he predicted, would "maintain the character of Lancaster."[58]

Even as construction workers brought new life to dilapidated houses in Old Town, only a few blocks away recently renovated buildings were falling into disrepair. Redevelopment director Patterson was so upset by signs of blight in the Adams and Duke Street project areas that he sent a memo to Democratic City Councilman Ronald E. Ford, chair of the Redevelopment Committee, urging that the city take immediate action to arrest and reverse the deterioration. As part of the urban renewal process, every structure in those project areas had been inspected and almost all of them had been brought up to city code. Within a decade many of those same structures were vacant, boarded up, or had obvious structural problems, such as porches in danger of collapse. "Hundreds of thousands of dollars were spent on housing rehabilitation" only a few years earlier, he wrote. "One finds that difficult to believe, if you drive through that neighborhood today." Patterson hoped that his criticisms would result in a strengthening of the city's housing code, which lacked effective enforcement provisions; he also chided district magistrates who, he charged, tended to be "extremely lenient with violators of the city housing code."[59]

What Patterson intended as an internal memorandum became a major political issue when the *New Era* published most of its contents under the alarming headline "New Slums Rise in Renewal Areas, Redeveloper Charges." Republican Mayor Scott accused Patterson and Ford of collusion in calling for systematic inspections of all buildings in the city. Councilman Edward M. Sager blamed the Redevelopment Authority, the local Model Cities agency, and the previous mayoral administration for the problem. "Instead of rehabilitating the people and the buildings in the hard-core slum area, which was small," he charged, Monaghan and the program administrators "destroyed the buildings and used federal funds to spread the people into the stabilized area around them." The *Intelligencer Journal*, by contrast, praised Patterson for his vigilance in attempting to prevent neighborhood decline and placed the blame for conditions in the southeast squarely on Scott, whose "'penny-wise and pound foolish' budgeting" cut city inspections. A *New Era* editorial entitled "New Slums Replace Old Ones" asserted that the "general air" in the renewal neighborhoods "is one of dilapidation" and called for "a more concerted effort" to prevent the spread of blight.[60]

Patterson's testimony before City Council on June 14 convinced most listeners that the problem of recurring blight was real and that the city needed to study causes and seek solutions. But even as the political storm subsided, the contrast between Old Town, an island of prosperity, and deteriorating buildings only a block or two away that were on the verge of becoming new slums, pointed to the ultimate failure of residential renewal. Old Town was almost exclusively white, the adjoining blocks experiencing decline were overwhelmingly black and Hispanic. A decade earlier, housing consultant Bryant had envisioned the southeast as an economically and demographically diverse neighborhood, with the ability to maintain a strong sense of community even while experiencing constant change. Instead of fulfilling Bryant's vision of a self-regenerating neighborhood, however, redevelopment resulted in a continuing pattern of residential segregation. In this, Lancaster's experience conformed with that of other cities, such as Philadelphia, Detroit, and Chicago, where historians have studied the interplay of race, public housing, and renewal.[61]

The failure of will that derailed Lancaster's program of scattered-site public housing exemplifies how the local housing authority and members of City Council were able to subvert federal antidiscriminatory goals and regulations. Because of white resistance to integration, the 96 units of scattered-site housing owned by the Housing Authority in 1990 were not randomly distributed throughout the city: 6 units were located in the northwest quadrant, 18 in the northeast, 24 in the southwest, and 48 in the southeast. The Housing Authority's 516 apartment units in Susquehanna Court, Franklin Terrace, Church Street Towers, and Farnum Street East, 92 percent of the public housing in the city, were located in the southeast. Despite federal fair-housing and nondiscrimination laws, Lancaster's public housing was concentrated in an area many white Lancastrians still call "the Ward." In 1980, twenty-three years after the Citizen Housing Committee first examined housing conditions in the city, the Lancaster Redevelopment Authority ceased operations. Despite two decades of redevelopment and millions of dollars of public and private spending, the southeast was still home to Lancaster's poor and the overwhelming majority of its racial and ethnic minorities. In striking ways urban renewal had widened streets, installed sidewalks and new infrastructure, transformed the southeast as physical space. But the Redevelopment Authority's success was limited because of resistance to scattered-site housing and the persistence of discrimination in housing and employment throughout the metropolitan area. The southeast, the crucial point where race and public policy intersected in Lancaster, remained a place apart.[62]

PART IV

Consequences

CHAPTER 7

SUNNYSIDE
The Persisting Failure of Planning and Renewal

The Adams-Musser Towns and Church-Musser projects encompassed most of the southeast quadrant of the city. One area excluded from the improvement projects undertaken by the Lancaster Redevelopment Authority was Sunnyside, a peninsula of approximately 129 acres, across the Conestoga River from the historic boundary of the city. At the time the city housing committee first studied residential blight in Lancaster, in 1957, the southern third of the peninsula was home to hundreds of residents who lived in dwellings without water, sewer, and other utilities, most of whom were unable to afford better housing. Sunnyside had long been impoverished; one newspaper characterized it as a "touch of Appalachia" and described its ramshackle structures as "Lancaster's secret shame." Although located only a little more than a mile from Penn Square, Sunnyside is remote from Lancaster's urban culture and is economically, socially, and psychologically separate from the city. Twenty years after the conclusion of urban redevelopment in Lancaster, Sunnyside remains a place apart, testament to the failure of renewal to improve housing conditions while maintaining a sense of community among residents.[1]

The Sunnyside peninsula (Fig. 40) was formed by the south-flowing Conestoga River, which bends northward to avoid limestone bedrock and then turns south again in its meandering course to the Susquehanna. Especially in the southern two-thirds of the peninsula, there is only a thin covering of soil. The presence of subsurface rock made the digging of wells and septic systems exceedingly difficult and, as civic leaders eventually discovered, would make the construction of water and sewer lines prohibitively expensive. The landscape has several different physical characteristics, ranging from steep hillsides to rolling meadows to areas that are in floodplains. One newspaper reporter poetically described the scenery near the precipitous hillsides at the southern end of the peninsula as "wild, rocky and beautiful," but such characteristics are generally incompatible with standard subdivisions or street systems. When the lower third of the Sunnyside peninsula was platted for development, its roadways and potentially developable lots had slope gradients that were quite steep, so much so that in later years they exceeded Lancaster subdivision ordinance and FHA regulations.[2]

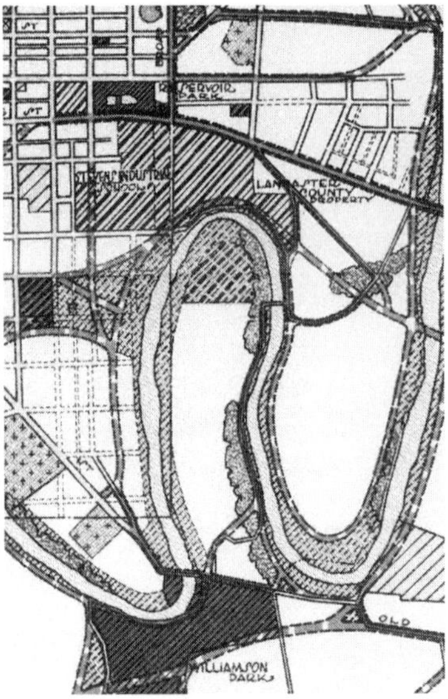

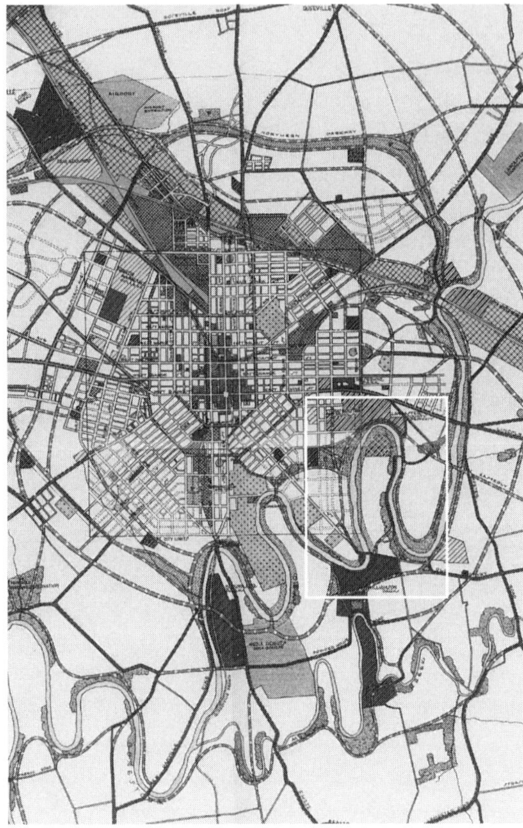

FIG. 40 *The Sunnyside peninsula (above) from John Nolen's 1929 plan for Lancaster (right). From* Lancaster, Pennsylvania Comprehensive City Plan, 1929 *(for the City Planning Commission, 1929).*

Sunnyside shares a host of characteristics with other areas that might be described as urban backwaters or other-side-of-the-tracks neighborhoods—places with little or no infrastructure, poor, alienated populations, inferior housing, and a tenuous relationship with the dominant local political, economic, and social institutions. In some cases, as in Lancaster and the working-class suburbs of turn-of-the-century Toronto, which contemporaries described as "shacktowns" and shacklands, these areas were not originally platted as part of the city but were later incorporated as a result of annexation. In other cases they were left largely undeveloped because topography made the cost of grading the site to conform to the existing street system prohibitively expensive. This has generally been the case in smaller cities rather than larger ones, where high property values resulted in development even of difficult sites, though some distant parts of major metropolitan areas are remarkably similar to Sunnyside. Moreover, as places in which poverty has passed from generation to generation, such neighborhoods usually have not been adjacent to growing industrial areas with opportunities for occupational mobility.[3]

Although most areas that shared Sunnyside's physical and social characteristics were demolished as part of urban redevelopment programs in the post–World War II era, Sunnyside is a textbook example of the tenuous meanings of community and the limits of planning in reconciling residents' needs with those of the city as a whole. During the 1960s and 1970s, when federal initiatives ranging from urban renewal to Model Cities extended to smaller cities, public officials in Lancaster attempted to chart a new future for the peninsula. One major impediment to change was the resistance of residents who, although predominantly renters, defended Sunnyside as a community and perceived planning as a threat to their way of life. The behavior of Sunnyside residents was remarkably similar to that of Italians in the West End of Boston during their struggle against urban redevelopment. "Lower-class people," sociologist Herbert J. Gans concluded in *The Urban Villagers,* "are likely to be more hostile to planners and caretakers than less deprived populations. Living so close to the edge of despair, they have developed ways of immunizing themselves against the outside world, and against false hope." The other great obstacle to improving the physical condition of Sunnyside was equally tenacious: a widely accepted history that functioned to deny the existence of a residential community defined by attachment to place and a sense of reciprocity in human interaction.[4]

In 1971 Lancaster's Model Neighborhood Agency commissioned FRIDAY, a Philadelphia architecture and planning firm, to study Sunnyside and plan for its future. The agency selected FRIDAY because of the firm's "reputation of working closely with residents in rehabilitation," and at their first meeting with residents at the Sunnyside Mennonite Church on February 23, planners Donald Matzkin and Peter Artac explained that their task was "to develop a community plan for Sunnyside based on what the people themselves want." However well-intentioned the planners, residents were skeptical at best. One man described the proceedings that evening as "like listening to an old record. As I see it, it's the same old thing." A woman echoed that sentiment: "You told us no more tonight than you told us before. I heard this same stuff back in 1960 and it's still the same." Some residents sought assurance that the planners would not recommend demolition of their houses, while others disagreed strenuously about what the goals of any planning program should be. The discussion became so heated that Linda Odum, executive director of the local Model Cities program, reportedly told residents, "If you don't want us we'll take our maps and programs and leave." Peter Artac put the best interpretation on the frustration all participants experienced that evening when he claimed to be encouraged by the meeting because residents were "very enthusiastic."[5]

Matzkin returned to Lancaster on March 10 and, at another public meeting, attempted to "overcome the distrust, anger and fear of Sunnyside residents who have long been promised that something will be done in their neighborhood." Although he once again pledged that the FRIDAY study would incorporate the hopes and concerns of residents, participants remained unconvinced. One resident, Sandy Black, angrily stated, "Why don't you just tear it down? Do what you want, tear it down. Go ahead, plan for us, just push everyone out and tear it down." People debated whether they should form committees to discuss issues the planners suggested, whether or not landlords should serve as members of those committees, and, as Mrs. Black's remarks indicated, whether the city intended to address the interests of residents in any new plan. The meeting was contentious, concluded organizer Kenneth Abernathy of the Model Neighborhood Agency, as has been the history of planning efforts to improve the quality of life in Sunnyside. But for all the plans, little happened; three years after FRIDAY submitted its preliminary report, a local newspaper noted that Sunnyside "still ranks as the most over-studied and underdeveloped area of the city."[6]

Matzlin and Artac were not the first planners to confront the ire of Sunnyside residents and the legacy of previous planning efforts. They undoubtedly began their task with optimism, confident that their professional skill would help resolve long-standing problems, certain that their plan would mark a new beginning for Sunnyside and its people. Yet they too have become a minor part of the peninsula's history, a century-long struggle involving land, people, resources, and attitudes.

The history of Sunnyside may help explain why planners have been unable to transform the peninsula into a different kind of place. The name "Sunnyside," which evokes images of innocent youth, sounds as if it were invented by a subdivider, but apparently its use antedates the development of the residential community there. According to the larger community's collective memory, Sunnyside was not always a battleground, not always blighted, not always an impoverished area. Local tradition maintains that in the early twentieth century it was a vacation spot, only a mile from downtown, where middle- and upper-middle-class Lancastrians built summer cottages to escape the heat of the city. The Rocky Springs line of the Conestoga Transportation Company, which ran through Sunnyside, would have provided easy access to the cottages. To be sure, the modest dwellings lacked wells or public water service, but this was a rustic resort, not unlike Mt. Gretna, a nearby Chautauqua. According to a newspaper account of Sunnyside's history, published in 1980, the "area's woods, rocky hills and commanding view made it an ideal vacation spot, and soon dozens of summer cottages plus a handful of regular frame and brick homes that were used all year began springing up." Sunnyside remained a popular resort until widespread ownership of the automobile introduced competition from coastal resorts such as Atlantic City, or until the Great Depression, and then its slow decline began. The story, embellished in varying degrees, has become etched in the public memory.[7]

Perhaps mythology is more accurate, given the degree to which Sunnyside's history diverges from this account. On August 29, 1912, two developers from Paterson, New Jersey, Frank H. H. Boody and James K. O'Dea, acquired 43 acres, the lower third of the Sunnyside peninsula, from the estate of Samuel T. Davis, a Lancaster physician. What kind of community Boody and O'Dea envisioned is impossible to determine from surviving documents, but this much is certain: civil engineer F. H. Shaw subdivided the property into 531 lots, virtually all of which were 20 feet wide, though with varying depths because of the curvilinear roads that wound through the community. "The original subdivision plan for Sunnyside," the Lancaster City Planning Commission concluded in 1960, "although adequate in design for the normal development, was, in this case, improperly superimposed upon a topography totally unsuitable for it." The commission's report also noted that the street plan "does not in any way conform to the extreme topographical conditions of the area," with the result that many of the roads platted in 1912 "have never been opened to their full cart-way width and many of them are physically impossible to construct."[8]

Only a couple of days after taking possession of the property, Boody and O'Dea began selling lots ranging in price from $29 to $79 (Fig. 41). The terms were easy—five dollars down and fifty cents a week—but the deed remained with the subdividers until completion of the purchase. In addition, Boody and O'Dea felt it necessary to include a provision in the transaction to ensure that "no dwelling costing less than four hundred ($400) shall be erected and no tent or shanty shall be erected on said premises." These terms suggest that Sunnyside may have attracted a different, less prosperous clientele than that usually attributed to it. Subsequent sales (17 transactions to 14 individuals in September and October 1912, and 9 sales to 6 other individuals in the summer of 1913) confirm that purchasers were working-class Lancastrians. Although only the occupations for males can be determined from city directories, those jobs included candymaker, horseshoer, carriage body maker, upholsterer, cigarmaker, trolley conductor, bricklayer, carpenter, and laborer.

FIG. 41 *Advertisement offering Sunnyside lots for sale,* Lancaster New Era, *September 4, 1912 (Lancaster Newspapers Inc.).*

Tax records for West Lampeter Township in 1921 identified tenants living in summer houses, presumably at Sunnyside, whose occupations were listed in directories as laborers, painters, tailors, and a candymaker—respectable jobs, to be sure, but not the kind traditionally associated with the middle- and upper-middle classes in the early decades of the twentieth century.[9]

If the first generation of Sunnyside residents does not conform to local lore, it also seems likely that the cottages were much more modest than collective memory suggests. A number of the structures may well have been owner-built dwellings similar to those erected by working-class residents on the periphery of several North American cities in the late nineteenth and early twentieth centuries. These shacktowns generally formed just outside the city limits, in places where municipal regulations were ineffective or nonexistent. Given their appearance and the proximity of the trolley tracks, other Sunnyside residences appear to have been inexpensive mail-order houses marketed by companies such as Sears and Alladin. In the absence of fee-simple ownership, purchasers of lots under the terms explained in the advertisement presumably would have been unable to secure a mortgage for improvements to their properties.[10]

Whether or not Sunnyside ever enjoyed a golden era, by 1933 it was clearly a distressed area. The Residential Security Map of Lancaster, prepared in that year, redlined the entire peninsula. The red color assigned to Sunnyside made it unlikely that residents who owned lots would be able to secure financing for building on or improving their properties. The typescript accompanying the Residential Security Map was equally negative: it identified the properties as the least desirable in Lancaster, with valuations of $300 to $800, and characterized residents as "squatters, itinerants and loafers in shacks." Six years later, when Works Progress Administration photographer

FIG. 42 *Lewis Hine photograph of Sunnyside, 1939, showing houses along the side of the peninsula, a city dump in the foreground, and a covered bridge crossing the Conestoga River to the right (National Archives and Records Administration, Washington, D.C.).*

Lewis Hine toured Sunnyside with camera in hand (Fig. 42), he described the houses as shacks, and residents as low-paid workers.[11]

Sunnyside's future became intertwined with Lancaster's in 1929, when John Nolen prepared the city's first comprehensive plan. Although Sunnyside was then part of West Lampeter Township, the city planning commission included the peninsula in the Nolen study because its jurisdiction extended three miles beyond the municipal boundaries. Nolen's plan reserved the northern part of the peninsula as the site for a future county prison but called for the preservation of existing stands of trees, especially along the eastern edge of Sunnyside, and reserved land adjacent to the river for a parkway corridor. Nolen envisioned a time when "the Lancaster region will have a parkway along the Conestoga Creek reaching to the Susquehanna River," and called for immediate steps to preserve public access to the river for that eventuality. Lancaster's second comprehensive plan, prepared by Michael Baker in 1945, also incorporated Sunnyside. Without describing existing housing, the Baker plan again called for developing the area adjacent to the Conestoga River as parkland, with the interior of the peninsula devoted to single-family and multifamily residential purposes. Although some of the riverbank was "in uses which are contrary to the best interests of the community and which detract from the scenic resources of Conestoga Creek," as Nolen had done the Baker plan recommended development as a linear park and parkway.[12]

Neither West Lampeter Township nor the city took steps to implement the recommendations for the peninsula incorporated in the Baker plan, and in 1950 Sunnyside remained an impoverished community. Most of the houses were continuing to deteriorate, and residents received few services from the municipality, West Lampeter Township. In that year Raymond Grimm, a trash hauler and farmer from nearby Willow Street who had acquired the trolley right-of-way, moved eight railroad boxcars to the property. Although he initially claimed that the boxcars were to be used for storing hog feed, after placing the structures on the ground Grimm made a few improvements—adding a door and windows, dividing them into three 8.5-by-14-foot rooms (a central kitchen and a bedroom at either end)—and then he rented them to tenants for about twenty dollars a month. Sunnyside residents objected to the boxcars, both because they were unsightly and because they feared that the units would attract undesirable tenants from Lancaster City, where there was a severe shortage of adequate housing and a growing African American population. Despite their protests, and an unsuccessful attempt to prevent occupancy through litigation, the township approved use of the boxcars, in large part, it seems, because in the absence of a housing code it did not have the legal authority to prevent such use. The Lancaster County Commissioners also approved the boxcars so long as they conformed to minimum housing and health standards.[13]

Expressions of community concern over the presence of the boxcars receded until a fire consumed one of the structures on March 16, 1954. A two-year-old child, Reba K. Waltman, died in the fire, which resulted in yet another public outcry against the boxcars, but again nothing was done to remedy the situation. Conditions in Sunnyside continued to deteriorate, and the municipality, West Lampeter Township, provided virtually no public services.[14]

At the request of an overwhelming majority of residents, who hoped that a larger governmental entity would be able to provide greater services, Lancaster City annexed Sunnyside in September 1955. Shortly thereafter, Mayor Kendig C. Bare informed residents that city services would be extended to Sunnyside "as promptly as economically feasible." Police and fire protection was simple enough, as were emergency repairs to streets. More problematic were water and sewer connections, because of the cost of extending those lines through the rocky peninsula, but Bare promised that this infrastructure would be constructed "as finances permit." The following year the mayor praised Sunnyside's location and announced a long-term goal of improvement that would eliminate all substandard housing, beginning with Grimm's boxcars.[15]

In the years following annexation the city failed to deliver on Bare's promises. To be sure, shortly after annexation the city's Board of Health began a program of housing inspections and promptly condemned the boxcars. As they were vacated the boxcars could not be reoccupied, but although the board condemned other houses, as was true of Lancaster's slum clearance program throughout the 1950s, the city temporized on demolition, even of vacant buildings. Thus in February 1960 the Lancaster City Planning Commission concluded that since 1955 "the area has remained virtually stagnant insofar as physical upgrading is concerned" and was "perhaps the most undesirable residential area within the whole of the Lancaster Metropolitan Community."[16]

When Lancaster began its program of urban redevelopment in 1957, visiting federal officials suggested that Sunnyside not be included in the General Neighborhood Renewal Plan the city was preparing. Two years later the planning commission described Sunnyside as "an area of extensive blight typified by poorly and improperly constructed dwelling units totally deficient of inside plumbing facilities." Commission staff then commenced a study to determined how best to rehabilitate the peninsula, which was published as *Sunnyside: People, Conditions, Needs* in February 1960 (Fig. 43). At the time, approximately 450 persons resided at Sunnyside, virtually all of them white. Of the roughly 135 residences, 92 percent were substandard; perhaps 25 percent were occupied by squatters, another 25 percent were owner-occupied. The majority of residents had incomes of less than $2,500 a year, and an unspecified but significant percentage relied on social welfare payments for their subsistence. Average rents ranged from $15 to $20 per month for squalid dwellings that lacked sewer and water connections as well as adequate heat and ventilation. These conditions notwithstanding, the planning commission described Sunnyside as "an area of outstanding natural beauty" and termed it "perhaps among the most desirable areas in Lancaster County for natural beauty."[17]

In determining alternative futures for Sunnyside, the planning commission found that fulfilling Bare's promise of city services was prohibitively expensive. Its report estimated that street paving and lighting and the extension of sewer and water service would cost $482,000. Given the low assessed value of Sunnyside properties, the commission calculated that it would take 200 years of taxes simply to pay for infrastructure improvements. "Therefore," it concluded, "such action is entirely out of the question unless accom-

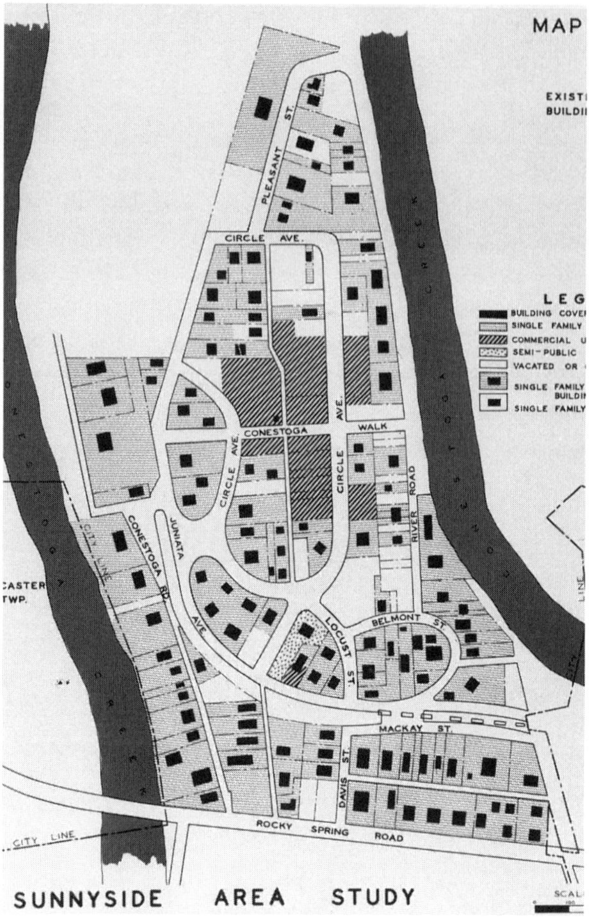

FIG. 43 *The Sunnyside residential community as developed. With the exception of minor deviations at the southern end of the subdivision, the streets conform to the 1912 plat. Note the site of "Boxcar Row" just above Mackay Street. From* Sunnyside: People, Conditions, Needs *(Bureau of Planning, City of Lancaster).*

panied by comprehensive remedial action resulting in improved land-use and higher tax returns."[18]

Each of the alternatives the planning commission suggested was predicated upon the clearance of all existing structures on the Sunnyside peninsula. Only such drastic action would make the area suitable for more advantageous uses. The first alternative the commission envisioned was "a scattered-site development of high-priced homes"—residences located on spacious lots that would combine "a sense of country living within easy access of the City." A second alternative, construction of low-cost public housing, was less attractive because Sunnyside was outside the boundaries of the urban renewal area; as a result, the city would not be able to count the cost of extending infrastructure throughout the peninsula as part of its match of federal and state redevelopment grants. Other possible futures the planning commission sketched included devoting Sunnyside to recreational use, especially if it proved feasible to construct a dam and enlarge the river into a substantial body of water, or to take advantage of the isolation of the peninsula and the presence of an existing automobile scrapyard by locating "commercial junk yards and automobile graveyards" there. Even if the city undertook such minimal steps as repairing roads, installing streetlights, and extending a water line to the community, those improvements would only "delay that which must eventually take place—the complete physical renewal of the Sunnyside community." Thus the planning commission recommended that "Sunnyside should, at the appropriate time, be completely cleared of all existing structures and uses." This action, the report concluded, should be undertaken by the city's Redevelopment Authority when the first urban renewal projects were completed.[19]

At the commencement of planning the city invited the participation of Sunnyside residents to "determine its rehabilitation needs and to explore the feasibility of an urban renewal project within its boundaries." Urban renewal had not yet come to signify demolition in February 1960, as it would in subsequent years, because in Lancaster no structures had yet been razed by the Redevelopment Authority. While it is impossible to determine what Sunnyside residents anticipated would be the outcome of the planning process, a local newspaper announced the planning commission's findings under a boldface headline: "City Urged to Clear Out Sunnyside & Start Anew." On one level the report must have confirmed what residents had been experiencing since annexation: that the city had no desire to bear the financial burden of extending essential services to Sunnyside and had little concern for the people who lived there. Perhaps more important, announcement of an urban renewal clearance program for Sunnyside marked a major turning point in the debate about the peninsula's future. The promises of better services that were not kept, after all, meant that things would remain the same, whereas the 1960 plan for redevelopment portended the destruction of residents' homes and the severing of kinship and communal ties.[20]

Despite its implications for residents, *Sunnyside: People, Condition, Needs* was met with a resounding silence. Minutes of the planning commission and of City Council reveal no objections to the proposed clearance program, nor do letters to the editors of the three local newspapers. The silence could not have been the result of ignorance, because a number of residents had served on the Sunnyside Citizens Committee that advised the planners. It is possible that residents simply could not comprehend the complexities of the planning and redevelopment process, a phenomenon Herbert Gans discovered in his analysis of the effects of urban renewal on Boston's West End neighborhood. Even if that were the case, the absence of protest surely resulted from a sense of powerlessness in a community in which more than half of the households were occupied by tenants—many of whom were months behind in their rents, if claims of landlords can be believed—and another quarter were squatters. Some owners may have been reluctant to protest because so many of the properties were in arrears for taxes; others may have anticipated that an ambitious redevelopment program would enhance the value of their holdings.[21]

An equally telling silence ensued in government. The planning commission reviewed the Sunnyside report at its meeting of February 10, 1960, just before its release, and "decided to discuss this report in more detail as other aspects of the Urban Renewal Program make themselves visible in the months ahead." Perhaps because the staff devoted so much energy to launching renewal projects elsewhere in the city, there would not be another reference to Sunnyside in planning commission minutes for more than a year. City Council similarly allowed the Sunnyside proposal to languish unacknowledged. Given the magnitude of the money the city would have to commit to match federal and state urban renewal grants, as well as the 1957 decision to defer improvements to Sunnyside until after redevelopment programs elsewhere were well advanced, Lancaster simply did not have the resources to undertake the capital expenditures Sunnyside desperately needed.[22]

For the next seven years the debate over Sunnyside's future vacillated between spurts of energetic planning and developmental stasis. In June 1962, for example, Burrell Cohen, then director of the Lancaster Redevelopment Authority, proposed a major improvement program that included significant resources for the peninsula. Sometime between staff recommendations and the issuance of the city's Capital Improvement Program, the Sunnyside initiative had become a $350,000 budget line for construction of a municipal golf course, which was not built. Four years later the planning commission undertook a property survey and an engineering study of the peninsula, at which time Louis Milan, the third director of the city's Redevelopment Authority, predicted that "this should be the year for certain specific action" to improve Sunnyside. Again, no significant improvement followed.[23]

Sunnyside's relationship with city government became more antagonistic toward the end of the decade. In November 1967 the Sunnyside Community Action Council, aided by neighborhood organizers from the Community Action Program, asserted that residents "are entitled to the same privileges as other taxpayers" and submitted a petition requesting that the city address such long-standing issues as "water, [street] lights, and transportation for our children for primary and secondary education." Planning commission staff reviewed the petition and recommended consideration of "various short-range improvements in physical facilities and services." Among the steps the staff endorsed were extending a water line to "two or three common water sources within the Sunnyside area," modest improvements in roads and the construction of sidewalks, and better street lighting. These improvements were "compatible with the long-range renewal goals for the area," the planners informed City Council, not a change in policy. The planning commission then reiterated its position that "the complete physical and social renewal of the Sunnyside area is the only solution to the current problems of the area."[24]

In July 1968 Mayor Thomas J. Monaghan requested that City Council address Sunnyside's short-term needs by appropriating $17,000 to construct a water line to the community. Perhaps a dozen Sunnyside residents attended the July 9 meeting to urge Council to resolve the water issue. The spring in nearby Williamson Park that traditionally had provided Sunnyside with drinking water was polluted, and a recent outbreak of hepatitis in the community made a supply of pure water imperative. But if residents considered water the most important issue, the mayor and members of Council thought otherwise: they authorized construction of the water line as an interim solution only after designating the peninsula the city's "number one priority in the Community Renewal Plan so that a complete renewal of said area may be accomplished at the earliest possible time."[25]

By the summer of 1968 residents of Sunnyside knew what urban renewal meant. Since the publication of *Sunnyside: People, Conditions, Needs* in 1960, Lancaster had embarked on an ambitious program of slum clearance. Redevelopment projects completed or then under way had resulted in the demolition of 868 buildings in the southeast quadrant of the city, the vast majority of them residential, and had forced the relocation of almost 1,100 families and 250 individuals, as well as a substantial number of neighborhood businesses. City Council's designation of Sunnyside as the city's priority renewal project meant relocation, perhaps to public housing but almost certainly to a more congested setting than the peninsula. Thus residents interpreted Council's vote as kind of punishment: it was the "result of attention drawn to the area by agitation" for services that the city rightfully should already have been providing. The level of mistrust and misunderstanding was equally apparent the following year. At a meeting of the Citizen's Assembly in February 1969, residents of Sunnyside expressed their fear that Model Cities was simply slum clearance under another name.[26]

Despite the evident cleavages separating officials and citizens, and without conducting a survey to ascertain how residents of Sunnyside felt, Lancaster added the peninsula to its Model Neighborhood Program on March 11, 1969. Shortly thereafter, using $40,000 in Model Cities funding, the city extended a water line to the community and constructed a central water house for use by all residents. At the same time, city officials began inspecting Sunnyside and, relying upon powers incorporated in a more stringent housing code adopted the previous February, forcing owners to demolish condemned and vacant properties. The Grimm boxcars were finally removed on August 13, 1969, almost twenty years after they were placed in Sunnyside, and 5 other structures were slated for demolition at the same time. More would follow under Lancaster's Comprehensive City Demonstration Program, which in October 1969 designated an additional 19 Sunnyside properties for clearance. The Demonstration Program proposal had noted that many of the residents who had witnessed the demolition of the boxcars "feared that the City would continue until the homes they lived in were condemned and torn down also." Demolition of the 19 additional properties would be performed by Sunnyside residents, employed using Demonstration Program funds, who presumably would reassure neighbors that the city was razing only condemned structures that were unoccupied.[27]

Ironically, the first Model Cities efforts devoted to Sunnyside sent a mixed message. The water supply was a decided improvement, though a single water house obviously fell short of what residents wanted. At the same time, the demolitions were a telling reminder of what residents most feared: a clearance program that would eliminate their homes. Thus the action plan for the second year changed the name of the program from "Sunnyside Demolition Project" to "Sunnyside Improvement Project." It defended the demolitions as a "crucial focus of a city developmental strategy for Sunnyside" and argued that the first year's work provided "tangible evidence . . . that Lancaster is going to deal with the peninsula and the problems of its residents." The action plan nevertheless characterized the attitude of Sunnyside's residents toward the city in terms of "violent distrust and accumulated frustration." Because of the demolitions, residents eyed the Model City program with only slightly less hostility than they had viewed earlier planning efforts.[28]

As Model Cities staff tackled the dilemma of Sunnyside, in 1969 a team of planning consultants from Cleveland, Ohio, began compiling a massive long-range Community Improvement Program plan for the Lancaster City Planning Commission. The firm, Dalton, Dalton, Little & Newport, characterized existing conditions in Sunnyside as very poor because of major physical, environmental, and social deficiencies. Of the 122 residences then standing on the peninsula, it projected that 77 percent should be cleared and almost 22 percent rehabilitated, which left only two dwellings rated standard. The report called for total clearance of all substandard housing and removal of the junkyard. Lancaster faced an immediate need for a substantial increase in the number of homes for moderate-income families, the Dalton firm asserted, and Sunnyside was an ideal location because of its proximity to downtown, its relatively undeveloped state, and its natural beauty. The plan proposed the construction of several eight-story apartment buildings, totaling 600 new units, near the center of the peninsula, as well as clusters of two-story houses near the north and south ends of Sunnyside that would add another 600 units to the peninsula. To provide services for residents of the 1,200 units, the plan called for construction of a "small convenience shopping center," a community center, and a school, all to be located near the apartment buildings. It also designated three new bridges crossing the Conestoga to improve access to Sunnyside, and a "loop parkway traversing the perimeter of the peninsula along the creek." Small parks would be located adjacent to the parkway, and the quarry used for fishing and boating. Two-thirds of the cost of infrastructure development and site preparation, estimated at $4,918,300, could be paid through federal grants, the remainder from local funds. Such a comprehensive program was essential to the future of Lancaster, the Dalton plan urged, because "of all redevelopment areas in the City, Sunnyside offers the greatest potential for a dramatic reversal of 'image' and an ideal opportunity to provide a large amount of new housing for the moderate-income market."[29]

For all its pages and charts and plans, the Dalton study, completed in draft in 1970, was an anachronism. Its call for razing existing structures on the peninsula and constructing moderate-income housing would have forced the relocation of virtually all Sunnyside residents, who would not have been able to afford the increased cost of shelter. Residents had become increasingly vocal about defending their community in the late 1960s, and the Dalton plan would have incited an angry response. The days of the bulldozer as a blunt instrument in urban renewal were ending. So too was the era of a strong federal commitment to cities and the urban population. By the time the Dalton study was reviewed by local and federal officials, revised, and published in May 1973, virtually every significant source of federal money to undertake the projects it outlined had been cut or eliminated.[30]

Lancaster officials undoubtedly reviewed a draft of the Dalton report in late 1970 or early 1971. In the previous two years, several Redevelopment Authority applications for planning or projects involving Sunnyside had been denied, and the peninsula was still not certified as eligible for federal urban renewal programs. A 1971 report tersely summarized the absence of governmental assistance to the peninsula when it noted that "even the Federal Government is reluctant to come to grips with the situation in Sunnyside"—perhaps the ultimate legacy of the 1957 decision not to include the peninsula within Lancaster's General Neighborhood Renewal Plan. As a result, in 1971 Sunnyside's future remained as uncertain as it was in 1960, when the Planning Commission issued the first study calling for clearance of all extant structures.[31]

Setbacks in the search for federal funds made the city seek alternative strategies for improving Sunnyside. In 1971 the local Model Neighborhood Agency commissioned the firm FRIDAY to undertake a study of the Sunnyside community. Planners Donald Matzkin and Peter Artac noted long-standing nuisance problems—the automobile junkyard and, more ominously, a rapidly expanding quarry operation that was illegally engulfing adjoining land—and paid special attention to the sociological characteristics of Sunnyside. The population remained overwhelmingly white and poor. Thirty percent of the 70 resident families received some form of public assistance, another 30 percent had annual incomes of less than $3,000. The pattern of nonresident ownership had intensified: two individuals owned 35 percent of the land, and if the county-owned land were added to the aggregate, 95 percent of Sunnyside was controlled by absentee landlords. There were only a handful of resident owners of Sunnyside lots. Still, FRIDAY planners were heartened by the sense of community they found. Perhaps because of the peninsula's isolation, perhaps because of their embattled mentality, Sunnyside's residents shared "an attachment to place which is sadly missing in many neighborhoods, rich or poor; a loyalty to place and neighbors that transcends physical conditions." Although largely renters rather than owners, residents of Sunnyside nevertheless had developed a sense of identity as a community, and a powerful attachment to the peninsula.[32]

The FRIDAY plan envisioned the "ultimate replacement of almost every structure in Sunnyside," but it hoped to accomplish this "with minimum dislocation of the residents and minimum disruption of their living pattern in the process." Thus it effectively divided the peninsula in thirds. The lower third, the existing Sunnyside community, "should continue to be single family detached dwellings serving low and middle income families." For the middle third FRIDAY proposed turning the quarry into a small marina surrounded by commercial facilities and a community center. The upper third "should be predominantly townhouses and/or apartment units serving the middle and upper-middle income markets." The plan also proposed a walking and biking trail along the Conestoga, construction of bridges to provide more convenient access to the peninsula, as well as passive recreational facilities such as tot lots and sitting areas. FRIDAY projected a development of approximately 735 residential units, with the cost of infrastructure and site improvements estimated at between $2.25 and $3.2 million, and building construction at between $9.9 and $13.7 million. To assess the feasibility of the preliminary scheme, FRIDAY then advised the city to undertake a market study of housing needs, conduct analysis of subsurface conditions to establish accurate costs for infrastructure development, and apply for federal grants for the sewer and water project. The city should pursue these steps aggressively, FRIDAY advised, because "Sunnyside could and should be a lovely, unique place to live instead of an eyesore and a health hazard."[33]

Based on this preliminary plan, the Model Neighborhood Agency commissioned FRIDAY to prepare a second document that would establish a series of options, including cost analysis, for development of the peninsula. The second report, submitted in March 1973, reiterated many of the conceptual themes sketched in preliminary form sixteen months earlier. It also treated geology, hydrology, and environmental questions extensively. The most revealing aspect of the second report, however, was its analysis of finances. FRIDAY estimated that in order to make the Sunnyside project attractive (and profitable) to a private developer, the city would probably have to assume the cost of terracing the quarry, constructing bridges, and site preparation, as well as to subsidize land acquisition—incentives totaling almost $1.5 million. The city would also have to waive real estate taxes during the five-year developmental process. Either because of the cost or because its suggestions contravened the broader, citywide comprehensive plan, Lancaster officials apparently did not distribute the FRIDAY reports widely. A newspaper article summarizing the Dalton plan alluded to the second FRIDAY plan as "another study, prepared for Model Cities . . . [that] has been kept mysteriously secret."[34]

The Dalton study and the two FRIDAY reports represent the last comprehensive planning efforts devoted to Sunnyside. Each is a professional document in the best sense of that term, yet they differ vastly in content and proposals. The Dalton study, commissioned by the city, examined Sunnyside as a small part of a much larger urban mosaic. Given the overall needs of the city, especially for middle-income housing and increased tax revenue, the Dalton plan called for development that would have displaced the existing Sunnyside community. By contrast, the FRIDAY reports, commissioned by the Model Neighborhood Agency, examined only Sunnyside; the overall needs of the city seemed peripheral to those of residents of the peninsula. Indeed, the first FRIDAY study conceded that after extensive conversations with residents the planners developed "a deep concern for the members of this community"—an empathy that was evident in their recommendations for treatment of the southern end of the peninsula. The Dalton team presented a package of recommendations that would enable the city to seek federal grants to develop Sunnyside, whereas the FRIDAY report posited the need for local public investment to make private development attractive. Yet for all their differences the Dalton and FRIDAY studies have one thing in common: neither pointed the way to immediate development of the Sunnyside peninsula.[35]

The years since FRIDAY submitted its preliminary sketch plan have seen little progress in resolving Lancaster's enduring dilemma of what to do with Sunnyside and its people. In 1972 Tropical Storm Agnes swept across the peninsula. Damage resulting from powerful winds and extensive flooding necessitated the demolition of numerous properties, especially in the floodplain. In the aftermath of the devastating storm, when numerous other cities in Pennsylvania received significant funding for rebuilding, Sunnyside was again overlooked. Using $54,000 from Model Cities, in 1973 the city constructed an educational resource center with classrooms for Early Childhood Education and Neighborhood Education Services programs. Welcome though the school services may have been, this was not the multipurpose community center with showers, a laundromat, and recreational rooms residents had requested in interviews with FRIDAY planners in 1971.[36]

By 1980 Sunnyside's population had been reduced to 54 households and 175 individuals. Slightly more than 90 percent of residents were white, the remainder African American. Three of ten individuals had incomes below the poverty line, relatively few had completed high school, and the vast majority of residences were still without water and sewer connections. Sunnyside remained a "community in trouble." The fate of the educational resource center symbolized the dimensions of these difficulties: because interest and use had declined as operating costs increased and vandalism became a problem, in 1980 the School District of Lancaster sold the building at public auction for $9,800. Sadly, a structure that represented one decade's hope for a revitalized community became the next decade's concession of failure.[37]

During the 1980s Sunnyside finally achieved one of the principal goals that had led to annexation by Lancaster so many years earlier. On August 6, 1983, the *Lancaster New Era* published an anguished letter inviting Mayor Arthur Morris to tour Sunnyside. There he would see "streets neglected for years" as well as the "lack of city water" and the absence of numerous other services. Should the mayor be inclined to come, the letter writer advised: "Bring your jungle cutting crew so we can walk the 'city streets.'" The following January several residents attended a public hearing to determine citizen priorities in the allocation of Community Development Block Grant (CDBG) funds. Their argument that the city had to assume the cost of installing water and sewer lines at last found an ally in Morris, a former city engineer, who promised to try to find a way to meet Sunnyside's needs. Two months later Morris announced the allocation of $100,000 in CDBG funds for the beginnings of an eight- to ten-year phased project to supply Sunnyside with water and sewer service. Subsequent allocations from CDBG, from the Lancaster Water and Sewer authorities, from liquid fuels taxes for road improvements, even $84,000 in funds from the city's jobs program, accounted for the $1.5 million cost of improvements.[38]

Construction of water and sewer lines, as well as road improvements, necessitated the demolition of several additional Sunnyside structures. The city refused to place utility lines in the floodplain, so houses there could not be connected to services and would no longer be in compliance with city codes. Morris defended the need to raze six buildings—although not all of them were actually in flood-prone areas—stating that the "structures all have serious housing code violations, and we have serious doubts about the economic and structural feasibility of rehabilitation." Seven churches joined Sunnyside residents in protesting the city's plan of action, and a spokesman for the local Habitat for Humanity chapter, attorney Melvin H. Hess, urged the city to "concentrate not just on monetary factors but think of the community." Morris pushed ahead with the projects, including demolition, Habitat erected a new dwelling for one of the residents who had to relocate, and the city helped the other families find new homes. New water and sewer lines, paved and lighted streets, and other utilities finally brought Sunnyside into the twentieth century at the end of the 1980s. After completion of construction, however, rents began to rise. "Some people can no longer afford to live in Sunnyside," resident Elaine Stolzfus explained. "There are some pains that go with the improvement." Ironically, the changes Sunnyside residents had wanted for so long brought consequences they had not anticipated; the community that had defended itself against planners, bureaucrats, and public officials could not completely insulate itself against landlords who saw the opportunity to raise rents.[39]

Neighborhoods such as Sunnyside, which once existed in virtually every American city, tell their histories incompletely, through the lines of human endeavor, however modest the material world generations of residents left behind, however faded the once-bright promise of human aspirations. These places stand as poignant metaphors for the limits of planning and renewal. As an isolated community within Lancaster, Sunnyside's needs have often diverged from what planners and elected officials considered the city's priorities. At the time when federal community action and antipoverty programs attempted to protect the rights of residents and promote "maximum feasible participation" in the political process—empowerment in today's discourse—the city was struggling to prevent the acceleration of flight to suburbia and maximize its tax base. Even in the absence of a competition for scarce resources, Sunnyside's future has been hostage to the broader community's unwillingness to work with residents in shaping the optimal future for the peninsula.[40]

At the beginning of the twenty-first century, Sunnyside's future remains uncertain. There are numerous unresolved questions: environmental contamination at the quarry and junkyard, the city's resources if it chooses to redevelop the lower third of the peninsula, and the fate of residents who would be affected by those plans. What commitment the federal government makes to urban America, especially program initiatives that include smaller cities as well as major metropolitan areas, will determine what resources the city can draw upon to improve Sunnyside as physical environment and social space. But what may have sealed Sunnyside's fate—the residential community on the southern end as well as county-owned open space on the northern two-thirds of the peninsula—was the decision by the Board of County Commissioners in 1997 to use its property as the site of a juvenile detention center. This enormous block structure, designed to enclose more than 100,000 square feet, will occupy the central portion of the largest piece of undeveloped land in Lancaster. The county has invited developers to propose residential and commercial development on the remaining 25 acres of land. Construction of the juvenile detention center began in the year 2000, forty years after the first planning commission study, *Sunnyside: People, Condition, Needs.* While the redevelopment of county-owned land will undoubtedly affect what remains of the residential community to the south, many of the human welfare issues that first planning document identified have never been adequately addressed.[41]

Unresolved as well is the larger community's attitude toward Sunnyside and its people. The mythic but enduring version of Sunnyside's history—the once-pleasant cluster of vacation cottages that became a rural slum—implicitly suggests that Sunnyside's woes are the fault not of the subdividers, whose speculative plat failed to take account of topography and subsurface rock and to provide any infrastructure, or of the initial purchasers, who surely would never have allowed their properties to deteriorate to this level, but of later residents. The widely held attitude toward Sunnyside and its residents also denies the existence of community, of people who value the place, who have an attachment to locale and to each other despite physical conditions that might lead an outsider to conclude that the area was a hopeless slum. In a subtle but highly effective way, then, the myth of Sunnyside's decline has for generations allowed Lancaster to absolve itself of responsibility for the peninsula, and for the people who live there. In the absence of a consensus that Sunnyside and its residents are essential to the interests of the city, no planning efforts undertaken to date could possibly have succeeded. Especially when examined in conjunction with the failure of residential renewal in Lancaster, Sunnyside stands as a haunting reminder that urban neighborhoods are the product of ideas, attitudes, and sometimes even mistakes inherited from the past, as well as the networks of community residents have forged.

CHAPTER 8

LEGACY
A Historic City in the Suburban Age

In the two decades following the organization of the Lancaster Redevelopment Authority in 1957, a succession of mayors, administrators, and planners attempted to revitalize the central business district and the southeast quadrant of the city. Lancaster suffered from blight, planners assured civic leaders, which they described as a combination of declining property values and deteriorating buildings that threatened to spread throughout the city. In commencing an ambitious urban redevelopment program, elected officials attempted to solidify the downtown retail center against competition from suburban malls and to provide adequate housing for citizens. With urban renewal Lancaster turned to the federal government, for the first time in its history, for substantial financial help.[1] Federal aid came with a series of expectations of performance that modernized the administrative structure of the city. The first professional planning staff was one product of the renewal program, as was the first housing code, a new comprehensive plan, and elements of a Workable Program for Community Improvement that was required by the Housing and Home Finance Agency.

Urban renewal federalized the nation's cities by tying funding to specific projects and mandating compliance with federal regulations, including the nondiscrimination provisions of the Civil Rights Act of 1964. The very structure of urban renewal made almost inevitable some conflict between experts and bureaucrats in regional and national offices, on one hand, and elected municipal officials, who jealously guarded local prerogatives, on the other. Especially when local leaders attempted to place all public housing in the area where most of Lancaster's minorities lived, and to block the implementation of a scattered-site housing program, federal officials sought to change the social geography of the city. It is perhaps the most telling indication of how concerted local opposition could thwart federal mandates that all public housing was built in the southeast quadrant of the city: no scattered-site public housing was located elsewhere, in Lancaster City or its adjacent suburbs, during these years.

What was built was significant, though arguably not as significant as what was torn down. Indeed, for almost a decade the most powerful statement of urban renewal's impact on the city was the vacant block on North Queen Street. Conscious of how essential a vital downtown was to the city, in 1974 the presidents of two local corporations, Armstrong Cork Company and National Central Bank, committed millions to build new facilities on the west side of Lancaster Square. Their decision to invest in downtown was the catalyst that finally brought the North Queen Street renewal project to completion.

As the steel frame and brick walls of Armstrong House and the National Central Bank building rose throughout 1975 and 1976, there was a palpable optimism downtown. The opening of Armstrong's new seven-story office building and design center in June 1977 marked a major turning point in the revitalization of the central business district, as did completion of the new bank building, on the former site of the YMCA at North Queen and West Orange streets, three months later. As employees were moving into the bank's new headquarters, Wilson D. McElhinny, its president, described an "aura of confidence" about the city's future.[2]

That feeling of confidence was a long time coming. During the twenty years since the organization of the Lancaster Redevelopment Authority in June 1957, the explosive growth of surrounding suburbs made Lancaster's economic health precarious, as new shopping malls to the north, east, and west of the city attracted consumers who had formerly patronized downtown. Moreover, the demolition of the 100-block of North Queen Street had eliminated a significant part of the tax base that supported public education as well as municipal government. In the succeeding twelve years the Redevelopment Authority had sought a developer with the right plan for the site. The second block of North Queen Street may have been Lancaster's "most spectacular and most expensive redevelopment project," as one newspaper reported in 1970, but no one described it as a resounding success. Victor Gruen's proposed Lancaster Square generated critical acclaim, but attracting the tenants to anchor the new retail space proved exceedingly difficult, especially after the opening of Park City, a large regional shopping center northwest of the historic city, in September 1971. When no new buildings rose in place of the ones that had been razed, downtown seemed doomed to extinction. The looming presence of Gruen's concrete screen on the vacant west block came to symbolize the failure of urban redevelopment. The east block fared little better: the Hilton Hotel had not earned the affection of Lancastrians who cherished the Beaux Arts character and reassuring presence of the Brunswick, and the closing of Hess's Department Store in August 1973 shattered the long-standing hope that downtown would remain the retail center of the metropolitan area. As the west block became known as "our hole in the ground," North Queen Street took on the characteristics of what McElhinny called "a pretty psychologically depressed area." The linking of the absence of a vibrant streetscape with psychological as well as economic depression was astute. The west block, he recalled, "had remained empty and idle for such a long period of time and was a gaping eyesore and reminder to everybody that the downtown area was deteriorating." Only dramatic steps would change attitudes and stimulate faith in the future of the central business district.[3]

As the Lancaster Square buildings neared completion, the confident attitude they inspired spread throughout the city. Mayor Richard M. Scott shared McElhinny's expectation that the success of these buildings would advance the ultimate if elusive goal of revitalizing the entire city. Perhaps fittingly, the final piece of the west block was the removal of the skating rink and other elements of Gruen's plan, and the creation of a plaza, shaded by honey locusts, for passive recreation. Scott termed the new park "the symbol of the renaissance of our central city." The *Intelligencer Journal* hailed the completion of the west side of Lancaster Square as "another milestone in the rebirth of downtown." What once had been an enduring reminder of failure had become "one of the most attractive downtowns to be seen in cities of this size." The *New Era* similarly praised the completion of the west block as an "excellent accomplishment" but pointed to the largely vacant east side of the street—where the former Hess's department store building stood empty, adjacent to storefronts intended for smaller retail businesses that were also unoccupied—as a remaining challenge.[4]

The transformation of the center city was progressing elsewhere too. The renovations to buildings in Old Town Lancaster were under way, a project that promised to bring an infusion of prosperous residents to homes within walking distance of downtown retail. The Redevelopment Authority had commenced upgrading the infrastructure of North Queen Street, while the city had undertaken the restoration of Central Market, an 1889 Romanesque Revival building that continued to bring farmers, and customers, downtown. The old City Hall, on the northwest corner of Penn Square, had served a number of functions over the course of the twentieth century, and during the mid-1970s it was being restored in preparation for its use as a cultural institution, the Heritage Center Museum of Lancaster County. As part of the center city improvement program, the Redevelopment Authority was renovating the plaza in front of the old City Hall, adding brick paving, trees, seating walls, historical plaques, and an information kiosk. Most important of all was the construction of a major addition to the Fulton Bank building on the northeast corner of Penn Square. The traditional crossroads of urban life in Lancaster, Penn Square had been designated the highest priority in the city's final urban renewal project, Crosstown, in 1972. While Crosstown embraced a sprawling area of more than 200 acres of central and southwest Lancaster, the heart of this renewal program was the area around Penn Square.[5]

In the 1970s Penn Square was a textbook example of what planners described as blight. The commercial and governmental center of the county for more than two centuries, Penn Square and adjacent blocks had been particularly hard hit by the suburbanization of retail and the resulting decline of other businesses that it supported. A number of downtown storefronts that once displayed premium goods had, by the 1970s, become purveyors of discount merchandise; others stood vacant, neon signs testifying to former uses and to a once-thriving retail economy. Property values were declining, and evidence of decay was visible even to the untrained eye. The northeast corner of the square, opposite the Watt & Shand department store, the commercial anchor of downtown, attracted the planners' particular attention. The art deco Fulton Bank stood next to three small buildings, a White Cross discount store, the Famous Maid clothing shop, and Delmonico's Cafe, which Mayor Scott praised as a "beautiful building" but whose decline paralleled that of the central business district over the previous twenty years. In March 1972 the Redevelopment Authority proposed to demolish the three small commercial buildings and erect on the site a modern five-story commercial structure. Once again the authority staff was willing to place a critical piece of the city's real estate in the hands of an unnamed but "very interested" developer.[6]

The reaction to the Penn Square proposal was mixed. Thomas Monaghan, Lancaster's mayor at the beginning of the Crosstown urban renewal project in 1972, generally favored the plan, though he preferred a more ambitious project that addressed Penn Square immediately and as a totality which included Central Market. Even while conceding that the White Cross building was an eyesore, City Council once again expressed reservations about any new demolition while Lancaster Square remained on the drawing board. Benjamin High described a meeting in which councilmen assured the new head of the Redevelopment Authority, Donald Hostetter, that they wanted revitalization to succeed. "But we didn't mean tear down the whole town," High stated. Hostetter pledged that there would be no demolition until the commencement of building on the west side of Lancaster Square. Some businessmen criticized the continuing emphasis on downtown at the expense of the rest of the city, others expressed concern that more land was being subjected to redevelopment when so much had been torn down and so little built. Monaghan, who knew that consensus was critical to the success of the revitalization process, quickly defended Crosstown, explaining the importance of the Penn Square improvements to the entire city and the ways in which a revitalized square, together with the completion of Lancaster Square, would stand as the two ends of an urban retail dumbbell. Despite considerable misgivings, on April 11, 1972, City Council approved the demolition of the northeast corner of the square—the White Cross, Delmonico's, and Famous Maid buildings—but only after several downtown businessmen pledged to continue paying property taxes at the current level for six years even if the land stood vacant.[7]

The Redevelopment Authority then began the process of applying for federal and state grants and appraising the properties prior to acquisition. Drawing upon the Workable Program for Community Improvement, the Redevelopment Authority presented Crosstown as a step in creating "a central city which has the ability to draw the resident with middle and upper income earning potential back into the City." But, in what Monaghan attributed to cutbacks in urban programs by the Nixon administration, HUD rejected the city's application for funding. The Redevelopment Authority then turned to the state Department of Community Affairs, which in April 1973 awarded Lancaster $2.4 million to fund the first two years of the Crosstown project. Major initiatives funded in the two-year grant included acquisition and demolition of the White Cross, Delmonico's, and Famous Maid buildings, improvements to the Central Market area (including the establishment of direct access to the market from North Queen Street, which Monaghan advocated), and a residential rehabilitation program along the Water Street corridor in the southwest quadrant of the city.[8]

Demolition of the Penn Square buildings continued to be delayed while the Redevelopment Authority devoted most of its energies to the west side of Lancaster Square. When City Council finally approved going ahead with Crosstown in February 1974 and the Redevelopment Authority initiated condemnation proceedings on the Penn Square properties in May, the owner of Delmonico's contested the value placed on the property. Not until the following July did the authority advertise for proposals for the acquisition and development of the site and set an August 1 date for vacating the buildings. Three parties expressed interest in the site: William F. Hoke, president of Fulton Bank, informed the Redevelopment Authority of the bank's desire to expand its operations downtown by building a major addition on the site; Revco Drug Stores, a Cleveland-based chain, saw the project as an opportunity to replace its small downtown store with a larger modern retail facility; and Charles Conrad, a local architect, represented investors interested in erecting an office building on the square. The Redevelopment Authority was particularly interested in what Hostetter termed "the esthetic contribution and architectural contribution" that each of the proposals would make to the downtown.[9]

On September 16, 1974, the Redevelopment Authority announced that Fulton Bank had been chosen as the developer of the Penn Square site. At a ceremony in which the bank and the authority presented the design, Hoke expressed pride in the Fulton's "major role in the revitalization of downtown Lancaster." Together with the plans for Armstrong House and the National Central Bank building on Lancaster Square, announced earlier that month, the Fulton expansion was a catalyst that, civic leaders expected, would stimulate reinvestment in center city. The project design, prepared by Buchart Associates, proposed a four-story structure where the buildings slated for demolition still stood, a site plan that preserved the recessed square that framed Lancaster's handsome Civil War monument. Buchart's drawings promised to transform what had been a montage of eclectic buildings into a unified red-brick composition that was colonial in appearance (Fig. 44). On the eve of the nation's bicentennial celebration, Hoke proudly announced that the bank was "fully committed" to the colonial design. Pointing to the old City Hall across Queen Street, a late Georgian building erected in 1799, he found in traditional architecture a key to the city's future. "It seems appropriate," Hoke stated, "that we reach back into Lancaster's colonial heritage and have it become an integral part of the revitalization of Penn Square." Perhaps wisely, no one attempted to explain the incongruity of sheathing a stone art deco building in brick colonial garb or placing a mansard roof at the top of a Georgian revival building.[10]

Reaction to the selection of the Fulton as developer and to the design as unveiled was generally enthusiastic. Richard Scott, who succeeded Monaghan as mayor in January 1974, described the building as "exactly what the city wants and needs. It will be a great addition to the downtown area." Scott expressed particular pleasure with the selection of the Fulton project because the "architecture fits the character of our city." Wesley Shope, president of the Chamber of Commerce, was likewise enthusiastic. The Fulton proposal was a "further indication that the downtown is alive and well." Some members of the Redevelopment Authority's architectural review committee clearly were less than enthusiastic about the design and submitted a minority report. Instead of releasing the majority and minority reports, the Redevelopment Authority board issued a statement concluding that the "colonial approach of the Fulton Bank suits the city and its residents much better than any of the other more modernistic approaches." Ironically, even as it was celebrating progress, a colonial crossroads that had evolved into a Victorian industrial city was mythologizing its past in Georgian revival bricks and mortar.[11]

Although the Fulton initially hoped that its building program would be completed in time for the bicentennial summer of 1976, not until the fol-

FIG. 44 *Fulton Bank and Penn Square, c. 1976 (Fulton Financial Corporation).*

lowing spring was the project ready for occupancy. On Friday, May 20, 1977, the bank hosted a garden party on the brick-paved plaza formed by the two wings of the L-shaped building. More than 5,000 people enjoyed coffee and donuts, listened to a band, watched an old-time organ-grinder and his monkey, and toured the remodeled and newly constructed sections of the bank. At a brief dedication ceremony, William Hoke once again stated that the Fulton was "proud to be one of the leaders in the revitalization of downtown." Mayor Scott then thanked the Fulton for "a tremendous contribution to the revitalization of our center city." The new building brought more than 100 additional workers to the bank and, civic leaders hoped, a new infusion of economic life to the center of the city. Together with the completion of the west side of Lancaster Square and improvements to the northwest quadrant of Penn Square, the Fulton symbolized a downtown renaissance, a city that had triumphed in its twenty-year battle against blight. To celebrate these achievements, and to showcase the attractions of the new downtown to office workers as well as suburban shoppers, during the summer of 1977 the city sponsored a series of lunchtime brown-bag concerts on Fridays. Merchants expressed delight with the crowds that attended the inaugural concert, and remarked on the festive atmosphere resulting from so many people on the streets and in the stores. Downtown, they optimistically hoped, was once again becoming a destination of choice.[12]

Still another component of the city's revitalization program, though several blocks from Penn Square, was the Lancaster Neighborhood Center, a starkly modern structure on Rockland Street that stands as the major physical achievement of the national Model Cities program in Lancaster. As was true of the Lancaster Square buildings and the Fulton Bank expansion, projects completed around the time of the bicentennial but with origins several years earlier, proponents had advocated construction of the Neighborhood Center for almost a decade before its dedication. Drayton S. Bryant had suggested the idea of a community center in the southeast in his 1967 study of housing and services for the Church-Musser renewal area. Such a building, he believed, could bring together a number of social service agencies and nonprofit organizations that were dispersed throughout the southeast quadrant. In mid-February 1971 the Model Neighborhood Agency proposed erecting a building to house agencies essential to the well-being of residents. The Model Neighborhood Agency then sought the involvement of a number of social service providers as potential tenants, including the Lancaster Community Action Program (CAP), which agreed to lease space for its Head Start program and its family planning center. In an application seeking federal funds for two-thirds of the estimated $1.6 million project, the Model Neighborhood Agency included letters of support from CAP, the Urban League, the School District of Lancaster, the YWCA, and physicians committed to establishing a health clinic to serve poor and minority residents of the area. These organizations were potential tenants of the center, as were groups such as Planned Parenthood, Legal Services, the Spanish Center, and a day-care center, which also submitted letters endorsing the application for funding. On March 30, 1971, the Redevelopment Authority approved the application for federal funds to erect the community center.[13]

The proposed Neighborhood Center was a striking building of metal and glass (Fig. 45) designed by FRIDAY, the Philadelphia architecture and planning firm that was then studying the Sunnyside peninsula for the Model Neighborhood Agency. In the preliminary plan the building's four stories, which would enclose approximately 40,000 square feet of space, cascaded down the hill along South Duke Street. Where once modest nineteenth-

FIG. 45 *The Lancaster Neighborhood Center, designed by FRIDAY, a Philadelphia architecture and planning firm, constructed in 1974 and 1975 (author photo).*

century brick and frame dwellings and the venerable Higbee School defined a densely built streetscape, the Neighborhood Center would stand surrounded by grass and parking, an unabashedly modern presence that, its designers surely hoped, symbolized a better future for residents of the southeast.[14]

Almost immediately the proposed Neighborhood Center sparked the opposition of City Council, which was dominated by Republicans hostile to many redevelopment programs and particularly to Model Cities. Although the Model Neighborhood Agency was largely beyond the control of local officials, City Council did have to approve its budget and grant applications. Councilman Richard Filling expressed dismay that City Council had not been kept informed of the planning process, wondered how the architects had been selected, and worried that the building would be mismanaged and become a financial responsibility of the municipality. Unless there were satisfactory answers to these concerns, Filling warned that he and his colleagues might withhold approval of the Neighborhood Center. He was joined by Council President Jack B. Metzger and fellow members Benjamin High and Julia Brazill, each of whom voiced their disapproval to the *Lancaster New Era.*

Brazill was so incensed that she threatened to vote to cancel the entire Model Cities program. Linda Odum, director of the local Model Neighborhood Agency, informed a *New Era* reporter that she had, in fact, briefed council on March 15 on the proposed building and the application for a federal grant her staff was preparing and had promised to bring plans to City Council as soon as they were completed. With an April 1 deadline for applications, her staff and the architects preparing preliminary plans worked day and night to get the paperwork completed and the sketches prepared. Odum explained to the reporter that she was bringing the completed proposal for review at the earliest possible moment.[15]

Although the Department of Housing and Urban Development promised a $1 million community facilities grant to help construct the Lancaster building, those funds could not be released until City Council approved use of Model Cities funding for the remainder of the cost. Thus the fate of the Neighborhood Center became a hotly contested political issue, debated principally in the press, in which local officials sought to assert their prerogatives over those of the Model City agency and federal administrators. Filling proposed a requirement that tenants sign ten- to twenty-year leases, ostensibly as a way of ensuring that the city would not have to assume responsibility for maintaining the building. But given the uncertainty of long-term funding for agencies that relied on donations or annual appropriations from federal or state programs, such leases were out of the question, as Filling knew. Moreover, opposition to the building from powerful interests in the city undoubtedly made some organizations wary of the project. The YWCA, which in preliminary plans would have occupied the second largest amount of space for a teen drop-in facility, announced that it would be unable to afford the cost of the estimated annual rent. Filling also proposed a different kind of building that would meet the space needs of the Salvation Army and the Neighborhood Center, but this proved unrealistic because it would have violated the Salvation Army's bylaws and perhaps its tax-exempt status, and might also have jeopardized the commitment of HUD funding. After City Council tabled a vote on the use of Model Cities funds to construct the Neighborhood Center, Odum and members of the Model Neighborhood Citizens Assembly organized a letter-writing campaign in the hope of persuading Council to release the monies.[16]

In succeeding weeks, as opponents continued to raise concerns about the building's cost and projected maintenance, the local press began to deride the proposed structure as an "expensive white elephant." Filling's insistence that the Neighborhood Center charge enough in rent to cover its operating costs resulted in a preliminary figure of roughly $3 per square foot, which was low compared to downtown office space but high when measured against the rents that interested social service agencies were then paying. The School District of Lancaster, which had considered relocating its Adult Basic Education and Head Start programs to the Neighborhood Center, wavered in its commitment to the new building and decided in the fall of 1971 that it could provide those programs in existing facilities. As the fate of the building hung in the balance, Mayor Thomas Monaghan criticized City Council for its unrealistic requirements: "It's rather mystifying that they want every square foot rented ahead of time," he stated. "We never would have moved in the downtown if we had waited for commitments before tearing anything down." The board of the Lancaster Redevelopment Authority similarly supported construction of the Neighborhood Center, but City Council continued to balk. In early August, Filling, High, and Brazill objected to its proposed location, in the southeast, and suggested instead that it be constructed in a central place: the North Queen Street renewal project. Finally, on September 8, 1971, City Council defeated a motion that would have authorized the Model Neighborhood Agency to submit the project to the federal government—which effectively prevented HUD from releasing the $1 million grant reserved for the Neighborhood Center—and for good measure then voted to deny the use of Model Cities funding in the construction of the building.[17]

Monaghan was determined to build the Neighborhood Center. When the Boys Club of Lancaster approached the city and offered to buy the old Higbee School site, where it intended to erect a new club facility, the mayor saw an opportunity to undercut Council's concern that the Neighborhood Center would become an expensive municipal responsibility. He agreed to sell the lot at the corner of Rockland and Dauphin streets to the Boys Club if the club agreed to manage the Neighborhood Center. When the board of the Boys Club expressed reluctance to take on that responsibility, Monaghan sweetened the deal by offering to include a swimming pool in the adjacent federally funded building that the Boys Club could use in its programming. The Boys Club finally assented to Monaghan's proposal, and with the highly regarded Boys Club added to the mix, opposition to the Neighborhood Center all but disappeared. At a special meeting on June 1, 1972, City Council unanimously approved the submission of an amended neighborhood facilities application, for a slightly smaller building with a swimming pool, and also authorized the use of Model Cities funds as the local share of the building's costs.[18]

The Lancaster Redevelopment Authority then sold part of the site of the old Higbee School to the Boys Club, which planned to erect its new facility at the corner of Dauphin and Rockland streets, and the remainder to the city, which made the adjacent tract along Rockland Street, south of the Boys Club, the site of the Neighborhood Center. At that time six tenants had agreed to lease space on three floors of the proposed building, with the other floor reserved for a health clinic. The Boys Club commenced work on the James Hale Steinman Memorial Building in the fall of 1972, while groundbreaking for the Neighborhood Center took place in December 1973. At the groundbreaking James Ford, chair of the Citizens Assembly, called the new building the realization of a dream, but the achievement of that dream remained difficult. Less than six months after construction began, three of the original tenants—the Addictive Diseases Unit of Lancaster General Hospital, the Spanish Center operated by Catholic Social Services, and Tri-County Legal Services—made arrangements to lease space in different locations, and other tenants were no longer sure of their commitment to the Neighborhood Center. Cost overruns, combined with City Council's determination not to spend any city money on the building, forced the Model Neighborhood Agency to reduce construction costs and eliminate equipment.[19]

The Neighborhood Center was dedicated on May 4, 1976, seven months after its doors opened and nine years after Drayton Bryant first suggested the construction of a building that would bring a number of social service agencies under one roof. The four-story building cost $2.1 million, almost equally contributed by HUD and Model Cities. Federal and state officials spoke at the dedication, as did Mayor Scott and Alfred C. Alspach, president of the Boys Club. The building was fully occupied with an impressive range of agencies, from Head Start to CAP to a health clinic for the southeast. Unfortunately, the Neighborhood Center, which had been conceived in controversy, would remain mired in controversy. Within three years Jack Canan, the chief city planner, denounced the award-winning building as "poorly designed," while the lack of insulation resulted in astronomical heating bills in winter and an occasional tropical shower in summer, the latter caused when the soaring temperature indoors set off the sprinkler system. The panel of lights above the swimming pool simply collapsed into the water one night, and a catalog of other flaws in design or construction continued to detract from the effective operation of the building for years to come. From an administrative standpoint the building was an expensive problem, and successive mayoral administrations, Democratic and Republican alike, kept it at arm's length. Still, residents embraced this modern structure as their own, and over the years it has remained remarkably free from graffiti and vandalism. By this important if imprecise measurement, the Neighborhood Center was more successful than City Hall ever realized.[20]

In 1980 the Lancaster Redevelopment Authority prepared to cease operations. Its final report, which covered the years from 1978 to 1980, focused on Church-Musser, the final federally funded urban renewal program, and Crosstown, a state-financed initiative that had its beginnings earlier in the decade and that, since completion of the Penn Square project, was largely a building conservation program for the southwest quadrant of the city. While the document's official title was printed in small white letters against a dark background, a photograph of a handsomely restored dwelling dominated the cover. Beneath the photograph, in a type size much larger than the official title, were words that announced the theme of the brochure: the city's revitalization. The text conceded that urban redevelopment was an "important chapter in the history of Lancaster" and an essential strategy for eliminating the junkyards and substandard housing that were so prevalent in the southeast. One passage described renewal as having been "born as an idea in the hearts and minds of the people"—an unacknowledged paraphrase of John Adams's famous description of the American Revolution—while another quoted the preamble to the 1949 Housing Act promising "a decent home in a suitable living environment for every American family." Although much of the report celebrated what redevelopment had accomplished, there were glimpses of ambivalence about the consequences of renewal. The text treated the earlier stages of redevelopment, which were characterized more by demolition than by rehabilitation, as warfare waged with a bulldozer and a wrecking ball. Charles K. Patterson, the last director of the Lancaster Redevelopment Authority, recounted in 1980 how the program worked: in the initial stages, federal officials "told us to totally replan the area. Don't do it piecemeal, they said. Don't put a band-aid on it. Perform major surgery."[21]

Instead of providing a retrospective on the full range of urban renewal activities and projects, the Redevelopment Authority's final report celebrated Church-Musser, and especially the housing rehabilitation that had been accomplished during the 1970s. Some photos captured modest homes that had been brought up to code, others showed dwellings that had been brightened by new paint, still others presented the smiling faces of people who had transformed once-substandard buildings into comfortable dwellings, or who benefited from the efforts of the Redevelopment Authority in undertaking improvements to their homes. Perhaps tellingly, five photographs spread over two pages chronicled Old Town Lancaster, while the accompanying text described the two-block area as "the phoenix of Lancaster's Urban Renewal efforts." The report lauded Old Town as a private-sector housing rehabilitation project but failed to point out that the vacant buildings slated for demolition had been condemned, acquired, and left empty by the Redevelopment Authority a decade earlier. With its brick sidewalks and interior streets, underground wiring, and old-fashioned lampposts, Old Town was "a lesson in nostalgia—a blend of the best of the old with the best of the new." Although Old Town attracted an affluent and largely white clientele, the one resident identified in the report was an African American academic, Marion Oliver, who was an administrator at nearby Millersville University. Because Old Town combined upscale housing with proximity to the black community, Oliver described it as "the best of all possible worlds."[22]

Where the report looked back on the history of urban renewal in the city, it did so with a series of quotes, four from African American residents involved in redevelopment or social services, the fifth from the director of the Spanish American Civic Association. Although the Redevelopment Authority described its efforts in the southeast as a battle against squalor, Vern Fisher of Neighborhood Services related that residents displaced by renewal "*felt* they were moved from good houses to houses that were not quite as good." Lionel Cunningham, a former member of the Redevelopment Authority board, attributed many of the problems of the southeast to absentee landlords, with the result that Church-Musser produced "very little change." While Carlos Graupera acknowledged that the Redevelopment Authority's program had resulted in significant improvements in the southeast over the previous decade, he worried that the benefits had not reached all residents and regretted the housing projects that he considered an unfortunate legacy of renewal.[23]

The Redevelopment Authority offered its own conclusions in a single page of commentary. Conversations with numerous residents gave the authority mixed reviews on its efforts. The "overall impression we garnered," the report stated, "was one of a difficult and complex problem still lacking a complete solution." Defending Church-Musser as a successful renewal program, it nevertheless conceded that the renovation of housing was only one essential step. Indeed, upgrading the housing stock usually resulted in higher rents, which many residents could not afford. Moreover, the prevalence of absentee landlords contributed to the spread of blight even as the effects of the recession of the 1970s hit the city's minority population particularly hard. Ultimately, urban renewal as a whole had serious shortcomings, in large part because it treated housing as a "separate and solvable problem, rather than as one of a network of problems that feed upon and aggravate each other." Despite the expenditure of more than $20 million in public funds and the demolition of approximately 900 buildings in the four projects (Adams, Duke, Higbee, and Church-Musser), the report concluded that urban renewal was "in itself an incomplete solution to the problems of the Southeast Area."[24]

If the Redevelopment Authority's final report was circumspect in assessing the impact of urban renewal, the mayors who led the city between 1957, when K. C. Bare called for the establishment of a Redevelopment Authority, and 1974, when the Nixon administration dismantled urban renewal and replaced it with community development block grants, were eager to place their interpretation on events. Bare pointed to Barney Google Row as an example of the kind of squalid conditions that led him to advocate an urban redevelopment program for the city. While he regretted the red tape and federal directives that, at least initially, limited the range of actions to demolition and new construction, he believed that urban renewal "did well for Lancaster." George Coe, who presided over the commencement of demolition on North Queen Street, praised renewal for "getting rid of a lot of old fire traps, buildings that were ready to fall in anyway," and for eliminating the deplorable conditions that had existed in the southeast. While he decried Lancaster Square as a monstrosity, Coe concluded that urban renewal had put the city "back on the right track toward rejuvenation." Thomas Monaghan, whose first term had preceded Coe's administration and whose second and third terms followed it, conceded that the "bulldozer approach" had been used too extensively in the city. The lone Democrat to lead the city during these years, Monaghan praised Bare for bringing a "new breath of life into the community in the postwar period" and expressed regret that systematic opposition by city and county Republicans impeded the effectiveness of the renewal efforts. Monaghan, who was widely if erroneously blamed for initiating the demolition of the west block of North Queen Street, attributed the slow pace of downtown revitalization to two events, the death of Goldie Hoffman, the developer of Lancaster Square, and the sudden closing of Hess's Department Store. The loss of the lead developer and the flagship new retail facility discouraged other potential developers and tenants, which resulted in the west side of the block standing vacant for more than a decade.[25]

As the former mayors had done, Charles K. Patterson turned the closing of the agency he headed into an occasion for reflection on the accomplishments of the Redevelopment Authority. Patterson praised the impetus behind urban renewal—the desire to rid the city of slums and to revitalize the downtown economy—and conceded that the city did not have the resources to tackle widespread blight without a massive infusion of federal aid. One of the most important accomplishments of renewal, he asserted, was the elimination of substandard housing and nuisance uses such as junkyards throughout the southeast. Patterson was less sanguine about the North Queen Street project and commercial renewal in general. He rightly pointed to one of the crucial assumptions in the various urban renewal acts, the belief that if a public authority acquired and cleared a site, private-sector redevelopers would act in the best interests of the municipality. This was "the biggest pitfall in urban renewal," he noted. "In most places, including Lancaster, private developers didn't rush in." Given the long-standing and ultimately misguided assumption that a redeveloped downtown would be a retail center, the construction of a ring of shopping centers around the city, punctuated by the opening of Park City in September 1971, made Lancaster Square an anachronism before the first stores opened. Lancaster's long, painful experience in redeveloping North Queen Street convinced business and civic leaders that private investment, not federal programs, was the key to downtown revitalization. Patterson recalled that "a resolution to the problem evolved from a segment of the business community and city leadership who recognized [that] the only salvation was to have an intensive effort of the part of community leaders to start new construction, new development, to solve the problem." The new Armstrong and National Central Bank buildings, as well as the Fulton Bank and other improvements to Penn Square and North Queen Street, were, to Patterson and other civic leaders, a strong foundation for the continuing revitalization of downtown.[26]

Given their personal investment in the process, the mayors were more positive about the changes resulting from urban renewal than any other group. And what they wrought dramatically transformed key areas of the city between 1960 and 1980. In addition to the completion of Lancaster Square and the improvements to Penn Square, a large part of the southeast had been physically improved. Adjacent to a widened South Duke Street was a tree-lined promenade unimaginatively named the Duke Street Mall. Just south of Juniata Street, the red-brick Duke Manor garden apartments occupied the site where an automobile junkyard once stood, and the entire block to the north, formerly a densely built hive of human activity, had been cleared. The Boys Club and the Lancaster Neighborhood Center replaced the small houses that had lined the west side of Rockland Street as well as the old Higbee School, while farther to the north a new Higbee (now the Martin Luther King Jr. Elementary School) was surrounding by grass and asphalt. Still farther to the north stood the new sanctuary of Faith United Church of Christ (now San Juan Bautista Spanish Catholic Church) and Church Street Towers, a high-rise apartment house for the elderly.

In striking ways urban renewal resulted in the impress of modern planning on the historic fabric of the city. If mixed use had plagued the southeast, redevelopment resulted in the relocation of almost every commercial and industrial establishment away from residential neighborhoods. If density of building had detracted from the quality of life, whole blocks of dwellings were demolished and replaced by grass. If narrow streets and a severe shortage of parking had characterized a community that developed long before the automobile, street-widenings and new housing arrangements that provided off-street parking valiantly tried to bring the old city into conformity with the demands of modern transportation. In Lancaster, as in cities across the United States, what planners considered logical steps to renew a decaying downtown and a deteriorating old neighborhood reflected what architectural critic Herbert Muschamp has termed "the postwar mythology of progress." Their plans resulted in the physical transformation of Lancaster, though what residents experienced was far different from the mayors' celebratory assessments of civic improvement: in the eyes of many residents, urban renewal changed Lancaster for the worse.[27]

This sense of loss was particularly true in the southeast, where a stable and cohesive African American neighborhood had existed throughout most of the twentieth century. One lifelong resident characterized the southeast prior to renewal in terms of a "sense of community, particularly along South Duke Street," which was the location of barbershops, restaurants, a nightclub, and other small businesses owned by African Americans. Another resident described the southeast as a "viable, socially alive" neighborhood and characterized South Duke Street as a vibrant business community. Several black churches ministered to the spiritual needs of residents; other institutions, including service clubs and fraternal lodges, gave meaning to everyday life. Throughout the southeast the face-to-face relationships historians and anthropologists consider an essential component of traditional communities defined the patterns of human interaction. A number of residents, now adults, recall being disciplined by neighbors when they were children; others remember a safe area where no one locked the front door and where neighbors were friends who could be counted on in times of need; still others remark about the sense of belonging they felt. And undoubtedly as a result of segregation, African American doctors, lawyers, ministers, teachers, and other professionals lived and worked in the southeast. These individuals were leaders of their community and examples of economic success. For all the density documented in census records, the nearby junkyards and noisome industries, the dreadful condition of buildings along Mercer Avenue and other alleys on the interior of blocks, collective memory portrays the southeast as a special place. Urban renewal destroyed the neighborhood as a physical space, and in displacing longtime residents and disrupting the overlapping contexts of everyday life, unraveled the social cohesion that many black Lancastrians attributed to their former neighborhood.[28]

One of the community leaders quoted in the Redevelopment Authority's final annual report, MacDonald Stacks of CAP, pointed out that urban renewal had changed Lancaster by providing "increased housing opportunities." He explained that because so much demolition had occurred in what traditionally had been minority neighborhoods, renewal broke down segregation by forcing residents of the southeast to move into different areas of the city. Analysis of census data from 1960 through 1980 confirms Stacks's assessment. In 1960, 2,478 of the city's total African American population of 2,628 residents, 94 percent, lived in the Seventh Ward (census tracts 8, 9, 14, and 15); in 1980, 1,073 Africans Americans lived outside the Seventh Ward (census tracts 8, 9, 15, and 16), 27 percent of the total African American population of 5,052, as did 2,308 Hispanics, 35 percent of the total Hispanic population of 6,540 in the city.[29]

Stacks did not attempt to assess the impact of population dispersion on the African American community, and census data are mute on the subject. Nevertheless, the dynamic of change was more complex than Stacks could explain in the brief passage quoted in the Redevelopment Authority report (Appendix, Table 4). Census data from these years reveal a series of profound transformations in the southeast. One development directly related to the breakdown of segregation was a sharp decline in the total population of the traditional heart of the minority neighborhood, the part of the southeast west of South Ann Street (that is, all but census tract 8). The population of census tract 9, the area between East Vine and Chester streets, declined by one-third, from 5,193 in 1960 to 3,386 in 1970, and then to 3,216 in 1980. Aggregating the two census tracts in the southern part of the 7th Ward, 14 and 15 in 1960, and comparing them with tracts 15 and 16 in 1970 and 1980 (which covered almost exactly the same area), reveals that the population of the area below Chester Street declined by one-eighth, from 5,278 in 1960 to 4,599 in 1970, and then to 4,465 in 1980. The loss in population was in large part an intended consequence of urban renewal, which attempted to alleviate the overcrowding of a densely built neighborhood by demolishing substandard housing and replacing buildings with open space, especially along South Duke Street.[30]

But the changing composition of the population was, if possible, more noticeable than the aggregate numbers. In 1960 the nonwhite population of the 7th Ward, 2,478 residents, represented 4 percent of the city's population of 61,055; in 1980 the combined black and Hispanic population of census tracts 8, 9, 15 and 16 (8,211 residents) represented 15 percent of the total population of 54,725. By 1980 most minorities lived outside census tract 9, the traditional heart of the African American community. The largest changes occurred in the area east of South Ann Street, which had 2 nonwhite residents (of 3,094 residents) in 1960 and 2,716 (of 4,170 residents) in 1980, and in the southernmost reaches of the quadrant, where the two public housing developments, Susquehanna Court and Franklin Terrace, as well as the Duke Manor Apartments, had been built. In 1960, census tracts 14 and 15 had 908 nonwhite residents (17 percent of 5,278 residents); in 1980 census tracts 15 and 16 had 3,526 nonwhite residents (71 percent of 4,968 residents). Shortly after the commencement of renewal in the southeast, in 1966, Paul Miller, then director of the Redevelopment Authority, had expressed concern that a second ghetto was emerging around the original area where minorities had resided. Fourteen years later the demolitions undertaken by the Redevelopment Authority, combined with the persistence of discrimination in housing and a rapidly growing Hispanic population, resulted in precisely the outcome Miller feared, a larger, spreading area of minority concentration in an old, declining neighborhood.[31]

Demographic change in the city caused ripples in the surrounding suburbs. Lancaster's white population, 58,427 in 1960, declined to 44,373 in 1980, a drop of almost 25 percent. Many of the whites who moved from Lancaster relocated to nearby communities. The six adjacent townships that are Lancaster City's immediate suburbs—East Hempfield, East Lampeter, Lancaster Township, Manheim Township, Manor, and West Lampeter—had a total population of 80,097 in 1980, an increase of 26,947 (51 percent) over the previous twenty years. Of this total only 630 were black (0.78 percent) and 667 Hispanic (0.83 percent) (Appendix, Table 5). Nationally, 27 percent of the African American population lived in suburbs in 1980, as did 40 percent of the Hispanic population. The differential between the national pattern and the Lancaster pattern of minority residence in suburbs is dramatic: a city where blacks and Hispanics represented more than 21 percent of the population was surrounded by suburbs where the same minorities represented 1.6 percent of all residents. Thus even as a once-segregated minority population spread throughout Lancaster, municipal boundaries proved to be more than lines drawn on a map. Federal and state fair housing laws notwithstanding, minorities seeking places to live found the city limits to be a barrier as formidable as Howard Avenue had been to earlier generations of African Americans.[32]

Urban renewal occurred simultaneously with the dramatic growth of suburbs, in Lancaster as elsewhere in the United States. During the postwar years Lancaster's suburbs experienced a construction boom, at first of single-family homes and then gradually of new commercial and industrial facilities as well. A newspaper account of Manheim Township's growth in the twelve years after World War II described suburbanization as "the most spectacular happening in this area during the past decade." Almost overnight more than twenty housing developments were built in the township. In 1957 builders were completing one new house every third day, a figure that might seem small when compared with a Levittown, but which accommodated a 40 percent increase in population between 1950 and 1958. One journalist described Manheim Township's growth as "a building boom [that] began like water bursting a dam," a simile that hardly overstated the impact of growth in the eyes of longtime residents. One individual who was born in the township shortly after the war recalls driving along one of the principal roads leading north from Lancaster City. The countryside he observed as a youth was pastoral, the neat farmsteads and massive barns testifying to fertile soils and generations of skilled agriculturists. An occasional old village dotted the countryside, and every few miles a tavern or inn stood on the side of the road, but otherwise there was no residential or commercial development beyond the immediate outskirts of the city. Over the course of his life most of those centuries-old farms have been lost. As Amish and Mennonite farm families moved away, a unique cultural landscape, a place of remarkable beauty and historical significance, was transformed into shopping centers, subdivisions, and single-family homes that epitomized all that was wrong with suburban growth. Many of the new subdivisions that sprang up in townships surrounding Lancaster validated Lewis Mumford's description of the typical postwar suburb as "a multitude of uniform, unidentifiable houses" that promoted conformity. His vision of a humanely designed and scaled residential community was transformed by market forces and government policies into a "low-grade uniform environment."[33]

The pattern of suburban development that characterized the 1950s accelerated in succeeding decades. Manheim Township's population, for example, grew from 14,855 in 1960 to 26,042 in 1980, an increase of 75 percent; East Hempfield, to the west of the city, grew from 8,417 in 1960 to 15,152 in 1980, an increase of 80 percent; and Manor Township, southwest of Lancaster, grew from 6,939 in 1960 to 11,474 in 1980, an increase of 65 percent. As was true in most metropolitan areas, the city's economic woes worsened even as the ring of overwhelmingly white suburban townships surrounding Lancaster was experiencing increasing prosperity. In 1958 Lancaster had 191 manufacturing establishments that employed 17,406 workers. Nineteen years later the number of manufacturers had dropped to 150 employing 15,200 workers. During the same period the number of manufacturers in Lancaster

County increased from 632 to 770 and employees from 42,295 to 56,400. In 1958 the city was home to 196 wholesale establishments employing 2,479 workers; in 1977 the number of wholesale establishments had dropped to 152 and the work force to 1,963. During the same period the number of wholesale establishments in Lancaster County increased from 429 to 591 and the work force from 4,275 to 7,174. In 1958 Lancaster City could boast of 908 retail establishments that employed 5,692 workers; by 1977 the number of retail businesses had dropped to 717 even though the number of employees had risen slightly to 5,865, but these totals include four department stores and more than 100 other businesses at Park City and therefore disguise the sharp drop in downtown retail. During the 1960s and 1970s Lancaster lost more than 10 percent of its work force.[34]

The dimensions of this loss are critical. As a result of the outmigration of jobs and a changing metropolitan economy, employment in manufacturing, wholesale, and downtown retail in Lancaster City dropped by more than 3,000 jobs. Because of the dramatic decline in the number of jobs, the city's unemployment rate, an enviable 3.8 percent in 1960, rose to 9.1 percent in 1980. Equally important, what had been lost were the kinds of jobs that had enabled generations of blue-collar workers with modest educational attainments to buy the red-brick row houses and duplexes that dominated Lancaster's streetscape and to provide for their families.[35] Most of the new jobs that resulted from the redevelopment of North Queen Street and Penn Square—banks and Armstrong House—were white-collar positions, which hardly matched the skill level of most of the city's work force. As good jobs became more and more difficult to find in close proximity to residential areas, particularly in the southeast, many residents began experiencing difficulty making ends meet. In 1979 the mean family income in Lancaster County was $23,058, while in Lancaster City the mean was $16,904. Census tracts 8, 9, 15 and 16, which encompassed the vast majority of the southeast quadrant, ranged from $12,264 (tract 16) to $14,508 (tract 8). In 1979 some 40 percent of residents in census tract 16 existed below the poverty line, as did 30 percent of African Americans in Lancaster and 17 percent of all city residents.[36]

Even as increasing numbers of residents of Lancaster City were experiencing economic distress, suburban townships were enjoying the fruits of middle-class life. Census data from 1979 demonstrate that the mean family income in adjacent suburbs ranged from $23,510 in East Lampeter and $24,401 in West Lampeter, to $28,260 in Lancaster Township and $30,674 in Manheim Township. Poverty levels were significantly below those of Lancaster City, ranging from 2.8 percent of families in Manheim Township and 3 percent in East Hempfield and Lancaster townships, to 3.5 percent in

Manor and 4.6 percent in East Lampeter townships. A better-educated work force, abundant jobs, and an increasing standard of living characterized life in Lancaster's suburbs in 1980. So did many other attributes that contemporaries considered essentials of suburban life, including good schools, low taxes, and a relatively crime-free environment.[37]

Before World War II, a traditional pattern of land use had defined the Lancaster County landscape. A prosperous county seat stood at its center, and other, smaller urbanized boroughs and villages dotted the countryside, surrounded by rich farmland. By 1980, suburbanization had transformed the metropolitan landscape: the national pattern of affluence on the urban periphery, and concentrated poverty at the center, had come to define Lancaster. But there was nothing inexorable about this development. In 1985, Kenneth T. Jackson concluded that "suburbanization was not an historical inevitability created by geography, technology, and culture, but rather the product of governmental policies." Jackson identified a number of federal programs that promoted new growth on the "crabgrass frontier," including FHA and Veterans Administration mortgage policies that directed housing loans to suburbs, federal and state subsidies for road building and the financing of infrastructure such as schools, sewer lines and waste treatment plants, and the deductibility of home mortgage interest and real estate taxes, which in 1981 amounted to a $35 billion subsidy for the nation's homeowners, most of whom lived in suburbs. In the years since 1980 most incentives for development have continued to direct investment toward the suburbs rather than the cities that desperately need it. In *When City and Country Collide,* agricultural economist and planner Tom Daniels cataloged a stunning number of federal policies that affect housing, economic development, transportation, agriculture, federal lands, and the environment, most of which have promoted growth on the metropolitan fringe. Many of these effects are the result of what sociologist Robert K. Merton termed the "law of unanticipated consequences" rather than of conscious intent, but the result has been the same: federal policies have caused the destruction of farmland and open space and have redirected to distant suburbs the scarce resources desperately needed to revitalize the nation's cities.[38]

The explosive growth of Lancaster's suburbs in the years since World War II was in part the product of thousands of individual decisions about the best place to live, raise a family, or locate a business.[39] Yet it is important to recognize that those decisions were not made in a vacuum, to acknowledge that suburbanization was also directly and indirectly subsidized by federal and state spending programs and federal tax policies. During the same years in which its suburbs burgeoned, Lancaster City was also deeply affected by federal policies, though with far less success than policy makers or planners anticipated. In the postwar era, Lancaster, like most older cities, desperately needed help. As a result of the lack of investment in buildings and infrastructure during the Great Depression and World War II, many older commercial buildings had deteriorated to the point of obsolescence; many residences, which lacked even the most rudimentary sanitary facilities, became unfit for human habitation. The junkyards and hazardous industries that stood in close proximity to homes in the southeast represented serious threats to the well-being of residents. Given these conditions, there is no doubt that redevelopment and some demolition was essential.

But the kind of urban renewal program that would be undertaken would determine the future of the city and especially affect the minority population that lived in Lancaster's southeast quadrant. Tragically, the Lancaster Redevelopment Authority undertook not curative actions but what Charles K. Patterson called radical surgery. Urban renewal resulted in the demolition of 926 buildings, necessitating the relocation of almost 1,100 families and 350 individuals, the vast majority in the southeast, and also necessitated the demolition of 171 businesses. The Redevelopment Authority was also responsible for rehabilitating almost 1,600 structures, most of them residential, while the Lancaster Housing Authority erected 710 new housing units, most of which were public housing apartments for the elderly. Government funding for the various projects totaled roughly $37,100,000 (at a net cost, after sale of land to developers, of $28,700,000), two-thirds of which came from Washington.

This public spending, together with perhaps as much as $30 million in private-sector investment, failed to revitalize downtown Lancaster and maintain the attractiveness of neighborhoods by improving the quality of residential life. Thus at the end of the renewal process the city was vulnerable to the forces of decline. Despite the organization in 1979 of the Greater Lancaster Corporation, a corporate-sponsored agency to promote downtown, economic and social conditions in the city worsened over the following decade: in 1990 more than one in five residents of Lancaster lived in poverty; the white population, 43,133 in 1980, declined to approximately 36,000 in 1990, a decade in which the African American and Hispanic residents increased from 21 to 35 percent of the total population. And as jobs continued to migrate to the suburbs, the unemployment rate for African Americans rose to 33 percent and for Hispanics to 44 percent, with the result that hyperconcentrations of poverty existed in the southeast. The combination of an urban redevelopment program that disrupted a traditional African American neighborhood, the influx of large numbers of Hispanics, and the migration of jobs, wealth, and a substantial percent of the city's white population to the suburbs in the years between 1960 and 1980 left Lancaster a city that was poorer and less economically viable than at any time since the beginnings of industrialization more than a century and a half earlier. Ultimately, urban redevelopment exacted human as well as financial costs that continue to haunt the city and its people, that continue to detract from the quality of metropolitan life. This is the nation's story, America's collective tragedy.[40]

Appendix

TABLE 1. *Lancaster city population, 1940–1990*

		Percent Change	Nonwhite	Percent Nonwhite
1940	61,435	—	—	—
1950	63,774	4	1,123	1.7
1960	61,055	–4.3	2,628	4.3
1960*	59,881	–6.1	—	—
1970	57,690	–5.5	4,525	7.8
1980	54,725	–5.1	10,252	18.7
1990	55,551	1.5	16,183	29.1

SOURCES: U.S. Bureau of the Census, *Census of Population*, 1940, 1950, 1960, 1970; U.S. Bureau of the Census, *1980 Census of Population and Housing, Census Tracts, Lancaster, Pa., Standard Metropolitan Statistical Area* (Government Printing Office, 1983); Pennsylvania State Data Center, *2001 Lancaster County Data Book* (Pennsylvania State Data Center, 2001).

**Population within 1950 area of the city.*

TABLE 2. *Population, six suburban townships, 1950–1980*

	1950	1960	1970	1980
East Hempfield	4,322	8,417	11,739	15,152
East Lampeter	5,166	7,399	8,834	9,760
Lancaster Twp.	6,859	10,020	10,329	10,833
Manheim	9,289	14,855	21,539	26,042
Manor	4,461	6,939	9,769	11,474
West Lampeter	4,119	5,520	6,374	6,836
Totals	34,216	53,150	68,584	80,097

SOURCES: U.S. Bureau of the Census, *Census of Population*, 1950, 1960, 1970, 1980.

TABLE 3. *Retail sales, 1948–1967 (in thousands)*

	City	County	Manheim Twp.	Lancaster Twp.
1948	90,806	215,371	—	—
1954	120,513	268,262	—	—
1958	139,069	309,049	—	—
1963	111,020	387,430	4,942	1,491
1967	138,357	508,209	50,721	20,885

SOURCES: U.S. Bureau of the Census, *Census of Business: Retail Trade—Area Statistics* for 1948, 1958 (which also contains 1954 figures), 1963, and 1967, except city retail sales for 1958, which is based on sales management data as reported in *Lancaster Moves Ahead* (Lancaster City Planning Commission, 1959), 45. This figure is probably somewhat inaccurate; the same report for total county retail sales was $296,338,000, 4.1% below the amount reported using census data.

TABLE 4. *Minority population in Lancaster, 1960–1990*

	African American	Hispanic
1960	2,628	—
1970	4,269	2,077
1980	5,052	6,540
1990	6,777	11,444

SOURCES: U.S. Bureau of the Census, *Census of Population*, 1960, 1970, 1980, 1990; *County and City Data Book 1977.*
Note: The Census of 1970 identifies "persons of Spanish Heritage"; the 1980 and 1990 Censuses enumerate "persons of Hispanic origin . . . of any race."

TABLE 5. *Population by race, suburban townships, 1980*

	Population	Blacks	Hispanics	Total Nonwhites
East Hempfield	15,152	114 (0.8%)	132 (0.9%)	246 (1.6%)
East Lampeter	9,760	85 (0.87%)	99 (1.0%)	184 (1.87%)
Lancaster	10,833	157 (1.4%)	180 (1.7%)	337 (3.1%)
Manheim	26,042	151 (0.6%)	130 (0.5%)	281 (1.07%)
Manor	11,474	57 (0.5%)	79 (0.7%)	136 (1.18%)
West Lampeter	6,836	66 (0.97%)	47 (0.69%)	113 (1.65%)
Totals	80,097	630 (0.78%)	667 (0.83%)	1,297 (1.61%)

SOURCE: U.S. Bureau of the Census, *Census of Population*, 1980.

Notes

INTRODUCTION

1. See Lancaster Redevelopment Authority, *1978–1980 Comprehensive Report* (Lancaster, Pa., 1980).

2. Ibid., 10, 2.

3. Ibid., 2; Paul R. Diller, letter to Mrs. Goldie Hoffman, October 29, 1968, Bureau of Planning, City of Lancaster. On the effects of government programs and policies in promoting suburban growth, see Kenneth T. Jackson, *Crabgrass Frontier: The Suburbanization of the United States* (New York, 1985), 190–218, 248–51; Tom Daniels, *When City and Country Collide: Managing Growth in the Metropolitan Fringe* (Washington, D.C., 1999), 107–34; and Thomas W. Hanchett, "The Other 'Subsidized Housing': Federal Aid to Suburbanization, 1940s–1960s," in John F. Bauman et al., eds., *From Tenements to the Taylor Homes: In Search of an Urban Housing Policy in Twentieth-Century America* (University Park, Pa., 2000), 163–79.

4. Jerome H. Wood Jr., *Conestoga Crossroads: Lancaster, Pennsylvania, 1730–1790* (Harrisburg, Pa., 1979); James T. Lemon, *The Best Poor Man's Country: A Geographical Study of Early Southeastern Pennsylvania* (Baltimore, 1972); Wilbur Zelinsky, "The Pennsylvania Town: An Overdue Geographical Account," *Geographical Review* 67 (April 1977): 127–47; Thomas R. Winpenny, *Industrial Progress and Human Welfare: The Rise of the Factory System in Nineteenth-Century Lancaster* (Washington, D.C., 1982), 87–98, 121–23; John Ward Willson Loose, *The Heritage of Lancaster* (Woodland Hills, Calif., 1978), 83–149.

5. Robert S. and Helen Merrell Lynd, *Middletown: A Study in American Culture* (New York, 1929), 97–98. See also Richard Wightman Fox, "Epitaph for Middletown: Robert S. Lynd and the Analysis of Consumer Culture," in Richard Wightman Fox and T. J. Jackson Lears, eds., *The Culture of Consumption: Critical Essays in American History, 1880–1980* (New York, 1983), 103–41.

6. Works Progress Administration, *Real Property Survey: Lancaster, Pennsylvania* (n.p., 1936), 18, 27, 31 and passim. The obsolescence of much of the city's building fabric is a theme of Michael Baker Jr., *A Comprehensive Municipal Plan: City of Lancaster, Pennsylvania* (Rochester, Pa., 1945).

7. These various data are drawn from the following census reports: *Census of Population*, 1950, 1960, 1970, and 1980; *Census of Population and Housing*, 1960, 1970, and 1980; and *County and City Data Book*, 1962.

8. John D. Fairfield, *The Mysteries of the Great City: The Politics of Urban Design, 1877–1937* (Columbus, Ohio, 1993); Jon C. Teaford, *The Rough Road to Renaissance: Urban Revitalization in America, 1940–1985* (Baltimore, 1990), 11.

9. U.S. Housing Act of 1949, 81st Cong., 1st sess., ch. 338, July 15, 1949, in 63 Stat., 413–44; "Urban Redevelopment Law," Act of 1945, P.L. 991, no. 385; Lancaster Redevelopment Authority, Minutes, July 9, 1957, Bureau of Planning,

City of Lancaster. The literature on the Housing Act and the beginnings of urban renewal is vast, but see especially James Q. Wilson, ed., *Urban Renewal: The Record and the Controversy* (Cambridge, Mass., 1966); Mark I. Gelfand, *A Nation of Cities: The Federal Government and Urban America, 1933–1965* (New York, 1975), 136–56; Teaford, *Rough Road to Renaissance,* 105–21; Marc A. Weiss, "The Origins and Legacy of Urban Renewal," in Pierre Clavel et al., eds., *Urban and Regional Planning in an Age of Austerity* (New York, 1980), 53–80; John H. Mollenkopf, *The Contested City* (Princeton, 1983), 72–81; Alexander von Hoffman, "A Study in Contradictions: The Origins and Legacy of the Housing Act of 1949," to be published in *Housing Policy Debate;* Gail Radford, *Modern Housing for America: Policy Struggles in the New Deal Era* (Chicago, 1996). Arnold Hirsch uses the term "containment" to describe housing policy in *Making the Second Ghetto: Race and Housing in Chicago, 1940–1960* (Chicago, 1998), as does Thomas J. Sugrue in *The Origins of the Urban Crisis: Race and Inequality in Postwar Detroit* (Princeton, 1996).

10. U.S. Housing Act of 1949, 414–24.

11. Although the terms "renewal" and "redevelopment" quickly became conflated in policy discourse, redevelopment—clearance and rebuilding—was the intent of the 1949 act, while the term "renewal" has generally been associated with the Housing Act of 1954, which made possible the rehabilitation or restoration of existing buildings rather than wholesale clearance. In Lancaster, public officials and citizens used the terms interchangeably.

12. Von Hoffman, "A Study in Contradictions"; Judith A. Martin and Antony Goddard, *Past Choices / Present Landscapes: The Impact of Urban Renewal on the Twin Cities* (Minneapolis, 1989), 1, 3, 177; June Manning Thomas, *Redevelopment and Race: Planning a Finer City in Postwar Detroit* (Baltimore, 1997), 3; Roger Biles, "Public Housing and the Postwar Urban Renaissance, 1949–1973," in Bauman et al., *From Tenements to the Taylor Homes,* 143–62.

13. Peirce F. Lewis, "Small Town in Pennsylvania," *Annals of the Association of American Geographers* 62 (June 1972): 328.

14. Zelinsky, "Pennsylvania Town," 127–28.

15. Sinclair Lewis, *Main Street: The Story of Carol Kennicott* (New York, 1920), n.p.

16. My analysis in this and the following paragraphs has been influenced by the writings of a number of talented historians, including Mollenkopf, *Contested City;* Teaford, *Rough Road to Renaissance;* Hirsch, *Making the Second Ghetto;* John F. Bauman, *Public Housing, Race, and Renewal: Urban Planning in Philadelphia, 1920–1974* (Philadelphia, 1987); and Sugrue, *Origins of the Urban Crisis.*

17. Discussion of an arterial highway was a component of most planning studies undertaken in Lancaster during the 1950s and 1960s. The city completed a Major Thoroughfare Plan as part of its new comprehensive plan in the mid-1960s, but when that plan was never completed the planning commission published a separate document to make the case for significant road improvements in 1968. That document called for creation of a north-south arterial highway with four major traffic interchanges within the city, significant improvements to existing roads, and enhancements to existing roads within the central business district. See Lancaster City Planning Commission, *Major Thoroughfare Plan* (1965, 1968).

18. Robert R. Archibald, *A Place to Remember: Using History to Build Community* (Walnut Creek, Calif., 1999), 43–46.

19. Lancaster Redevelopment Authority, *1978–1980 Comprehensive Report*, 2.

CHAPTER 1

1. A local newspaper stated: "The row of 14 houses has been condemned almost annually for about 20 years but the mayor's statement today is the first promise of direct action." "Mayor to Push for Elimination of 'Google Row,'" *Lancaster New Era*, September 12, 1956.

2. "85 P.C. Negro Homes Unfit to Live In," *Lancaster New Era*, May 13, 1944.

3. Ibid.; Michael Baker Jr., *A Comprehensive Municipal Plan: City of Lancaster, Pennsylvania* (Rochester, Pa., 1945), 96–97 (hereafter cited as *Baker Plan*).

4. "85 P.C. Negro Homes Unfit to Live In," *Lancaster New Era*, May 13, 1944; "'Barney Google Row' 1st Target in War on Slums," *Lancaster New Era*, January 11, 1950; *Baker Plan*, 96–97.

5. In 1936, 86.3 percent of all residential structures in Lancaster were brick; only 8.9 percent were frame. See Works Progress Administration, *Real Property Survey: Lancaster, Penna.* (n.p., 1936), 31.

6. Deed of transfer from Emanuel C. Reigart to Patrick Kelly, March 13, 1861, Recorder of Deeds, Lancaster County Courthouse, describes the property as containing two springs and its use as farmland; "City Starts Demolition of 'Google Row,'" *Lancaster New Era*, July 10, 1957; deed of transfer from Anna Cohn to Barney Cohn, October 24, 1934, Recorder of Deeds, Lancaster County Courthouse, mentions "fifteen (15) frame Dwelling houses" on the site; *Baker Plan*, 65, 98. The dating of Shantytown to World War II is corroborated by the absence of any housing in the area in block statistics compiled as part of the 1940 federal census. See U.S. Department of Commerce, Bureau of the Census, *Sixteenth Census of the United States, Housing*, pamphlet reporting block statistics for Lancaster, table 3, "Characteristics of Housing for Wards by Blocks: 1940." The blocks comprising Shantytown, 17th Ward blocks 492–496, contained only three structures in 1940.

7. For information on the comic strip, see Ron Goulart, ed., *Encyclopaedia of American Comics* (New York, 1990), 20–22; for the Billy Rose / Con Conrad song, see David Ewen, ed., *American Popular Songs from the Revolutionary War to the Present* (New York, 1966), 31–32. The Rose/Conrad song is included in *100 Best Songs of the 20s and 30s* (New York, 1973). It is also possible that the row of shacks was named after its longtime owner, Barney Cohn. In its condemnation proceedings the Board of Health referred to the 700 block of Southeast Avenue as "Barney Cohen [*sic*] Row," which the Board termed its "more sedate name." "Barney Google Row Doomed by Board of Health," *Lancaster Intelligencer Journal*, June 7, 1950.

8. Information on Leroy T. Hopkins Sr. and early residents of Barney Google Row provided by Leroy T. Hopkins Jr. For evidence of the activities of the Klan in Pennsylvania during these years, see Philip Jenkins, *Hoods and Shirts: The Extreme Right in Pennsylvania, 1925–1950* (Chapel Hill, N.C., 1997); Emerson Hunsberger Loucks, *The Ku Klux Klan in Pennsylvania: A Study in Nativism* (Harrisburg, Pa., 1936); Donald A. Crownover, "The Ku Klux Klan in Lancaster County, 1923–1924," *Journal of the Lancaster County Historical Society* 68 (Easter 1964): 63–77; and Andrew T. Kuhn, "The Ku Klux Klan in Lancaster County," ibid., 98 (Fall 1996): 106–23. For the history of blacks in Conestoga Township, see Leroy T. Hopkins Jr., "Hollow Memories: African Americans in Conestoga Township," ibid., 101 (Winter 2000): 145–66. See also *Baker Plan*, 65, and "178 Homes Here Unfit to Live In, More Than 100 Called 'Hopeless,'" *Lancaster New Era*, February 8, 1950.

9. *Real Property Survey, Lancaster, Penna.*, 60. Planner Michael Baker estimated that the annual income from rents paid by tenants of Barney Google Row was 40 to 50 percent of the total capitalization of the property (*Baker Plan*, 97).

10. For discussions of earlier federal involvement in housing, see Christian Topalov, "Scientific Urban Planning and the Ordering of Daily Life: The First 'War Housing' Experiment in the United States, 1917–1919," *Journal of Urban History* 17 (November 1990): 14–45; Gail Radford, *Modern Housing for America: Policy Struggles in the New Deal Era* (Chicago, 1996), 111–98; Marc A. Weiss, *The Rise of the Community Builders: The American Real Estate Industry and Urban Land Planning* (New York, 1987); Paul Conkin, *Tomorrow a New World: The New Deal Community Program* (Ithaca, N.Y., 1959); Joseph L. Arnold, *The New Deal in the Suburbs* (Columbus, Ohio, 1971); and Kenneth T. Jackson, *Crabgrass Frontier: The Suburbanization of the United States* (New York, 1985).

11. *Baker Plan*, 85; U.S. Housing Act of 1949, 81st Cong., 1st sess., ch. 338, July 15, 1949, in 63 Stat., 413–44. The literature on the Housing Act and the beginnings of urban renewal is vast, but see especially James Q. Wilson, ed., *Urban Renewal: The Record and the Controversy* (Cambridge, Mass., 1966); Mark I. Gelfand, *A Nation of Cities: The Federal Government and Urban America, 1933–1965* (New York, 1975), 136–56; Jon C. Teaford, *The Rough Road to Renaissance: Urban Revitalization in America, 1940–1985* (Baltimore, 1990), 105–21; Marc A. Weiss, "The Origins and Legacy of Urban Renewal," in Pierre Clavel et al., eds., *Urban and Regional Planning in an Age of Austerity* (New York, 1980), 53–80; and John H. Mollenkopf, *The Contested City* (Princeton, 1983), 72–81.

12. "City Health Board Ready to Crack Down on Slums," *Lancaster New Era*, January 5, 1950; "'Barney Google Row' 1st Target in War on Slums," ibid., January 11, 1950; "Owners of 178 Unfit Houses Get Notices to 'Clean Up,'" ibid., February 15, 1950; "'Barney Google Row' to Be Razed," *Lancaster Intelligencer Journal*, June 3, 1950; "City May Ask Aid in Finding Homes for Slum Families," *Lancaster New Era*, June 6, 1950; "75 Families Ordered to Quit Shantytown Homes," ibid., June 7, 1950; "City Health Board Ready to Crack Down on Slums," ibid., January 5, 1950. For Baltimore's code-enforcement program, see Teaford, *Rough Road to Renaissance*, 113–20. For Charles's housing standards, see "List of Minimum Requirements in Housing Issued," *Lancaster Intelligencer Journal*, April 11, 1951. For the eventual adoption of a housing code, see Thomas J. Monaghan to David M. Walker, Regional Administrator, Housing and Home Finance Agency, October 30, 1958, Bureau of Planning; and "Lancaster City Housing Code," *Journal of City Council*, January 19, 1960, 109–33, February 16, 1960, 152–54.

13. The problem of finding replacement housing for residents of condemned buildings was recognized at the very outset of the city's campaign against slums but remained unsolved for years. See, for example, "City Health Board Ready to Crack Down on Slums," *Lancaster New Era*, January 5, 1950; "City May Ask Aid in Finding Homes for Slum Families," ibid., June 6, 1950; "New Problem Develops in Slum Battle," *Lancaster Intelligencer Journal*, June 29, 1950.

14. "75 Families Ordered to Quit Shantytown Homes," *Lancaster New Era*, June 7, 1950; *Baker Plan*, 97–98; "Goodhart Raps Housing 'Blunders,'" *Lancaster Intelligencer Journal*, November 5, 1949; *Journal of City Council*, January 2, 1950, 57.

15. "Mayor's Message," *Journal of City Council*, January 2, 1951, 33; "Mayor Stud-

ies Shack Problem at Housing Project," *Lancaster New Era,* March 20, 1951; "6 Shacks in Shantytown Eliminated," ibid., August 1, 1951; "County Aids in Bringing an End to Shantytown," *Lancaster Intelligencer Journal,* January 3, 1951; "21 at Public Meeting Vote Slum 'Fact-Finding' Group," *Lancaster New Era,* May 22, 1951; "Bureau of Health," *Journal of City Council,* January 2, 1951, 6.

16. "Shantytown Population Is Gradually 'Melting Away,' City's Slum Report Shows," *Lancaster New Era,* February 21, 1952; "Shantytown Residents Say 'How Dare You?'" ibid., February 22, 1952; "13 Dwellings Taken from Slum Roster," ibid., April 7, 1952; "Mayor's Report," *Journal of City Council,* July 22, 1952, 259; ibid., January 5, 1953, 34; "Bureau of Health," ibid., January 5, 1953, 21.

17. "This Is Sunnyside," *The Sunday News,* July 15, 1956; "Mayor's Message," *Journal of City Council,* January 2, 1951, 33; "Bureau of Health," ibid., January 7, 1952, 29; ibid., January 5, 1953, 21; ibid., January 4, 1954, 6–7; ibid., January 4, 1955, 10.

18. See, for example, Harold K. Hogg's statement that the figure of 41 substandard dwellings reported in 1954 "does not include Barney Google Row or Shanty Town." "Bureau of Health," *Journal of City Council,* January 4, 1954, 6, January 5, 1953, 21; City of Lancaster, Board of Health, Minutes, September 12, 1956, November 19, 1956; "Mayor to Push for Elimination of 'Google Row,'" *Lancaster New Era,* September 12, 1956; "City Gives Official Sanction to Erase Barney Google Row Blight," *Lancaster Intelligencer Journal,* October 12, 1956.

19. City of Lancaster, Board of Health, Minutes, November 19, 1956.

20. Ibid., December 13, 1956; Benj. F. Charles to Mrs. Anna Gottlieb [*sic*], February 20, 1957, typescript copy in Board of Health, Minutes; "Conditions as Found 700 Block Southeast Ave., February 16, 1957," typescript report in Board of Health Minutes; Board of Health, Minutes, March 13, 1957.

21. "12 Families Stay in Google 'Row,'" *Lancaster New Era,* April 2, 1957; "Court OKs City Plan to Raze 'Google Row,'" ibid., June 20, 1957; "City Will Buy 1 'Google' Home," ibid., June 21, 1957; "Google Row Appeal Looms," ibid., June 24, 1957; "City to Purchase All Google Row," ibid., June 29, 1957; "City Pays $7,000 for Google Row," ibid., July 1, 1957; "City Starts Demolition of 'Google Row,'" ibid., July 10, 1957; "Squatter Families Plop into Empty Google Row," ibid., July 8, 1957.

22. "City Starts Demolition of 'Google Row,'" *Lancaster New Era,* July 10, 1957; "Barney Google Row Almost Gone," ibid., July 13, 1957; "When Slums Are Razed Where Do People Go?" ibid., July 31, 1957.

23. "15th and Last House Razed on Barney Google Row," *Lancaster New Era,* August 26, 1957; "Shantytown Shack Is Razed," ibid., August 13, 1957; "Only 6 Dwellings Remain Standing in Shantytown," *Lancaster Intelligencer Journal,* September 25, 1957; "City Condemns Four Houses in 7th Ward as 'Unfit for Humans,'" *Lancaster New Era,* January 25, 1957.

24. Both Arnold Hirsch, in *Making the Second Ghetto: Race and Housing in Chicago, 1940–1960* (1983; reprint, Chicago, 1998), and Thomas J. Sugrue, in *The Origins of the Urban Crisis: Race and Inequality in Postwar Detroit* (Princeton, 1996), use the term "containment" to describe a housing policy that attempts to restrict the location of public housing to neighborhoods where a preponderance of racial minorities already live.

25. Information on the southeast drawn from Sanborn maps and city directories; typescript accompanying the Residential Security Map, Lancaster, Pennsylvania, Home Owners' Loan Corporation Records, National Archives and

Records Administration, Washington, D.C.; Works Progress Administration, *Real Property Survey: Lancaster, Penna.* (n.p., 1936), 32–33, 54–55, and passim; *Baker Plan*, 85–98. See also "Slum Areas 12 Years Ago Still Slums Today," *Lancaster New Era*, April 1, 1957. In 1958 the Lancaster Redevelopment Authority concluded: "The southeast quadrant of the City[,] bounded by East King Street on the north and South Queen Street on the west, provided clear and unquestionable evidence as containing the worst characteristics of blight and deterioration in the City." *General Neighborhood Renewal Plan Application for Adams-Musser Towns Project, Urban Renewal Area*, October 30, 1959, 8, copy in Bureau of Planning, City of Lancaster.

26. K. C. Bare, "Annual Report of the Mayor," *Journal of City Council*, January 8, 1957, 2; "Report of the Mayor, First Quarter 1957," ibid., April 16, 1957, 186; "Mayor Says City May Act to Build Adequate Houses," *Lancaster New Era*, January 8, 1957; "Slum Tour Bares Crowding & Filth," ibid., March 14, 1957; "Slums Solution Seen as Urgent," ibid., March 16, 1957.

27. Members of the Citizen Housing Committee were quoted in "Slums Solution Seen as Urgent," *Lancaster New Era*, March 16, 1957; Lancaster Redevelopment Authority, Minutes, July 9, 1957, Lancaster Redevelopment Authority Records, Lancaster County Historical Society.

28. Kenneth T. Jackson, *Crabgrass Frontier: The Suburbanization of the United States* (New York, 1985), 195–203; idem, "Race, Ethnicity, and Real Estate Appraisal: The Home Owners' Loan Corporation and the Federal Housing Administration," *Journal of Urban History* 6 (August 1980): 419–52; Raymond A. Mohl, "Making the Second Ghetto in Metropolitan Miami, 1940–1960," ibid., 21 (March 1995): 395–427.

29. "Report of the Citizen Housing Committee," *Journal of City Council*, May 21, 1957, 267; J. A. Schram, statement recorded in *The Complete Report on Lancaster Looks Ahead: A Forum, September 18, 19, and 20, 1956* (Lancaster, Pa., 1956), 175; U.S. Bureau of the Census, *Census of Housing: 1950. Block Statistics, Lancaster, Pennsylvania* (Washington, D.C., 1952), table 3; interview with Thomas Hyson, August 3, 1998; U.S. Bureau of the Census, *Census of Population and Housing: 1960. Census Tracts, Lancaster, Pa.*, table P-1.

30. Members of the Citizen Housing Committee were quoted in "Slums Solution Seen as Urgent," *Lancaster New Era*, March 16, 1957.

31. "Report of the Citizen Housing Committee," 266–68.

32. Ibid., 268–72, 265–66, 280–81; "Slum Solution Seen as Urgent," *Lancaster New Era*, March 16, 1957; resolution creating the Redevelopment Authority of the City of Lancaster, *Journal of City Council*, May 21, 1957, 280–81; "Urban Redevelopment Law," Act of 1945, P.L. 991, no. 385; Lancaster Redevelopment Authority, Minutes, July 9, 1957; "City Provides $100,000 for Slum Clearance," *Lancaster New Era*, May 21, 1957.

33. See, for example "When Slums Are Razed Where Do the People Go?" *Lancaster New Era*, July 31, 1957; and Jerry Sapienza's five-part series "Housing Disgrace," ibid., September 13–17, 1957.

34. Lancaster Redevelopment Authority, Minutes, July 9, 1957; "City Seen Qualified to Get U.S. Aid for Urban Renewal," *Lancaster Intelligencer Journal*, October 10, 1957.

35. This assessment of the residents of Hickory Tree Heights is based on Lancaster City Housing Authority, Minutes, November 10, 1960.

36. See, for example, the statements by Alfred Alspach, chair of the Lancaster Housing Authority, and by home-builder

Emanuel Murry in *Lancaster Looks Ahead,* 168, 163.

37. "85 P.C. Negro Homes Unfit to Live In," *Lancaster New Era,* May 13, 1944; B. F. Charles to Mrs. Anna Gottlieb [*sic*], February 20, 1957, typescript copy in Board of Health, Minutes.

38. John O. Shirk, *The Lancaster Housing Study* (Lancaster Redevelopment Authority, 1966), 7, 39–40, 95–97, examines the pattern of housing discrimination; the 1944 statistic is from "85 P.C. Negro Homes Unfit to Live In," *Lancaster New Era,* May 13, 1944, while census figures are drawn from Shirk, *Lancaster Housing Study* and from Dalton, Dalton, Little & Newport, *Community Improvement Program: Lancaster, Pennsylvania,* May 1973, 2–8; Lancaster City Planning Commission, *Lancaster Looks Ahead, Volume I* (1959), 28.

39. J. A. Schram, quoted in *Lancaster Looks Ahead,* 175; Shirk, *Lancaster Housing Study,* 7, 39.

CHAPTER 2

1. Wilbur Zelinsky, "The Pennsylvania Town: An Overdue Geographical Account," *Geographical Review* 67 (April 1977): 127–47.

2. "Experts Point Out Ways to Relieve City's Traffic Problems," *Lancaster New Era,* August 14, 1926; John Nolen, *Lancaster, Pennsylvania Comprehensive City Plan, 1929* (Cambridge, Mass., 1929); Albert W. Gotch to John Nolen, November 21, 1929, March 5, 1930, John Nolen Papers, Department of Manuscripts and University Archives, Kroch Library, Cornell University, Ithaca, New York. For the political context of these planning efforts, see Richard J. Gerz Jr., "Urban Reform and the Musser Coalition in the City of Lancaster, 1921–1930," *Journal of the Lancaster County Historical Society* 78 (Easter 1974): 49–110.

3. Works Progress Administration, *Real Property Survey: Lancaster, Pennsylvania* (n.p., 1936), 18, 27, 31, and passim.

4. *Real Property Survey: Lancaster,* 27; D. E. Cary, "Annual Report of the Mayor," in *Journal of City Council,* January 2, 1945, 20; Jon C. Teaford, *The Rough Road to Renaissance: Urban Revitalization in America, 1940–1985* (Baltimore, 1990), 10–43. See also John F. Bauman, "Visions of a Postwar City: A Perspective on Urban Planning in Philadelphia and the Nation, 1942–1945," *Urbanism Past and Present* 6 (Winter-Spring 1990–1991): 1–11. Alison Isenberg's forthcoming book, *Downtown Democracy: The Aesthetics and Values of Main Street Investment in the Twentieth Century,* documents the efforts of downtown merchants in a number of cities to fight the effects of the Great Depression by undertaking modernization of storefronts.

5. Michael Baker Jr., *A Comprehensive Municipal Plan: City of Lancaster, Pennsylvania* (Rochester, Pa., 1945), 62–63, 77–79 (hereafter cited as *Baker Plan*).

6. Ibid., 52–53, 194–207; Kenneth T. Jackson, *Crabgrass Frontier: The Suburbanization of the United States* (New York, 1985), 257–61. For a broader discussion of the critical importance of the automobile and traffic in these years, see Scott L. Bottles, *Los Angeles and the Automobile: The Making of the Modern City* (Berkeley and Los Angeles, 1987); and Alan A. Altshuler, "The Intercity Freeway," in Donald A. Krueckeberg, ed., *Introduction to Planning History in the United States* (New Brunswick, N.J., 1983), 190–234.

7. *Baker Plan,* 208–11; "Completed Bypass Seen from Air," *Sunday News,* November 22, 1953; Jack Brubaker, "Brawl over Sprawl Begins in the 1950s," ibid., August 1, 1999.

8. "Plan Proposed to Divert Heavy Traffic," *Lancaster Intelligencer Journal,* December 11, 1952.

9. See, for example, "Annual Report Bureau of Traffic," *Journal of City Council,* January 4, 1955, 3–6; ibid., January 2, 1956,

3–7; Ned L. Wall, "New Approach Must Be Made to Cope with City's Traffic," *Lancaster Intelligencer Journal,* July 5, 1957.

10. "Annual Report Bureau of Traffic," *Journal of City Council,* January 4, 1955, 3–6; ibid., January 2, 1956, 3–7.

11. "Updating of Baker Plan Seen as 1955 Project," *Lancaster Intelligencer Journal,* November 5, 1954; K. C. Bare, "Report of the Mayor," *Journal of City Council,* April 26, 1955, 185–86.

12. K. C. Bare, "Annual Report of the Mayor," *Journal of City Council,* January 4, 1955, 47; "Growth of Area Spurs Formation of Planning Units," *Lancaster Intelligencer Journal,* January 19, 1955. For Klein's support of regional planning, see "Community Planners Cross Boundaries to Solve Problems," *Sunday News,* November 22, 1953.

13. "Move Made to Up-Date Baker Plan," *Lancaster Intelligencer Journal,* September 16, 1955; "Updating Baker Plan Discussed by Commission," ibid., October 1, 1955; Lancaster City Planning Commission, Minutes, February 2, 1956, Bureau of Planning, City of Lancaster.

14. See Lancaster City Planning Commission, Minutes; as an example of rampant suburbanization during this period, see "Commission Okays Plan on 283 Homes Off Route 30 East," *Lancaster Intelligencer Journal,* March 23, 1956; Andrew Torchia, "A Study in Suburbia—Manheim Township," *Lancaster New Era,* May 12–15, 1958; "The Announcement of the Forum," in *The Complete Report on Lancaster Looks Ahead: A Forum, September 18, 19, and 20, 1956* (Lancaster, Pa., n.d.). Hereafter cited as *Lancaster Looks Ahead.*

15. *Lancaster Looks Ahead,* 269, and passim.

16. Ibid., 40–41, and passim.

17. Ibid., 13, 16, and passim. For a thoughtful discussion of planned decentralization as a response to the Cold War, see Michael Dudley, "Sprawl as Strategy: City Planners Face the Bomb," *Journal of Planning Education and Research,* forthcoming.

18. *Lancaster Looks Ahead,* 52, 158, 42, and passim.

19. Ibid., 168, 163, and passim; Wolcott and McCarthy are quoted in John F. Bauman, *Public Housing, Race, and Renewal: Urban Planning in Philadelphia, 1920–1974* (Philadelphia, 1987), 93.

20. *Lancaster Looks Ahead,* 163; Bauman, *Public Housing, Race, and Renewal,* 120; William H. Whyte Jr., ed., *The Exploding Metropolis* (1958; reprint, Berkeley and Los Angeles, 1993), 51. The best explication of the ways in which federal policies redirected investment from downtown to the urban periphery is Kenneth T. Jackson's *Crabgrass Frontier.* On the Allegheny Conference and the Greater Baltimore Committee, see Teaford, *Rough Road to Renaissance,* 45–54; Roy Lubove, *Twentieth Century Pittsburgh: Government, Business, and Environmental Change* (New York, 1969), 106–41; and John Mollenkopf, *The Contested City* (Princeton, 1983).

21. *Lancaster Intelligencer Journal,* September 21, 1956; *Lancaster Looks Ahead,* 9, 269–70.

22. *Lancaster Looks Ahead,* 268–70; Groff and Bare are quoted in "City, County Gov't to Get Forum Data," *Lancaster Intelligencer Journal,* September 21, 1956.

23. Lancaster County Planning Commission, Minutes, Lancaster County Court House, Lancaster, Pennsylvania; Torchia, "A Study in Suburbia—Manheim Twp. Has Growing Problems—Like All Suburbs," *Lancaster New Era,* May 13, 1958.

24. "2d Proposal Presented for Area Planning," *Lancaster Intelligencer Journal,* October 19, 1956. One of the consultants interviewed, Michael Baker Engineers, had been responsible for the city's 1945

plan, while another, Clifton E. Rodgers & Associates of Harrisburg, would later be commissioned to undertake a study of Lancaster's central business district. See also "Area Planners Delay Action on Director," ibid., October 3, 1957; "Planners to Gently Woo Cooperation Within Area," ibid., October 14, 1959; Lancaster City Planning Commission, Minutes, February 2, 1956; and Lancaster County Planning Commission, Minutes, October 13, 1958, and August 10, 1959.

25. Ned L. Wall, "Planners' Crystal Ball Shows A New Lancaster 10 Yrs. Hence," *Lancaster Intelligencer Journal,* July 4, 1957. The only reference to the deliberations or findings of the group in City Planning Commission minutes is a decision, at the meeting of August 6, 1957, to order reprints of the newspaper series.

26. *Baker Plan,* 193–207; Wall, "Planners' Crystal Ball Shows a New Lancaster 10 Yrs. Hence," *Lancaster Intelligencer Journal,* July 4, 1957; idem, "New Approach Must Be Made to Cope with City's Traffic," ibid., July 5, 1957.

27. Wall, "Planners' Crystal Ball Shows a New Lancaster 10 Yrs. Hence," *Lancaster Intelligencer Journal,* July 4, 1957; idem, "Plan Aims at Converting Motorists to Pedestrians," ibid., July 17, 1957. On Gruen's Forth Worth plan and Jacobs's assessment, see Whyte, ed., *Exploding Metropolis,* 66–68, 162.

28. *Baker Plan,* 245–53; Ned L. Wall, "Plan Would Concentrate All Government Offices," *Lancaster Intelligencer Journal,* July 18, 1957; idem, "Penn Square Would Be Hub of Tree-Lined Central Mall," ibid., July 19, 1957. John Nolen, who frequently proposed civic centers in his plans, did not include one in his Lancaster report because "the present permanent location of many of Lancaster's public buildings does not give opportunity for the creating of a Civic Center group in the downtown district." Nolen, *Lancaster, Pennsylvania Comprehensive City Plan,* 55.

29. Ned L. Wall, "Ideas for City's Tomorrow Still Far from Completion," *Lancaster Intelligencer Journal,* July 20, 1957.

30. "City Democrats to Push Progress in Community Affairs," *Lancaster Intelligencer Journal,* October 8, 1957; T. J. Monaghan, inaugural address, in *Journal of City Council,* January 6, 1958, 67.

31. The reorganized planning commission was chaired by John H. Vanderzell, a professor of government at Franklin & Marshall College and an active supporter of Monaghan's Democratic Party. Robert M. Going, executive director of the Lancaster Redevelopment Authority, was also named to the planning commission at this time, as was Robert E. Flinchbaugh. "Vanderzell Elected Chairman of City Planning Commission," *Lancaster Intelligencer Journal,* February 7, 1958; Lancaster City Planning Commission, Minutes, February 6, 1958.

32. Lancaster City Planning Commission, *Lancaster's Central Business District: A Study* (1958), unpaginated introduction and 8, 10–12. Cohen's call for increased reliance on mass transit reiterated a proposal for downtown advanced by the Urban Land Institute. See Hal Burton, *The City Fights Back: A Nationwide Survey of What Cities Are Doing to Keep Pace with Traffic, Zoning, Shifting Population, Smoke, Smog, and Other Problems* (New York, 1954), 93–103. For a contrary position, one that predicted an increasing reliance on the automobile, see Francis Bello's essay "The City and the Car" in Whyte, ed., *Exploding Metropolis,* 53–80.

33. *Lancaster's Central Business District,* unpaginated introduction and 2, 3, 7, 8.

34. Ibid.; Lancaster City Planning Commission, *Lancaster Moves Ahead,*

vol. 1 (1959), 55, 61; *Baker Plan*, 85; Burrell B. Cohen, "Urban Renewal and the Future of the City of Lancaster," unpublished address, c. 1961, Lancaster Redevelopment Authority Records, Lancaster County Historical Society, Lancaster, Pennsylvania. For the Urban Land Institute's recommendations on adaptive reuse of older structures, see Burton, *The City Fights Back*, 115–24.

35. *Lancaster's Central Business District*, 2, 3, 11; *Lancaster Moves Ahead*, 38–39, 45–62.

36. Burton, *The City Fights Back*, 145–55; Teaford, *Rough Road to Renaissance*, 22; Lizabeth Cohen, "From Town Center to Shopping Center: The Reconfiguration of Community Marketplaces in Postwar America," *American Historical Review* 101 (October 1996): 1050–81; and, for the efforts of Bergenfield merchants in defending downtown retail in the face of the new malls, see Michael J. Birkner, *A Country Place No More: The Transformation of Bergenfield, New Jersey, 1894–1994* (Rutherford, N.J., 1994), 192–94.

37. *Lancaster Moves Ahead*, 46; "$2,500,000 Home Building Boom on in Lancaster and Suburbs," *Lancaster Intelligencer Journal*, October 25, 1951; "Huge Shopping Center Looms Here," ibid., November 15, 1955; "$1,500,000 Shopping Center for Ephrata," ibid., May 31, 1956; "Sears Planning Store at Lititz Pike Shop Center," *Lancaster New Era*, September 24, 1956; Andrew Torchia, "A Study in Suburbia—Manheim Township," ibid., May 12, 1958, Data demonstrating the increasing disparity in median family income of city and suburban households in metropolitan Lancaster is derived from the U.S. Bureau of the Census, *Census of Population and Housing, Census Tracts*, 1960 and 1970.

38. "Estimated 5,000 Witness Formal Opening Ceremony at New Shopping Center," *Lancaster Intelligencer Journal*, February 14, 1958; "Shopping Center Opens," *Lancaster New Era*, February 14, 1958; undated advertising supplement published as part of both newspapers, February 13, 1958; Cohen, "From Town Center to Shopping Center," 1050–81.

39. "New Shop Area West of City on Columbia Pike," *Lancaster New Era*, February 13, 1959; Ned L. Wall, "Businessmen Dealing for Lititz Pike Sites," *Lancaster Intelligencer Journal*, February 14, 1959. A third suburban retail mall, the Manor Shopping Center, located just west of the city, opened in August 1962. "5,000 Persons at Opening of Manor Center," *Lancaster New Era*, August 16, 1962.

40. Thomas Walter Hanchett, "Sorting Out the New South City: Charlotte and Its Neighborhoods," Ph.D. diss., University of North Carolina at Chapel Hill, 1993, 485–88; idem, "U.S. Tax Policy and the Shopping-Center Boom of the 1950s and 1960s," *American Historical Review* 101 (October 1996): 1082–110.

41. See, for example, Teaford, *Rough Road to Renaissance*, 129, 338 n. 5; Cohen, "From Town Center to Shopping Center."

42. U.S. Bureau of the Census, *Census of Business: Retail Trade Area Statistics*, 1948, 1958 (which also contains 1954 data), 1963, 1967; Lancaster City Planning Commission, *Lancaster Moves Ahead*, 45.

43. Lancaster City Planning Commission, *North Queen Street Study Area Report and Downtown Renewal Project 2 Certification*, August 15, 1962, 2, 7, and passim; Clifton E. Rodgers & Associates, *Downtown Lancaster . . . 1980* (1959), 3–4.

44. Lewis Mumford, *From the Ground Up: Observations on Contemporary Architecture, Housing, Highway Building, and Civic Design* (New York, 1956), 237–38.

CHAPTER 3

1. Information on the streetscape is drawn from Sanborn maps, photographs, and city directories; Michael Baker Jr., *A Comprehensive Municipal*

Plan: City of Lancaster, Pennsylvania (Rochester, Pa., 1945), 94.

2. Lancaster City Planning Commission, *Lancaster Moves Ahead,* (1959):55, 61–62; Burrell B. Cohen, "Urban Renewal and the Future of the City of Lancaster," unpublished address, c. 1961, Lancaster Redevelopment Authority Records, Lancaster County Historical Society, Lancaster, Pennsylvania; Clifton E. Rodgers & Associates, *Downtown Lancaster . . . 1980* (Lancaster City Planning Commission, 1959), 3. See also Howard Gillette, "Assessing James Rouse's Role in American City Planning," *Journal of the American Planning Association* 65 (Spring 1999): 151–65.

3. Rodgers, *Downtown Lancaster . . . 1980,* 3, 4. Society Hill Towers, designed by architect I. M. Pei, attracted a large number of prosperous citizens to old-town Philadelphia. On Boston's plan for high-rise luxury apartments adjacent to downtown, see Thomas H. O'Connor, *Building a New Boston: Politics and Urban Renewal, 1950–1970* (Boston, 1993).

4. Rodgers, *Downtown Lancaster . . . 1980,* 8–12.

5. Ibid., 13–16.

6. Ibid.; Burrell Cohen, "Your Questions Answered About Downtown Lancaster—1980" (typescript, c. 1960), 6–7, copy in Bureau of Planning, City of Lancaster.

7. Rodgers, *Downtown Lancaster . . . 1980,* 18–24.

8. Ibid., 18–21.

9. Ibid., 21. "Downtown Lancaster of the Future Shown City Leaders, Given $50 Million Price Tag," *Lancaster Intelligencer Journal,* October 28, 1959.

10. Rodgers, *Downtown Lancaster . . . 1980,* 23. In *The Federal Bulldozer: A Critical Analysis of Urban Renewal, 1949–1962* (Cambridge, Mass., 1964), Martin Anderson denied that significant tax benefits accrued to cities as a result of redevelopment. He termed this the "tax increase myth" (161–72).

11. "Downtown Lancaster of the Future Shown City Leaders, Given $50 Million Price Tag," *Lancaster Intelligencer Journal,* October 28, 1959. Victor Gruen articulated the principal components of the suburban shopping mall in *The Heart of Our Cities. The Urban Crisis: Diagnosis and Cure* (New York, 1964).

12. U.S. Housing Act of 1949, 81st Cong., 1st sess., ch. 338, July 15, 1949, in 63 Stat., 413–44; Ashley A. Foard and Hilbert Fefferman, "Federal Urban Renewal Legislation," in *Urban Renewal: The Record and the Controversy,* ed. James Q. Wilson (Cambridge, Mass., 1966), 71–125; Rodgers, *Downtown Lancaster . . . 1980,* 28; Lancaster City Council, *Journal of City Council,* May 21, 1959, 280–81; "Redevelopment Authority May Aid Midtown Plan," *Lancaster Intelligencer Journal,* October 31, 1959; "Corporation Planned to Push Downtown Plans," ibid., November 7, 1959; Cohen, "Your Questions Answered About Downtown Lancaster—1980," 9–11.

13. Rodgers was quoted in "Downtown Lancaster of the Future Shown City Leaders, Given $50 Million Price Tag," *Lancaster Intelligencer Journal,* October 28, 1959; "The Lancaster of the Future—Can It Be Made to Happen?" ibid.; "Corporation Planned to Push Downtown Plans," ibid., November 7, 1959.

14. "The Lancaster of the Future—Can It Be Made to Happen?"; "Downtown Lancaster of the Future Shown City Leaders, Given $50 Million Price Tag," *Lancaster Intelligencer Journal,* October 28, 1959; "Mixed Reaction to City Plan," ibid. On redevelopment in Boston, see O'Connor, *Building a New Boston,* 190–91, and passim, and Lawrence W. Kennedy, *Planning the City upon a Hill: Boston Since 1630* (Amherst, Mass., 1992), 157–92.

15. Cohen, "Your Questions Answered About Downtown Lancaster—1980," 2, 12.

16. These possible explanations for the reaction to the Rodgers plan are based on experience in other cities. See, for example, Herbert J. Gans, *The Urban Villagers: Group and Class in the Life of Italian-Americans* (New York, 1962); John F. Bauman, *Public Housing, Race, and Renewal: Urban Planning in Philadelphia, 1920–1974* (Philadelphia, 1987); June Manning Thomas, *Redevelopment and Race: Planning a Finer City in Postwar Detroit* (Baltimore, 1997).

17. "Coe Stresses Men and Finances in Platform for 'Better Lancaster,'" *Lancaster New Era,* September 12, 1961; "Coe Asks Aid of Voters to Move Ahead," ibid., November 6, 1961.

18. George B. Coe, "Downtown Renewal Project II," press release, August 2, 1962, Bureau of Planning, City of Lancaster; "City Unveils $10 Million Plan to Rebuild 2nd Block of N. Queen," *Lancaster New Era,* August 2, 1962; "Mayor Calls Plan 'Giant Step Forward,'" ibid.

19. "Mid-City Needs New Look, Survey Discloses," *Lancaster New Era,* August 2, 1962; "N. Queen St. Department Store Proposal Defended," *Lancaster Intelligencer Journal,* August 31, 1962; "Renewal Talk Centers on Department Store," *Lancaster New Era,* August 31, 1962.

20. "Dept. Store May Be Renewal 'True Test,'" *Lancaster Intelligencer Journal,* August 16, 1962; "Renewal Talk Centers on Department Store," *Lancaster New Era,* August 31, 1962; "The North Queen Renewal Area—As Planners See It," ibid.; "Thruway Is Planned to Center City," ibid.

21. For additional information on Gruen's dumbbell plan, see Peter G. Rowe, *Making a Middle Landscape* (Cambridge, Mass., 1991), 123–33.

22. "How City Rated 46 of 55 Buildings as Sub-Standard," *Lancaster New Era,* August 22, 1962; "Why City Applies 'Economic Blight' Tag to Queen St.," ibid., August 23, 1962; Lancaster City Planning Commission, North Queen Street Study Area Report and Downtown Renewal Project 2 Certification, August 15, 1962, 2, 7, and passim.

23. "A Look at Downtown Renewal Project 2," *Lancaster Intelligencer Journal,* August 9, 1962.

24. Ibid.; Jerry Sapienza, "What Merchants Think of N. Queen Renewal Program," *Lancaster New Era,* August 20, 1962; idem, "Property Owners' Reaction to Queen Renewal Is Mixed," ibid., August 21, 1962; idem, "Why City Applies 'Economic Blight' Tag to Queen Street," ibid., August 23, 1962; "N. Queen St. Plan Moving in High Gear," *Lancaster Intelligencer Journal,* August 23, 1962.

25. "Cohen Raps Idea to Delay Renewal," *Lancaster New Era,* August 24, 1962; "Suggestions for Renewal Delay Hit," *Lancaster Intelligencer Journal,* August 24, 1962; "N. Queen St. Plan Moving in High Gear," ibid., August 23, 1962; Prospective Developer Data for Submission of Redevelopment Proposals, Queen Street Renewal Area—Downtown Project II, October 1962, Bureau of Planning, City of Lancaster.

26. James Shand, Presentation to Lancaster City Council, Monday, January 28, 1963, copy in Bureau of Planning, City of Lancaster.

27. Donovan K. Smith, Chair, Lancaster Redevelopment Authority, "Selection of Developer—Queen Street Renewal Project—Downtown Lancaster," press release, February 6, 1963, Bureau of Planning, City of Lancaster. Other developers submitting proposals were Wheatland Engineering & Development Company of Lancaster; Alexander Garber, who had built the Host Resort in suburban Lancaster; and the Earle Lipchin Company, Baltimore. Two other prospective developers submitted proposals for

part of the complex. "All Four Proposals for N. Queen Had Pedestrian Malls," *Lancaster New Era,* February 8, 1963.

28. "Phila. Firm Is Named Developer of Multi-Million N. Queen Plan," *Lancaster New Era,* February 6, 1963; "Cohen Explains Why 'Prestige' Store Is Sought," ibid.

29. George B. Coe, "Selection of Developer—Queen Street Renewal Project—Downtown Lancaster," press release, February 6, 1963, Bureau of Planning, City of Lancaster; "North Queen Proposal," *Lancaster New Era,* February 11, 1963; "Council Clarifies Its Position on N. Queen Renewal," ibid., February 13, 1963.

30. "Council Clarifies Its Position on N. Queen Renewal," *Lancaster New Era,* February 13, 1963; "Cohen, Authority Planners Answer Renewal Criticism," ibid., February 14, 1963; [James Shand], Presentation to Special Review Committee, March 23, 1963; Robert R. Shoemaker to George B. Coe, March 22, 1963, all in Bureau of Planning, City of Lancaster; "C of C Clarifies Renewal Stand," *Lancaster New Era,* February 16, 1963.

31. "Mayor, Queen Review Board Agree on Duties," *Lancaster New Era,* March 1, 1963; Harris C. Arnold, letter to the editor, ibid.; Martin J. Murphy, letter to the editor, ibid., March 8, 1963; "City Endorses Economy League Renewal Study," ibid., March 25, 1963; "Downtown Unit Opposes Big Store & Garage," ibid., March 22, 1963; "9 Give Views on Queen Renewal to Review Unit," ibid., March 23, 1963.

32. "First Agreement on N. Queen Is Aired," ibid., March 18, 1963; "Developer OKs N. Queen Pact," ibid., April 4, 1963; "Text on Initial Queen Renewal Pact Released," ibid., April 8, 1963.

33. "N. Queen Renewal Approved by 10-Man Review Board," ibid., June 14, 1963; "City Slates Talks to Get N. Queen Renewal Started," ibid., June 15, 1963.

34. "City Slates Talks to Get N. Queen Renewal Started," ibid., June 15, 1963; "Queen Renewal Project Going into High Gear," ibid., June 17, 1963.

35. Lancaster Redevelopment Authority, Redevelopment Area Plan, Downtown Project No. II, June 1964; Paul F. Miller memorandum to Redevelopment Authority Board Members, May 21, 1964; Donovan K. Smith to Mayor and City Council, September 17, 1964; Redevelopment Proposal, Downtown Urban Renewal Project No. II, September 1964, all in Bureau of Planning, City of Lancaster.

36. This was a sentiment expressed by James Shand in his Presentation to Lancaster City Council, Monday, January 28, 1963, Bureau of Planning, City of Lancaster.

37. "Ground Rules for N. Queen Hearing," *Lancaster New Era,* September 29, 1964; "Hager's Asks Delay in Buying Queen Property," ibid.; "City Asked to Delay N. Queen Project, Get Local Developer," ibid., September 30, 1964; "All Comers to Be Heard on Renewal Plan," *Lancaster Intelligencer Journal,* September 30, 1964.

38. "Hager's Asks Delay in Buying Queen Property," *Lancaster New Era,* September 29, 1964; Minutes of Public Hearing held on September 30, 1964, at 10:30 A.M. on Proposal for Redevelopment of Downtown Urban Renewal Project No. II Queen Street, 20–22, 27, 37, Bureau of Planning, City of Lancaster.

39. Paul F. Miller, Text of Statement to Be Released by Members of Lancaster Redevelopment Authority on Monday Evening, November 30 1965, Bureau of Planning, City of Lancaster; "Queen St. Developer Given January Deadline," *Lancaster Intelligencer Journal,* December 1, 1965; "'Dropout' Seen as No Setback to North Queen," *Lancaster New Era,* January 7, 1965.

40. "'Dropout' Seen as No Setback to North Queen"; "GOP Accepts Coe Decision 'With Regret,'" ibid.

41. "Authority Oks Land Use Concept for N. Queen," *Lancaster Intelligencer Journal,* January 9, 1965.

CHAPTER 4

1. "City Clears Way for New Program on N. Queen St.," *Lancaster New Era,* January 13, 1965; "C of C Backs New Plan for N. Queen," ibid., January 15, 1965; "Federal Approval Given Queen Renewal Project," ibid., January 16, 1965; *Journal of City Council,* January 13, 1965, 33–35.

2. "Site Plan for N. Queen St. Redevelopment Unveiled," *Lancaster Intelligencer Journal,* February 23, 1965; Charles W. Fitzkee, "Nine Proposals Filed for N. Queen St.," ibid., May 11, 1965.

3. Charles W. Fitzkee, "Mall Featured in 2 Development Plans for N. Queen Area," ibid., May 28, 1965; Jerry Sapienza, "Local, Phila. Plans for Entire N. Queen Project Outlined," *Lancaster New Era,* May 28, 1965.

4. Ibid.

5. Lancaster Redevelopment Authority, Minutes, June 15, 1965; "Chamber Backs Local Queen St. Developer," *Lancaster Intelligencer Journal,* June 16, 1965; "Design Comm. Says Hoffman Idea Superior," ibid.; Donald W. Reidenbaugh to the Redevelopment Authority of Lancaster, June 15, 1965, copy in the files of Richard H. Barr Jr.; Richard H. Barr Jr. to the Redevelopment Authority of Lancaster, June 11, 1965, Barr files; A. C. Darmstaetter to Richard Barr, June 8, 1965, Barr files; Charles W. Fitzkee, "Second North Queen Corp. Is Selected for $15 Million Downtown Renewal Project," *Lancaster Intelligencer Journal,* June 16, 1965; *Journal of City Council,* June 16, 1965, 305; "Chronology of the Selection of Second North Queen Inc. as a Developer," typescript, August 31, 1967, Bureau of Planning.

6. "Agreement on Queen Renewal Property Ok'd," *Lancaster Intelligencer Journal,* April 6, 1965; "Queen Renewal Project's Execution Phase Begins," ibid., April 10, 1965; Lancaster Redevelopment Authority, Minutes, July 19, 1965, August 5, 1965; "Demolition Starts on N. Queen," *Lancaster New Era,* August 2, 1965; *Journal of City Council,* June 16, 1965, 304–5.

7. Interview with Richard H. Barr Jr., October 27, 1992. Miller was quoted in E. Wayne Schlegel, "The Past, the Present, the Future of City Renewal," *Lancaster Intelligencer Journal,* May 4, 1964; Paul R. Diller to Mrs. Goldie Hoffman, October 29, 1968, and Helen S. Chait to G. Theodore Storb, May 25, 1968, Bureau of Planning. In 1980, Charles K. Patterson, then the executive director of the Lancaster Redevelopment Authority, agreed with this assessment of the decision to clear the North Queen Street site. "We carried out the plans," he told a *New Era* reporter, "but they didn't always go the way the planners foresaw it. One plan was that if land were (cleared), investors would move in at once and build and rejuvenate." Patterson conceded that "this was the biggest pitfall in urban renewal." In most places, including Lancaster, private developers did not rush in (Jack Pollard, "After 20 Years & $30 Million, City's Renewal Era Is Ending," *Lancaster New Era,* June 24, 1980).

8. For the renewal strategies of Bacon, Logue, and Moses, see John F. Bauman, *Public Housing, Race, and Renewal: Urban Planning in Philadelphia, 1920–1974* (Philadelphia, 1987); Thomas H. O'Connor, *Building a New Boston: Politics and Urban Renewal, 1950–1970* (Boston, 1993); and Joel Schwartz, *The New York Approach: Robert Moses, Urban Liberals, and the Redevelopment of the Inner City* (Columbus, Ohio, 1993). See also Martin Anderson, *The Federal Bulldozer: A Critical Analysis of Urban Renewal, 1949–1962* (Cambridge, Mass., 1964).

9. "'Blight' Label May Be Fought," *Lancaster New Era,* May 18, 1965;

"Faranda Loses Battle with Renewal Auth.," *Lancaster Intelligencer Journal,* June 30, 1965; "Demolition Begins on Imperial Bar Building," *Lancaster New Era,* September 27, 1966; Anderson, *Federal Bulldozer.*

10. "Steps Taken for New N. Queen Demolition," *Lancaster Intelligencer Journal,* August 6, 1965; "Demolition Steps Started for More Buildings on North Queen," ibid., November 4, 1965; "Design Started on New Hager Store," *Lancaster New Era,* August 23, 1965.

11. "N. Queen St. 'Wasteland' More a Certainty Than Ever," *Lancaster Intelligencer Journal,* September 1, 1965; Monaghan's criticism of Coe's handling of redevelopment was quoted in "2 Views of Our Renewal," *Lancaster New Era,* October 15, 1965.

12. "Mishkin Seen Pulling Out of Queen Project," *Lancaster New Era,* December 20, 1965; "Queen Builder Has 10 Weeks to Find Partner," ibid., December 21, 1965; "Deadline Set for 2nd North Queen to Air Financing Plan," *Lancaster Intelligencer Journal,* December 21, 1965.

13. "New Backer Is Found for N. Queen Project," *Lancaster New Era,* February 15, 1966; "New N. Queen Backers Insist City Build Parking Garage," ibid., February 22, 1966; "2nd North Queen Financial Plan Okayed by Authority, Parking Garage Delayed," *Lancaster Intelligencer Journal,* March 1, 1966.

14. "2nd North Queen Names Architect," *Lancaster Intelligencer Journal,* April 13, 1966.

15. Ibid. On Gruen, see Howard Gillette Jr., "The Evolution of the Planned Shopping Center in Suburb and City," *Journal of the American Planning Association* 51 (Autumn 1985): 449–60; David R. Hill, "Sustainability, Victor Gruen, and the Cellular Metropolis," ibid., 58 (Summer 1992): 312–26; and M. Jeffrey Hardwick, "Creating a Consumer's Century: Urbanism and Architect Victor Gruen" (Ph.D. diss., Yale University, 2000). See also Victor Gruen, "Urban Renewal," *The Appraisal Journal,* January 1956, 23–29, copy in the Victor Gruen Collection, American Heritage Center, University of Wyoming (hereafter cited as Gruen Collection).

16. Gruen, quoted in Elwood Exley Jr., "Top Architect Working on N. Queen," *Lancaster New Era,* February 2, 1967; Victor Gruen, "The Future of Retailing Downtown," speech to the National Retail Furniture Association, Chicago, January 9, 1961, Gruen Collection. See also Gruen, "Is the Mall Good for Downtown: Affirmative Side," address at the National Retail Merchants Association, New York, January 13, 1959, and "Urban Planning for the Sixties," Address to the U.S. Conference of Mayors, May 13, 1960, both in Gruen Collection.

17. Victor Gruen, *The Heart of Our Cities. The Urban Crisis: Diagnosis and Cure* (New York, 1964), 63–72, 83–97.

18. Ibid., 190–204.

19. Ibid., 214–31; Garrett Eckbo, "Pilgrim's Progress," in Marc Treib, ed., *Modern Landscape Architecture: A Critical Review* (Cambridge, Mass., 1993), 212. See also William H. Whyte Jr., ed., *The Exploding Metropolis* (1958; reprint, Berkeley and Los Angeles, 1993), 66–68, 162.

20. Lancaster Redevelopment Authority, Minutes, July 28, 1966; Bob Kozak, "New Plan Enlarges Queen Project," *Lancaster New Era,* July 29, 1966; Charles W. Fitzkee, "Developer's New N. Queen Plan Features Public Square," *Lancaster Intelligencer Journal,* July 29, 1966; "Chamber Takes N. Queen Site Plan Position," ibid., July 30, 1966; "Queen Plan Enlarging Ups Cost," ibid.

21. Peter G. Rowe, *Making a Middle Landscape* (Cambridge, Mass., 1991), 124; Gruen, *Heart of Our Cities,* 243–65. The first redevelopment authority project completed in Lancaster was a parking garage. The authority had acquired and

cleared land adjacent to the Watt & Shand department store, which built a parking garage on the site. It had a walkway from the parking areas directly into the store. Gruen clearly expected that a municipal parking garage would serve a broader public purpose, and so placed the garage and the retail establishments in his plan to get shoppers into the downtown. As succeeding paragraphs indicate, the shift of the department store site across North Queen Street had a consequence the Gruen team may not have anticipated: the loss of a potential department store tenant for the project.

22. Bob Schaffner, "First Reaction to Plan Favorable," *Lancaster Intelligencer Journal,* July 29, 1966; "Reaction Is Split on New Project," *Lancaster New Era,* July 29, 1966; Lichtenstein and Clubb were quoted in Kozak, "New Plan Enlarges Queen Project."

23. Lizabeth Cohen, "From Town Center to Shopping Center: The Reconfiguration of Community Marketplaces in Postwar America," *American Historical Review* 101 (October 1996): 1050–81; Kenneth T. Jackson, "All the World's a Mall: Reflections on the Social and Economic Consequences of the American Shopping Center," ibid., 1111–21; David Schuyler, "Prologue to Urban Renewal: The Problem of Downtown Lancaster, 1945–1960," *Pennsylvania History* 61 (January 1994): 75–101; Bob Kozak, "City in Race with Shopping Centers," *Lancaster New Era,* August 1, 1966.

24. "Hager's Says 'No' to Plan," *Lancaster New Era,* July 29, 1966; George J. Zellem, "Hager's Says No to City 'Renewal,'" *Sunday News,* September 18, 1966; "Hager Store Signs Long-Term Lease in Shopping Center," *Lancaster New Era,* December 28, 1966; "Shop Center OK Aired by Hager's," ibid., December 28, 1966; "Penney Firm Signs Lease for Shop Center Store," *Lancaster Intelligencer Journal,* September 13, 1966.

25. Lancaster Redevelopment Authority, Minutes, August 1, 1966; "Chamber Takes N. Queen Site Plan Position," *Lancaster Intelligencer Journal,* July 30, 1966; "Queen Plan Approved, 6-Month Deadline Set," *Lancaster New Era,* August 2, 1966; *Journal of City Council,* August 9, 1966, 247.

26. Lancaster Redevelopment Authority, Minutes, August 1, 1966, January 31, 1967; Charles W. Fitzkee, "Developer Still Hasn't Accepted N. Queen Terms," *Lancaster Intelligencer Journal,* September 3, 1966; "17 Firms Listed as 'Interested' in N. Queen St.," *Lancaster New Era,* December 21, 1966; Elwood Exley Jr., "N. Queen Tenant List Stirs Up Controversy," *Lancaster New Era,* December 22, 1966; Bob Kozak, "Mayor Says Other Plans Under Study," ibid., December 22, 1966; "New Problems Beset Planning for N. Queen St.," ibid., December 23, 1966; "North Queen Deadline Tuesday," *Lancaster Intelligencer Journal,* January 28, 1967; Bob Holmes, "2nd North Queen Given Go Ahead to Proceed on Downtown Renewal," ibid., February 1, 1967; Elwood Exley Jr., "2nd North Queen to Start Building Motel by September 1," *Lancaster New Era,* February 1, 1967.

27. "City Moves to Enlarge N. Queen Renewal Area," *Lancaster New Era,* April 4, 1967; "The Brunswick's Last Ball," *Lancaster Intelligencer Journal,* May 2, 1967; "Last Walls of Hotel Brunswick Are Down," ibid., June 10, 1967; "N. Queen Demolition Site Shifts," ibid., June 21, 1967; "YMCA Building Yields to Wreckers," *Lancaster New Era,* August 11, 1967.

28. I am grateful to many residents of Lancaster for sharing their memories of the Brunswick, but particularly Paula Jackson, James McMullen, and Peggy Bender. See also Robert R. Archibald, *A Place to Remember: Using History to Build Community* (Walnut Creek, Calif., 1999), 33–34.

29. "Parking Authority OKs Queen Plans," *Lancaster New Era,* May 10, 1967;

Bob Holmes, "Construction Starts November 1 on N. Queen Hotel & Theater," *Lancaster Intelligencer Journal,* September 12, 1967; Lancaster Redevelopment Authority, Minutes, September 11, 1967.

30. "N. Queen Motel Project Begins," *Lancaster Intelligencer Journal,* November 2, 1967.

31. Broucht is quoted in "Storb Hits N. Queen Criticism," *Lancaster Intelligencer Journal,* November 1, 1967; "Have Delays and Red Tape Ended for North Queen?" *Lancaster New Era,* January 4, 1968; "N. Queen Contract Approved," *Lancaster Intelligencer Journal,* January 9, 1968.

32. R. Zane Wilson, "Phila. Group Buys Out Local Queen Partners," *Lancaster New Era,* March 27, 1968; "N. Queen Partners Here Sell," *Lancaster Intelligencer Journal,* March 28, 1968; Bob Holmes, "Plaza Adds $2.8 Million to Renewal," ibid., May 2, 1967; "Renewal Square Contract OK'd," *Lancaster New Era,* February 6, 1968.

33. "N. Queen Architecture Type Hasn't Been Set," *Lancaster New Era,* August 6, 1965; "Architecture for Renewal," ibid., January 7, 1966; "Renewal Style Under Debate," ibid., March 22, 1966; Verbatim transcript of public hearing held before the Lancaster City Council, June 12, 1967, Bureau of Planning.

34. "Redevelopment Board OKs Hotel Plan," *Lancaster New Era,* November 15, 1967; "Queen St. Movie House Lease Inked," *Sunday News,* February 23, 1969.

35. "City to Sell Land to Hess's Queen St. Store," *Lancaster New Era,* March 5, 1969; Dave Hennigan, "Hess's Unveils Design of Store," *Lancaster Intelligencer Journal,* July 31, 1969; Charles H. Kessler, "Hess's Closing Store Here Today," and Jack Moore, "Officials Dismayed by Closing," *Lancaster New Era,* August 27, 1973.

36. David J. Hladick, "Merchants See Business Boom in Queen Renewal," *Sunday News,* May 25, 1969; "Hess's Buys Land, Unveils Sketches," *Lancaster New Era,* July 31, 1969.

37. "Hess's Buys Land, Unveils Sketches," *Lancaster New Era,* July 31, 1969.

38. "Financing Arranged for Queen Office Building," *Lancaster New Era,* August 4, 1969; "City to Seek Bids for Queen Square Project," ibid., August 28, 1969; Dave Hennigan, "$3.3 Million Low Bid on City Square," *Lancaster Intelligencer Journal,* October 9, 1969; "Senator Hugh Scott to Speak at Dedication of Lancaster Square, a Revitalization Project," Lancaster Redevelopment Authority and Gruen Associates press release, September 20, 1971, Lancaster Redevelopment Authority Records, Lancaster County Historical Society; "Architect's Sketches Show Interior Plans for New Lancaster Square," *Sunday News,* April 12, 1970.

39. "New Hilton Inn Opens Today," *Lancaster Intelligencer Journal,* April 3, 1970; "Hess's to Open Doors Thursday," ibid., April 13, 1971; "Lancaster Square, Park City Ready for Dedication," *Sunday News,* September 19, 1971; Frank Arcuri, "New Square Brightens Downtown," *Lancaster Intelligencer Journal,* September 25, 1971; Jack Pollard, "New Lancaster Square Dedicated," *Lancaster New Era,* September 25, 1971; Lancaster Square Dedication 1971, brochure in the Lancaster Redevelopment Authority Records, Lancaster County Historical Society.

40. Dave Hennigan, "Developer Plans 13-Story Queen Apartment Units," *Lancaster Intelligencer Journal,* July 22, 1970; Gil Delaney, "Search Ordered for New Developer for N. Queen," ibid., February 10, 1972; "Mrs. Hoffman Dies, Was 52," ibid., March 16, 1971.

41. "D.C. Developer Under Contract, Lawyer Says," *Lancaster New Era,* April 7, 1971; "Big Step to N. Queen Completion," ibid.; Jack Pollard, "U.S. Refuses

Loan on Queen Square," ibid., July 16, 1971; Gil Delaney, "FHA to Back Financing for Queen Square," *Lancaster Intelligencer Journal,* July 17, 1971; Jack Pollard, "The Man Who Got N. Queen Moving Again," *Lancaster New Era,* August 21, 1971; "New Square Office Work Starts Soon," *Lancaster Intelligencer Journal,* September 28, 1971.

42. "New Partnership Formed to Finish N. Queen Square," *Lancaster New Era,* January 4, 1972; Delaney, "Search Ordered for New Developer for N. Queen," *Lancaster Intelligencer Journal,* February 10, 1972; Charles H. Kessler, "Hess's President Is 'Disappointed' Over Delays in Completing Square," *Lancaster New Era,* January 4, 1972.

43. Jack Pollard, "FHA Expected to Kill Loan for N. Queen," *Lancaster New Era,* April 13, 1972; Jack Pollard, "National Central Bank Relocating into High Rise," ibid., May 12, 1972; Pollard, "Bank Unveils Plans for 13-Story Office Building," ibid., August 3, 1972; "The Future Brightens," *Lancaster Intelligencer Journal,* August 4, 1972.

44. Jack Keyser, "Apartment-Store Eyed for Square," *Lancaster Intelligencer Journal,* August 19, 1972; Gil Delaney, "New N. Queen St. Complex Will Have 136 Apartments," ibid., December 7, 1972; "15-Story Apt., Retail Complex Set on N. Queen," ibid., December 19, 1972; "Completing Lancaster Square," *Lancaster New Era,* December 20, 1972; "The Way to a Better Downtown," ibid., January 9, 1973.

45. Jeff Forster, "Downtown Lancaster—Its Mood Is Optimistic," *Lancaster New Era,* March 27, 1973; A. M. Casale, "Bank Developer Told: Build or Lose $25,000," *Lancaster Intelligencer Journal,* June 13, 1973; Jack Pollard, "N. Queen Street Developers Ask 4th Extension," *Lancaster New Era,*" July 9, 1973; Jack Pollard, "N. Queen Bank Building Cut to 10 Floors," ibid., July 10, 1973; Jack Pollard, "Murry Pulling Out of North Queen Project," ibid., August 17, 1973; A. M. Casale, "Murry Permits Option to Expire on N. Queen Site," *Lancaster Intelligencer Journal,* August 18, 1973; Gil Delaney, "Loan Feud Perils N. Queen Project," ibid., August 31, 1973; William H. Chafe, *The Unfinished Journey: America Since World War II,* 2nd ed. (New York, 1991), 445–50.

46. Charles H. Kessler, "Hess's Closing Store Here Today," and Jack Moore, "Officials Dismayed by Closing," both in *Lancaster New Era,* August 27, 1973; "Hess's Closing and City's Future," ibid., August 28, 1973; Charles Shaw, "Downtown Renewal Set Back," *Lancaster Intelligencer Journal,* August 28, 1973. If Berman felt betrayed by the lack of progress on the part of the city and the redevelopment authority, his employees had even more reason to feel wronged: Hess's announced the closing so abruptly that Berman gave only one day's notice to his workers. See "Setbacks Delaying City Renewal," *Lancaster New Era,* September 12, 1973.

47. Scott is quoted in Jack Moore, "Officials Dismayed by Closing," *Lancaster New Era,* August 27, 1973; "Hess's Closing and City's Future," ibid., August 28, 1973; Jack Pollard, "City Acquires Options to N. Queen Sites," ibid., October 16, 1973; "Armstrong and NC Bank to Study Building of Offices in Center City," *Lancaster Intelligencer Journal,* October 16, 1973; "Queen Sites Reserved for Armstrong, Bank," ibid., October 20, 1973; "Make Downtown a Local Project," *Lancaster New Era,* October 16, 1973; John W. W. Loose, "Evolution of the Government of Lancaster: Village, Borough, City," *Journal of the Lancaster County Historical Society* 95 (Spring 1993): 58–71.

48. Jack Moore, "Armstrong & National Central to Build Queen Office Complex," *Lancaster New Era,* April 9,

1974; John M. Hoober III, "Scott Lauds Plan as 'Turnaround' for City," ibid.; "Armstrong, Bank to Build Offices in Queen Square," *Lancaster Intelligencer Journal,* April 10, 1974.

49. Jack Moore, "Armstrong, Bank Unveil Plans for 3 N. Queen St. Buildings," *Lancaster New Era,* August 30, 1974; Sam Taylor, "Architect Tells How He Decided on Design," ibid.; Gil Delaney, "Armstrong, Bank to Unveil Square Plans," *Lancaster Intelligencer Journal,* August 30, 1974.

50. Jack Pollard, "City Officials Delighted with Construction Plans," *Lancaster New Era,* August 30, 1974.

51. Taylor, "Architect Tells How He Decided on Design," ibid., August 30, 1974; "New Square Concrete to Be Razed in Nov.," *Lancaster New Era,* September 10, 1974. On Mellon Square, see Roy Lubove, *Twentieth-Century Pittsburgh: Government, Business, and Environmental Change* (New York, 1969), 124–26.

52. "Square Razing Begins," *Lancaster New Era,* December 18, 1974; Scott is quoted in Pollard, "City Officials Delighted with Construction Plans."

53. On federal subsidies for suburban development, see Kenneth T. Jackson, *Crabgrass Frontier: The Suburbanization of the United States* (New York, 1985), esp. 190–218; Thomas W. Hanchett, "U.S. Tax Policy and the Shopping-Center Boom of the 1950s and 1960s," *American Historical Review* 101 (October 1996): 1082–110; Hanchett, "The Other 'Subsidized Housing': Federal Aid to Suburbanization, 1940s–1960s," in John F. Bauman et al., eds., *From Tenements to the Taylor Homes: In Search of an Urban Housing Policy in Twentieth-Century America* (University Park, Pa., 2000), 163–79; and Tom Daniels, *When City and Country Collide: Managing Growth in the Metropolitan Fringe* (Washington, D.C., 1999), 107–34. See also Lewis Mumford, *From the Ground Up: Observations on Contemporary Architecture, Housing, Highway Building, and Civic Design* (New York, 1956), 237–38.

CHAPTER 5

1. "Report of the Citizen Housing Committee," *Journal of City Council,* May 21, 1957, 268–72, 265–66, 280–81; "City Provides $100,000 for Slum Clearance," *Lancaster New Era,* May 21, 1957.

2. Monaghan, Inaugural Address, January 6, 1958, in *Journal of City Council,* January 6, 1958, 66–69; City Council, Minutes, ibid., April 1, 1958, June 10, 1958, and July 22, 1958, 189–92, 329–31, 379; Ned Wall, "Consultants Outline Two Plans for Portions of 3rd, 7th Wards," *Lancaster Intelligencer Journal,* January 27, 1958; "500 Families Must Vacate in Slum Removal," *Lancaster New Era,* March 31, 1958; Lancaster City Planning Commission, Minutes, May 28, 1958; idem, Certification of Adams-Musser Towns Area for Urban Renewal, Certification No. 1, n.d. (May 28, 1958); idem, *General Neighborhood Renewal Plan Application for Adams-Musser Towns Project, Urban Renewal Area,* October 30, 1958, n.p. In April 1958 Cohen had submitted a survey and planning application for the Adams-Musser Towns area, but the Urban Renewal Administration determined that because of the cost of the project the city needed to prepare a General Neighborhood Renewal Plan application.

3. *General Neighborhood Renewal Plan Application for Adams-Musser Towns Project,* 2–3, 8–38, 39–45.

4. Ibid., 39–45; U.S. Bureau of the Census, *Census of Housing: 1950, Block Statistics, Lancaster, Pennsylvania.*

5. *General Neighborhood Renewal Plan Application for Adams-Musser Towns Project,* 45–47.

6. Ibid., 47–49.

7. "6-Part Forum Will Explain Urban Renewal," *Lancaster Intelligencer Journal,*

December 10, 1958; "Robin to Be 1st Speaker on Renewal," ibid., January 17, 1959; "City Renewal Seen Needing a Long View," ibid., February 5, 1959; "City Renewal Expert Maps Path to Take," ibid., January 22, 1959; "Forum Told of Renewal 'Homeless,'" ibid., February 19, 1959; "5 Problems to Be Met in City Renewal," ibid., March 5, 1959; "Last Renewal Forum Hears Conn. Expert," ibid., April 2, 1959.

8. "End 1st Phase of Slum Survey," *Lancaster New Era,* September 16, 1958; "Public Housing May Be Needed," *Lancaster Intelligencer Journal,* May 14, 1959.

9. "7th Ward Area Pinpointed as First to Be Redeveloped," *Lancaster New Era,* August 31, 1959; "1st Renewal Area in City Declared 75% Sub-Standard," ibid., September 29, 1959; Lancaster Redevelopment Authority Minutes, November 25, 1959, December 14, 1959; *General Neighborhood Renewal Plan for Adams-Musser Towns Urban Renewal Area,* November 1959; "School, Parks, Homes in City Renewal Plan," *Lancaster Intelligencer Journal,* October 5, 1959; "98 Houses to Be Razed in 1st Renewal Area," *Sunday News,* October 11, 1959; "Authority OKs Renewal Area Land Use Plan," *Lancaster Intelligencer Journal,* November 17, 1959; "City Receives Plan for Renewal," ibid.; "Authority Okays Plan for Renewal," ibid., November 26, 1959; "City Renewal Program Sketched," *Lancaster New Era,* November 28, 1959; "Outline Map for Renewal Is Approved," *Lancaster Intelligencer Journal,* December 15, 1959.

10. Minutes of Public Hearing, May 19, 1961, typescript copy included in Application for Loan and Grant, Adams-Musser Towns Urban Renewal Area, Project I, Bureau of Planning, City of Lancaster.

11. "C of C Housing Proposal Wins Quick Approval," *Lancaster Intelligencer Journal,* April 9, 1960; "Is Public Housing a Need in 7th Ward?" *Lancaster New Era,* May 26, 1960; "City School Board Hit on Renewal," *Lancaster Intelligencer Journal,* June 14, 1960; "Dispute Over Public Housing Mounts in City," *Lancaster New Era,* June 14, 1960; "School Move on Renewal Plan Urged," *Lancaster Intelligencer Journal,* June 16, 1960; Jerry Sapienza, "Is Public Housing Necessary to Help Clear Out Slums?" *Lancaster New Era,* June 23, 1960.

12. "Is Public Housing a Need in 7th Ward," *Lancaster New Era,* May 26, 1960; Jerry Sapienza, "Is Public Housing Necessary to Help Clear Out Slums?" ibid., June 23, 1960; Michael Katz, *Improving Poor People: The Welfare State, the "Underclass," and Urban Schools as History* (Princeton, 1995), 21. Sapienza described one privately funded experiment in low-income housing, a 20-unit complex built by philanthropist Gerard Lambert in Princeton, New Jersey, which was later sold to the Princeton Housing Authority. The complex was not intended or priced for the "lowest income groups," though this was precisely the cohort that would need public housing in Lancaster as redevelopment forced the relocation of hundreds of families. See also Joel Schwartz, *Fighting Poverty with Virtue: Moral Reform and America's Urban Poor* (Bloomington, Ind., 2000).

13. "Dispute over Public Housing Mounts in City," *Lancaster New Era,* June 14, 1960; "City School Board Hit on Renewal," *Lancaster Intelligencer Journal,* June 14, 1960; "City Program Aims to Improve Economic Health," ibid., July 5, 1960.

14. Ralph Moyed, "Suggestion Made for Housing Plan," *Lancaster Intelligencer Journal,* June 25, 1960.

15. *Journal of City Council,* June 28, 1960, 334–37; "Mayor Attacks School Board for Questioning Public Housing Plans," *Lancaster New Era,* June 28, 1960; "Monaghan Warns of Aid Loss on

Renewal," *Lancaster Intelligencer Journal,* June 29, 1960; "Monaghan's Statement to Council on Renewal Poser," ibid.

16. *Journal of the Board of School Directors of the School District of Lancaster,* July 14, 1960, 2–12; "Tax Waiver Refused for City Renewal," *Lancaster Intelligencer Journal,* July 15, 1960; "Mayor Will Try to Save Portion of Urban Renewal," ibid., July 16, 1960.

17. *Journal of the Board of School Directors,* July 14, 1960, 11; "Mayor Will Try to Save Portion of Urban Renewal," *Lancaster Intelligencer Journal,* July 16, 1960.

18. "Fedl. Aide Says City Alone Has Renewal Answer," *Lancaster Intelligencer Journal,* July 20, 1960; "Redevelopment Authority Will Remain on Duty," ibid., July 26, 1960.

19. "Action Group's Report Given Cool Reception," *Lancaster Intelligencer Journal,* July 27, 1960; "Cost to School District Called Main Question in Urban Renewal," ibid., August 2, 1960; information on residential segregation in Hickory Tree Heights provided by James G. Shultz and Leroy T. Hopkins Jr.; average income of Hickory Tree Heights residents was presented in Lancaster City Housing Authority, Minutes, November 10, 1960; median family income is derived from U.S. Bureau of the Census, *Census of Population and Housing: 1960. Census Tracts, Lancaster, Pa.*

At an August 1, 1960, public forum on urban renewal, John Truxal defended the Lancaster Housing Authority against a suggestion of discrimination at Hickory Tree Heights, asserting: "At no time has a Negro been denied admission because of his race." It is significant that Truxal did not state that the housing complex was integrated. "Questions, Answers at Renewal Forum," *Lancaster Intelligencer Journal,* August 2, 1960.

20. Monaghan, quoted in "Action Group's Report Given Cool Reception," *Lancaster Intelligencer Journal,* July 27, 1960; "Bankers See No Way to Finance Housing," *Lancaster Intelligencer Journal,* July 28, 1960.

21. "Cost to School District Called Main Question in Urban Renewal," *Lancaster Intelligencer Journal,* August 2, 1960; "Questions, Answers at Renewal Forum," ibid.; "City, School Board Meet Wednesday," ibid., August 9, 1960; "Signing of Public Housing Pacts Expected Today," ibid., August 11, 1960.

22. *Journal of the Board of School Directors,* August 11, 1960, 46, 52–59; *Journal of City Council,* Special Meeting, August 11, 1960, 420–21; "Text of Forster's Statement," *Lancaster Intelligencer Journal,* August 11, 1960; "Signing of Public Housing Pacts Expected Today," ibid., August 11, 1960; "School Board Okays Housing Agreement," ibid., August 12, 1960.

23. Minutes of Public Hearing, May 19, 1961, typescript copy included in Application for Loan and Grant, Adams-Musser Towns Urban Renewal Area, Project I, Bureau of Planning, City of Lancaster.

24. Ibid.; "Council Chamber Jammed for Hearing on Renewal," *Lancaster Intelligencer Journal,* May 19, 1961; "Council Stamps Okay on Renewal Program," ibid., May 20, 1961; *Proposal for the Redevelopment of Project I of the Adams-Musser Towns Urban Renewal Area, May 19, 1961,* Bureau of Planning, City of Lancaster.

25. Lancaster Redevelopment Authority Minutes, May 14, 1962, December 26, 1962; Charles W. Fitzkee, "Bogar Company Picked as 'Renewal One' Developer," *Lancaster Intelligencer Journal,* May 15, 1962; "Bogar to Build 119 Renewal Homes," *Lancaster New Era,* May 15, 1962;

26. Lancaster Redevelopment Authority Minutes, May 14, 1962; Cohen was quoted in "Bogar to Build 119 Renewal Homes."

27. The first Bogar unit sold for $11,167 on January 31, 1964, and eight others sold between March 25 and June 30, 1964, at prices ranging from $10,900 to $12,125 for the end-of-row house with a larger lot. One other property sold on October 5, 1964, while the final one was purchased on January 6, 1965, almost a year after the first unit. The lowest price was $300 to $600 above the range Burrell Cohen established as the purchase price in announcing the selection of Bogar as developer; the average price, $11,379, was $779 to $1,079 above the expected price, a level only middle-income residents could afford. Information on dates of sale and purchase price derived from real estate transfers for the following addresses: 715, 717, 721, 723, 727, 729, 731, 735, 737, 741, and 743 Rockland Street, all in Recorder of Deeds Office, Lancaster County Court House.

28. Bogar Disposition Contract, Contract No. 2, April 1964, and H. F. Huth Engineers, Preliminary Layout Composite Plan of Residential Tracts No. 6, 7 & 8 in Project Number One—Adams-Musser Towns Urban Renewal Area . . . , September 25, 1962, both in Bureau of Planning; "Bogar Dropped from S. Duke St. Renewal Plans," *Lancaster New Era,* September 11, 1965; Bob Kozak, "City Has Trouble Getting Developer for S. Duke Block," ibid., July 16, 1965; Lancaster Redevelopment Authority Minutes, July 19, 1965, September 20, 1965, November 3, 1965; Donovan K. Smith, press release announcing the collaboration of the Bell Development Corporation and the Penn Central Conference of the United Church of Christ to develop garden apartments as a joint venture, September 20, 1965, Bureau of Planning; "Bell Corp., UCC Enter Duke St. Renewal Picture," *Lancaster Intelligencer Journal,* September 21, 1965; "Ground Broken for UCC Housing Project," ibid., July 13, 1968; "Local UCC Cited for Concern," ibid., August 11, 1969; "UCC Curbs Plans on Housing," ibid., Jun 17, 1970; "FHA May Take UCC Apartments," ibid., August 18, 1971. A 1967 newspaper story announcing the beginnings of the Church-Musser urban renewal project reported that the ash fill had raised the cost of construction of the UCC homes between $500 and $600 per unit. See "Church-Musser Project Core Boring to Begin," *Lancaster Intelligencer Journal,* September 12, 1967.

29. Lancaster Housing Authority Minutes, September 5, 1962, January 17, 1963, March 14, 1963, April 11, 1963, June 13, 1963; "Housing Unit Site Atop Ash Dump; May Raise Costs," *Lancaster New Era,* February 15, 1963; Charles Kessler, "Why an Ash Dump Was Picked as Site for Public Housing," ibid., February 25, 1963; Charles Kessler, "Ashes to Add $50,000 to Public Housing Cost," ibid., March 15, 1963.

30. Cohen was quoted in Kessler, "Why an Ash Dump Was Picked as Site for Public Housing"; Lancaster Housing Authority Minutes, March 14, April 11, and June 13, 1963; Jerry Sapienza, "Authority Opposes Ash Pit Location for Public Housing," *Lancaster New Era,* April 9, 1963; "Housing Authority Gives Statement on Renewal Site," *Lancaster Intelligencer Journal,* April 13, 1963; "Plan Okayed for Housing on S. Duke," ibid., August 15, 1963; Lancaster Redevelopment Authority, *Annual Report 1966,* 7; Paul F. Miller memorandum to Redevelopment Authority Board Members, October 2, 1965, Bureau of Planning; Charles Betts, "A Look at Susquehanna Courts: First Federal Housing Project Nearly Ready," *Lancaster New Era,* November 6, 1965; "Public Housing Occupants Move In," *Lancaster Intelligencer Journal,* December 2, 1965.

31. The assertion that 73 families would require public housing seems problematic. Six months earlier, reporter Jerry Spaienza estimated that approximately 77 of the 134 families who lived in

the project area were eligible for public housing. Those earlier figures were surely provided by the redevelopment authority, so it seems likely that the December 1963 estimates reflected awareness of the number of apartments that would become available in the Susquehanna Court complex. Federal officials had demonstrated the importance of an adequate supply of replacement housing when they halted approval of the Higbee and Duke street projects until public housing was available for residents displaced by clearance. See Lancaster Redevelopment Authority, Proposal for the Redevelopment of Project II-A of the Adams-Musser Towns Urban Renewal Area, December 18, 1963; Jerry Sapienza, "100 City Buildings Razed for Renewal," *Lancaster New Era,* June 11, 1963; "Lack of Housing Delays Duke St. Renewal a Year," ibid., October 12, 1963.

32. Lancaster Redevelopment Authority, Proposal for the Redevelopment of Project II-A of the Adams-Musser Towns Urban Renewal Area, December 18, 1963; Minutes of Public Hearing on Proposal for the Redevelopment of Project II-A of the Adams-Musser Towns Urban Renewal Area, December 18, 1963, City Clerk's Office, Lancaster; Jerry Sapienza, "100 City Buildings Razed for Renewal"; "Lack of Housing Delays Duke St. Renewal a Year," *Lancaster New Era,* October 12, 1963; "School Dist. Gets Higbee School Land," *Lancaster Intelligencer Journal,* September 10, 1965; "New Higbee School Is Dedicated Here," ibid., January 8, 1967; Lancaster Redevelopment Authority, *Annual Report 1965,* 14, and *Annual Report 1967,* 8.

33. Lancaster Redevelopment Authority, Adams Urban Renewal Project, November 1964; "Architectural Historian Excited by Buildings Here," *Lancaster Intelligencer Journal,* June 22, 1963; Miller was quoted in Minutes of Public Hearing, April 28, 1965, 14, Bureau of Planning.

34. Charles Fitzkee, "Renewal Property Owners Will Be Well Informed," *Lancaster Intelligencer Journal,* January 29, 1963; idem, "Cooperation of Home Owners Required for Rehabilitation Plan," ibid., January 30, 1963; George J. Zellem, "Homes to Be Spared in Renewal Improved," *Sunday News,* May 5, 1963; "City Initiates Rehabilitation Grant Program," *Lancaster Intelligencer Journal,* April 23, 1966; "Rehabilitation Going Well," ibid., October 4, 1966.

35. Lancaster Redevelopment Authority, Adams Urban Renewal Project, November 1964; "U.S. to Get Plans for Adams Renewal Homes," *Lancaster New Era,* November 20, 1964; "Standards Set for Fixing-Up Renewal Area," ibid., February 20, 1964; Bob Kozak, "Adams Renewal Project to Rid City of Eyesore," ibid., October 7, 1965.

36. Bob Holmes, "Demonstration House to Aid Blight Fight," *Lancaster Intelligencer Journal,* August 10, 1967; "Armstrong to Rehabilitate 7 Renewal Homes," ibid., August 23, 1967.

37. Charles Fitzkee, "First Steps Taken for 223 More Public Housing Units," *Lancaster Intelligencer Journal,* September 13, 1963; "Lack of Housing Delays Duke St. Renewal a Year," *Lancaster New Era,* October 12, 1963; "New Public Housing Site Under Option," ibid., December 11, 1963.

38. "Public Housing in Old Homes Here Is Urged," *Lancaster New Era,* September 13, 1963; "New Public Housing Site Under Option," ibid., December 11, 1963; Jerry Sapienza, "City May Scatter Its Public Housing," ibid., February 24, 1964.

39. Tompkins was quoted in Minutes of Public Hearing on Proposal for the Redevelopment of the Adams Urban Renewal Project, April 28, 1965, 30.

40. Housing Subcommittee's Statement Concerning Public Housing, June 6, 1966, typescript copy in Bureau of

Planning; Paul F. Miller to Theodore R. Schwalm, August 4, 1966; Lancaster Redevelopment Authority, Minutes, August 15, 1966; "400-Unit Housing Resolution Tabled," *Lancaster Intelligencer Journal,* November 11, 1966; "Case Presented for 400 New Low-Rent Units Here," ibid., December 10, 1966.

41. "More Public Housing Units Eyed in City," *Lancaster New Era,* November 10, 1966; Filling and Bucher are quoted in "Action on 400 Housing Units Delayed Again," ibid., January 13, 1967; "Low-Rent Housing Plan Stalled Again," *Lancaster Intelligencer Journal,* January 13, 1967; Thomas J. Monaghan to D. B. Bucher, January 13, 1967, and D. B. Bucher to T. J. Monaghan, January 14, 1967, both in D. B. Bucher personal files, courtesy of Dave Bucher. See also "Mayor Clashes with Public Housing Official," *Lancaster New Era,* January 16, 1967.

42. Mrs. Leonard Sloane to Richard M. Filling, January 16, 1967; Subcommittee on Housing, Lancaster City-County Human Relations Committee to Thomas J. Monaghan, April 10, 1967, both in Bureau of Planning.

43. Esbenshade to T. Monaghan, April 7, 1967; R. Zane Wilson, "Public Housing Dispute—What's It All About?" *Lancaster New Era,* January 20, 1967.

44. John O. Shirk, *The Lancaster Housing Study* (Lancaster Redevelopment Authority, 1966), 19–20, 50.

45. Shirk, *Lancaster Housing Study,* 8, 31, 47; "$6 Million Public Housing Program Unveiled for City," *Lancaster New Era,* October 7, 1970; "Should Unmarried Couples, Credit Risks, Be Allowed [in] Public Housing?" ibid., November 16, 1965; Bob Kozak, "Can the Slums' 'Unwanted Families' Make a New Start in Public Housing," ibid., November 17, 1965; Paul F. Miller to Redevelopment Authority Board Members, December [1965]; Jack E. Keyser, "Rejection Rate for Housing 'Excessive,'" *Lancaster Intelligencer Journal,* December 17, 1965; Bob Schaffner, "Higbee Area Citizens Rap 'Unfairness' in Housing," ibid., April 29, 1966. Schaffner quoted one individual who described the pattern of successive relocations as transforming citizens into "poverty-stricken, powerless people."

46. Shirk, *Lancaster Housing Study,* 39–41; "Encroachment of Negro Ghetto Feared in City," *Lancaster Intelligencer Journal,* April 23, 1966; "94 Minority Families Are Living Outside of City's Southeast Area," *Lancaster New Era,* January 30, 1967; Bob Holmes, "City Losing in Fight to Curb Blight," *Lancaster Intelligencer Journal,* January 31, 1967; idem, "Ghetto Housing Trend Stopped, Not Reversed," ibid., February 2, 1967. The 1970 Census of Housing demonstrates the migration of the minority population to census tracts 8, 15, and 16, south and east of what traditionally had been the city's African American community. See U.S. Bureau of the Census, *1970 Census of Housing. Block Statistics, Lancaster, Pa., Urbanized Area,* table 2.

47. Shirk, *Lancaster Housing Study,* 51–52.

48. R. Zane Wilson, "Public Housing Dispute—What's It All About?" *Lancaster New Era,* January 20, 1967.

CHAPTER 6

1. Drayton S. Bryant Associates, *Ongoing Neighborhood Self-Renewal: Recommendations for Housing Programs and Related Services, Church-Musser Renewal Area, Lancaster, Pa.* (May 1967), 2–3, 11, 17; Bob Kozak, "Largest Renewal Plan Given U.S. OK," *Lancaster New Era,* August 30, 1965; "City Applies for Church-Musser Renewal Funds," ibid., September 22, 1965; Bob Kozak, "People to Help Plan Own Renewal," ibid., May 14, 1966.

2. This summary of the activities of the NAACP and the civil rights struggle

is based on conversations with Leroy Hopkins Jr. See also "NAACP to Demonstrate at 2 Stores," *Lancaster Intelligencer Journal,* July 20, 1963; "Demonstrators to March at Rocky Springs Park," ibid., July 30, 1963; "Rights Marchers at Pool Explain What It's About," ibid., August 12, 1963; "Housing auth. Chided by NAACP on 20 Rejections," ibid., November 23, 1965; "NAACP Airs Complaints on Public Housing," ibid., June 14, 1966; "NAACP Attacks Junkyard Peril," ibid., July 18, 1967; "Junkyards War Waged by NAACP," ibid., July 20, 1967; "NAACP Lists Filth Spots Here," ibid., August 8, 1967.

3. R. Zane Wilson, "NAACP Makes Threats on City House Shortage," *Lancaster New Era,* October 5, 1967; Barbara L. Little, "Minority Housing Demanded," *Lancaster Intelligencer Journal,* October 5, 1967; "Home for Aging Plan Is Dropped," ibid., December 8, 1967.

4. Bryant, *Ongoing Neighborhood Self-Renewal,* 61, 10–21; John O. Shirk, *The Lancaster Housing Study* (Lancaster Redevelopment Authority, 1966).

5. Bryant, *Ongoing Neighborhood Self-Renewal,* ix, vii.

6. Ibid., vii, 7–9, 61–62.

7. Ibid., 21–27. Based on his experience in Philadelphia in the 1950s, Bryant realized that the surrounding neighborhood had a significant impact—positive or negative—on public housing projects and, implicitly, on their residents. His warning against the concentration of additional projects in the southeast quadrant was surely an attempt to prevent the physical and social decline he had witnessed in Philadelphia's Richard Allen Homes. See John F. Bauman, *Public Housing, Race, and Renewal: Urban Planning in Philadelphia, 1920–1974* (Philadelphia, 1987), 133–35; and John F. Bauman, Norman P. Hummon, and Edward K. Muller, "Public Housing, Isolation, and the Urban Underclass: Philadelphia's Richard Allen Homes, 1941–1965," *Journal of Urban History* 17 (May 1991): 264–92.

8. Bryant, *Ongoing Neighborhood Self-Renewal,* 33, 46–47, 50–61.

9. Ibid., 51, 53, 56–57.

10. Ibid., 53–54, 56–57, 7–9.

11. Ibid., 69–72.

12. Ibid., 57–58. Bryant held out an alternative to market-rate housing—a low- to moderate-income development similar to the 221(d)3 apartments being constructed by the United Church of Christ and Bell Development Corporation across South Duke Street—but warned that additional subsidized housing would "further identify this section as only the low-income area." Such a reputation, and the absence of a range of income groups, would make neighborhood self-regeneration difficult if not impossible (ibid., 58).

13. Ibid., 75, 83–85.

14. Elwood Exley Jr., "Unveil Building Plans for Church-Musser," *Lancaster New Era,* May 22, 1967; Bob Holmes, "New Renewal Approach Urged," *Lancaster Intelligencer Journal,* May 23, 1967; "Renewal Residents Shun Talks," *Lancaster Intelligencer Journal,* July 14, 1967. Milan may have modified elements of Bryant's plan because he anticipated difficulty in implementation, especially in attracting market-rate developers and upper-income households to the southeast. In May 1967 he told reporter Bob Holmes, "There is little doubt that if we accept this new basic concept, we will have a much tougher job, but one that probably would be more worthwhile for the city as a whole."

15. "Church-Musser Renewal Approve[d]," *Lancaster New Era,* January 5, 1968; Goodhart explained the Housing Authority's policy in "Housing Chairman Won't Call Hearing," ibid., March 18, 1969; Milan was quoted in R. Zane

Wilson, "The City's Housing Dilemma," ibid., July 17, 1968; Lancaster Housing Authority, Minutes, February 9, 1967, March 9, 1967; P.L. 88-352, in *United States Statutes at Large, 1964* (Washington, D.C., 1965), 252.

16. Lancaster Housing Authority, Minutes, February 9, 1967, March 9, 1967; "Housing Chairman Won't Call Hearing," *Lancaster New Era*, March 18, 1969; Lancaster Forum for Low and Moderate Cost Housing, typescript, November 29, 1967, 4–7, 14–16, 25–26, Bureau of Planning; Robert T. Schaffner, memo to Thomas R. Wenger, June 19, 1968, Bureau of Planning; Charles K. Patterson to Louis G. Milan, April 2, 1969, Bureau of Planning.

17. Lancaster Forum for Low and Moderate Cost Housing, 5–6, 26–28; "Housing Meeting: The Kind We Need," *Lancaster New Era*, December 2, 1967.

18. R. Schaffner, memo to T. R. Wenger, June 19, 1968.

19. R. Zane Wilson, "U.S. Halts New Renewal Demolition Here Until More Housing Is Built," *Lancaster New Era*, July 15, 1968.

20. "Public Housing Sites Sought Outside SE Area," *Lancaster New Era*, July 18, 1968; Goodhart was quoted in "Housing Chairman Won't Call Hearing," ibid., March 18, 1969; Lancaster Housing Authority, Minutes, August 8, 1968, April 24, 1969.

21. "7 Public Housing Sites Eyed Outside SE Area," *Lancaster New Era*, October 28, 1968; "Housing Chairman Won't Call Hearing," ibid., March 18, 1969; Discussion by Mr. George B. Coe, vice-chairman, Lancaster Housing Authority, and Howard R. Riegert, executive director, Lancaster Housing Authority Minutes, April 24, 1969, which was also printed as "City Housing: Questions & Answers," *Lancaster New Era*, April 25, 1969.

22. "School Board Members Rap Public Housing," ibid., December 13, 1968; "U.S. Okays Four Sites for Low-Cost Housing," *Lancaster New Era*, March 12, 1969; "Public Housing Zoning Denials Being Appealed," ibid., July 8, 1969; Lancaster Housing Authority Minutes, April 24, 1969.

23. "Filling Urges Hearing on 4 Housing Sites," *Lancaster New Era*, March 17, 1969; "County Needs Public Housing, Mayor States," ibid., March 20, 1969. On white resistance to integration in other cities, see especially Thomas J. Sugrue, *The Origins of the Urban Crisis: Race and Inequality in Postwar Detroit* (Princeton, 1996), 209–29; and Arnold Hirsch, *Making the Second Ghetto: Race and Housing in Chicago, 1940–1960* (1983; reprint, Chicago, 1998).

24. "County Needs Public Housing, Mayor States," *Lancaster New Era*, March 20, 1969; "Shirk Raps Monaghan on Housing Issue," ibid., March 21, 1969; "City Will Go Ahead with Housing Plans," ibid., March 26, 1969; "Southwest Area Residents Plan Housing Fight," ibid., April 3, 1969; letters to the editor published in the *Lancaster New Era* between March 13 and mid-April 1969 (the quote is from a letter signed by "A Heartsick 8th Ward Resident," March 20, 1969); A. Scott Henderson, "'Tarred with the Exceptional Image': Public Housing and Popular Discourse, 1950–1990," *American Studies* 36 (Spring 1995): 40; "Charred Cross Found on Public Housing Site," *Lancaster New Era*, April 8, 1969.

25. "Another Public Housing Site Hit," *Lancaster New Era*, March 22, 1969; "Eden Manor Fight on Public Housing Eyed at Meeting," ibid., March 28, 1969; J. Hershey, letter to the editor, ibid., March 25, 1969; Kenneth L. Olsen, "Public Housing: Controversy with 2 Points of View," ibid., April 7, 1969.

26. For letters in defense of public housing or residents of the southeast, see H. Parmer, *Lancaster New Era*, March 21,

1969, Mrs. William Benedict, ibid., March 22, 1969, and the Executive Committee of the Southeast Area Council, ibid., March 22, 1969; the letter of Mrs. Hugh C. Evans, President of the League of Women Voters, was published on March 28, 1969; Human Relations Committee to Monaghan, April 10, 1969, and Milton B. Stanley, president of the board of Neighborhood Services, to Monaghan, April 22, 1969, both in Bureau of Planning.

27. Filling was quoted in "Housing Chairman Won't Call Hearing," *Lancaster New Era,* March 18, 1969; Monaghan was quoted in "County Needs Public Housing, Mayor States," ibid., March 20, 1969; Riegert was quoted in "City Wants to Extend Street at Housing Site," ibid., April 9, 1969.

28. George Tresnak, "Housing Sites Vetoed Outside Southeast Area," *Lancaster Intelligencer Journal,* June 10, 1969; J. A. Jarvis et al., "Report of the Fact-Finding Committee on Public Housing," typescript, July 1969, copy in Bureau of Planning.

29. "Special Meeting Thursday on Public Housing," *Lancaster New Era,* April 23, 1969; "Don't Rezone Pitney Road, Planners Urged," ibid., April 16, 1969; "Public Housing Zoning Denials Being Appealed," ibid., July 8, 1969;

30. Tresnak, "Housing Sites Vetoed Outside Southeast Area"; "Public Housing Outside of SE Area Is OKd," ibid., January 23, 1970; Louis G. Milan to members of the Lancaster Redevelopment Authority board, April 24, 1970, and Minutes of Meeting, Lancaster Redevelopment Authority and Housing Authority of the City of Lancaster, April 27, 1970, both in Bureau of Planning.

31. Jack Pollard, "$6 Million Public Housing Program Unveiled for City," *Lancaster New Era,* October 7, 1970; "Public Housing Plans Revealed," *Lancaster Intelligencer Journal,* October 8, 1970.

32. Gil Delaney, "SW Citizens Call for 500 to Protest Housing," *Lancaster Intelligencer Journal,* October 20, 1970; Gil Delaney, "Council Packed as 530 Protest Public Housing," ibid., October 28, 1970; Jack Pollard, "Councilmen Opposed to Project Housing," *Lancaster New Era,* October 28, 1970.

33. Jack Pollard, "Councilmen Opposed to Project Housing," *Lancaster New Era,* October 28, 1970; Sugrue, *Origins of the Urban Crisis.*

34. Jack Pollard, "U.S. Bars More Public Housing in Southeast," *Lancaster New Era,* November 3, 1970.

35. Bill Fisher, "City Has 90 Days to Revise Housing Plan," *Lancaster New Era,* December 1, 1970; "Revised Plan for Housing Unveiled Here," ibid., December 3, 1970; "New Housing Plans Disclosed," *Lancaster Intelligencer Journal,* December 3, 1970; Gil Delaney, "City Drafts List of 18 Possible Housing Sites," ibid., January 6, 1971; Jack Pollard, "5 Public Housing Sites Proposed in SW," *Lancaster New Era,* February 2, 1971; Gil Delaney, "Public Housing Developers Favor S.W. Area," *Lancaster Intelligencer Journal,* February 3, 1971.

36. Jack Pollard, "4 Public Housing Sites Set; 'Low Income' Homes to Sell for $22,000–$26,000 Each," *Lancaster New Era,* March 31, 1971; Gil Delaney, "4 Sites Selected for $22,000–$26,000 Homes," *Lancaster Intelligencer Journal,* April 1, 1971; idem, "$26,000 Homes Said 'High' for Public Housing," ibid., April 2, 1971; "Median City Home Valued at $11,700," ibid.

37. Gil Delaney, "City Scattered Site Housing Dealt Setback," *Lancaster Intelligencer Journal,* April 13, 1971; "HUD Mad About Stall on Housing," ibid., April 14, 1971; "Public Housing to Start," ibid., April 16, 1971.

38. Jack Pollard, "SW Public Housing Is KOd by Costs," *Lancaster New Era,* August 8, 1972; idem, "2 Housing Projects

Dead, 3rd in Trouble," ibid., November 28, 1972.

39. Jack Pollard, "Miller Jr. Hits Housing Plan for SW Area," *Lancaster New Era,* July 9, 1974; idem, "Zoners Vote 3 to 0 to Kill Controversial SW Housing Project," ibid., July 11, 1974.

40. My understanding of the sense of community among minority residents of the southeast was strengthened by conversations with Thomas Hyson and Leroy Hopkins Jr. See also John O. Shirk, *The Lancaster Housing Study* (Lancaster Redevelopment Authority, 1966), 39–41; "Encroachment of Negro Ghetto Feared in City," *Lancaster Intelligencer Journal,* April 23, 1966. For comparisons with the second ghettos that emerged in other cities, see Hirsch, *Making the Second Ghetto,* and Raymond A. Mohl, "Making the Second Ghetto in Metropolitan Miami, 1940–1960," *Journal of Urban History* 21 (March 1995): 395–427.

41. *Journal of City Council,* March 25, 1969, 166–67; Arthur Miron, *A Study of Lancaster Housing* (Lancaster Redevelopment Authority, 1969), 50; "City Changes Mind About Church-Musser," *Lancaster New Era,* October 9, 1969; "HUD Advises City on Shift of Church-Musser," ibid., October 11, 1969; "Church-Musser Cost Increased by $4.7 Million," ibid., December 2, 1969; Monaghan was quoted in Jack Pollard, "Church-Musser Gets Grant of $3.5 Million," ibid., May 15, 1969.

42. See, for example, Gil Delaney, "SE Sanitary Food Market Coming Down," *Lancaster Intelligencer Journal,* October 3, 1970; "Church-Musser Razing to Start," ibid., January 16, 1971; "Old Duke St. School Ready for Razing," *Sunday News,* May 9, 1971; "Design Assailed on New Salvation Army Building," *Lancaster Intelligencer Journal,* January 16, 1973.

43. Louis G. Milan described the grant and loan programs in response to questions posed during a public hearing held April 22, 1969. A transcription of the hearing was included in Church-Musser Urban Renewal Project, Application for Loan and Grant, Part II, April 1969, R-308, 10, while the various programs to provide low- and moderate-income housing were presented in ibid., R-301, 14, copy in Bureau of Planning.

44. Bob Holmes, "Low-Cost Housing Gets Push by City," *Lancaster Intelligencer Journal,* April 18, 1968; R. Zane Wilson, "150 Low-Cost Homes Planned for SE Area," *Lancaster New Era,* May 22, 1969; Neal Mitchell Associates Inc., undated presentation packet explaining the firm's innovative framing system, copy in Bureau of Planning; Wolf Von Eckardt, "Building Blocks for the Slums," *Washington Post,* July 14, 1968; "City Negotiates on Mitchell Homes," *Lancaster New Era,* May 20, 1969; "Mitchell Sites to Cost $90,750," ibid., December 1, 1969; "Builder Must Pre-Sell 150 Mitchell Homes," ibid., March 13, 1970; "Hillrise Homes Not in Demand," *Lancaster Intelligencer Journal,* July 11, 1970.

45. "$2 Million New Housing Project Slated in City," *Lancaster New Era,* January 22, 1971; Gil Delaney, "Mid-City Drops Plans for Co-op, Will Rent Units," *Lancaster Intelligencer Journal,* March 16, 1971; "Hillrise Housing Project to Get Underway October 1," *Lancaster New Era,* September 16, 1971; Jack Pollard, "Hillrise Apts. Built Without Any Insulation in Walls," ibid., February 4, 1977.

46. Jack Pollard, "18 Dauphin St. Homes Will Be Renewed with Private Money," *Lancaster New Era,* September 14, 1970; Connie Grzelka, "Dauphin St. Private Renewal a 'Success,'" ibid., August 17, 1971. Although the project ultimately proved a success, when first announced, a developer from nearby East Petersburg, Robert Showalter, protested the sale of the properties to Rock-Towne, arguing that the houses should have been sold through a competitive bidding process.

City Council delayed the sale while it investigated, only to find that the redevelopment authority's action was perfectly legal and an efficient way of getting housing back on the market. See Gil Delaney, "Council Balks at Sale of 17 Homes," *Lancaster Intelligencer Journal,* October 14, 1970, and "Controversial Homes Sale Is Approved," ibid., October 16, 1970.

47. Jack Pollard, "Phila. Man Gets Renewal Job Here," *Lancaster New Era,* May 18, 1973.

48. Jack Pollard, "'Shoddy' Work Charged in SE Homes' Renewal," ibid., May 2, 1975.

49. A. M. Casale, "Minor Errors Uncovered in Rehab Housing Probe," *Lancaster Intelligencer Journal,* May 6, 1975; Jack Pollard, "2 Former Employes [*sic*] Criticize Bhar Homes," *Lancaster New Era,* May 10, 1975; idem, "Residents Tell of 'Defects' in 26 Bhar Homes," ibid.; idem, "25 March to Air Bhar Complaints," ibid.; A. M. Casale, "City Renewal Unit Defends Bhar Rehab Housing Work," *Lancaster Intelligencer Journal,* May 15, 1975; Jack Pollard, "Storb Answers Mayor on Bhar Complaints," *Lancaster New Era,* May 15, 1975; "Renewal Board Member Hits Bhar Homes," ibid., May 16, 1975; Jack Pollard, "Scott Says Bhar Probe Shows Major Defects," ibid., May 21, 1975.

50. "Bhar Requests 'Guarantee' of Homes to Fix," *Lancaster New Era,* November 16, 1975; "Redevelopers Act to Speed Bhar Repairs," ibid., December 16, 1975; Lancaster Redevelopment Authority, Minutes, December 15, 1975; "Bhar Firm Finished as Chief City Home Rehab Specialist," *Lancaster Intelligencer Journal,* June 16, 1976.

51. Gary Mayk, "Rehab Housing: Why Did It Flop in Southeast Lancaster?" *Lancaster Intelligencer Journal,* June 13, 1978.

52. Jack Pollard, "After 20 Years & $30 Million, City's Renewal Era Is Ending," *Lancaster New Era,* June 24, 1980; "Church-Musser Cost Increased by $4.7 Million," ibid., December 2, 1969.

53. Jim Hersh, "Largest Restoration Project to Begin Soon in SE Area," *Lancaster Intelligencer Journal,* September 17, 1976; Jack Pollard, "Entire City Block of Homes Will Be Sold for Redevelopment, Resale," *Lancaster New Era,* December 9, 1976.

54. Bryant, *Ongoing Neighborhood Self-Renewal,* 53–54, 56–57; Lancaster Redevelopment Authority, Amendment to Part I of Application for Loan and Grant, Church-Musser Project, December 1969, R-224, copy in Bureau of Planning; J. Hersh, "Largest Restoration Project to Begin Soon in SE Area."

55. Patterson was quoted in Gary Mayk, "Sale of 2 City Blocks Marks Start of Old Town Project," *Lancaster Intelligencer Journal,* April 19, 1977.

56. Jack Pollard, "Wanted: Someone to Invest $1 Million in City's Future," *Lancaster New Era,* November 6, 1976; idem, "No Developer Bids to Renew SE Block," ibid., December 15, 1976; Prospectus for Development: "The Triangle," 4, and Prospectus for Development: "Washington Square," 3–4, both in Bureau of Planning; Jack Pollard, "3 Firms Bid on 2 Tracts in City," *Lancaster New Era,* March 9, 1977; Gary Mayk, "72 Homes Planned for E. Vine Triangle," *Lancaster Intelligencer Journal,* April 19, 1977.

57. Mayk, "72 Homes Planned for E. Vine Triangle"; Gary Mayk, "Sale of 2 City Blocks Marks Start of Old Town Project," *Lancaster Intelligencer Journal,* April 19, 1977; Jack Pollard, "59 Deteriorated City Homes to Be Restored," *Lancaster New Era,* April 19, 1977; "Old Town Project: A Boost for City," ibid., April 20, 1977; "Transforming the Old into Something New," *Lancaster Intelligencer Journal,* August 18, 1977.

58. Bryant, *Ongoing Neighborhood Self-Renewal,* vii, 7–9, 61–62; Gockley was

quoted in G. Mayk, "Sale of Two City Blocks Marks Start of Old Town Project."

59. Jack Pollard, "New Slums Rise in Renewal Areas, Redeveloper Charges," *Lancaster New Era,* May 23, 1978.

60. Scott was quoted in "City Plans Meeting on New Slum Charge," *Lancaster Intelligencer Journal,* May 24, 1978; Sager was quoted in Jack Pollard, "City to Meet June 13 on 'New Slums,'" *Lancaster New Era,* May 24, 1978; "Our New Slums," *Lancaster Intelligencer Journal,* May 25, 1978; "New Slums Replace Old Ones," *Lancaster New Era,* May 24, 1978.

61. "'New Slums' Evidence to Be Presented," *Lancaster New Era,* June 13, 1978; Gary Mayk, "Rehab Housing: Why Did It Flop in Southeast Lancaster," *Lancaster Intelligencer Journal,* June 13, 1978; Mayk, "Council to Meet with Scott About Southeast Housing," ibid., June 14, 1978; Jack Pollard, "Council Urged to Probe City Blight," *Lancaster New Era,* June 14, 1978. On the role of public housing in promoting residential segregation in other cities, see Bauman, *Public Housing, Race, and Renewal;* Sugrue, *Origins of the Urban Crisis;* Hirsch, *Making the Second Ghetto;* Arnold Hirsch, "Choosing Segregation: Federal Housing Policy Between *Shelley* and *Brown,*" in John F. Bauman et al., eds., *From Tenements to the Taylor Homes: In Search of an Urban Housing Policy in Twentieth-Century America* (University Park, Pa., 2000), 206–25; and Roger Biles, "Public Housing and the Postwar Urban Renaissance, 1949–1973," ibid., 143–62.

62. The distribution of housing units is derived from maps of Lancaster City Housing Authority housing program units (January 1998) and scattered-site units (August 1999), courtesy of Lancaster City Housing Authority.

CHAPTER 7

1. A. M. Casale, "20 Years of Promises, Sunnyside Unchanged," *Lancaster Intelligencer Journal,* July 27, 1974. For details of the 1971 meeting, see "Residents Skeptical of New Sunnyside Program," ibid., February 24, 1971.

2. Susan FitzGerald and Pete Mekeel, "A Pocket of Poverty, A Community Apart," *Lancaster New Era,* December 15, 1980.

3. Richard Harris, *Unplanned Suburbs: Toronto's American Tragedy, 1900 to 1950* (Baltimore, 1996).

4. "Model Cities Sets Sunnyside Plan," *Lancaster Intelligencer Journal,* February 23, 1971; "Residents Skeptical of New Sunnyside Program," ibid., February 24, 1971; Herbert J. Gans, *The Urban Villagers: Group and Class in the Life of Italian-Americans* (New York, 1962), 273.

5. Citizen's Assembly Minutes, February 16, 1971, and March 22, 1971, Bureau of Planning; "Model Cities Sets Sunnyside Plan," *Lancaster Intelligencer Journal,* February 23, 1971; details of the meeting are drawn from "Residents Skeptical of New Sunnyside Program," ibid., February 24, 1971, and Bill Fisher, "Planners, Citizens Clash in Sunnyside," *Lancaster New Era,* February 24, 1971. Fisher offered a different version of Odum's remark: "Maybe you don't want anything to happen. Then we will take our programs and maps and leave."

6. "Renewal Has Rough Going in Sunnyside," *Lancaster Intelligencer Journal,* March 11, 1971; A. M. Casale, "20 Years of Promises, Sunnyside Unchanged."

7. The story has been repeated by dozens of residents and has been published in most of the planning reports devoted to Sunnyside as well as in newspaper accounts. For a particularly useful example, and the source of the quotation, see Susan FitzGerald and Pete Mekeel, "So How Did Sunnyside Get This Way?" *Lancaster New Era,* December 16, 1980.

8. Martha H. Davis, deed of transfer to Frank H. H. Boody et al., August 29,

1912, Recorder of Deeds, Lancaster County Courthouse, Deed Book B, vol. 21, 581–83, 598–600; Lancaster City Planning Commission, *Sunnyside: People, Conditions, Needs* (February 1960), 2, 9.

9. Advertisement, "Great Land Sale! Sunnyside, House Lots, Bungalow Sites," *Lancaster New Era,* September 4, 1912. For 1912 and 1913 purchasers, consult the Grantor index, Recorder of Deeds, Lancaster County Courthouse, s.v. "Boody, Frank H. H. et al." For an example of the deed restriction, see Frank H. H. Boody et al. to Grover C. Waitz, Deed Book B, vol. 21, 596–97; for tenants, see West Lampeter Township tax assessment books, 1913, 1915, 1921, Lancaster County Historical Society, Lancaster, Pennsylvania. The reference to tents in the restriction may indicate that Boody and O'Dea did not want Sunnyside to become a camp meeting.

10. Richard Harris presents an astute analysis of owner-built housing in Toronto in *Unplanned Suburbs,* 16–18, 109–40, 200–232. For information on similar housing in other cities, see Ann Durkin Keating, *Building Chicago: Suburban Developers and the Creation of a Divided Metropolis* (Columbus, Ohio, 1988), Carolyn S. Loeb, *Entrepreneurial Vernacular: Developers Subdivisions of the 1920s* (Baltimore, 2001); and John Bodnar et al., *Lives on Their Own: Blacks, Italians, and Poles in Pittsburgh, 1900–1960* (Urbana, 1982).

11. Residential Security Map, Lancaster, Pennsylvania, Home Owners' Loan Corporation Records, National Archives and Records Administration, Washington, D.C.; Lewis Hine, photograph and manuscript notebook, Works Progress Administration Records, National Archives and Records Administration, Washington, D.C. See also Kenneth T. Jackson, "Race, Ethnicity, and Real Estate Appraisal: The Home Owners' Loan Corporation and the Federal Housing Administration," *Journal of Urban History* 6 (August 1980): 419–52; and Raymond A. Mohl, "Making the Second Ghetto in Metropolitan Miami, 1940–1960," ibid., 21 (March 1995): 395–427.

12. John Nolen, *Lancaster, Pennsylvania Comprehensive City Plan, 1929* (Cambridge, Mass., 1929), 37–38; Michael Baker Jr., *A Comprehensive Municipal Plan: City of Lancaster, Pennsylvania* (Rochester, Pa., 1945), 180. The Nolen plan did not address the condition of existing housing at Sunnyside.

13. "Ask Sunnyside Boxcar Ban," *Lancaster New Era,* June 6, 1950; "Sunnyside Residents Protest Boxcars for Use as Homes," ibid., June 9, 1950; "Suit to Ask Housing Ban on Boxcars," ibid., June 28, 1950; "Sunnyside Boxcar Rebuilt as House," *Lancaster Intelligencer Journal,* September 27, 1950; "Boxcar Homes Made Unlikely by New W. Lampeter Twp. Ordinance," ibid., October 14, 1950; "Court Approves Boxcar Homes," *Lancaster New Era,* October 25, 1950. The estimated rent of $20.00 per month is based on the 1954 rent of $22.50 per month, as reported in "Housing Probe Launched in Wake of Boxcar Fire," ibid., March 17, 1954.

14. "Probe Here in Tot's Fire Death at Box-Car Home," *Lancaster Intelligencer Journal,* March 17, 1954; "Housing Probe Launched in Wake of Boxcar Fire," *Lancaster New Era,* March 17, 1954.

15. Lancaster, City Council, *Journal of City Council,* September 6, 1955, 337–39, September 13, 1955, 349–50; "Mayor Details Plans for Sunnyside Improvements," *Lancaster New Era,* July 3, 1956; "Sunnyside Asking Water, Sewers," ibid., October 31, 1956; "Mayor Sees End to Boxcar Homes," ibid., November 2, 1956; "Mayor Promises Sunnyside Group City Will Aid Civic Betterment," *Lancaster Intelligencer Journal,* November 2, 1956; George Tresnak, "Sunnyside—100 Acres

of Poverty & Problems," ibid., August 12, 1968. According to the resolution of City Council, approximately 85 percent of Sunnyside residents favored annexation. Years later, after numerous studies but little physical improvement to the community, at least some residents of Sunnyside took a more cynical view of annexation. The city's intent, they came to believe, was not to upgrade infrastructure on the peninsula but to make possible the annexation of "more lucrative areas that lay beyond the Conestoga River to the east." See Susan FitzGerald and Pete Mekeel, "So How Did Sunnyside Get This Way?" *Lancaster New Era,* December 16, 1980.

16. "Box Cars Being Ended as Homes," *Lancaster New Era,* September 11, 1957; "4 Vacant Boxcar Homes Posted as Being 'Unfit,'" ibid., December 11, 1957; "City Health Board Spurns New Plea for Boxcar Dwellings," *Lancaster Intelligencer Journal,* November 13, 1957; "They've Left the Boxcars of Sunnyside," ibid., November 29, 1958. See also "Annual Report—Bureau of Health," *Journal of City Council,* January 6, 1958, 20; *Sunnyside: People, Conditions, Needs,* 2. One condemned Sunnyside home was demolished in April 1958, but not because of health violations; it was torn down to provide space for a parking lot adjacent to the Sunnyside Mennonite Mission. The boxcars stood until August 1969. "Raze Condemned Sunnyside Home," *Lancaster New Era,* April 5, 1958; "Sunnyside's 8 Boxcar Homes Being Razed," ibid., August 13, 1969.

17. "City Seen Qualified to Get U.S. Aid for Urban Renewal," *Lancaster Intelligencer Journal,* October 10, 1957; "Annual Report—City Planning Commission," *Journal of City Council,* January 13, 1959, 122; "Planners Will Make Full Study of Sunnyside Need," *Lancaster Intelligencer Journal,* July 29, 1959; *Sunnyside: People, Conditions, Needs,* 2, 5, 6, 10.

18. *Sunnyside: People, Conditions, Needs,* 13.

19. Ibid., 13–23.

20. "Sunnyside Area Planning Gets Citizen Assist," *Lancaster Intelligencer Journal,* August 6, 1959; "City Urged to Clear Out Sunnyside & Start Anew," *Lancaster New Era,* February 24, 1960.

21. Gans, *Urban Villagers,* 288–304. For percentages of homeowners, renters, and squatters, as well as the number of tax-delinquent properties, see *Sunnyside: People, Conditions, Needs,* 2, 5, 6. How many Sunnyside tenants were behind in monthly rent payments is impossible to determine, but this was a frequent complaint of landlords. See, for example, George Tresnak, "What Will Eliminate Blight in Sunnyside?" *Lancaster Intelligencer Journal,* August 13, 1968; and idem, "Sunnyside Residents Fear Renewal," ibid., August 14, 1968.

22. Lancaster City Planning Commission, Minutes, February 10, 1960.

23. "Cleanup of Sunnyside Is Eyed by City," *Lancaster New Era,* June 20, 1962; Lancaster City Planning Commission, *Capital Improvement Program: An Element of the Comprehensive Plan, 1962–1968,* July 1962; "Renewal Project Tabbed for Sunnyside This Year," *Lancaster Intelligencer Journal,* February 9, 1966.

24. William J. Geist, "Is City Ignoring Sunnyside Needs?" *Lancaster New Era,* December 20, 1967; Lancaster City Planning Commission, Minutes, December 7, 1967, February 29, 1968; Thomas R. Wenger to Charles S. Sharrocks, December 21, 1967, and Wenger to Members of City Council, February 29, 1968, both in Bureau of Planning. Eighty-five residents signed the petition, which was dated November 2, 1967.

25. *Journal of City Council,* July 9, 1968, 358–62, July 23, 1968, 406–8; "Mayor Urges Starting New Urban Renewal Project in

Sunnyside," *Lancaster New Era,* July 10, 1968.

26. George Tresnak, "Sunnyside Residents Fear Renewal," *Lancaster Intelligencer Journal,* August 14, 1968; Citizen's Assembly Meeting, Minutes, January 27, 1969, February 24, 1969. See also "Planner Questions New Sunnyside Proposal," *Lancaster Intelligencer Journal,* February 28, 1969; "Sunnyside Is Included in Model Neighborhood," *Lancaster New Era,* March 12, 1969.

27. *Journal of City Council,* March 11, 1969, 155–57; Francis X. Healy Jr., Assistant Regional Administrator for Model Cities, gave federal approval to include Sunnyside within the Model Neighborhood Area in a letter to Mayor Thomas J. Monaghan March 25, 1969, Bureau of Planning; "Sunnyside Is Included in Model Neighborhood," *Lancaster New Era,* March 12, 1969; Lancaster City Planning Commission, *Environmental Assessment for the Sunnyside Public Improvements Project* [1984], 1; *Lancaster Comprehensive City Demonstration Program,* October 1969, 334–37; Citizen's Assembly Minutes, Coordination Committee Meeting, March 15, 1972, Bureau of Planning; "Sunnyside's 8 Boxcar Homes Being Razed," *Lancaster New Era,* August 13, 1969.

28. *Lancaster Comprehensive City Demonstration Program,* October 1969, 334–37; Lancaster Model Neighborhood Program, Plan for Action Year 2, October 1, 1971-September 30, 1972, 122–25.

29. Dalton, Dalton, Little & Newport, *Community Improvement Program: Lancaster, Pennsylvania,* May 1973, 10-27–10-30.

30. Ibid., preface; A. M. Casale, "20 Years of Promises, Sunnyside Unchanged," *Lancaster Intelligencer Journal,* July 27, 1974.

31. See, for example, FRIDAY, *Sunnyside Planning Project: Interim Report,* November 30, 1971, 4; Harry W. Staller, Chief, Processing Control and Reports Branch, Region III, Department of Housing and Urban Development, letter to Louis G. Milan, Lancaster Redevelopment Authority December 17, 1970, Bureau of Planning; "Model Cities Sets Sunnyside Plan," *Lancaster Intelligencer Journal,* February 23, 1971.

32. FRIDAY, *Sunnyside Planning Project: Interim Report,* 16–17, 56, 10.

33. Ibid., 14, 49, 75–76, 79–80.

34. FRIDAY, *Sunnyside Planning Project—Phase II,* March 1973, 2–3, 4–8, and passim; A. M. Casale, "20 Years of Promises, Sunnyside Unchanged," *Lancaster Intelligencer Journal,* July 27, 1974.

35. FRIDAY, *Sunnyside Planning Project: Interim Report,* 45.

36. Marvin I. Adams, "Groundbreaking Starts New Education Building," *Lancaster Intelligencer Journal,* June 12, 1973; FRIDAY, *Sunnyside Planning Project: Interim Report,* 36–47.

37. Eugene Kraybill, "Symbol for Sunnyside Winds Up on the Block," *Lancaster Intelligencer Journal,* October 28, 1980; Susan FitzGerald and Pete Mekeel, "So How Did Sunnyside Get This Way?" *Lancaster New Era,* December 16, 1980; *Environmental Assessment,* 1–2.

38. Letter to the Editor, *Lancaster New Era,* August 6, 1983; Mary Jane Lane, "Sunnyside's Discontented Join Forces," *Sunday News,* February 19, 1984; David Sturm, "Mayor Defends Decision on CD Funding Requests," *Lancaster Intelligencer Journal,* March 29, 1984.

39. "6 Sunnyside Homes May Be Condemned Under City Plan," *Lancaster New Era,* July 15, 1988; Leslie R. Klein, "7 Churches Offer to Renovate 6 Old Sunnyside Homes," *Lancaster Intelligencer Journal,*" July 28, 1988; idem, "20th Century Finally Finds Sunnyside," ibid., May 6, 1989.

40. Nicholas Lemann, *The Promised Land: The Great Black Migration and How It Changed America* (New York,

1991), 111–221; and, for the consequences of this failure of will, William Julius Wilson, *When Work Disappears: The World of the New Urban Poor* (New York, 1996).

41. Gil Smart, "Sunnyside Fight Over," *Sunday News,* April 30, 2000; Todd R. Weiss, "Work Starts on Sunnyside Despite Legal Challenges," *Lancaster New Era,* March 7, 2000.

CHAPTER 8

1. Perhaps because of the political conservatism of the city, and the dominance of a Republican machine, there were no significant New Deal–era projects undertaken in the city.

2. Charles Shaw, "'Aura of Confidence' Felt Downtown, McElhinny Says," *Lancaster Intelligencer Journal,* August 26, 1977.

3. Ibid.; "Renewal in the City," ibid., November 20, 1970; Paul R. Diller to Mrs. Goldie Hoffman, October 29, 1968, Bureau of Planning, City of Lancaster. See also Chapter 4, above, for a more comprehensive discussion of the North Queen Street project.

4. Scott was quoted in Gary Mayk, "Lancaster Square Key to Downtown Prosperity," *Lancaster Intelligencer Journal,* September 9, 1977; Wilson D. McElhinny to Mayor Richard M. Scott, September 19, 1977, Bureau of Planning; "Another Milestone," *Lancaster Intelligencer Journal,* August 29, 1977; "Lancaster Square Plaza Dedicated, Returned to City," *Lancaster New Era,* September 8, 1977; "Now Finish Lancaster Square," ibid., September 9, 1977.

5. See above, Chapter 6, for a discussion of Old Town; Jim Kinter, "Heritage Center Opens Today," *Lancaster Intelligencer Journal,* May 4, 1976. For the importance of Penn Square, see David Hladick, "Penn Square Plan Unveiled," *Sunday News,* December 28, 1969; Gil Delaney, "$20 Million Crosstown Renewal Plan Unveiled," *Lancaster Intelligencer Journal,* March 18, 1972; and Lancaster NDP Supplement: Crosstown URA / Penn Square NDP (Lancaster Redevelopment Authority, December 1972). For other improvements, see Jack Pollard, "City Moves to Renew 400 Homes in S. Prince St. Area," *Lancaster New Era,* April 12, 1973; idem, "Queen Beautification Project Is Speeded Up," ibid., April 15, 1975, and idem, "Arches Dropped from Old City Hall Plaza Plan," ibid., August 21, 1975.

6. Lancaster NDP Supplement: Crosstown URA / Penn Square NDP, ND 303: 4–6; Delaney, "$20 Million Crosstown Renewal Plan Unveiled"; Jack Pollard, "Office Building Proposed for White Cross Site on Square," *Lancaster New Era,* March 18, 1972; Charles H. Kessler, "Penn Square Store Officials Back Plan for Razing 'Eyesore' Building," ibid.; Jack Pollard, "Council Approves Razing Buildings in Penn Square," ibid., April 12, 1972; Ernest Schreiber, "Scott Tries to Save Delmonico Facade," ibid., August 26, 1974. Information on the appearance of the northeast corner of the square was provided by John W. W. Loose, an educator and prolific historian who for many years was president of the Lancaster County Historical Society.

7. Pollard, "Office Building Proposed for White Cross Site on Square"; "Redevelopers OK Downtown Renewal Plan," *Lancaster New Era,* March 21, 1972; "Council Reaffirms Anti-Razing Views," ibid., April 5, 1972; Pollard, "Taxes Pledged If Penn Square Buildings Razed," ibid., April 10, 1972; idem, "Council Approves Razing Buildings in Penn Square," ibid., April 12, 1972; Gil Delaney, "Council Reverses Stand, Supports Crosstown Plan," *Lancaster Intelligencer Journal,* April 12, 1972; Pollard, "City Asks Pa. for Penn Square Renewal Funds After U.S. Turndown," *Lancaster New Era,* April 2, 1973.

8. Lancaster NDP Supplement: Crosstown URA / Penn Square NDP, ND 303: 4–6; Pollard, "City Asks Pa. for Penn Square Renewal Funds After U.S. Turndown," *Lancaster New Era,* April 2, 1973; idem, "$2.4 Million Pa. Grant OKd for Renewal," ibid., April 19, 1973.

9. *Journal of City Council,* February 12, 1974, 60–62; Jack Pollard, "Council OKs Beginning of Crosstown," *Lancaster New Era,* February 13, 1974; "Crosstown Project to Start," *Lancaster Intelligencer Journal,* February 13, 1974; Jack Pollard, "Redevelopers Act on 1st Phase of 'Crosstown,'" *Lancaster New Era,* May 21, 1974; A. M. Casale, "Penn Sq. High-Rise Developer Is Sought," *Lancaster Intelligencer Journal,* July 10, 1974; Charles Shaw, "Fulton Bank Wants to Build," ibid., August 16, 1974; Sam Taylor, "Fulton to Build 'Colonial' Bank Bldg. in Penn Square," *Lancaster New Era,* September 17, 1974.

10. A. M. Casale, "Fulton to Build Penn Square Offices," *Lancaster Intelligencer Journal,* September 17, 1974; Taylor, "Fulton to Build 'Colonial' Bank Bldg. in Penn Square."

11. Ibid.

12. Casale, "Fulton to Build Penn Square Offices"; "Downtown Bank Dedicates Remodeled Headquarters," *Lancaster Intelligencer Journal,* May 21, 1977; "Fulton Bank Hosts Party on the Square," *Lancaster New Era,* May 20, 1977; "Business Spurts as Downtown Reawakens," ibid., May 31, 1977.

13. Drayton S. Bryant Associates, *Ongoing Neighborhood Self-Renewal: Recommendations for Housing Programs and Related Services, Church-Musser Renewal Area, Lancaster, Pa.* (May 1967), 75, 83–85; "CAP Directors OK Proposed New Building," *Lancaster New Era,* March 26, 1971; "Redevelopers OK Community Building," *Lancaster Intelligencer Journal,* March 30, 1971; "$1.5 Million Sought for New Gov't Building; Council Irked," *Lancaster New Era,* March 30, 1971; "Council Briefed, Director Claims," ibid.; Lancaster Redevelopment Authority, Minutes, March 29, 1971; "14 Agencies to Share Center in SE Area," *Lancaster New Era,* April 8, 1971. On Model Cities, see John A. Andrew III, *Lyndon Johnson and the Great Society* (Chicago, 1998), 131–62; Bernard Friedan and Marshall Kaplan, *The Politics of Neglect: Urban Aid from Model Cities to Revenue Sharing* (Cambridge, Mass, 1975); and Charles Haar, *Between the Idea and the Reality: A Study in the Origin, Fate, and Legacy of the Model Cities Program* (Boston, 1975).

14. "$1.5 Million Sought for New Gov't Building; Council Irked," *Lancaster New Era,* March 30, 1971.

15. Ibid.; "Council Briefed, Director Claims," ibid.

16. Gil Delaney, "YW Pulls Out of SE Area Building," *Lancaster Intelligencer Journal,* June 12, 1971; Jeff Forster, "Why SE Center Has 'Lost' Tenants," *Lancaster New Era,* May 2, 1974; "Model City Criticism Challenged," *Lancaster Intelligencer Journal,* June 14, 1971; "Model City Building Questioned," ibid., June 22, 1971; "Model City, Salvation Army Building Joint Venture Collapses," ibid., June 26, 1971; "Model Cities Asks Support Be Shown," ibid., June 29, 1971. Mayor Thomas Monaghan reported receiving 453 postcards in support of the Neighborhood Center; Council President Metzger also acknowledged receipt of cards in support of the building, though he did not specify a number. *Journal of City Council,* August 24, 1971, 237.

17. Keith Jones, "Few Agencies Committed to SE Building," *Lancaster Intelligencer Journal,* July 23, 1971; "Mayor Raps Council on New Building," ibid., July 31, 1971; "Redevelopers Back Model Cities Building," ibid., August 3, 1971; *Journal of City Council,* September 8, 1971, 256–57. Filling, High, and Brazill were among the five who voted against the Neighborhood Center.

18. Much of the material in this paragraph reflects the recollections of Robert Kiernan, of the Boys Club and Girls Club of Lancaster, who participated in the negotiations with Monaghan and whose organization managed the Neighborhood Center for more than twenty years. Kiernan, conversation with the author, January 27, 2000; *Journal of City Council,* June 1, 1972, 196–97; "Council Approves SE Area Building," *Lancaster Intelligencer Journal,* June 2, 1972. The reactions of Council members to the role of the Boys Club were quoted at length in the *Lancaster Intelligencer Journal,* but there was no discussion recorded in the minutes of the meeting in which members approved the building.

19. Jack Pollard, "Higbee Site to Be Sold for $32,000," *Lancaster New Era,* August 21, 1972; "Groundbreaking Eyed Next Month for New Boys Club," *Lancaster Intelligencer Journal,* August 22, 1972; "SE Area Center Work Begins," *Lancaster New Era,* December 10, 1973; Jeff Forster, "Why SE Center Has 'Lost' Tenants," ibid., May 2, 1974; A. M. Casale, "Funds to Complete SE Building Lacking," *Lancaster Intelligencer Journal,* June 1, 1974.

20. "Mayor to Dedicate SE Area Center," *Lancaster New Era,* May 4, 1976; "Neighborhood Center Dedicated," *Lancaster Intelligencer Journal,* May 5, 1976; "2 Million City Bldg. Needs Insulation," *Lancaster New Era,* October 18, 1979; Robert Kiernan, conversation with the author, January 27, 2000.

21. Lancaster Redevelopment Authority *1978–1980 Comprehensive Report* (Lancaster, Pa., 1980), 1–3, 5, 10, 19; Patterson is quoted in Jack Pollard, "After 20 Years & $30 Million, City's Renewal Era Is Ending," *Lancaster New Era,* June 24, 1980.

22. Lancaster Redevelopment Authority, *1978–1980 Comprehensive Report,* 5–9.

23. Ibid., 16–18.

24. Ibid., 19. The figures on public expenditures and demolitions are drawn from Pollard, "After 20 Years & $30 Million."

25. Bare, Coe, and Monaghan were quoted in Pollard, "After 20 Years & $30 Million."

26. Patterson was quoted in Pollard, "After 20 Years & $30 Million." Walter L. Creese, a historian of Anglo-American architecture and urban planning, has observed that the "assumption that slum housing land would become belatedly valuable for commercial development was disproved over and over by the downtown redevelopment failures of the 1950s. It was an economic illusion, but it held a tight grip on governmental imaginations." This expectation continued to shape renewal policy into the 1960s. See Creese, *The Search for Environment: The Garden City Before and After,* expanded ed. (Baltimore, 1992), 356.

27. In describing modern planning in this way I am drawing upon the classic criticisms of the postwar city by Lewis Mumford, especially *The City in History: Its Origins, Its Tranformations, and Its Prospects* (New York, 1961); and Jane Jacobs, *The Death and Life of Great American Cities* (New York, 1961). The incisive commentaries of Ada Louise Huxtable have also been important to my thinking, especially *Will They Ever Finish Bruckner Boulevard?* (1963; reprint, Berkeley and Los Angeles, 1989) and *Architecture, Anyone? Cautionary Tales of the Building Art* (1986; reprint, Berkeley and Los Angeles, 1988). See also Herbert Muschamp, "From an Era When Equality Mattered," *New York Times,* February 20, 2000, Arts & Leisure section, 41.

28. In characterizing the African American community before urban renewal I have drawn upon conversations with the Rev. Louis Butcher, Ronald Ford, Gwen Glover, Professor Leroy Hopkins, and Tom Hyson.

29. Stacks, quoted in Lancaster Redevelopment Authority, *1978–1980 Comprehensive Report,* 16. Statistical data are

drawn from U.S. Bureau of the Census, *Census of Population and Housing, Census Tracts,* 1960, 1970, 1980, various tables.

30. *Census of Population and Housing, Census Tracts,* 1960, 1970, 1980, various tables.

31. Ibid.; "Encroachment of Negro Ghetto Feared in City," *Lancaster Intelligencer Journal,* April 23, 1966.

32. U.S. Bureau of the Census, *1980 Census of Housing, General Housing Characteristics, Pennsylvania,* tables 3, 3a, 4, 4a; William H. Frey and Elaine L. Fielding, "Changing Urban Populations: Regional Restructuring, Racial Polarization, and Poverty Concentration," *Cityscape: A Journal of Policy Development and Research* 1 (June 1995): 16–20 and fig. 6.

33. "$2,500,000 Home Building Boom on in Lancaster and Suburbs," *Lancaster Intelligencer Journal,* October 25, 1951; Andrew Torchia, "A Study in Suburbia—Manheim Township," *Lancaster New Era,* May 12, 1958; idem, "A Study in Suburbia—Manheim Twp. Has Growing Problems, Like All Suburbs," ibid., May 13, 1958; Mumford, *The City in History,* 486. My description of Manheim Township's transformation has benefited from conversations with a number of individuals but especially Melvin H. Hess.

34. Data in this paragraph are drawn from U.S. Bureau of the Census, *County and City Data Book 1962,* tables 2, 6; *County and City Data Book 1983,* tables B, C; *Census of Population and Housing, Census Tracts, 1980,* table P-11; *1980 Census of Population: General Social and Economic Characteristics,* table 137.

35. This assessment of educational level of Lancaster residents in 1980 is based on the percent of adults age twenty-five or older who completed high school, 53.9 percent for males and 50.4 percent for females, which compared with 59 percent for both male and female workers in Lancaster County (a percentage that reflects the number of Old Order Amish and Mennonite adults, principally farmers, who never completed high school) and 67.1 percent for males and 64.2 percent for females in Lancaster city and adjacent suburbs. See *1980 Census of Population: General Social and Economic Characteristics,* table 119.

36. U.S. Bureau of the Census, *County and City Data Book 1962,* tables 2, 6; *County and City Data Book 1983,* tables B, C; *Census of Population and Housing, Census Tracts, 1980,* table P-11; *1980 Census of Population: General Social and Economic Characteristics,* table 137.

37. *1980 Census of Population: General Social and Economic Characteristics,* tables 161a, 168a.

38. Kenneth T. Jackson, *Crabgrass Frontier: The Suburbanization of the United States* (New York, 1985), 293–94; Thomas W. Hanchett, "The Other 'Subsidized Housing': Federal Aid to Suburbanization, 1940s–1960s," in John F. Bauman et al., eds., *From Tenements to the Taylor Homes: In Search of an Urban Housing Policy in Twentieth-Century America* (University Park, Pa., 2000), 163–79; Tom Daniels, *When City and Country Collide: Managing Growth in the Metropolitan Fringe* (Washington, D.C., 1999), 107–34; Robert K. Merton, *Social Theory and Social Structure,* enlarged ed. (New York, 1968), 105n., 115–16.

39. I am paraphrasing historian Sam Bass Warner, who characterized the suburbanization of Boston in the late nineteenth century as "the product of hundreds of thousands of separate decisions." See Warner, *Streetcar Suburbs: The Process of Growth in Boston, 1870–1900* (Cambridge, Mass., 1962), 3.

40. Pollard, "After 20 Years & $30 Million." Data from 1990 are drawn from Ed Klimuska, *Lancaster: A Fading Rose,* a compilation of articles published in the *Lancaster New Era,* November 9–20, 1992, 4–6.

Index

Page numbers in italics refer to illustrations.